TEACHING WESTERN AMERICAN LITERATURE

POSTWESTERN HORIZONS

GENERAL EDITOR
William R. Handley
University of Southern California

SERIES EDITORS
José Aranda
Rice University

Melody Graulich
Utah State University

Thomas King
University of Guelph

Rachel Lee
University of California, Los Angeles

Nathaniel Lewis
Saint Michael's College

Stephen Tatum
University of Utah

TEACHING WESTERN AMERICAN LITERATURE

Edited by Brady Harrison and Randi Lynn Tanglen

UNIVERSITY OF NEBRASKA PRESS · LINCOLN

Library of Congress Cataloging-in-Publication Data
Names: Harrison, Brady, 1963– editor. |
Tanglen, Randi Lynn, editor.
Title: Teaching Western American literature / edited
by Brady Harrison and Randi Lynn Tanglen.
Description: Lincoln: University of Nebraska
Press, [2020] | Series: Postwestern horizons |
Includes bibliographical references and index.
Identifiers: LCCN 2019035105
ISBN 9781496220387 (paperback)
ISBN 9781496221278 (epub)
ISBN 9781496221285 (mobi)
ISBN 9781496221292 (pdf)
Subjects: LCSH: Western stories—Study and teaching. |
American literature—Study and teaching. | West
(U.S.)—In literature—Study and teaching.
Classification: LCC PS41 .T44 2020 |
DDC 808/.042071—dc23
LC record available at https://lccn.loc.gov/2019035105

Set in Adobe Garamond by Laura Buis.
Designed by N. Putens.

CONTENTS

TABLES

ACKNOWLEDGMENTS

First and foremost we would like to thank all the contributors to *Teaching Western American Literature* for their diligence, hard work, and faith in this project. This book has traveled a long (and sometimes dusty) road from conception to realization, and the contributors have stayed the course with good humor and kindness.

We would also like to thank William Handley, editor of the Postwestern Horizons series, Alicia Christensen and Abigail Stryker, our editors at the University of Nebraska Press, and the anonymous readers for their time, energy, goodwill, and attention to detail. This book is much stronger and smarter for their guidance and careful criticisms; they have been the best sort of participants in the growth and development of this book. We are also grateful for all the hard work of the staff at the University of Nebraska Press in turning a rather monstrous manuscript into the fine book you now have in hand.

Finally, and perhaps most of all, we would like to thank all of our colleagues and friends at the Western Literature Association for all their books, articles, conference papers, and conversations on the literature of the American West and on how to teach the works we value and admire most. Quite simply, this book could not have happened without all of you and your graciousness, intelligence, wit, and more.

TEACHING WESTERN AMERICAN LITERATURE

Introduction

Teaching Western American Literature

BRADY HARRISON AND RANDI LYNN TANGLEN

In these pages both experienced and beginning teachers will find clear, practical, and adaptable strategies for designing or updating courses in western American literature or, more broadly, in western studies. Our contributors, drawing on years (and sometimes decades) of experience and on a wealth of pedagogical practices, offer guidance in developing both undergraduate and graduate courses dedicated to the study of writers from throughout the North American West. They take readers through their rationales for syllabus design and text selection, and they model ways to develop units on specific authors, regions, or subjects, and a few even bring us along on journeys beyond the classroom and out into the literal places of the West. Our veteran teachers not only reveal the vitality and range of western writing and ways to bring primary and secondary sources to life in the classroom but also show how to engage students in many of the debates currently playing out in western studies and its many allied fields, including African American studies, American studies, border studies, critical race theory, cultural studies, disability studies, ecocriticism, gender studies, global studies, human rights, Indigenous studies, Native American studies, place studies, queer theory, and more. Well versed in western literature, history, and current and canonical scholarship in western studies, our scholar-teachers take up, either implicitly or explicitly, a wide array of definitions and competing visions of the West—the Black West, global West, Indigenous West, new West, postwestern West, quotidian West, real West, rhizomatic West, transnational West, true West, and more—and explore different ways to bring these terms and concepts to life for students, whether the classroom be in the Pacific Northwest, the desert Southwest, the Great Plains, New England, or even farther afield. Focused on the nuts and bolts of teaching western literature courses, our contributors also show how they immerse students, from first-year enrollees to doctoral candidates, in the latest debates and newest (and traditional) topics in western studies.

If some of our contributors offer models for designing courses dedicated solely to the study of western literature, others detail how they incorporate western writing, themes, or scholarship into a variety of courses aimed not only at literature students but also at students in a wide array of disciplines and fields. In one chapter, for example, an award-winning instructor (who is also an accomplished scholar and administrator) details how to develop a general-education, second-level writing course around the topic of the popular western. At this particular scholar's institution—as at many others—the course must focus on the writing process, and it takes the "American experience," broadly defined, as its subject matter; given such liberty, the course enrolls students from every conceivable major and seeks to engage them in a compelling (and perhaps even fun) subject. In a step-by-step manner our author explains how to ground a gen-ed course in the literature and films of the American West. In other chapters contributors offer strategies for incorporating individual western writers—or whole units on western writing—into, say, American literature survey courses or classes on environmental justice or queer theory. Other chapters suggest ways in which instructors can ground, at least in part, courses in African American, cultural, or Native American studies in western literature, film, music, art, and more. Our collection, in other words, does not focus exclusively on developing literature courses for literature majors and minors but much more broadly offers strategies for designing courses in multiple disciplines that include, or could include, western writers, history, and subjects.

As readers will also discover, we do not have one particular type of institution or student in mind when thinking about and designing courses or sections of courses in western American literature. Our contributors teach at a variety of private and public colleges and universities, and they work with a diverse range of students. In most chapters our teacher-scholars are very clear about the size and scope of the places where they teach, about the kinds of courses they can or must offer (and at what level), and about the sort of students they seek to attract and engage. Some of our contributors teach, for example, at small liberal arts colleges where students enroll in traditional disciplines in the humanities and sciences; others work at small colleges that foreground programs in education or nursing and where students tend to take literature or writing courses, if at all, as electives or to fulfill general-education requirements. Still others work at regional or comprehensive universities, and some work at research institutions that can offer specialized graduate seminars in western American literature. In one chapter the author-instructor meditates on how to design graduate seminars that will appeal not only to MA students in literary studies but also to MFAS in creative writing and MS candidates in environmental studies (and perhaps a few interested students from graduate programs in anthropology, history, or Native American studies). In another chapter the author explores how to engage non-American students in classrooms outside of the United States, and while some of our contributors teach at institutions located in the American West, others work in the Midwest or Northeast, and they foreground what they might reasonably expect their students to know about the West, western history, or western works of literature or art and discuss what historicizing or background they must offer according to the interests, knowledge, and experiences of their students. We hope that our contributors, taken collectively, supply enough strategies and ideas about how to teach western American literature that any interested instructor will be able to adapt the courses or modules detailed in these pages to their own institutional, departmental, professional, and pedagogical needs.

In addition to walking readers through course development and implementation, our contributors offer practical classroom activities, projects, and goals; they present the big picture and also get into the nitty-gritty of how to generate class discussions and how to design a variety of traditional and nontraditional assignments. For example, one of our contributors describes an assignment that could be used in either a composition or an environmental writing course: after reading and discussing Wallace Stegner's famous "Wilderness Letter," the students must write a letter themselves. In it they must confront a pressing cultural, political, or social issue and must address, stamp, and send that letter to an actual agency, group, or person involved in that issue. Following Stegner's assertion that citizens must turn words into actions, the students become advocates and learn in the process about persuasion, passion, polemics, and more. Another of the contributors argues for addressing, directly and in class discussions, affective responses to literature while also asserting that the emotional responses students have to various western texts can be interrogated and used as a means to deepen critical inquiry. The chapter explores how to draw out and make use of difficult emotions as a means to understand character and conflicts in literary works; as the author puts it, "we laugh, we cry, we analyze." In yet another chapter an author lays out in precise terms how to teach a western novel—or, by implication, almost any literary or cultural text—by situating it in three interlocking frames: national, transnational, and human rights. The author then provides a detailed account of the historical and scholarly sources she includes in the reading list to help establish these frames. All of the contributors to this book offer specific classroom activities and objectives and describe—and offer rationales for—the research and writing (and other) assignments that grow out of the readings, discussions, and activities.

While the contributors model a range of courses, assignments, pedagogical practices, and course objectives and while they hold a variety of theoretical investments that shape their pedagogical practices, they all share a common passion for teaching and a conviction that the field of western literary studies needs to engage in more critical conversations about instruction and pedagogy. The annual meetings of the Western Literature Association (WLA) have consistently featured panels on teaching and pedagogy that have been well attended and well received, and the WLA's online syllabus exchange indicates the field's long-standing concern with critical pedagogy and social justice teaching around issues such as place, power, and identity.[1] Yet the field—and perhaps the profession as a whole—has yet to provide a venue in which to explore in a sustained way the intersections of our research and our pedagogy. Like our other scholarly endeavors, our teaching is a "form of community property that can be shared, discussed, critiqued, exchanged, built upon," yet we too rarely have the opportunity to share our teaching as a means of scholarly exchange and discourse.[2] Our collection, as an intervention, draws upon energies already at play in the field and seeks not only to reinforce the work that has been done but also to spark further conversations and to reinforce the connection between our scholarship and our teaching.

As the chapters in this collection make clear, the contributors see teaching and scholarship as part or particle of the same critical endeavor; put another way, they show how teaching is inextricably tied to and generative of scholarship even as scholarship is tied to and generative of teaching. In one chapter, for example, a very experienced teacher and scholar details how thinking about ways to develop new courses intersected and intertwined with her research and scholarship. As she remarks, thinking about courses helped push her toward deeper reading in areas such as bioregionalism and critical regionalism even as she was also following the research "of my western studies colleagues" on affect theory and studies of the everyday. All of this led in turn to the chapter that appears here: her chapter, as readers will see, works brilliantly not only as a how-to on developing graduate-level seminars but also as a work of scholarship that will inspire further research on the "western quotidian." If we generally think of our research as impacting our teaching—all those hours in the library and at the desk may pay dividends at conferences or in print, but they really come alive in the classroom—as this chapter and, we hope, the book as a whole make clear, teaching also impacts and brings energy to research. This in turn finds new life in conversation with students and colleagues, and we hope that new developments in the field can likewise be generated from the deep thinking and reflections on the western literature classroom that readers will find in these pages.

If we take a step back, we can see that the field of western literary and cultural studies has always been focused on bringing the latest research and scholarship into the classroom. The discipline has, for example, long questioned the dominant myth of the cultural, symbolic, and geographic meaning of the West, in both the teaching and the research produced by the field.[3] Indeed, this approach is useful for helping beginning students whose notions of the American West may conjure "a preponderance of images, ideas, and historical artifacts from the post–Civil War, pre-twentieth-century period, the so called 'Old West.'"[4] But as the essays in this volume indicate, this earlier framework for theorizing and teaching the West has been reevaluated due to questions that have arisen out of the fields of "Indigenous studies, environmental humanities, queer theory, feminism, borderlands criticism, transnational studies, settler colonial theory, and postcolonial criticism."[5] Today the field is primarily conceptualized by a critical regionalism "that . . . questions the who, what, and where of the West and speaks beyond" the traditional tropes long associated with the representation and study of the western United States.[6] Neil Campbell's more recent notion of critical "regionality" provides the opportunity to shape western American literature pedagogy around "a continual fixing and resetting of the self-world relationship," leading to a "cherished[,] positive, questioning, and productive disturbance."[7] In the classroom these "productive disturbances" foster the critical inquiry and analysis that many educators see as central to a humanities and liberal arts education, however much these may be under siege.

When applied to western American literature course and syllabus design, these new concerns, questions, and energies create classroom possibilities for enlarging the geographical and historical definitions of what counts or has counted as western American literature. The work of Susan Kollin and others asks scholars and teachers dealing with the American West to make "visible how the hemispheric division of the planet, the global colonial matrix of power, and settler colonialism histories all underpin the dominant logic and founding myths of the American West."[8] Many of the chapters in this collection likewise challenge narrow definitions and boundaries and seek to enlarge and diversify our sense of the West. One chapter, for example, reminds us to think about how the border between the United States and Canada unreasonably (and unnecessarily) limits our vision, definitions, and historical knowledge of "western" literature. At the same time, other chapters, focusing on teaching works set in the Southwest and building upon the work of Gloria Anzaldúa, José Aranda, Annette Kolodny, Patricia Limerick, and others, also invite us to develop a more hemispheric, transnational view of the "American" West.[9]

As a field informed by the assumptions of critical pedagogy, the field of western literary studies also self-reflexively examines how academia reproduces social power relations, especially settler-colonialist dynamics that emerge out of the standard historicity of knowledge about the West. Recent scholarship on western studies and pedagogy, for example, calls on instructors to disrupt the authoritative settler-colonial narrative of the West by bringing forward Indigenous worldviews that help students to think about "Indigenous Wests" and that "center contemporary Native aesthetics, perspectives, and methodologies."[10] Chadwick Allen's *Trans-Indigenous: Methodologies for Global Native Literary Studies* (2012), for example, considers a methodology that addresses the global Indigenous and Indigenous self-representation. Lisa Tatonetti's *The Queerness of Native American Literature* (2014) dislodges "heteronormative settler genealogies," and she reminds us in her chapter in this collection that "the West has always been queer" and Indigenous. As readers will see, several of the chapters herein build upon these calls to action by foregrounding Indigenous literatures, cultures, histories, worldviews, and more.

This process of foregrounding a diversity of worldviews, as well as literary and cultural texts, in the field of western studies also extends to Latinx, African American, Asian American, and other experiences and works. In one chapter, for example, two leading scholars of the African American West model courses that engage a range of texts (and critical sources) that many scholars may not know much about but that clearly form part of the broader and deeper western experience. As these scholars note, many students very likely will not know much about black western literature, history, music, art, or films (beyond perhaps *Blazing Saddles* or *Django Unchained*), and they offer detailed strategies for developing courses or sections of courses on the African American West. Other chapters explore how to teach Chicana/o writing set in and about the West in a variety of literature, cultural studies, and environmental justice courses. As these chapters, as well as the work of Frederick Luis Aldama, Rolando Hinojosa-Smith, Priscilla Solis Ybarra, and others, remind us, the American West contains many voices and a diversity of experiences and literary and artistic forms that must be part of the critical and classroom conversation.

Environmentalism and environmental justice have also long been scholarly and pedagogical concerns in western studies. The Association for the Study of Literature and Environment (ASLE), for example, grew at least in part out of the WLA: at the 1992 annual WLA conference, held in

Reno, Nevada, a group of like-minded teacher-scholars met to discuss the notion of founding an organization (complete with annual conference and journal) dedicated not only to the study and promotion of environmental literature but also and equally to pedagogical and social activism. ASLE has since grown to a membership of more than 1,400, and its website features invaluable resources for instructors interested in teaching environmental literature.[11] As readers will see, several of our chapters, building on the work undertaken in collections such as Cheryll Glotfelty and Harold Fromm's *The Ecocriticism Reader: Landmarks in Literary Ecology* (1996) and Ken Hiltner's *Ecocriticism: The Essential Reader* (2015), likewise stress the need for a profound ecological awareness and activism in the western studies classroom. Other recent works that emphasize the intersections of western studies and environmental studies include Jennifer K. Ladino's *Reclaiming Nostalgia: Longing for Nature in American Literature* (2012) and Amy T. Hamilton's *Peregrinations: Walking in American Literature* (2017).[12]

Feminist interventions in western literary studies, spurred by the "new western history" movement, have likewise broadened classroom approaches to the literature we teach. From Kolodny's *The Land Before Her: Fantasy and Experience of the American Frontiers, 1630–1860* (1984), Jane Tompkins's *West of Everything: The Inner Life of Westerns* (1992), and Nina Baym's recovery work in *Women Writers of the American West, 1833–1927* (2011), gender has been a vital category for teaching in the field. The more recent recovery work of Christine Bold in *The Frontier Club: Popular Westerns and Cultural Power, 1880–1924* (2013) extends earlier feminist recovery work to the Indigenous archive, bringing audacious new voices into the field and our classrooms. Victoria Lamont's *Westerns: A Women's History* (2016) creates new possibilities for teaching women and the West with her discovery of women's role in the shaping of the western literary genre, and Cathryn Halverson's work introduces western women writers' strategic use of the home as a site of autonomy and resistance. Krista Comer's work helps us envision a western literature feminist pedagogy that "deploy[s] feminism as an opportunity for more engaged, public, methodological, and intellectual practices and would expose as weak the idea that feminism is a special interest project, a narrow identity concern."[13] In one way or another, perhaps all of the chapters in this book reveal the influence of the work of these scholars, and others, on our conceptualizations of gender and the West.

As we argue above and as the chapters in this volume illustrate, these critical directions in western literary studies are not necessarily created outside the realm of the classroom but are often generated from the classroom and its concerns; that is, western literary studies' essential research questions are also the field's essential pedagogical questions, and they are deeply connected to the real-world concerns of the classroom, our students, and the learning we do together. The field has many rich classroom directions and pedagogical opportunities, and the real challenge is to make them focused and relevant to our classrooms and students. In these pages we hope that instructors from a diversity of fields and backgrounds will find clear, practical suggestions on how to incorporate western writing into a wide array of courses at a wide array of institutions. If, by times (and like faculty in all fields), western studies scholars do not agree on interpretations or critical methodologies or pedagogical practices, we all agree that western American—indeed, western North American—writing deserves even more critical attention and that western writing deserves far more time, space, and attention in classrooms across the United States and beyond.

Chapters in This Volume

As in most scholarly collections, our clusters or groupings of chapters are meant to be suggestive rather than proscriptive or limiting. We see all of the chapters as being in conversation with one another, and we hope that the advice, strategies, models, assignments, and classroom activities that they offer can be adapted to suit any number of courses and settings. As we note above, we have no ideal student, course, or type of school in mind, and we hope that instructors in colleges, comprehensive universities, and research institutions alike will—with proper attribution, of course—borrow, steal, retool, revise, adopt, or otherwise make use of any or all of the ideas and strategies presented in these pages. Our contributors are accomplished instructors with many years of experience—and trial and error, as well as trial and success—informing their approaches, courses, modules, assignments, and more. Above all we hope that readers will find these chapters to be both helpful and hopeful (we return to the latter notion in the conclusion to this introduction).

Our first cluster of chapters, "Teaching the Literary Wests," showcases diverse ways of understanding, defining, and presenting the West to students in a wide array of courses and settings. Chadwick Allen's "Teaching the Popular Western in the Second-Level Writing Course" opens our collection with clear, practical advice on how to design and implement writing courses built around the literature of the American West. As the author notes, he draws upon his experience in designing gen-ed writing courses at large, public universities, but his strategies and course model could be adapted in any number of settings. In particular he foregrounds teaching such works as *The Virginian* and *Fools Crow* and offers a concrete set of suggestions for developing syllabi, assignments, and classroom practices around the title "Rereading the Popular Western." Along the way he offers careful guidance on how to include and make use of secondary materials. In the next chapter, "Quirky Little Things and Wilderness Letters: Using Wallace Stegner to Teach Cultural Studies and the Responsibilities of Citizenship," Melody Graulich, drawing upon Clifford Geertz's concept of "thick description," demonstrates how to use Stegner's *Angle of Repose* to teach research-based approaches to cultural studies of the West in introductory and advanced American studies, literature, and composition courses at institutions of any size or scope. Graulich describes how she has her students focus on one of the "quirky little things"—allusions, historical references, and more— that most readers would skip past and asks students to undertake a thick description of that one detail as a means to build interpretations based on historical research. As readers will quickly deduce, this strategy can be easily adapted to any number of similarly rich, allusive, and historically and culturally attuned texts. In many of these same courses Graulich also asks her students to read Stegner's "Wilderness Letter" and to write—and send—a letter on a pressing social, political, or environmental issue to an individual or group involved in that issue; the students not only learn about audience and persuasion but become engaged citizens and social actors in the process.

Chapter 3, "Teaching the Black West," by Kalenda Eaton and Michael K. Johnson, offers two models for a course in black western studies.

The first course, The African American West and the African American Western, emphasizes genre—in particular the development of the black western in literature and film—and also models how to bring key critical sources into upper-division classes. The second course, Literatures of the Black West, proceeds chronologically and explores the diversity of black western experiences. Both courses can be adapted to the undergraduate and graduate levels at a variety of institutions, and the chapter offers a wealth of material that may not be very familiar to faculty working in western studies or its allied fields. Johnson, for example, offers direction on how to teach Frank X Walker's poem sequence *Buffalo Dance: The Journey of York* and films such as Sidney Poitier's *Buck and the Preacher* and Boots Riley's *Sorry to Bother You*, and Eaton introduces students to writers and artists they may not know, offering texts ranging from an excerpt from Garci Rodríguez de Montalvo's sixteenth-century adventure novel *Las Sergas de Esplandián*, to Sutton Griggs's *Imperium in Imperio*, to Toni Morrison's *Paradise*.

In our second cluster, "Affect, Indigeneity, Gender," the chapters explore how to teach complex emotions, issues, histories, cultures, genders, and more in a variety of undergraduate and graduate courses at an array of institutions and in a diversity of courses. In chapter 4, "Gender, Affect, Environmental Justice, and Indigeneity in the Classroom," Amy T. Hamilton confronts the complexities of teaching Native American literature to a largely white student population and in particular explores the place, in both undergraduate and graduate Native American studies courses, of emotional responses to literary texts. Asking a not-so-simple question— "To emote or not to emote?"—she models how affective responses can be interrogated as places or moments to deepen critical inquiry. Drawing on the latest work in affect, feminist, environmental, and Indigenous studies, Hamilton shows how she seeks to draw upon the emotional energy in the process of analyzing such works as Diane Glancy's *Pushing the Bear: A Novel of the Trail of Tears* and Luci Tapahonso's poem "In 1864." As Hamilton contends, by confronting the emotions of characters, speakers, and readers, readers can come to understand how powerful emotions such as grief, loss, and despair exist at the heart of the colonial, western experiences of conquest, displacement, and exploitation.

In chapter 5, "Teaching Queer and Two-Spirit Indigenous Literatures, or The West Has Always Been Queer," Lisa Tatonetti offers clear,
detailed strategies for teaching queer Indigenous poetry and fiction, both
in American and Native American undergraduate literature surveys and
in specialized graduate seminars on queer Indigenous studies. Since, as
Tatonetti notes, many students may not know much about Indigenous
history or the history of the West beyond the popular, heteronormative
narratives of white pioneers that celebrate the settling of the West while
simultaneously downplaying or erasing the decimation and displacement
of Native Americans, teaching queer Indigenous literature, as well as the
narratives of sovereignty and indigeneity that sustain them, revises, corrects,
and enlarges a student's understanding of the literature, history, and cultures
of the West. Tatonetti models how to incorporate a mix of critical works
from Indigenous and queer studies into a range of courses and focuses
on how to teach the poetry and fiction of Maurice Kenny, Beth Brant,
and others. In the third chapter in the cluster, Amanda R. Gradisek and
Mark C. Rogers offer "An Interdisciplinary Approach to Teaching Gender
in Western American Literature." Here the authors discuss strategies for
developing collaborative, cross-disciplinary courses in western literature.
As they note, with the number of students in the humanities in decline
across the United States, faculty at a variety of institutions may not have
sufficient interest or numbers to offer specialized courses housed only in
literature departments. Given this decline, Gradisek and Rogers show how
to design honors courses in western literature and film that seek to engage
students who are focused on preprofessional majors and job training. The
authors ground their course in the study of gender in western literature
and film, focusing on strategies for teaching Willa Cather's *The Professor's
House* and Leslie Marmon Silko's *Ceremony* alongside such western film
classics as *Shane*, *True Grit*, *The Searchers*, and *Unforgiven*.

As the title of part 3, "Place and Regionality," suggests, the chapters in this
cluster, drawing upon the latest work in place-based learning, bioregionalism,
critical regionalism, field studies, and more, explore how to teach place and
region both in and out of the classroom. In chapter 7, "Moving Beyond the
Traditional Classroom and *So Far from God*: Place-Based Learning in the
U.S. Southwest," Karen R. Roybal, adapting teaching strategies from her

course Interdisciplinary Approaches to Chicana/o Literature, models how to teach southwestern literature as a key element in environmental justice courses that include extensive, hands-on fieldwork. The author describes how to build on working relationships with women of color–run organizations as a means of getting students out of the classroom and onto farms where they can assist in planting and learn about food justice initiatives. The chapter offers practical strategies for teaching Ana Castillo's novel *So Far from God* while also visiting some of its settings; the combination, the author argues, takes the students deep into the particular social, political, gendered, and environmental realities of the communities they visit and on which the works they read are based. In chapter 8, "Quotidian Wests: Exploring Regionality through the Everyday," Nancy S. Cook walks readers through the process of developing cutting-edge graduate seminars that appeal to students in both literary studies and creative writing (and other disciplines). Drawing on the latest research in western, affect, and regional studies, among other fields, Cook models how to design seminars centered not only on place, region, and microregion but also, following the work of Kathleen Stewart and others, on feeling and the everyday. In particular Cook offers practical guidance on how to integrate primary and critical sources, how to attend to the interests and strengths of students according to their fields or programs, and how to design both short and long writing assignments appropriate to advanced students.

In chapter 9, "Western Writers in the Field," O. Alan Weltzien, like Roybal, takes advantage of the small college "block" schedule (where students take only one class at a time) to take students out of the classroom and into the field to visit the settings of the narratives of Thomas Savage and Norman Maclean, among other Montana and western writers. As Weltzien argues, visiting the actual places described in literary works can bring them alive for students in ways that reading, classroom discussions, and writing critical essays usually cannot. Drawing on current research on "high-impact" pedagogies, he explores the dynamic learning that occurs when students travel from their classrooms to Savage's settings, ranging from Dillon to Salmon, Idaho, and to Maclean's Big Blackfoot River and Mann Gulch. In preparation for these adventures the students not only read the primary texts but also take a great deal of responsibility, via strategies of the flipped classroom, for teaching one another about both the works and their locales. In chapter 10 we turn to yet another dimension of contemporary western studies pedagogy: the recovery of texts, especially by women, and the designing of courses dedicated to regions sometimes overlooked in the broader enterprise of literary and cultural studies. As Laura Laffrado argues in "Placing the Pacific Northwest on the Literary Map: Teaching Ella Rhoads Higginson's *Mariella, of Out-West*," the Pacific Northwest remains, in Kollin's phrase, "largely undertheorized," and Laffrado offers step-by-step, concrete suggestions for both how to teach a newly recovered work and how to engage with regional literatures that do not receive a great deal of critical attention or acclaim.[14] Drawing on the work of Baym and Lamont, among others, Laffrado presents strategies for teaching Higginson, offers instruction on how to incorporate online databases and digital archives into the classroom, suggests how to read the novel alongside acknowledged American classics such as *My Ántonia* and *The Adventures of Huckleberry Finn*, discusses supplementary critical materials on women's literary regionalism, and more. As Laffrado contends, introducing neglected texts can not only deepen our students' sense of American literature, place, and region but also introduce them to the dynamics of canon formation and the inclusion and exclusion of texts.

In our final cluster, "Hemispheric/Global Wests," contributors explore how to teach western literature from a variety of transnational and global perspectives. In chapter 11, "National, Transnational, and Human Rights Frames for Teaching María Amparo Ruiz de Burton's *The Squatter and the Don*," Tereza M. Szeghi models how to teach a major western novel in an American literature survey course and, by implication, in an array of literature, history, and cultural studies classes. Offering guidance on how to build relevant secondary and historical sources into a syllabus, the author walks readers through the process of teaching the novel through three interlocking frames and details an assortment of engaging and helpful in-class and out-of-class activities and assignments, including critical essays, poster presentations, and more. The chapter also considers how to teach the novel in conversation with works such as Alexander Posey's *The Fus Fixico Letters* and Helen Hunt Jackson's *Ramona*. The next chapter, "Able-Bodies, Difference, and Citizenship in the West: Teaching James Welch's *The*

Heartsong of Charging Elk in a Global Context," by Andrea M. Dominguez, foregrounds many of the issues central to contemporary western studies: globalization, indigeneity, masculinity, gender, identity, history, regionalism, place, intersectionality, assimilation, citizenship, and more. Like Szeghi, Dominguez offers a meticulous description of how to teach one landmark work, thereby modeling how to teach a diverse range of works that explore colonialism, disability, diaspora, and resistance. Instructors at all levels and at all institutions can draw upon and adapt the careful, detailed, and practical activities and exercises for helping students to develop historical and critical contexts necessary for understanding Welch's novel and then follow and build upon the case studies, sample activities, and research assignments. This chapter, like many of the others and in the spirit of critical interrogation, also asks teachers to think about their pedagogical practices and how they may be implicated in forms of oppression and exclusion.

Appropriately, our collection ends with a call to look beyond our traditional views of the West and of where western North American literature might be taught. In "Teaching Western Canadian Literature in the Croatian Context: A Case Study," Vanja Polić reminds us that the United States does not have a monopoly on "the West," on "the western experience," or on thinking critically about the West and its literature and cultures, and she affirms that the western and the North American West remain matters of international, even global, interest. Here Polić confronts—and offers effective strategies for dealing with—the challenges of designing courses on Canadian and American writing for non–North American classrooms. Drawing on literary and cultural theorists as diverse as Gilles Deleuze, Félix Guattari, Mikhail M. Bakhtin, Sherrill Grace, Linda Hutcheon, and many others and offering practical advice on how to provide instruction in Canadian geography, history, culture, and literatures to students largely unfamiliar with the land north of the forty-ninth parallel (an issue perhaps not unfamiliar to American teachers of Canadian literature), Polić provides guidance on how to contextualize the similarities and differences between the two nations, their histories, and the ways in which writers from each country variously take up (and revise, ironize, trouble, or otherwise confront) the conventions and underlying myths and ideologies of the western. The author also offers strategies for teaching primary texts ranging from Guy

Vanderhaeghe's *The Englishman's Boy* to Aritha van Herk's performance piece "Shooting a Saskatoon (Whatever Happened to the Marlboro Man?)." As Polić concludes, critical reflection on the history and literatures of other countries may encourage students to take their theoretical knowledge and analytical skills and apply them not only to their own literatures and cultures but to all accounts presented as "received truth."

Western American Literature and a Pedagogy of Hope

To close, we can address a question fundamental to our enterprise: why compile a volume on teaching when literary studies, and the humanities more broadly, seem to be in a state of ongoing decline? As we look around and see literature and language programs enduring cuts or closures and see liberal arts colleges being forced to shut their doors, we could give up, could accept that the study of literature and culture no longer matters or has become irrelevant in the global, technology-driven marketplace.[15] Or we can think hard about what we do, and why it matters, and seek to communicate that not only to our students—and ourselves—but to the social and political worlds around us. As the work in this volume reveals, the study of literature develops skills, vision, and a passion for what it means to be human both across time and at a particular moment and in a particular place. The study of literature allows us to see not only into poems, stories, or films but also into the social, cultural, political, economic, and ethical worlds that we inhabit and that inhabit us. The study of literature offers profound pleasures and invites us to see as deeply as we can into the scope and nature of our existence, and it asks profound questions about how we should be and how we should regard and treat one another and our world.

So why a volume on how to teach western American literature? For the not-so-simple reason that we must teach as well, as creatively, as intensely, and as thoughtfully as we can because what we offer matters and our survival depends on doing the best work we can. Written during and in some cases in response to a daunting political moment in the United States in the aftermath of the 2016 presidential election, the essays in this volume represent the human capacity to change and to grow from the deep study and understanding of western American literature. Paulo Freire's *Pedagogy of the Oppressed* was published in 1968, just three years after the establishment of the Western Literature Association. Although Freire's work was not translated into English until the 1970s, the field of western American literary and cultural studies and the field of critical pedagogy both originated when the academy itself was changing in response to student activism for women's rights and civil rights and the American Indian Movement (AIM). These movements' intellectual aims were similar to those of Freire's critical pedagogy: to question systems of domination in order to promote greater critical consciousness and social change. This volume indicates that in our classrooms today western American literary and cultural studies educators have a role in ameliorating the impacts of an unjust and sometimes toxic political climate.[16]

The activist author bell hooks writes that "educating is always a vocation rooted in hopefulness," a concept at the heart of each of the pedagogical contributions to this volume on teaching western American literature.[17] These chapters collectively are an antidote to the cynicism and despair that have overtaken many in the larger culture and in the academy. As Parker J. Palmer reminds us, teaching is an act of courage, and these are times that need the "courage to keep one's heart open . . . so that teacher and students and subject can be woven into the fabric of community that learning, and living, require."[18] Pedagogical hope and courage have always been part of the field of western literary studies' values, and similar to hooks and Palmer, the authors in this volume together convey a spirit of hope, courage, and generosity.

NOTES

1. Along with panels devoted specifically to teaching and pedagogy, since 2015 the WLA has invited K–12 educators to their annual conference to present their innovative teaching ideas to the WLA membership. See WLA, "Syllabus Exchange."
2. Shulman, "Teaching," 7.
3. Henry Nash Smith's *Virgin Land* advanced the study of the West beyond the prevailing clichés and conventional understandings of the region. Annette Kolodny's "Letting Go Our Grand Obsessions" took this earlier work even further by dismantling the traditional geographic and linguistic definitions of frontier literature.
4. Witschi, "Imagining the West," 4.
5. Kollin, "Postwestern," 61.
6. Comer, "Exceptionalism, Other Wests, Critical Regionalism," 160.

7. Campbell, "Regionality," 73, 72. For more on the relationship between critical regionalism and western literary studies, see Campbell, *Cultures of the American New West*, *Rhizomatic West*, and *Affective Critical Regionality*.

8. Kollin, "Postwestern," 59. See also Coronado, *World Not to Come*.

9. Still other works, such as Hamilton and Hillard's coedited collection *Before the West Was West*, expand both the geography and time frame of what is considered western American literature by examining notions of the frontier in works usually taught as early American literature.

10. Bernardin, "Introduction," 2.

11. For more, see "Course Spotlights," ASLE, https://www.asle.org/teach/course-spotlights/.

12. See also Christensen and Crimmel, *Teaching about Place*; and Ybarra, *Writing the Goodlife*.

13. Comer, "Toward a Feminist Turn," 12. See also Comer's previous work, *Landscapes of the New West* and *Surfer Girls in the New World Order*.

14. Kollin, "North and Northwest," 414.

15. For further takes on the current state of the humanities, see, for example, Hayot, "Humanities"; and Kay, "Academe's Extinction Event."

16. See Tanglen, "Pedagogy."

17. hooks, *Teaching Community*, iv.

18. Palmer, *Courage to Teach*, 111.

BIBLIOGRAPHY

Allen, Chadwick. *Trans-Indigenous: Methodologies for Global Native Literary Studies*. Minneapolis: University of Minnesota Press, 2012.

Baym, Nina. *Women Writers of the American West, 1833–1927*. Urbana: University of Illinois Press, 2011.

Bernardin, Susan. "Introduction." In "Indigenous Wests: Literary and Visual Aesthetics." Special issue, *Western American Literature* 49, no. 1 (2014): 1–6.

Bold, Christine. *The Frontier Club: Popular Westerns and Cultural Power, 1880–1924*. New York: Oxford University Press, 2013.

Campbell, Neil. *Affective Critical Regionality*. London: Rowman & Littlefield International, 2016.

———. *The Cultures of the American New West*. Edinburgh: Edinburgh University Press, 2000.

———. "Regionality." *Western American Literature* 53, no. 1 (2018): 69–73.

———. *The Rhizomatic West: Representing the American West in a Transnational, Global, Media Age*. Lincoln: University of Nebraska Press, 2008.

Christensen, Laird, and Hal Crimmel, eds. *Teaching about Place: Learning from the Land*. Reno: University of Nevada Press, 2008.

Comer, Krista. "Exceptionalism, Other Wests, Critical Regionalism." *American Literary History* 23, no. 1 (2011): 159–73.

———. *Landscapes of the New West: Gender and Geography in Contemporary Women's Writing*. Chapel Hill: University of North Carolina Press, 1999.

———. *Surfer Girls in the New World Order*. Chapel Hill: University of North Carolina Press, 2010.

———. "Toward a Feminist Turn." *Western American Literature* 53, no. 1 (2018): 11–20.

Coronado, Raúl. *A World Not to Come: A History of Latino Writing and Print Culture.* Cambridge MA: Harvard University Press, 2016.

Freire, Paulo. *Pedagogy of the Oppressed*. 1968. New York: Bloomsbury Academic, 1970.

Glotfelty, Cheryll, and Harold Fromm, eds. *The Ecocriticism Reader: Landmarks in Literary Ecology*. Athens: University of Georgia Press, 1996.

Halverson, Cathryn. *Playing House in the American West: Western Women's Life Narratives, 1839–1987*. Tuscaloosa: University of Alabama Press, 2013.

Hamilton, Amy T. *Peregrinations: Walking in American Literature*. Reno: University of Nevada Press, 2017.

Hamilton, Amy T., and Tom J. Hillard, eds. *Before the West Was West: Critical Essays on Pre-1800 Literature of the American Frontiers*. Lincoln: University of Nebraska Press, 2014.

Hayot, Eric. "The Humanities as We Know Them Are Doomed: Now What?" *Chronicle Review*, July 1, 2018. https://www.chronicle.com/article/The-Humanities-as-We-Know-Them/243769.

Hiltner, Ken. *Ecocriticism: The Essential Reader*. New York: Routledge, 2015.

hooks, bell. *Teaching Community: A Pedagogy of Hope*. New York: Routledge, 2003.

Kay, Andrew. "Academe's Extinction Event." *Chronicle Review*, May 10, 2019. https://www.chronicle.com/interactives/20190510-academes-extinction-event?cid=wcontentgrid_hp_2b.

Kollin, Susan. "North and Northwest: Theorizing the Regional Literatures of Alaska and the Pacific Northwest." In *A Companion to the Regional Literatures of America*, edited by Charles Crow, 412–31. Hoboken NJ: Blackwell, 2003.

———. "Postwestern." *Western American Literature* 53, no. 1 (2018): 59–62.

Kolodny, Annette. *The Land Before Her: Fantasy and Experience of the American Frontiers, 1630–1860*. Chapel Hill: University of North Carolina Press, 1986.

———. "Letting Go Our Grand Obsessions: Notes toward a New Literary History of the American Frontiers." *American Literature* 64, no. 3 (1992): 1–18.

Ladino, Jennifer K. *Reclaiming Nostalgia: Longing for Nature in American Literature*. Charlottesville: University of Virginia Press, 2012.

Lamont, Victoria. *Westerns: A Women's History*. Lincoln: University of Nebraska Press, 2016.

Palmer, Parker J. *The Courage to Teach: Exploring the Inner Landscape of a Teacher's Life*. San Francisco: Jossey-Bass, 1998.

Shulman, Lee S. "Teaching as Community Property: Putting an End to Pedagogical Solitude." *Change* 25, no. 6 (1993): 6–7.

Smith, Henry Nash. *Virgin Land: The American West as Symbol and Myth*. Cambridge MA: Harvard University Press, 1950.

Tanglen, Randi Lynn. "Pedagogy." *Western American Literature* 53, no. 1 (2018): 53–88.

Tatonetti, Lisa. *The Queerness of Native American Literature*. Minneapolis: University of Minnesota Press, 2014.

Tompkins, Jane. *West of Everything: The Inner Life of Westerns*. New York: Oxford University Press, 1993.

Witschi, Nicolas. S. "Imagining the West." In *A Companion to the Literature and Culture of the American West*, edited by Nicolas S. Witschi, 3–10. Chichester, West Sussex: Wiley-Blackwell, 2001.

WLA. "Syllabus Exchange." Edited by Cheryll Glotfelty and Matt Lavin. Western Literature Association. Accessed March 16, 2018. http://www.westernlit.org/syllabus-exchange/.

Ybarra, Priscilla Solis. *Writing the Goodlife: Mexican American Literature and the Environment*. Tucson: University of Arizona Press, 2016.

PART 1

Teaching the Literary Wests

1

Teaching the Popular Western in the Second-Level Writing Course

CHADWICK ALLEN

The western is dead. Long live the western!

Esteemed readers of this volume: let us begin with a collective eye roll at five decades of pronouncing the western "dead." As in the past, these perennial declarations are easily quelled in our contemporary moment. Witness the sustained controversy surrounding the Disney Corporation's 2013 update of *The Lone Ranger* (anchored by international megastar Johnny Depp playing a deranged version of the masked mystery rider's Indian companion, Tonto, first voiced into stoic life on radio in 1933) or the sustained praise surrounding HBO's 2016 first season of its sci-fi thriller *Westworld* (a reboot of the cult-classic film from 1973). These and other high-buzz examples of recently popular westerns—beyond television's *Westworld*, for 2016 one thinks of *The Magnificent Seven*, a star-studded, multiracial remake of the equally star-studded but more racially homogenous original film from 1960, itself an American revisioning of the Japanese masterpiece *Seven Samurai* from 1954—should help quell, too, the accompanying dictum that today's undergraduates will find the genre's frontier landscapes old-fashioned, its stock of cowboy characters and its brand of six-gun violence unappealing, its inwardly focused and nationalistic themes susceptible to that most dreaded contemporary adjective deployed in U.S. classrooms, "unrelatable." Such pronouncements depend on limited understandings of both our students and popular westerns. Although most undergraduates are unlikely to have grown up watching classic film westerns on either large or small screens, let alone reading classic western novels, comics, and stories in print or listening to classic western dramas broadcast over the airwaves, they nonetheless are attracted to the central role these stories have played and continue to play in the formation of American identities. As Disney, HBO, and other production companies understand, the western is incredibly elastic as a vehicle for examining every facet of what it might mean to be an American, in any historical period—not only multiple pasts but the present and both near and distant futures—and ultimately what it might mean to be human. Indeed, popular westerns from every era and across every medium and form can be appropriate for a wide range of artistic and intellectual investigations and thus for a wide range of courses organized around literary, cultural, or rhetorical analysis.

Popular Westerns and/as Gen Ed

For the nearly two decades I worked at a large public university in the Midwest, I regularly taught popular westerns in the honors version of the second-level writing course. This course fulfilled a general-education requirement, and it was taken by all undergraduates regardless of major, including those who had received prior credit for the first-level writing course. Instructors were recruited from across campus, although primarily from the Department of English; all were expected to introduce students to academic writing practices within a specific discipline and to coach students through a sequence of relevant assignments in research, writing, and revision. So long as our courses focused on the writing process and explored some aspect of the broad theme "the American experience," we were free to choose specific topics, readings, and objects of study. Over the years I experimented with a number of choices but developed an especially effective set of syllabi and classroom practices around the title "Rereading the Popular Western." Students in these honors classes were typically sophomores and majoring in subjects outside the arts and humanities, often in lab-based sciences, international relations, or business. More often than not, mine was the first course to introduce these students to frontier studies, western literature—broadly defined—and critical ways of thinking about land, territory, indigeneity, settler colonialisms, racialized and gendered relations to place and power, and the refractions of these issues and problematics through a range of popular genres and media.

By definition, the second-level writing course does not allow for coverage, so my primary goal was to employ a limited set of literary texts to spur student writing, thinking, and research. In one version students read a chronological sequence of iconic narratives of U.S. frontiers. We begin with the first Daniel Boone narrative from the late eighteenth century, followed by two dime novels from the mid- and late nineteenth century, followed by Owen Wister's "art" novel, *The Virginian*, from the turn of the twentieth century. With these texts as grounding, at the end of the term we examine a late twentieth-century response to these earlier, dominant representations of U.S. frontiers: the American Indian historical novel *Fools Crow*, by James Welch, the acclaimed Blackfeet and Gros Ventre writer. Students engage relevant scholarship in each unit. Course requirements include informal writing assignments as well as formal essays, in-class workshops and exercises, a library assignment, and brief oral presentations. Through this focused examination of selected popular westerns, students learn to think critically about iconic narratives of American belonging, and they learn to write clearly and concisely about how such narratives do their work.

Adventures in Reading—and *Rereading*—Daniel Boone

This version of the course begins with "The Adventures of Col. Daniel Boon," originally published as an appendix to John Filson's *The Discovery, Settlement and Present State of Kentucke* (1784). Filson's Boone narrative establishes a number of important tropes for classic and ongoing representations of U.S. western frontiers: a hypermasculine white male hero, a highly charged and symbolic landscape, a host of natural and human obstacles to the hero's cause (including grossly stereotyped Indigenous peoples), a limited but crucial role for both white women and non-Indigenous people of color. The Filson text also works well for reviewing basic rhetorical analysis. I first have students read the narrative cold, without any contextualization, to see how they react to and interpret the text on their own. Most students accept the narrative as the voice and writing of Boone himself, and they are thus surprised—but also intrigued—when they discover it was actually penned by Filson, a schoolteacher and surveyor from Pennsylvania who deployed Boone's rugged frontier persona, with its perceived authenticity and charisma, in order to create a positive ethos for his book and to help promote his real interest, which was to sell Kentucky land he was speculating following the Revolutionary War. After describing their initial reactions, students are prompted to analyze the Boone narrative more systematically by following a set of standard questions one might ask of any text: What is the narrative's genre or genres? In whose voice or voices is it told? Who is the author? What is the narrative's message? What is its purpose? How are the message and purpose related? Who are the narrative's primary and secondary audiences? What strategies does the author use to convey the narrative's message to the audience and fulfill the purpose in writing it? How effective are these strategies? And so on. Once students have approached the questions on their own or in small groups, class discussion reveals that the text is not at all what it seems and that there is much more to frontier literature and the popular western than simple tales of (white masculine) travel, conquest, violence, or adventure.

Students are then asked to reread the Boone narrative from a now more informed position and to pair Filson's text with historian Frederick Jackson Turner's seminal 1893 essay "The Significance of the Frontier in American History," which clearly draws from Filson's work and that of other early purveyors of U.S. frontier mythology. Moreover, students are given a specific prompt for what will be the first of five informal writing assignments they will complete early in the term: "Use Turner's definitions of the frontier and its significance to analyze some aspect of Filson's Boone narrative." Students are asked to address the prompt directly, to give their essay a title, and to make sure their essay contains a clear argument and includes detailed support; they are allowed to write no more than two double-spaced pages in a standard 12-point font. Spurred by their notes from class discussion, many students gravitate toward the text's extensive representations of the white male hero as a homespun "philosopher" or of the newly encountered landscape as a "howling wilderness." An ambitious few focus on the text's more limited but no less fascinating representations of white women (the hearty Mrs. Boone and her daughters, who signify the arrival of "civilization"), Indigenous nations (Boone's would-be captors, the fierce but apparently witless "Shawanese"), and people of color (the black servant/slave who rescues a white woman and her children from marauding "savages").

The purpose of these brief informal papers is for students to practice writing thesis statements and to practice structuring and supporting arguments, as well as for students to practice writing concisely. These papers are also opportunities for students to experiment with their writing voice and academic style in a series of highly focused but relatively low-stakes assignments, since I typically count the five informal essays together as no more than 10 percent of the overall course grade and since I stress my willingness to reward students for taking risks with their writing and for demonstrating improvement. In addition, students are asked to read one of their five informal essays out loud in class. In the honors writing course setting, that typically means no more than four students will read out loud for a particular prompt. The other students are charged with listening closely to each essay as it is read and identifying its thesis and the main supporting evidence for its specific points. When the class reports back what they collectively heard and understood, authors receive immediate feedback on how well their strategies are working for their intended audience. All students are exposed to multiple strategies for responding to the essay prompt; they learn in concrete terms that there is always more than one effective way to approach any writing assignment. Brief class discussion can point out and weigh the relative merits of each strategy and consider how each might be improved. Although some students are intimidated by the idea of reading their work aloud to peers, the assignment inevitably helps build community, and nearly all students report on their course evaluations how valuable they find this exercise.

To complete this first unit, students are asked to review the Filson and Turner texts and to next read literary scholar Annette Kolodny's 1992 response to Turner's thesis and its ongoing legacy: her critical essay "Letting Go Our Grand Obsessions: Notes toward a New Literary History of the American Frontiers." Students respond to a second informal writing prompt: "Use Kolodny's definition of frontier literature to analyze some aspect of Filson's Boone narrative. Also, discuss the differences between employing Turner's versus Kolodny's ideas and methodologies in reading this text." Students begin to see how contemporary scholars build from the work of predecessors to construct new theories, offer new analyses, and make new arguments about classic works. And they begin to grapple with the complexity of incorporating multiple sources into a single essay.

Passages of Tragedy and Wonder: Dime Novels and Close Reading

The second unit focuses on the nineteenth-century dime novel tradition. Students read Bill Brown's useful introduction to *Reading the West: An Anthology of Dime Westerns*, along with the earliest of the collected works, Ann Stephens's *Malaeska: The Indian Wife of the White Hunter* (1860). For the third informal writing assignment, students are asked to connect the new reading back to the prior unit: "Compare either (1) how the hero is handled in *Malaeska* to how the hero is handled in Filson's Boone narrative, or (2) how the landscape is handled in *Malaeska* to how the landscape is handled in Filson's Boone narrative." In a typical semester or quarter there is time to assign only two of the four dime novels collected in Brown's anthology. I often pair *Malaeska*, with its emphasis on the stereotypically tragic Indian heroine and her even more tragic "half-breed" son, with Edward Wheeler's *Deadwood Dick, Prince of the Road; or, The Black Rider of the Black Hills* (1877), with its emphasis on the stereotypically robust (and yet wonderfully beautiful and homoerotic) white male hero. For the fourth informal writing assignment I prompt students to make a focused comparison: "Choose some aspect of the dime western and compare how it is handled in Stephens and Wheeler." Students can build upon an earlier analysis of how the dime novels handle the iconic western hero (What happens when the "lone" explorer, hunter, or gunman is part of a community?) or highly symbolic landscapes (What happens when untamed "wilderness" is revealed to be already inhabited by Indigenous peoples?), or they can explore additional points of interest, such as the dime novels' depictions of urban life in already-decaying eastern cities and booming western towns. Both dime novel prompts are meant to help students select a topic and begin to build a thesis for the first formal essay assignment.

For the first formal essay students are asked to focus specifically on developing their close reading skills. They are to choose a brief passage— from a couple of lines to a full page—from one of the dime novels in Brown's anthology that they find in some way intriguing, significant, and/ or problematic. Their completed essays should run three to four pages, and they should offer a reading of the chosen passage that (1) clearly identifies where the passage fits into the larger plot and structure of the novel; (2) presents a close reading and interpretation of the passage that addresses its role in the development of the novel's plot and theme(s), its specific structure, its use of language, and its development of symbolism, imagery, and/or metaphor; and (3) makes an argument about the passage's interest or significance. Students are free to engage any of the primary or secondary texts we have read thus far. In my experience many students are drawn to the novels' surprisingly complex portrayals of gender identities and performances of gender roles—the female masculinity of the character Calamity Jane featured in *Deadwood Dick*, for instance—and how these identities and performances intersect with ethnicity, race, and class on the one hand and with specific urban, rural, and wilderness landscapes on the other.

Before devoting class time to workshopping drafts of the first formal assignment, I like to guide students through a model essay. Obviously this is easier to accomplish in subsequent rather than first offerings of the course. Over time I have created a set of good—but, importantly, *not perfect*—models for each formal essay assignment. Each time I offer the course I ask the authors of strong essays for permission to modify their work for use in future classes, with their names removed. I edit the essays for any problems with grammar, syntax, or usage, and, as necessary, I make minor revisions that strengthen the essays' titles, thesis statements, topic sentences, transitions, uses of quotations, citations of sources, and so forth. I have found it most effective to hand out hard copies of the model in class and to read the essay out loud, stopping after each paragraph to point out significant structural and rhetorical features and how they work. Students find the explicit naming of the model essay's significant components and the explicit discussion of basic issues of composition—how to engage the reader's attention and interest with an essay's title and opening sentences, how to introduce a specific passage selected for analysis, how to make transitions between points, how to extend discussion of a particular point across two paragraphs, how to conclude a brief essay without simply repeating the introduction and thesis—helpful and often demystifying. Many may have never discussed essay composition in general or the expectations for a particular assignment at this level of concrete detail. And discussion of a model should elevate the quality of subsequent peer-to-peer workshops, since students will have a common frame of reference and vocabulary.

Scenes of Heroic Whiteness: *The Virginian*, Close Reading, and Critical Reception

We then shift from the dime novel tradition to a third unit, on Owen Wister's 1902 western "art" novel, *The Virginian*. Students first read Robert Shulman's useful introduction to the novel and its contexts in the Oxford World's Classics edition, which I prefer to teach, along with the novel's first twelve chapters. After an initial discussion of the novel's opening, and after reading through chapter 28, students complete a fifth and final informal writing assignment. I like to use a deceptively simple prompt: "Thus far, is Wister's hero similar to or different from the heroes of the dime novels we read? Be specific." Answering the prompt turns out to be more complex than students at first assume. Additional class time is devoted to discussing the remainder of the novel, and students begin work on their second formal assignment. For the second formal essay, I ask students to continue developing their close reading skills. Building from the first assignment, they choose a scene from *The Virginian*—rather than a brief passage—that they find in some way intriguing, significant, and/or problematic. Their three- to four-page essay should (1) clearly identify where the scene fits into the larger plot and structure of the novel; (2) offer a close reading and interpretation of the scene that addresses its role in the development of the novel's plot, subplot(s), and theme(s), its specific structure, its use of language, and its development of symbolism, imagery, and/or metaphor; and (3) make an argument about the scene's interest or significance. We again spend time in class talking through a model essay and workshopping students' drafts.

We complete the unit on *The Virginian* with a focus on effective strategies for understanding and responding to the work of other readers, critics, and scholars. Students are assigned the collection *Reading "The Virginian" in the New West*, edited by Melody Graulich and Stephen Tatum and published in 2003 to mark *The Virginian*'s centennial. The eleven essays in that volume demonstrate a wide range of critical approaches to Wister's novel and its multiple relevant contexts. Most students will have read little formal literary or cultural criticism prior to taking this course; the collection's variety gives them a sense of the breadth of possibilities for literary analysis and research, as well as a sense of the range of effective styles for academic writing. To get us started, I typically lead discussion of several of the essays over at least two class periods. In the first class we discuss Graulich's introduction to the collection, which provides more useful context, and Tatum's essay "Pictures (Facing) Words," which analyzes the impact of the illustrations included in the early editions of the novel. In the second class we pair Louis Owens's essay "White for a Hundred Years" with Jennifer Tuttle's essay "Indigenous Whiteness and Wister's Invisible Indians"; read together, these essays demonstrate two related but distinct approaches to analyzing Wister's engagements with issues of race and indigeneity. In class discussions we focus on how these scholars build their arguments and support their analyses, as well as on how they build and sustain interest in their topics. In other words, as in our discussions of model student essays, in addition to discussing the details of the authors' arguments about Wister's novel and the western literary tradition, we explicitly discuss how each author constructs and sustains his or her critical perspective and scholarly voice.

Working in small teams, students then present six of the remaining essays to each other in class. Each presentation team is responsible for (1) reading their chosen (or assigned) essay outside of class; (2) meeting either in person, over the phone, or online to discuss the chosen essay; (3) preparing a well-organized and effective twenty-five- to thirty-minute presentation of their essay; and (4) preparing a one-page handout of their main points to distribute in class. In addition, students on the team are asked to write a brief statement of their individual contribution to the team and hand it in on the day of the presentation. In the formal assignment I tell students each presentation should (1) give a summary of the essay's main arguments; (2) discuss the essay's critical methodologies and use of textual evidence, outside research, and/or theory; and (3) offer an assessment of the essay's persuasiveness and/or effectiveness, as well as its potential usefulness for further study of *The Virginian* or other literary texts.

Native Points of View: *Fools Crow*, Reading Comprehension, and Research

The final unit of this version of the course places even more responsibility on students, and it explicitly tests their reading comprehension and critical thinking skills. Whereas I take the lead in guiding students through analyses of the Boone narrative, the dime novels, and *The Virginian*, both through class discussions and assigned prompts for informal writing, I now ask students to read James Welch's historical novel *Fools Crow* on their own. The novel is set in a historical time frame and northern plains frontier location similar to that of Wister's novel—specifically, the fifteen years leading up to the January 1870 massacre of a band of Blackfeet camped along the Marias River in northern Montana—but it is told primarily from Native American rather than from white settler points of view. Given all that students have learned about representations of U.S. frontiers and about western genres in the course thus far, how well can they read, understand, and analyze this new text? Students are thus asked to read Welch's novel in its entirety, with no class discussion, and then to take an in-class exam that covers the novel's primary and secondary characters, major plot and subplots, dominant symbols and themes, narrative structure and point of view, textual innovations, and style. These last aspects of the novel are especially generative but also often especially challenging. Welch is a direct descendant of one of the survivors of the Marias River Massacre, and one of his several significant innovations in the novel is an attempt to render nineteenth-century Blackfeet worldviews, perspectives, and voices through the English language. The exam consists of multiple choice and short answer questions, as well as prompts for two brief essays. I share the structure of the exam with students ahead of time, and I discuss strategies for taking in-class exams. Like the reading of their informal essays aloud in class, students often find the idea of an in-class reading comprehension exam daunting. But here too students typically see the value of this test of their abilities. I frame the exam as a diagnostic, and I explain that it is meant primarily for the students' own use in gaining a realistic sense of the current state of their skills, and thus I count the exam as no more than 10 percent of the students' final course grade. Exam scores typically include a few in the A range and D range, with the majority falling in the B and C range; in the honors section this spread can be a new and humbling experience. The in-class discussion of the graded exams is often incredibly productive for students.

At the same time students are reading *Fools Crow* on their own and preparing for the in-class exam, they also complete a library assignment and produce a brief annotated bibliography. Early in the term the class visits the library and meets with a research librarian in the humanities to learn about relevant databases and other useful resources for research. Now, as we approach the end of the term, students are tasked with locating four scholarly sources—typically I ask for one book, two articles in scholarly journals, and one internet site—relevant to writing about Welch's novel. I like to ask students to use specific finding aids introduced in the session with the librarian: I might ask that they find one of their articles using JSTOR or Project Muse, for instance, and the other using the MLA International Bibliography. The assignment has two graded components: students are asked to write a complete and correct scholarly citation for each of their four sources, following MLA style guidelines, and they are asked to write a brief argument, from a couple of sentences to a short paragraph, for how each source could be relevant to writing an academic essay about *Fools Crow*.

For the third formal essay, due during finals week, students practice responding to another scholar's arguments and synthesizing research and analysis. I like to give students several options for the final essay, so they can write about either or both of the novels from the second half of the term, depending on their interests. One configuration of options for a four- to five-page final essay looks like this:

Option A. Find an interesting critical essay or book chapter that makes an argument about Wister's *The Virginian*. You may choose one of the essays from *Reading "The Virginian" in the New West* or an essay or book chapter you locate on your own. Your essay should (1) offer its own argument about some aspect of Wister's novel, (2) respond to the published article as part of its analysis and argument (note that "respond" is a neutral term—you may agree or disagree with the article, or partially agree, and so on), and (3) provide a full citation for the article or book chapter in a list of works cited that follows MLA style.

Option B. Find an interesting critical essay or book chapter that makes an argument about Welch's *Fools Crow*. (You may use your research from the library assignment and annotated bibliography.) Your essay should (1) offer its own argument about some aspect of Welch's novel, (2) respond to the published article as part of its analysis and argument (note that "respond" is a neutral term—you may agree or disagree with the article, or partially agree, and so on), and (3) provide a full citation for the article or book chapter in a list of works cited that follows MLA style.

Option C. Write a comparative essay on some aspect of *The Virginian* and *Fools Crow* that also responds to the work of at least one critic. Your essay should (1) offer its own, comparative argument about some aspect of the two novels, (2) respond to the published article as part of its analysis and argument (note that "respond" is a neutral term—you may agree or disagree with the article, or partially agree, and so on), and (3) provide a full citation for the article or book chapter in a list of works cited that follows MLA style.

Many students will continue to explore issues already discussed at length in class and covered in earlier writing, such as representations of the western hero or landscape, with the advantage of familiarity and relative expertise—a newly gained sense of analytical comfort. They may thus have greater confidence as they work through the assignment and may be able to offer more incisive arguments and stronger prose. Only a few of the more ambitious students typically choose the comparative option, but its articulation in the prompt and its discussion in class will often encourage students to think in more complex ways about the particular novel they choose as their focus. All three options give students opportunities to continue to refine skills they have practiced all term.

In another version of the course, rather than assign both *The Virginian* and *Fools Crow*, I assign only one of these lengthy novels. A reading comprehension exam on that novel is followed by in-class discussion of specific chapters led by teams of student discussion leaders. Students then write a longer and more fully developed final essay that offers a close reading of a major scene or set of linked scenes, supported by significant outside research. *Fools Crow* is well suited to this kind of assignment, since students can research a wide range of topics related to Blackfeet, other Native American, and U.S. settler cultures and histories in the mid- and late nineteenth century, as well as their many significant intersections. I have seen students research everything from the spread of smallpox on the northern plains to the specific flora and fauna utilized by the Blackfeet characters in the novel to the impact of specific treaties on the movement of settlers to the development of the Gatling gun and other weapons technologies to the court-martial proceedings of the cavalry officer responsible for the Marias River Massacre. As with the earlier formal assignments, I guide students through a model essay before they begin workshopping drafts of their own projects.

Beyond Print: Popular Westerns in Aural and Visual Media

In still other versions of the course, after students encounter the eighteenth-century Boone narrative and the nineteenth-century dime novels, I introduce additional popular media through which the western genre developed in the twentieth century, rather than continue to focus exclusively on print texts. During one or more class periods, for instance, I might have students listen to and discuss examples of westerns on radio, such as half-hour episodes from the long-running juvenile series *The Lone Ranger* (1933–55) and the long-running adult series *Gunsmoke* (1952–61). Recordings of these and other radio westerns are available online and from several commercial companies, such as Radio Spirits (www.radiospirits .com). Most students will be unfamiliar with the aural medium as a vehicle for drama, and many will be intrigued by the obvious continuities and adaptations carried over from the dime novel tradition, as well as by the creative use of sound effects, musical motifs, extradiegetic narration, dialogue, silence, and other techniques from classic radio of the 1930s through the 1950s. I typically assign at least one relevant critical essay to provide grounding in radio history and scholarship, such as my own essay "Sight in the Sound: Seeing and Being Seen in *The Lone Ranger* Radio Show." If the course schedule allows, I might then spend one or more class periods screening and discussing half-hour episodes of popular television westerns from the 1950s and 1960s. If the class has listened to an episode of *The Lone Ranger* from radio, I will screen the 1949 pilot from the television series so that we can discuss continuities and adaptations across aural and visual media.

Most of a final unit on nonprint westerns, however, is typically devoted to film, given the medium's significant role in both the innovation and the popularity of the genre across and beyond the twentieth century. Film is a medium with which students may feel familiar, but many will have never studied its history or formal properties. I like to introduce students to basic film terms and concepts—excerpts from a standard work such as *Film Art*, by David Bordwell, Kristin Thompson, and Jeff Smith, serves this purpose well—and screen in class an early film western such as *Stagecoach* from 1939, directed by the highly influential John Ford and starring a young John Wayne as the iconic (and handsome) western hero and the ancient Monument Valley as the iconic (and majestic) western landscape. There is a large body of scholarship on this film, developed from many theoretical perspectives, and I often assign one or more essays that engage the film's relevant contexts and innovative techniques in ways that will resonate with earlier class discussions; examples are Michael Coyne's "Mirror for Prewar America: *Stagecoach* and the Western, 1939–1941" and Richard Slotkin's "John Ford's *Stagecoach* and the Mythic Space of the Western Movie." After class discussion of the film's distinctive strategies—juxtapositions of panoramic exterior vistas with intimate interior settings, highly stylized patterns of musical motifs, particular camera shots and angles, light and shadow—along with its narrative pacing, specific dialogue, and so forth, I divide the class into teams to screen and research an additional film outside of class. I provide students with a brief list of classic westerns from the 1950s that help establish what are now considered key aspects of the genre (e.g., *High Noon* from 1952, *Shane* from 1953, *The Searchers* from 1956) and post-1970 westerns that innovate these conventions in obviously interesting ways (e.g., *Little Big Man* from 1970, *Blazing Saddles* from 1974, *The Outlaw Josey Wales* from 1976, *Dances with Wolves* from 1990, *Unforgiven* from 1992, *The Ballad of Little Jo* and *Posse* from 1993, *Maverick* from 1994, *The Quick and the Dead* from 1995). Both the classic and the revisionist films allow students to continue their examinations of conventions that began with the Boone narrative and developed across the dime novel, radio western, and television western traditions. Moreover, the films provide opportunities for students to investigate the ways in which well-established conventions for representing frontier heroes and landscapes can flex, stretch, bend, even break when writers and producers respond to changing attitudes about controversial issues (e.g., excessive violence deployed in the name of frontier conquest in the historical past or in the name of foreign wars in the recent past or present) or to changing assumptions about controversial categories (e.g., conceptions of citizenship, race, indigeneity, gender, and/or sexuality and the resultant sense of individuals' and communities' attendant rights and responsibilities). I have typically not had students work on post-1990s westerns, because less published criticism tends to be available, although the scholarship is always evolving; other instructors may wish to make different choices.

Film teams are asked to conduct relevant research on their film's production history (when, who, how, where); their film's popular and critical reception (reviews, commentary, scholarly analysis); and their film's historical, social, and cultural contexts (both for when and where the film is set and for when and where the film was made). They then prepare a well-organized and effective group presentation of thirty to forty minutes that actively involves all members of the team, gives a brief synopsis of the film, provides an overview of the film's relevant contexts, summarizes the relevant film commentary, and offers one or more critical analyses. In addition, each team prepares a one-page handout about its film and the highlights of its presentation for the class. For their final essays students write a focused analysis of this or another film western, supported by outside research. Building from their earlier assignments and group presentations, students typically develop close readings of a particular scene or set of related scenes that draw from research on relevant historical and social contexts. An example would be how *The Ballad of Little Joe* or *The Quick and the Dead* subverts the western's conventional gender roles in order to develop the potential for feminine heroes within the characters' storyworld of the nineteenth century and for feminist critiques of the genre's patriarchal and hypermasculinist definitions of heroism in the filmmakers' production world of the late twentieth century. The students may also draw from research on relevant genre criticism, with an example being how *Blazing Saddles* or *Maverick* deploys parody and slapstick humor in order to launch critiques of the racialized and gendered stereotypes that form the base of the genre's recognizable conventions.

Required Credits and the Popularity of Westerns

The honors students who find themselves in my required second-level writing courses are always happy to discover how much they learn about composition and research and how much they improve their skills of analysis. More ambivalently, these highly disciplined sophomores on their way to careers in marketing or medicine are often surprised to discover, as well, that they are capable of more than simply soldiering through the assigned texts—that many enjoy (yes, *enjoy*) reading, listening to, or viewing popular westerns and contemplating their cultural significance, their rhetorical force and powers of persuasion, their potential to provoke affective response and to build personal meaning. This surprise is perhaps especially acute among the young women in these courses, who, even more so than the young men, typically have not imagined themselves as part of the genre's potential audience. During office hours more than one aspiring major in business or international relations has confessed to being moved by the melodramatic plight of Malaeska or to becoming absorbed in the complexities and contradictions of Molly Stark Wood, the eastern-educated and fiercely independent love interest of Wister's Virginian. Young women and men alike express surprise at finding interest in the Boone narrative's economic and political contexts and at feeling deep connections to characters on both sides of the embattled Indigenous-settler divide in Welch's *Fools Crow*. One young man, a bright non-Native premed biology major who had grown up in a rural county and hunted deer with his father and brothers, wrote a provocative, well-researched final essay exploring the novel's critique of overhunting and wasteful violence against animals perpetrated by white "mountain men"; he then spent the following summer volunteering at an Indian health clinic on a Montana reservation. Months or years after the course, students email me to report how their newfound knowledge has helped build connections with grandparents and other older relatives fond of westerns and how they now notice the ways western conventions are repeatedly deployed and refashioned in innovating ways in popular movies, television, and video games, in advertising and journalism, and, especially during campaign seasons, in the rhetoric of politicians seeking to appeal to certain understandings of national history, self-conception, and pride.

The popularity of westerns appears to be cyclical, if not constant. There is thus every reason to center popular westerns and the myriad issues they raise and explore in the second-level writing course and in other general-education requirements meant to help students think critically about the U.S. nation-state and the world. The western is alive and ever-changing (at least through the next cycle). Let us long teach the western!

In memory of Annette Kolodny (1941–2019), admired scholar, mentor, colleague, and friend, who taught me how to teach western literature.

BIBLIOGRAPHY

Allen, Chadwick. "Sight in the Sound: Seeing and Being Seen in *The Lone Ranger* Radio Show." *Western American Literature* 42, no. 2 (2007): 117–40.

Bordwell, David, Kristin Thompson, and Jeff Smith. *Film Art: An Introduction*. 11th ed. New York: McGraw Hill, 2016.

Brown, Bill, ed. *Reading the West: An Anthology of Dime Westerns*. Boston: Bedford, 1997.

Coyne, Michael D. "Mirror for Prewar America: *Stagecoach* and the Western, 1939–1941." In *The Crowded Prairie: American National Identity in the Hollywood Western*, 16–30. New York: St. Martin's Press, 1997.

Filson, John. *The Discovery, Settlement and Present State of Kentucke*. 1784. New York: Corinth Books, 1962.

Graulich, Melody, and Stephen Tatum, eds. *Reading "The Virginian" in the New West*. Lincoln: University of Nebraska Press, 2003.

Kolodny, Annette. "Letting Go Our Grand Obsessions: Notes toward a New Literary History of the American Frontiers." *American Literature* 64, no. 1 (1992): 1–18.

Slotkin, Richard. "John Ford's *Stagecoach* and the Mythic Space of the Western Movie." In *The Big Empty: Essays on Western Landscapes as Narrative*, edited by Leonard Engel, 261–82. Albuquerque: University of New Mexico Press, 1994.

Turner, Frederick Jackson. "The Significance of the Frontier in American History" (1893). In *The Frontier in American History*, 1–38. 1920. Huntington NY: Krieger, 1976.

Welch, James. *Fools Crow*. New York: Penguin, 1986.

Wister, Owen. *The Virginian*. Edited by Robert Shulman. 1902. New York: Oxford University Press, 2009.

2

Quirky Little Things and Wilderness Letters

Using Wallace Stegner to Teach Cultural Studies and the Responsibilities of Citizenship

MELODY GRAULICH

> A teacher enlarged people in all sorts of ways besides just his subject matter.
> WALLACE STEGNER

A few hundred pages into *Angle of Repose*, Lyman Ward's son urges him to write about Deadwood, a setting he feels will add "zing" to his book, asking, "Why leave out the colorful stuff?"[1] But Lyman, an award-winning historian and the narrator of the novel, while ostensibly writing a biography of his grandmother, is disinterested in the riotous Deadwood, with its motley mythic cast. "I don't give a damn if [Grandfather] once saw Wild Bill plain," he rejoins. "I'm much more interested in quirky little things that most people wouldn't even notice."[2]

After taking my Introduction to the Theory and Practice of American Studies seminar, which focuses on the North American West, my graduate students use the phrase "quirky little things" as if it's a universally cited critical concept, something like "the legacy of conquest," "borderlands," or "settler colonialism." After taking my Introduction to American Culture course, my undergraduates learn to apply the anthropologist Clifford Geertz's concept of "thick description" through an exploration of one "quirky little thing" from *Angle of Repose*. I use *Angle of Repose* to teach research-based approaches to cultural studies of the West.

But those are scholarly practices undergraduate students may never use beyond their university classrooms. Stegner also helps me address students' lives beyond academia. He offers a way for teachers of introductory college classes to engage their students in larger questions about the central importance of responsibility and advocacy in their future roles as citizens, particularly concerning environmental issues in the West. Near the end of this chapter I describe another assignment for an undergraduate nature writing class, an assignment that would work as well in any composition or writing class. It is based on Stegner's often reprinted "Wilderness Letter," originally written in 1960 to intervene in the definition of the purposes of wilderness in a study prepared by the Outdoor Recreation Resources Review Commission.

Introducing *Angle of Repose*

In *Angle of Repose* Lyman says of his grandmother's Leadville cabin in 1879, "[T]here assembled . . . an extraordinary collection of education, culture, talent, eloquence, reputation, political power, and intellectual force."[3] My students come to recognize that he might also be describing *Angle of Repose*, which gathers a far larger collection of literary and historical figures and facts into a cultural history of the early U.S. West, written by two scholars in the interdisciplinary American studies tradition: Lyman and Stegner. Or he might be describing other Stegner works, particularly his biographies of Bernard DeVoto and John Wesley Powell and his essays, which also focus on western subjects. Page Stegner has commented that when his father "created DeVoto's life, he created his own."[4] And Stegner might be reflecting on much of his own work when he suggests that if DeVoto "were to put a single label on what he had written in the Easy Chair, we would call it cultural criticism" and insist that "no manifestation of American life is trivial to the critic of culture."[5] Nor is any quirky little thing.

Angle of Repose can certainly be read as a fictional biography, based as it is on the life and letters of Mary Hallock Foote, and Stegner's four biographies, as well as many of his other writings, are similarly genre-crossing, as much cultural history as biography, their interdisciplinary methodology instructive to contemporary critics, while Stegner's willingness to read town dumps, folk songs, river canyons, illustrations, geological surveys and drawings, paintings, and personal letters as "texts" anticipates current scholarship. Curt Meine has even called Stegner a "geobiographer," one who explores "the relationship between biographical subject and biogeographical space," using "this relationship to examine forces, tensions, patterns, and themes at the heart of North America's cultural development."[6] In *The Uneasy Chair* Stegner praises DeVoto for his innovative narrative style, particularly well demonstrated in *The Year of Decision, 1846*: "'history by Synecdoche,' the concentration of large events and movements of population and clashes of attitude and interest within the single, sharp focus of a symbolic action or restricted period of time."[7] I suggest that Stegner borrowed—and adapted— this methodology from his friend to write cultural biography. (He frequently commented that he was not interested in the personal lives of Powell or DeVoto.) Instead of concentrating on action or time, he focuses on a single crucial figure, such as Mary Hallock Foote, who serves as a magnet, drawing together cultural, geographical, and political forces and events. As DeVoto himself wrote about the Powell biography, *Beyond the Hundredth Meridian*, "Mr. Stegner's subject is nineteenth century America and the part the West played in creating twentieth century America"; Dan Flores calls the book a "history of ideas" of the West.[8]

In *Angle of Repose* Stegner borrows extensively—and controversially— from the life, writings, and drawings of Foote to create a historical novel in which he achieves one of his major goals: to connect the past and the present in the American West, as he argues most cogently in "History, Myth, and the Western Writer."[9] He creates a narrator, Lyman Ward, an award-winning historian who greatly resembles Stegner in his attitudes toward both past and present. Raised by his grandmother, Molly Ward, a celebrated illustrator and writer, and his grandfather, Oliver Ward, a groundbreaking engineer, Lyman seeks to reconstruct their lives through research into family archives and the cultural and intellectual history of the late nineteenth century. In particular, he would like to understand what happened to create what he views as a rupture in his grandparents' marriage around 1890, some forty years before the two died. Some critics believe he is motivated by the recent failure of his own marriage. Lyman is aided and sometimes challenged by his assistant, a rebellious product of the 1960s California youth movements, which further allows Stegner to draw parallels and contrasts between the West's pasts and presents. The Ward story concludes with a family catastrophe that never occurred in Foote's life, allowing Stegner to present what I at least see as a cynical view of the Wards' marriage, though Lyman's interpretation and authority as a narrator are hotly contested issues among scholars. Lyman, however, perhaps uses his exploration of his grandparents' lives to come to some resolution—an "angle of repose"—in his own personal life.

Within the first week of class I give my students a list of cultural and historical figures, events, institutions, and movements mentioned in *Angle of Repose*, some only once (the painter Mary Cassatt, for instance) or twice (*Little Women* author Louisa May Alcott). Some are recurrent: the picturesque, the geological surveys, the Hudson River school of painters, which I have learned I have to distinguish from other "schools," such as the Cooper Union School of Art, Massachusetts Institute of Technology, and University of California, Berkeley, which are also present in the novel. (I offer a list in the appendix to this chapter, but readers will find other examples, as will students.) Some are well known: Mark Twain, Rudyard Kipling, Gary Snyder; others are little known today: railroad magnate Henry Villard or Richard Watson Gilder, the influential editor of *Century Magazine*. Some establish a theme: the group of scientists and engineers who intersect with the Wards' lives in the West, for example, or the Wobblies. Some point to historical controversies or events: the "Grant pigpen," Clarence King, Stanford White, or a potential "mixed" marriage to Emma Lazarus, who was Jewish. Many reference cultural norms concerning gender: "corsets," "*ohne Büstenhalter*," "women's lib," *The Scarlet Letter*, or "Masaccio's Eve." Some occur only offstage, such as the Chinese miners who work at the New Almaden mine but who are never seen, or the mine outside of Potosí, Bolivia, where Oliver hopes to work but never does and which I learned from a student report was not only the highest but also one of the world's largest cities in 1672 (two hundred thousand people). Most serve as a kind of shorthand reference for Stegner to create his deeply textured social, political, and cultural landscapes; one such obvious example is "Edith Wharton's version of New York."

I ask each student to turn in a list of five details in which they are interested, and I then assign students one "quirky little thing" to discuss in a paper and an oral presentation no more than ten minutes long. In the graduate seminar this assignment comes early in the semester and, as I will discuss later, offers a template for future assignments. For the undergraduates this assignment serves as their "big" research paper for the semester, due at the end, when they present their oral reports. I have learned over the years not to assign too many students in the thirty-person undergraduate class the same details. Inevitably a large number of them want the well-known *Scarlet Letter*, but by the third oral report on the novel the student-presenter will be demoralized at having nothing new to offer. With the advent of Google, not available when I first gave this assignment, students can quickly search through the list. If I know the students and their interests—for instance, if one is a geology or art major—I often make suggestions.

Blinks, Winks, and the Interpretation of Culture

We then turn to Clifford Geertz's influential concept of how human activities and cultural production can only be understood when "thickly described."[10] By reading *Angle of Repose* as "thick description," my students develop a valuable methodology (as a literary critic, I might even call it a theoretical framework) through learning to borrow Lyman's interest in "quirky little things," an interest certainly shared by his creator, who wrote that "[t]he fiction writer is an incorrigible lover of concrete *things*."[11]

While the graduate students read Geertz, I enact for the undergraduates an explanation of the most relevant point, which is Geertz's well-known discussion of the difference between a "blink" and a "wink." This lesson offers a valuable opportunity for comic relief and great fun for any teacher who likes to ham it up. Some readers of this chapter have suggested that perhaps some instructors might feel uncomfortable using an exercise such as this one, which foregrounds sexuality and gender identity, so educators must use their own judgment. I will just say immodestly that my students have always enjoyed this classroom exercise; I have never had a complaint about it.

I call a male student to the front of the room and walk past him, giving him a broad wink. Acting as if some can't see me, I say, "My eye is closing and then opening." I ask the students to interpret our interaction. They offer predictable ideas: if I know him, one thing; if I don't, perhaps another.

Then I repeat with a female student. They immediately recognize how a cultural assumption inflects their interpretations, and we discuss how those assumptions have changed over time, especially with the growing acceptance of LGBTQ rights. We also read my wink in political contexts, discussing, for instance, how they would feel about my behavior if I were *really* me, their teacher, and they were my students, thus raising issues of the inappropriate use of power and authority.

Then I offer various scenarios. For example, "Let's say I had Susan in class last year and really liked her. She wants into this class, but it's full. I tell everyone who's not preregistered to leave, but then I [here I wink broadly at Susan]. What's going on here?" Another scenario: "You're out in the desert West, and a dust storm comes up." I pantomime excessive blinking and wipe dust out of my eyes. "Anyone wear contact lenses?" By this point we've begun to distinguish between winks—whose meaning is determined by cultural context, by the necessity of what Geertz calls "thick [cultural] description" to understand meaning—and blinks, which are physiological. The contact wearers believe they "blink." But then I point out that even that gesture *could* be culturally inflected by asking *why* they wear contacts. Perhaps because of cultural beliefs that glasses aren't "attractive" (wink?) or perhaps because they like to play sports (blink?). (A year prior to my writing this chapter *not one student* admitted to ever having heard the satiric line from Dorothy Parker's 1925 poem "News Item" that used to torment young women of my generation: "Men seldom make passes / At girls who wear glasses.")

So a "thin description" would simply describe what physically happened—as in my line "My eye was closed and then opened again" (note the passive, which removes agency)—whereas a "thick description" attempts to describe the full cultural context in which actions (or historical figures or writers or artists or events or places) acquire meaning.

Creating Together a "Thick Description" of the Cultural Context of *Angle of Repose*

As we turn to *Angle of Repose* I want my students first to recognize the novel, as I suggested before, as an excellent example of what "thick description" looks like, then to internalize what should be obvious—that the most important quality they can develop as readers and scholars is that intense curiosity and attention to detail captured in the phrase "quirky little things that most people wouldn't even notice." This quality is at the heart of interdisciplinary scholarship, and Stegner is an exemplar. The students' challenge is to offer their classmates a thicker description of their particular detail, which in turn allows for a focused interpretation based on historical research. Readers can enjoy the novel without knowing the role *Godey's Lady's Book* played in policing women's behavior in the nineteenth century or fully understanding why Oliver so admires John Wesley Powell or why Lyman has such disdain for eastern "Brahmins" or some of the ideas of Walt Whitman or the philosopher Paul Goodman. But the reports reveal that even cursory research leads to far richer cultural knowledge. This is a "chicken or egg" assignment: the student's detail acquires meaning within the cultural context of the novel, but at the same time, more information about the detail opens doors into the novel's hidden rooms, into its motifs, themes, and meanings—a fuller understanding they can share with their classmates.

Let me develop one example from my own work, from an essay in which I examine more fully Stegner's exploration of connections and conflicts between West and East: "Book Learning: *Angle of Repose* as Literary History." (For more examples of possible readings of "quirky little things" from the novel, turn to that essay.) My detail is "the single issue of February 1885" of *Century Magazine*, mentioned once in *Angle of Repose*.[12] *Century Magazine*, established and long edited by Richard Watson Gilder, on whom the character Thomas Hudson is based, was one of the most influential cultural media figures in the United States in the late nineteenth century.

Although Lyman's description of Thomas Hudson, longtime friend of Susan Ward, is ambivalent, fraught with a western male's attitudes about effete intellectuals and the eastern literary establishment, he respects Hudson's role as an editor, saying, "I wouldn't be surprised if he found and published two thirds of the best literature of four decades."[13] One of those writers is of course Susan Ward, and Hudson puts her in good company. According to Lyman, one of her stories—he does not identify which one—appears in that February 1885 issue of *Century Magazine*, which also includes installments of Twain's *The Adventures of Huckleberry Finn*, William Dean Howells's *The Rise of Silas Lapham*, and Henry James's *The Bostonians*. In fact Stegner makes a small but significant historical change: while Mary Hallock Foote's story "A Cloud on the Mountain" appeared in the November 1885 issue of *Century Magazine*, along with the first installment of her novel *John Bodewin's Testimony*, none of her stories appears in the February issue. And in what might appear to be an extraneous detail, Stegner points out that the February issue contains "the ninth and tenth chapters" of *Silas Lapham*.[14] Yet, like many of Stegner's cultural facts, this change and this detail validate Lyman's interest in "quirky little things" and set up an implicit conversation between and about books.[15]

The Rise of Silas Lapham is about class in the Gilded Age; a smart but uneducated farm boy from New England, whose brothers have headed west, becomes a self-made millionaire and struggles to make sense of "civilized society." Chapter 9 explores the role of reading in U.S. society, a major theme in *Angle of Repose*. In that chapter the upper-class Tom Corey advises Irene Lapham on which books to buy for the library in her family's elegant new house on Beacon Hill; the celebrated authors he names of course appear in *Angle of Repose*. Irene, like her father, is less concerned with the authors than with the elegant bindings, but her sister Penelope, a reader, expresses a view of George Eliot that parallels Oliver Ward's in a literary debate with his wife: "I wish she would let you find out a little about the people for yourself."[16] At the chapter's end Tom and his Brahmin father discuss habits of reading among the civilized and the "noncultivated." Later in the novel the book theme reappears when Howells examines the influence of a best-selling sentimental novel, *Tears, Idle Tears* (called *Slop, Silly Slop* by Tom's ironical sister), on the actions of various characters.

Ever practical, Silas Lapham reads newspapers, and Howells recognizes the cultural work done by newspapers, books, and magazines such as *Century Magazine*—he was after all the editor of *Harper's Monthly* for many years—even if his hero sees books largely as interior decoration. Serving a similar function as satiric props in the Grangerford house of Twain's classic, books and book learning are also major themes throughout *The Adventures of Huckleberry Finn*. Tom Sawyer is clearly a victim—and a carrier—of what Twain called the Sir Walter Scott disease, that is, an obsession with romantic plots and language. (Lyman reads Scott with his grandmother but escapes infection.) Twain often associates books with "gentility," with hypocrisy, with efforts to exert power over others, and time and again he exposes characters unable to escape the kind of "about used up" sentimental language Oliver points out in some of Susan's descriptions or other "false" literary inheritances.[17] (And a parenthetical here: writing about his childhood, Stegner said that "almost everything I got from books was either at odds with what I knew from experience or irrelevant to it or remote from it.")[18] Both *The Rise of Silas Lapham* and *The Adventures of Huckleberry Finn* show us characters wrestling with the influence books have on their lives; both novels explore the struggle between romance and realism in U.S. culture, one of our most significant literary themes.

Stegner recognizes that Susan has a voice in this conversation. Hudson, who decides to make Susan his "western correspondent" and to publish her work along with these great novels, values her attempts to bring together romance and realism, to write in "her key of aspiration arising out of homely realism" in a "spirit of discovery" about the West.[19] Susan will carry not only books but also the great literary and intellectual debates of her time into the West. Particularly in *Angle of Repose* but throughout his body of work as well, Stegner represents western history as shaped by reading: Susan and Oliver, anachronistically, have the same debate about reading that the Virginian and Molly Wood carried on in 1902 regarding works by George Eliot and Ivan Turgenev.

In many subtle ways, such as his reference to chapter 9 of *Silas Lapham*, Stegner explores the conflicts and the interdependence between the two dominant literary movements of the late nineteenth century and suggests that western literature evolves from the marriage of these two points of view and style—romance and realism. In fact he marries them together. Lyman continues his grandmother's project when he realizes what he's really exploring in his book: "A marriage . . . A masculine and a feminine. A romantic and a realist."[20] (Note which gender goes with which point of view.) Think back here to my discussion of Stegner's effort to synthesize, to offer us dialogic conversations.

DeVoto once said, "I distrust absolutes. Rather I long ago passed from distrust of them to opposition. And with them let me include prophecy, simplification, generalization, abstract logic, and especially the habit of mind which consults theory first and experience only afterward."[21] I think Stegner shared DeVoto's view, and so do I. What I've just demonstrated is an assignment based on inductive reasoning, building from close reading, curiosity, and careful research. (In my undergraduate class I use Susan Glaspell's midwestern short story "A Jury of Her Peers" very early in the term to establish the dichotomy between inductive and deductive thinking.) One of the quickest ways to paralyze even a graduate student would be an assignment to write about romance and realism as a theme in the novel, an abbreviated version of which I have just offered, beginning with the February 1885 issue of *Century Magazine*. Notice and start with the quirky little things. Stegner even seems to suggest this is the way culture is created: "Culture is a pyramid to which each of us brings a stone."[22] I've always thought his "pyramid" is really a cairn, with Stegner leading the way. Writing that "at its best [literature] is a bolt of lightning from me to you, a flash of recognition and a feeling within the context of a shared culture," he shows my students how to read within a shared cultural context.[23] Here is a comment about this assignment from my former graduate student Allyson Jones:

> For years I tried to explain my field of study through statements such as, "American Studies is an interdisciplinary view of history. For example, I love learning about how literature, say *Uncle Tom's Cabin*, has shaped history, or how a piece of art reflects a political movement." Such a statement quickly grew old and never quite encapsulated my fascination. My interests finally found articulation in Stegner's "quirky little details." As I researched my assigned "details," my readings and writings gained depth. A single mention of Mary Cassatt in the middle of *Angle of Repose* led to an examination that enriched my understanding of and appreciation for the character of Susan Burling Ward. A study of the "west cure" enhanced my knowledge of Owen Wister and the cast of *The Virginian*. Researching Alice Fletcher and the Dawes Act augmented my reading of [D'Arcy McNickle's] *Wind from an Enemy Sky*. And so it continues. Each detail, no matter how "quirky" or "little," adds vibrancy to my studies, my writings, and my understanding of humanity.

As Allyson's comment suggests, this assignment becomes a kind of template for later assignments, as the graduate students continue to do oral presentations on quirky details from other books that help us understand other texts in richer cultural contexts. Because their subject matter is so narrowly focused, these oral presentations are almost always very successful, building students' confidence and providing their classmates with a wealth of social, historical, and cultural background, accessory to the shared reading.

I've been giving this assignment for thirty or so years. About twenty-five years ago one of my students, Elizabeth Wright, now a full professor, carried it with her to grad school at the University of New Mexico, where the first-year writing committee adopted it. Every first year student at UNM was required to read *Angle of Repose* and write papers on "quirky little things" as a way of initiating them into how to do scholarly research.

Teaching and Advocating Citizenship

But most of those undergraduate students will not become scholars, and what I really hope they take away from their writing about *Angle of Repose* is an insatiable sense of curiosity about our culture and history that will keep them reading and engaged in learning about what I now will call, in the political climate of 2017, our democratic processes. Let me turn to another assignment, one I have often used primarily in nature or environmental writing classes, to illustrate how Stegner can also map trails for general-education students. This assignment originates in his advocacy for conservation and other environmental issues, particularly in the West. He admired Powell as "the personification of an ideal of public service" and DeVoto for taking on causes, for being what we would now call a "public intellectual."[24] DeVoto, he said, "galvanized" him "the moment [he] showed signs of being an activist."[25] Twenty years after writing his "Wilderness Letter" in 1960, Stegner acknowledged in "The Geography of Hope" that he was probably inspired to do so by the activism of Sierra Club president David Brower, who "cattleprod[ded]" him into action.[26] The environmental historian Dan Flores echoes Stegner, calling "Wilderness Letter" a "worldwide classic of environmental history, . . . a galvanizing document."[27] I assign the letter hoping my students will be galvanized by reading it, as students have been in the past.

Stegner shows us the importance of turning words into deeds. In class we talk about the coalition between Stegner and Brower that led to the book *This Is Dinosaur: Echo Park Country and Its Magic Rivers* (1955), distributed to all members of Congress as a lobbying tool to prevent construction of a dam that would flood a canyon on the Green River. That book served as a template for later works, such as Terry Tempest Williams and Stephen Trimble's *Testimony* (1996), also distributed to all congressional members to help protect the redrock desert. We also discuss Stegner's later regret that, in saving the Echo Park section of Dinosaur National Monument from flooding, they had inadvertently sacrificed Glen Canyon, and we explore the inevitable consequences of our actions. In *his* actions, as well as in passages such as the one below, Stegner illuminates for the next generation what he saw as the responsibility of the writer:

> You speak of the writer's involvement in his society. I think too many writers are far too little involved. They sit in the middle of their own skulls, or their endocrines, and snipe at the saints, politicians, working people, housewives, and bureaucrats who have to keep the world running. This doesn't mean I am anti-literary. The highest thing I can think of doing is literary. But literature does not exist in a vacuum. . . . We are neither detached nor semi-detached, but are linked to our world by a million interdependencies. To deny the interdependencies, while living on the comforts and services that they make possible, is adolescent when it isn't downright dishonest.[28]

After reading Stegner's letter and discussing its influence and how it laid the groundwork for Stegner's work with Stewart Udall at the Department of the Interior and numerous conservation successes, my students write a letter themselves, about a social or political or cultural issue they care strongly about, to a *real* person or agency or group that has some influence over their chosen topic, and then they must find an address and mail the letter. One day in class they all read their letters aloud to each other, and we talk about the rhetorics of advocacy, about differences between polemics and persuasion, between Edward Abbey's and Stegner's writing on redrock country. (Later we get to Terry Tempest Williams.) Sometimes they have actually received a reply they can share. Students have written letters to county officials about the desecration caused by run-offs into Bear Lake, to the National Park Service about snowmobiles in Yellowstone, to whoever it is—I have forgotten, but the student knew—who dispenses licenses to fish in the Logan River, to potential donors for a Humane Society chapter in Cache County, Utah. One student managed to get policies changed in the Utah State University's Dairy Bar, where she worked. (Sadly, despite my persistent pushiness, none of them have managed to get the Styrofoam containers and plastic utensils removed from the student union.) As they listen to each other, I ask them to think about another of Stegner's recurring concerns: "the bonds that make individuals into a society."[29]

Of course I tell my students I don't really care what they write about, what position they take (when, in fact, I do). But this assignment reaches beyond environmentalism. I want to train students to be insightful, lifelong readers, but I also feel it's my responsibility, especially at a public land-grant university, to encourage them to become good citizens. *Responsibility*—now that's one of Stegner's favorite words. "I'm quite sure that what I least like about some kinds of people is irresponsibility," he groused to Richard Etulain. "I don't give a damn what their morals are or anything else, but their irresponsibility to something larger than themselves, to some kind of social stability or common tradition and standard, does seem to me a kind of delinquency."[30] His past, he says,

> probably leads me to take a moralistic view of writing, to think of it not only as an art, but also as a kind of cultural function. I suppose I'm constantly trying to bear in mind that having been very lucky, I also am very responsible, and that the only thing that makes civilization go forward is the responsibility of individuals, whether gifted or otherwise, small or large. All of us have the obligation somehow to have some kind of concern for the species, for the culture, for the larger thing outside of ourselves. I'm sure that's buried not too deeply in most of the books I've written.[31]

That's a lesson I hope my students learn from reading Stegner. And the "Wilderness Letter" ends with that audacious and oft-quoted phrase he used elsewhere as well, "the geography of hope," which has such resonance today. (I rewrite this passage two days after President Obama gave his farewell address to Congress, a week before the Trump administration was set to begin.) Stegner, as we know, challenged the angst and despair and emptiness of so much late twentieth-century literature; he always showed that individual acts mattered, and he recognized that taking responsibility is a way of alleviating guilt. I think it's important that he leaves today's young people with that message and that hope. (For a fuller consideration of these themes of social responsibility and citizenship, one could assign the whole of Stegner's *Where the Bluebird Sings to the Lemonade Springs*.)

Conclusion: Stegner and Education

As with many things, Stegner the university teacher often "ruminated"—his word—about education. In *Beyond the Hundredth Meridian* he relies on a repeated phrase to define what he sees as the source of the energy, curiosity, and independent thinking Powell and many of his colleagues brought to the West following the Civil War: unlike the figures he often sets up as Powell's foils (the Harvard-educated Henry Adams and Clarence King), they depended on "homemade educations" and learned on the job.[32] They also "demonstrated that fundamental affinity between Democracy and Science" that both Powell and Stegner saw as essential to U.S. society, certainly a crucial theme in these times of climate-change deniers in Congress.[33] And yet he saw his own working-class western boyhood and those of DeVoto and Walter Van Tilburg Clark as "culturally undernourished," deprived of "the civilized tradition of books, ideas, poetry, history, philosophy, all the instruments and residue of human self-examination" that they rushed hungrily toward.[34] One of many reasons I value Stegner is that he describes my own western childhood, a generation or two later, and now those of some of my students, also first-generation college students. We bring our stones to his cairn.

Appendix: Cultural or Historical Mentions in *Angle of Repose*

Literary Figures

Helen Hunt Jackson
Bret Harte
Mark Twain

Walt Whitman
Rudyard Kipling
George Eliot and Ivan Turgenev
Henry Adams
Nathaniel Hawthorne/ *The Scarlet Letter*
Henry James
Margaret Fuller
Gary Snyder
Emma Lazarus
Louisa May Alcott
George Washington Cable
Mary Murfree
E. L. Godkin
William Dean Howells
Thomas Donaldson
Hjalmar Hjorth Boyesen
Peter Quint (Henry James character)
Richard Watson Gilder
The Beechers (Harriet B. Stowe, Lyman, Henry Ward)
"Edith Wharton version of New York"
Ralph Waldo Emerson

Artists, Art Critics, Art Movements, Actors

F. J. Haynes
Joseph Jefferson
Stanford White
Thomas Moran
Albert Bierstadt
John La Farge
Mary Cassatt
John Ruskin
Lola Montez
Abbott Thayer
"Masaccio's Eve"
Hudson River school (art movement)

Pre-Raphaelite movement
William James Linton
"The picturesque"

Potosí, Bolivia
Mexican mines like the one in Morelia

Places

Fruitlands and Brook Farm (utopian communities)
"Edith Wharton version of New York"
Santa Cruz CA in 1880
Quaker communities in New York and New England
Leadville CO
Deadwood CO

Schools

Cooper Union School of Art
Massachusetts Institute of Technology in 1870
University of California, Berkeley, in the late 1960s
St. Paul's School, Concord NH

Events

Battle of the Little Big Horn
Free Speech Movement, University of California, Berkeley
Completion of the transcontinental railroad
Strikes in Leadville when the Footes were there
"Women's lib movement"
Panic of 1890

Other Important Figures

Peter Cooper (idealist thinker)
Chief Joseph of the Nez Percé
William Bancroft (for whom the Bancroft Prize is named)
Paul Goodman (philosopher who influenced 1960s radical politics)

Controversies, Scandals, Politics

Boss Tweed/Tammany Hall
"The Grant pigpen"

Clarence King and the diamond scam
Stanford White's murder by the husband of his lover

Miscellany

Corsets in 1880

Homosocial relationships between nineteenth-century women/what
Lyman calls "lesbianism"

What women were taught in nineteenth-century art schools

"Bra burning"—Shelly Rasmussen being "*ohne Büstenhalter*"

Quaker use of "thee" and "thou"

Birth control in 1880

NOTES

1. Stegner, *Angle of Repose*, 211.
2. Stegner, *Angle of Repose*, 211.
3. Stegner, *Angle of Repose*, 252.
4. Quoted in Benson, *Wallace Stegner*, 368.
5. Stegner, *Uneasy Chair*, 381.
6. Meine, "Wallace Stegner, Geobiographer," 123.
7. Stegner, *Uneasy Chair*, 72.
8. DeVoto, "Introduction," xxiii; Flores, "Bioregionalist of the High and Dry," 109.
9. This controversy largely concerns two issues: Stegner's unattributed use of Foote's language from letters and writings and the liberties he took in dramatically changing her life story, after following it so closely throughout much of the novel, by imagining that Susan Ward has an affair that leads to the death of her daughter. For more information about Stegner's use of Foote materials, see Walsh, "*Angle of Repose* and the Writing of Mary Hallock Foote." For information about the controversy, see Fradkin, *Wallace Stegner and the American West*. For Stegner's defense, see Stegner and Etulain, *Conversations with Wallace Stegner*.
10. Geertz, "Thick Description," 14.
11. Stegner, "Fiction," 5.
12. Stegner, *Angle of Repose*, 54.
13. Stegner, *Angle of Repose*, 54.
14. Stegner, *Angle of Repose*, 54.
15. Stegner, *Angle of Repose*, 211.
16. Howells, *Rise of Silas Lapham*, 82.
17. Stegner, *Angle of Repose*, 139.
18. Stegner, *Wolf Willow*, 26.
19. Stegner, *Angle of Repose*, 21.

20. Stegner, *Angle of Repose*, 211.
21. Quoted in Thomas, *Country in the Mind*, 39.
22. Stegner, "Living Dry," 59.
23. Stegner, "Coming of Age," 141.
24. Stegner, *Beyond the Hundredth Meridian*, vii.
25. Stegner and Etulain, *Conversations with Wallace Stegner*, 170.
26. Stegner, "Geography of Hope, 113.
27. Flores, "Biogregionalist of the High and Dry," 113.
28. Fradkin, *Wallace Stegner and the American West*, 213–14.
29. Stegner and Etulain, *Conversations with Wallace Stegner*, 197.
30. Stegner and Etulain, *Conversations with Wallace Stegner*, 197.
31. Stegner and Etulain, *Conversations with Wallace Stegner*, 196–97.
32. Stegner, *Beyond the Hundredth Meridian*, 10.
33. Stegner, *Beyond the Hundredth Meridian*, viii.
34. Stegner, "Finding the Place" 4; Stegner, "Walter Clark's Frontier," 176.

BIBLIOGRAPHY

Benson, Jackson. *Wallace Stegner: His Life and Work*. New York: Penguin, 1996.
DeVoto, Bernard. "Introduction." In *Beyond the Hundredth Meridian: John Wesley Powell and the Second Opening of the West*, by Wallace Stegner, xv–xxii. 1954. New York: Penguin, 1992.
Flores, Dan. "Bioregionalist of the High and Dry: Stegner and Western Environmentalism." In *Wallace Stegner and the Continental Vision: Essays on Literature, History and Landscape*, edited by Curt Meine, 107–20. Washington DC: Island Press, 1997.
Fradkin, Philip L. *Wallace Stegner and the American West*. New York: Knopf, 2008.
Geertz, Clifford. "Thick Description: Toward an Interpretive Theory of Culture." In *The Interpretation of Cultures*, chapter 1. New York: Basic Books, 1973.
Graulich, Melody. "Book Learning: *Angle of Repose* as Literary History." In *Wallace Stegner: Man and Writer*, edited by Charles E. Rankin, 231–53. Albuquerque: University of New Mexico Press, 1996. Also available at MelodyGraulich.com.
Howells, William Dean. *The Rise of Silas Lapham*. 1885. New York: Signet, 1980.
Meine, Curt. "Wallace Stegner, Geobiographer." In *Wallace Stegner and the Continental Vision: Essays on Literature, History and Landscape*, edited by Curt Meine, 121–36. Washington DC: Island Press, 1997.
Stegner, Wallace. *Angle of Repose*. 1971. New York: Penguin, 1992.
———. *Beyond the Hundredth Meridian: John Wesley Powell and the Second Opening of the West*. 1954. New York: Penguin, 1992.
———. "Coming of Age: The End of the Beginning" (1990). In *Where the Bluebird Sings to the Lemonade Springs: Living and Writing in the West*, 135–42. New York: Penguin, 1992.
———. "Fiction: A Lens on Life" (1982). In *On Teaching and Writing Fiction*, edited by Lynn Stegner, 1–10. New York: Penguin, 2002.

———. "Finding the Place: A Migrant Childhood" (1989). In *Where the Bluebird Sings to the Lemonade Springs: Living and Writing in the West*, 3–21. New York: Penguin, 1992.

———. "The Geography of Hope." Originally published in *The Living Wilderness* (December 1980). Available at Eco-Speak. https://web.stanford.edu/~cbross/Ecospeak /wildernessletterintro.html.

———. "History, Myth, and the Western Writer" (1969). In *The Sound of Mountain Water: The Changing American West*, 186–201. New York: Penguin, 1997.

———. "Living Dry" (1987). In *Where the Bluebird Sings to the Lemonade Springs: Living and Writing in the West*, 57–75. New York: Penguin, 1992.

———. *The Uneasy Chair: A Biography of Bernard DeVoto*. 1973. Lincoln: University of Nebraska Press, 2001.

———. "Walter Clark's Frontier" (1983). In *Where the Bluebird Sings to the Lemonade Springs: Living and Writing in the West*, 172–89. New York: Penguin, 1992.

———. "Wilderness Letter." Published in many venues in 1960. Available from the Wilderness Society. https://www.wilderness.org/articles/article/wallace-stegner.

———. *Wolf Willow: A History, a Story, and a Memory of the Last Plains Frontier*. 1962. Lincoln: University of Nebraska Press, 1980.

Stegner, Wallace, and Richard Etulain. *Conversations with Wallace Stegner on Western History and Literature*. Rev. ed. Salt Lake City: University of Utah Press, 1990.

Thomas, John L. *A Country in the Mind: Wallace Stegner, Bernard DeVoto, History, and the American Land*. New York: Routledge, 2000.

Walsh, Mary Ellen Williams. "*Angle of Repose* and the Writing of Mary Hallock Foote: A Source Study." In *Critical Essays on Wallace Stegner*, edited by Anthony Arthur, 184–209. Boston: G. K. Hall, 1982.

3

Teaching the Black West

KALENDA EATON AND MICHAEL K. JOHNSON

Drawing on our experience in writing about and teaching the literature and culture of the African American West, our chapter proposes two models for a course in black western studies. Both courses are modified versions of classes that we have taught individually at various times at our universities. Our shared goal is to elucidate enduring themes in the literature and culture of the African American West and to illustrate the wide range and variety of black western texts. Michael's course, The African American West and the African American Western, uses a thematic organization and places more emphasis on genre—on the development of the black western in literature and film. Kalenda's course, Literatures of the Black West, organizes that material chronologically and emphasizes exploring the key characteristics of black western experience and history. Both courses are designed for upper-level undergraduates, but we will also suggest additional critical readings (some of which will be listed in our bibliography) that might be adopted for a graduate-level course.

For students at both our schools, even at the upper level, many would be taking their first course in African American literature, and, given our location in the eastern United States, this would likely be the first time students focused on the region of the American West (and, outside of perhaps

Blazing Saddles or *Django Unchained*, their first encounter with the concept of black western history). Our courses are designed with awareness of the need for filling in those gaps.

The African American West and the African American Western (Michael's Course)

I designed The African American West and the African American Western to examine two types of black western narratives. One type adapts the mythology of the West by revising the conventions of the "western" so as to recreate the genre in a form that better expresses black experience. The other type (both fiction and nonfiction) more realistically portrays black westward migration. Myth and reality, however, often mingle in works about the American West. The course covers a wide variety of material and is best suited for an upper-level English, American/cultural studies, or ethnic studies course. Most of the materials (books, films, songs, etc.) also foreground debates about gender or the roles men and women play in society.

The course is organized around four units: exploration and migration, region, cultural studies, and the contemporary West. Migration focuses on texts that make movement westward (or western exploration) an important narrative element. Region focuses more on stories taking place within areas of settlement. Cultural studies emphasizes film and other media and is more focused on the genre of the western. The contemporary West examines black western stories set in the last part of the twentieth and first part of the twenty-first centuries.

Because students may not be familiar with African American literature, I generally include specific contextual readings in (nonwestern) African American literature. For the course instructor (or for a course with graduate students), I also recommend my book *Hoo-Doo Cowboys and Bronze Buckaroos: Conceptions of the African American West* as an additional resource. Much of the literature and other media suggested for use as course materials receives at least some discussion in the book. Film, music, and television might be viewed in class or out of class, especially material posted on YouTube or available through streaming services.

Introduction (Week One)

The course begins with Stephen Crane's short story "The Bride Comes to Yellow Sky" (1898). The story effectively illustrates key conventions of the western genre: the perceived conflict between western freedom and eastern civilization, the West's association with nature and wilderness in contrast to the East's association with mechanization and urbanization, the way that opposition lines up with opposing gender roles in the story (the Bride, representing the changes brought by civilization, arriving at the frontier via the powerful mechanical force of the train), the importance of the showdown as the climax of the western plot, and the story's own ambivalence about these genre tropes.

"The Bride Comes to Yellow Sky" neatly encapsulates the gender ideology that Jane Tompkins sums up in *West of Everything*: the "qualities devalued" in the western (civilization, the East, church-going, education, resolving conflict through means other than violence, etc.) are consistently "associated with women."[1] The story surprisingly also provides an introduction to the African American West or at least to the black westerner as depicted in white narratives. The key African American character in "Bride" is the black porter who observes with amusement the newlywed discomfort of the sheriff and his bride, who serves them breakfast with concealed condescension, who stoically brushes ashes from their clothing as they disembark, and who accepts his tip before continuing off, unremarked, on his own westward journey. His duality (a topic African American writers explore in more detail) is suggested by the disjunction between his thoughts and his actions, the way he hides his judgmental observations through the mask of servility. Might this porter, like Nat Love (who retires from cattle drives to begin porter work), have had a more adventurous western history that precedes his service employment? The presence of the porter suggests a western story that Crane only partially recognizes as one worth telling. Thus "The Bride Comes to Yellow Sky" also introduces the racial politics of the western genre. Characters of color are present in the story, but they are pushed to the margins. Crane's entertaining short story provides a good introduction to the western in its concise cataloging of the genre's conventions, ideologies, and absences.

The western presence of African American cavalry troops (popularly known as "buffalo soldiers") is one aspect of African American western history that is ready-made for genre representation. "Mission" (1959), an episode of the anthology series *Zane Grey Theatre* starring Sammy Davis Jr., may be the earliest representation of the African American West on television. In the episode African American soldiers are charged with the task of delivering a Native American chief to a peace negotiation (which another tribal group opposes). As an accompanying critical reading, Richard Slotkin's chapter "Regeneration through Violence: The Language of Myth" in *Gunfighter Nation* works well in conjunction with the episode. Does violent action against the Other work the same mythic power when an African American hero is the agent of that violence?

I close this unit with the music and video of "Old Town Road" by Lil Nas X, a cross-genre song from a rapper who evokes both country and western imagery in his lyrics (the song begins with the singer taking his horse to Old Town Road, where he plans to ride until he can't ride no more). Debuting at number 19 in March 2019 on the Billboard Hot Country Songs chart, the song was subsequently removed from that category and placed on the Hot Rap Songs chart, sparking a debate over whether the musical elements or the presence of a black performer caused the removal of the western-themed song. As an introductory assignment, students researching the wide-ranging online conversation about the song would reveal a lot about why the African American West remains a marginal concern for many American readers, viewers, and listeners. The official video for a remixed version of the song (a collaboration with country singer Billy Ray Cyrus) amusingly references the controversy in a western-themed adventure taking place partially in the past (1889) and partially in the present (2019).

Exploration and Migration (Weeks 2–4)

This section begins with excerpts from four classic works of African American literature: Frederick Douglass's *Narrative of the Life of Frederick Douglass* (chapter 10), Harriet Jacobs's *Incidents in the Life of a Slave Girl* ("The Jealous Mistress"), Booker T. Washington's *Up from Slavery* ("Boyhood Days" and "The Atlanta Exposition Address"), and W. E. B. Du Bois's *The Souls of Black Folks* ("Of Our Spiritual Strivings"). African American narratives of the West are "double-voiced," Henry Louis Gates Jr. writes, occupying "spaces in at least two traditions," American or European, and "one of several related but distinct black traditions."[2] The slave narrative is central to African American literature, and there are clear parallels between the slave narrative's emphasis on the journey north to freedom and postemancipation black narratives of westward migration. Excerpts from the texts above provide a sample of the literary tradition that turn-of-the-twentieth-century black western writers draw on, and through Du Bois and Washington students will get a sense of the postemancipation issues and debates that likewise inform those texts.

I begin the discussion of *The Life and Adventures of Nat Love* by showing three photographs: portraits of Du Bois and Washington (fashionably dressed in suits) and the iconic photograph of Nat Love in his cowboy outfit. I then ask my students, "In this group of images, which photograph does not belong?" This question opens a discussion of self-presentation and of the construction of masculinity in image and text. The violent masculinity that Love celebrates in his autobiography is perfectly in keeping with the myth of regenerative violence, but it is very much counter to the civilized manliness modeled by his contemporaries—African American intellectuals and activists such as Du Bois and Washington (who were concerned with dispelling white stereotypes that depicted black men as savage, dangerous, primitive). At the same time, Love's story of finding acceptance and equality by doing "useful work" (which sometimes involves reading brands on cattle and sometimes involves using his gun) is a Washingtonian parable of assimilation through providing needed labor. Love's text provides an excellent illustration of what Gates calls "double-voiced discourse." This is a central theme that the course explores and that is apparent across a range of texts. The doubling of thematic concerns through a single genre trope is a primary technique for transforming a western into a black western. Exploring the double-voiced discourse of black western texts will also help students come to know an important theme of African American literature in general.

Frank X Walker's *Buffalo Dance: The Journey of York* is a poem sequence that revisits the Lewis and Clark expedition from the perspective of York, William Clark's slave who journeyed with the Corps of Discovery. A contemporary retelling of the early nineteenth-century expedition,

York's journey west in some ways parallels Love's in that both are black men who are involved in the enterprise of westward expansion and find some measure of acceptance and relative freedom by providing useful skills. Love's journey is from southern slavery to western freedom, while York remains a slave, and his story (unlike Love's) is left for others to tell. Through the first-person poems, Walker reclaims and makes audible a muted voice in western history, and he does so with the purpose of also making visible the absences and ideologies that official accounts of that history obscure.

A film recommendation for this unit is *Buck and the Preacher* (1972), directed by Sidney Poitier and starring Poitier (as Buck) and Harry Belafonte (as the Preacher). The film is a rare mainstream Hollywood western with an African American director—and the rare film about groups of African American settlers migrating west. If Nat Love tells a story of protecting white property interests against outlaws and "savage" Indians, *Buck and the Preacher* inverts the frontier myth's opposition of civilized white/racialized savage other by positing a band of white supremacist "night riders" as the savage threat the settlers must face and defeat. For context, I teach the film with African American trickster tales (and this also might be a good place for a few clips from *Blazing Saddles*), as the Preacher is an interesting and ambivalent trickster figure, one whose tricks sometimes exploit the settlers and sometimes help them. Mel Watkins's *On the Real Side* provides a good overview of the characteristics of the African American trickster tale.[3] As an example of double-voiced discourse, *Buck and the Preacher* draws on two genres: the western and the trickster tale.

Region (Weeks 5–7): Great Plains Focus

For this section of the course I've chosen to focus on the Great Plains region, in part because of the historical importance of the writer and film-maker Oscar Micheaux and in part because a comparison of Dakota writers (Micheaux and Era Bell Thompson) reveals the way gender shapes the depiction of western experience. Micheaux's *The Homesteader* (1917) is a story of conquering the wilderness rather than a western shoot-out, but it provides a neat illustration of Tompkins's observation that "the interaction between hero and landscape" is at the center of the western, as "the land is everything to the hero; it is both the destination and the way."[4] Micheaux recasts the western's East-versus-West opposition to explore the double consciousness of the black homesteader, torn between an assimilationist desire for success in a white western community and maintaining a continuing sense of connection to black communities in the East. His *The Symbol of the Unconquered* (1920), which is the earliest extant film about the Black West, shifts toward the western's more human-centered antagonist. Responding in part to D. W. Griffith's 1915 film *The Birth of a Nation*, *Symbol* precedes *Buck and the Preacher* in casting a white vigilante group as the lawless and savage antagonist the hero faces. As an example of double-voiced discourse, *The Symbol of the Unconquered* addresses a specific African American contemporary concern (active black protest against *The Birth of a Nation*) through the conventions of the genre western (by casting the Klan as the antagonists of the frontier hero).

Era Bell Thompson's North Dakota homesteading memoir *American Daughter* (1946) offers a black woman's perspective on western settlement, one that is more interested in finding a relationship with the natural world than conquering the wilderness, an interest that is reflected in her poetic descriptions of the prairie landscape. As does Micheaux, Thompson also employs the western's East/West opposition to do double duty, not only as genre trope but also to explore double consciousness—the appeal of racial belonging she finds with African American communities in the East, the sense of belonging to the natural world that she finds appealing about life in the West. Thompson also emphasizes the importance of family to black western community building, especially the role of her mother in creating a sense of what bell hooks calls "homeplace" in a social environment that is isolating.[5] Thompson also gestures toward what Emily Lutenski calls the "borderlands West," a vision of the West that suggests "cross-racial networks" that go beyond black and white.[6] Those comments suggest two productive topics for discussing *American Daughter*: how Thompson does (or does not) imagine a black "homeplace" as frontier refuge and how Thompson does (or not) depict the West as a place of "cross-racial networks" where a multiracial America might be imagined and realized. Those topics also open up the discussion of double-voiced discourse to an exploration of multivocality.

Cultural Studies (Weeks 8–12)

The cultural studies unit includes a range of literary, television, and film narratives, with a focus on the western as genre. It also expands beyond the realist mode of earlier materials to include weird westerns (a hybrid form that joins the western to one or more of the speculative genres: science fiction, horror, fantasy, etc.).

This unit begins with an example of a "civil rights western," that is, a western story that introduces an African American character into a western plot that explicitly explores issues of racial equality and racial justice. "The Bounty Hunter" (1971), an episode of *Alias Smith and Jones* with Lou Gossett Jr. guest starring in the title role, uses the western plot to seriously address racial themes—the difficulty of being a black representative of the law in a racist society. The character type of the bounty hunter, working on behalf of the law but in some ways outside it, has developed into a kind of archetypal western role for African American characters. Lord Bowler (played by Julius Carry), one of the two bounty hunters at the center of the TV series *The Adventures of Brisco County, Jr.*, provides another example of this archetype, and the episode "Riverboat" (from 1993) reflects the series' combination of humor and adventure (and fondness for trickster tales). A recommended critical reading is my essay "Sammy Davis Jr., Woody Strode, and the Black Westerner of the Civil Rights Era," from *Hoo-Doo Cowboys and Bronze Buckaroos*.

Justina Ireland's young adult novel *Dread Nation* (2018) brings us to the weird western. Set in an alternate history nineteenth-century America in which the Civil War is interrupted by a sudden and overwhelming zombie outbreak, *Dread Nation* is part slave narrative, part horror story, and, once protagonist Jane McKeene is taken from "The Civilized East" to "The Cruel West" (as the sections of the book are titled), we have entered the western genre, as Jane (enslaved and trained as a bodyguard) is compelled to protect the white citizens of a dusty frontier town—and fight for her own freedom. By joining the weird to the western, the weird western provides another example of double-voiced discourse, but, appropriate for contemporary approaches to genre, the weird western opens up beyond duality to a multiplicity of voices and genre references.

Firefly is a television space western that might also be interpreted as an Afrofuturist western through the prominent role accorded to two characters: Zoë Washburne (Afro-Latina actress Gina Torres) and Shepherd Book (African American actor Ron Glass). As Adilifu Nama writes in "Subverting the Genre: The Mothership Connection," the term "Afrofuturism" is "a word used to describe the variegated expressions of a black futurist imagination in relation to black cultural production, technology, cyberculture, speculative fiction, the digital divide, and science fiction," as expressed in forms as varied as the free jazz of Sun Ra to science fiction novels by writers such as Octavia Butler and N. K. Jemisin.[7] The *Firefly* episode "War Stories" (2002), which centers on Zoë's leadership and battle skills, pairs well with *Dread Nation* in terms of presenting black women in weird western action hero roles. The time travel series *Timeless* connects science fiction to the western genre by going back in time to the Old West in the episode "The Murder of Jesse James" (2017), which features the series regulars teaming up with Bass Reeves (played by Colman Domingo), in an all too rare western focused on this legendary black western lawman. Episodes of the HBO series *Westworld* might also work well in this section of the course.

As for films related to this unit, I offer two options. For a film associated with the "civil rights western" part of the unit, Quentin Tarantino's controversial slave narrative western *Django Unchained* (2012) works well (and might include, especially for graduate students, critical readings from the *Safundi: The Journal of South African and American Studies* special issue on the film). For a film that could provide a transition from the Afrofuturist/weird western part of this unit to the contemporary section of the course, I recommend *Sorry to Bother You* (2018), directed by Boots Riley and starring LaKeith Stanfield and Tessa Thompson. Set in a near-future dystopian Oakland, *Sorry to Bother You* is very much a contemporary western regional story (although not a genre western) that is also an Afrofuturist narrative with science fiction and fantastic elements. Thematically, the film cleverly uses fantastic elements to suggest double consciousness and provides another example of the flexibility of the slave narrative as a genre that continues to form hybrid narratives.

Contemporary (Weeks 13–15)

The course concludes with two texts that set their stories in the contemporary African American West: Percival Everett's novel *Watershed* (1996), in Colorado, and Charles Burnett's film *To Sleep with Anger* (1990), in California. *Watershed*, with its story of Native Americans, endangered water supplies, and villainous agents of the U.S. government, evokes elements of the western without necessarily being one, as it also evokes the very real western history of Native American activism and protest in the West. Burnett's *To Sleep with Anger* places us in a Los Angeles setting that is suggestive of both the urban West and the rural South, and it stars Danny Glover as a dangerous and charming trickster. As a critical reading, Daniel Widener's "How to Survive in South Central," which provides an overview of Burnett's other Los Angeles films, also sketches out a social context for understanding *To Sleep with Anger* in conjunction with other late twentieth-century texts set in the section of the city historically known as South Central. Both *Watershed* and *To Sleep with Anger* suggest the continuity between African American southern and western experiences, and the double-voiced discourse in these texts might be interpreted as primarily involving two black traditions: the southern civil rights era/contemporary western (*Watershed*) and southern black rural culture/western black urban culture (*To Sleep with Anger*). As the course begins with an examination of the duality of black and white traditions in African American texts, the end suggests a more Afrocentric approach, one that decenters white traditions in favor of exploring the multiple black traditions present in these western texts.

Literatures of the Black West (Kalenda's Course)

Literatures of the Black West is a course heavily situated in literature and history. Texts that move across genres make an appearance, as do theoretical texts providing the basis for critical discussion. The original version of this course was called The Black West in Literature and Film, in an attempt to capture how literary and visual representations of a western mythos persist throughout African American cultural studies. However, the course has developed over the years and continues to change as I discover new readings or reconsider the old. I consciously focus on what it means to define a "Black West" to emphasize how certain authors are self-aware of a western sensibility woven into the fabric of African American experience. Rather than focus on how the "western" is *referenced* in African American or global black popular culture, literature, and film, in this course we study how specific black texts are western (geographically, practically, existentially) and vice versa. Some examples of what I mean by "referencing" include the East Coast rapper Kool Moe Dee (Mohandas Dewese) lyrically comparing New York turf wars to the "Wild Wild West," in the 1987 song of the same name. Other examples include the scenes in Perry Henzell's *The Harder They Come* (film and novel) in which the primary character is enamored of the cowboy westerns he watches at the movie theater in Kingston, Jamaica, and later proceeds to act out a dangerous outlaw fantasy. Others include the West African films stylized in the manner of the popular westerns of the mid-twentieth century, as Tsitsi Jaji discusses in "Cassava Westerns: Ways of Watching Abderrahmane Sissako." While these examples speak to the persistent relevance of the West or the western to global black communities, the Literatures of the Black West course is designed to fill in historical gaps. The course has therefore naturally evolved into one that consciously works to introduce culturally and politically important regional texts that challenge the absence of African Americans in western spaces.

Over the past few years I have taught Literatures of the Black West as an elective. I emphasize regionalism, place consciousness, and the role of migration in the structure and formation of black western literary narratives. This approach works well to connect students' preexisting knowledge about nationalism and the politics of exile, since students at my institution (Arcadia University) have a global learning curricular requirement. In the graduate version of the course we also discuss the relationship of the American West to individual identity formation, displacement, and social responsibility. There the thematic emphases are more on literary recovery, historical preservation, and what it means to define a separate black western identity. I have found that through these approaches students are able to learn the history of the black American West more broadly and to consider how those experiences are manifested in literary and artistic production.

My reading selection and overall approach have been influenced by consistent student reactions (surprise, confusion, excitement) I have observed over the years when incorporating western literature written by and about African Americans into my general courses. Initially the primary goal of a stand-alone course on black western literature was to explore general representations and make connections across genres. Through fiction and nonfiction, students would be tasked with identifying key characteristics of narratives reflecting black western experience and would, I hope, learn something new. However, based on my experiences I now structure the course in more of a chronological fashion. Most of the texts included here reference historical events in some sequential order, even if they are actually published later on the time line (e.g., historical fiction).

Module 1: Early Wests (Weeks 1–2)

The first module serves as an introduction to the course. I provide the foundation upon which students will build a greater understanding of major concepts. We discuss geography, migration, cultural exchange, and settlement. I assign Quintard Taylor's *In Search of the Racial Frontier* (1998) as a required anchor text. I intentionally thread this text throughout the course, and I return to it often for context when introducing each module. In the first three weeks students read the first two chapters, "Spanish Origins, 1528–1848" and "Slavery in the Antebellum West, 1835–1865." They learn of the relationship between Spanish and African inhabitants of the American West, and we discuss the importance of these early cultural exchanges. This is also where the reality of slavery in the western territories is first introduced. Beginning with a historical study proves useful later in the course, when select historical fiction refers to people and places from these periods. Other readings in the first module include an excerpt from Garci Rodríguez de Montalvo's adventure tale *Las Sergas de Esplandián* (1510), the sixteenth-century novel that introduces Queen Califia, the black "Amazonian" ruler who later provides the inspiration for the naming of California.

In another version of this course, instead of beginning with Quintard Taylor, I start with a lecture on the root causes for the "Great Migration" out of the American South and into the northern and western states in the nineteenth century. This lecture is enhanced two ways: (1) with a video or documentary providing a visual representation of African American mass migrations (e.g., *Goin' to Chicago*, or the fourth episode of from Henry Louis

Gates Jr.'s *The African Americans: Many Rivers to Cross*) and (2) with an interactive map from the New York Public Library digital project on black migration, *In Motion: The African American Migration Experience* (http://www.inmotionaame.org). After this discussion we then move "backward," to the sixteenth century, and have a larger conversation about how the movement of people documented in the nineteenth century was part of earlier African American migratory and settlement patterns to and within the western United States. After this series of discussions we address the Quintard Taylor chapters.

Students are required to submit "reading responses" during each module. The reading response represents critical engagement with the assigned text(s). Instead of a general reflection, the responses are positioned as an original analysis of a relevant theme (or critical question) posed by the student. Each answer covers no fewer than two pages (double-spaced). For this module, responses to Taylor, Montalvo, and the documentary are required. There is also an accompanying online discussion board on the course learning management system (LMS), in this case CANVAS, which provides a space where students can reflect on the materials they have encountered throughout the course.

Module 2: Nineteenth Century (Weeks 3–6)

The second module introduces students to important historical figures, political movements, and the establishment of all-black towns in the postslavery West. Students read travel narratives, novels, historical plays, speeches, and chapters from history books that represent the variety of experiences of African Americans in the western region. In this module there is frequent pairing of fiction and nonfiction writing. For example, "The Kansas Fever Exodus of 1879," from Nell Irvin Painter's *Exodusters: Black Migration to Kansas after Reconstruction* (1976), is paired with Pearl Cleage's historical play *Flyin' West* (1995). Cleage's play focuses on the lived experiences of multigenerational black women homesteaders in Kansas and their attempts to protect the land. Ida B. Wells's nineteenth-century editorials in the newspaper *Free Speech* in support of black western migration are placed in conversation with Frederick Douglass's opposition to the "exodus" as printed in a 1879 *New York Times* editorial debate (with R. T. Greener) titled

"Reasons for and against the Negro Exodus." The opinions by both Wells and Douglass are then paired with Sutton Griggs's novel *Imperium in Imperio* (1899). The novel famously presents debates regarding separatism versus integration within the American superstructure during Reconstruction, with a proposed separate but equal southwestern nation-state developed solely for African Americans.

A less studied text is Kenneth Young's travel narrative *As some things appear on the Plains and among the Rockies in mid-summer* (1890). The pamphlet employs freedom of movement across the western United States as a metaphor for African American upward mobility on the cusp of the twentieth century. Young's American West is vast and barren, with very little evidence of human existence. We discuss how his account supports the rhetoric of Manifest Destiny while at the same time presenting his own social criticism of American racism and bigotry. Young's text is paired with a chapter from Bruce Glasrud and Charles Braithwaite's *African Americans on the Great Plains: An Anthology* (2009). Michael Johnson's "'This Strange White World': Race and Place in Era Bell Thompson's *American Daughter*" is a good companion piece from this anthology.

The readings in this module are paired to elicit discussion about the role of the creative writer in the retelling of African American western history and the intellectual debates arising during mass migration and settlement. The emphasis on Reconstruction-era America introduces conversations about land rights, the role of African Americans in the homesteading movement, and debates on how best to chart a path of black progress in nineteenth-century America. I round out the module with a discussion of chapter 5 from Fay Yarbrough's *Race and the Cherokee Nation: Sovereignty in the Nineteenth Century* (2008). The chapter titled "The Cherokee Freedmen's Story: The Boles Family" opens the thorny discussion on the topic of Native American displacement, slave ownership, and legacies of black indigeneity.

The second module introduces a new assignment. Beginning in the fourth week, students help curate an archive of material through what is called "Student Suggestions for Further Reading." By the beginning (Sunday) of each of the weeks that follow, students are required to provide two or three sources (e.g., video/audio, website, print, or a book/article title with bibliographic citation) relevant to the covered readings, discussions, or assignments. This exercise is designed to serve as a tool for further research and to give students the opportunity to enhance the course by contributing to a living archive of literature/films/ephemera about African Americans in the American West. The primary requirements are that the suggestions be relevant to the weekly discussion and that students provide a brief explanation of why they chose the source(s). The topics and references change throughout the semester.

For example, a reading on the western territory and armed conflict might inspire someone to post a link to the Honey Springs Battlefield historic site and visitor center, located in an Oklahoma state park designed to educate the public about the role of African American and Native American soldiers who fought a Civil War battle there.

Midterm Assignment (Week 7)

The midterm assignment is the first short essay. The assignment gives students the opportunity to consider connections between fictional and nonfiction representations of the Black West. During the seventh week, students are required to analyze one of the assigned literary texts through the lens of western culture and society, western space(s), migration/settlement, racial politics, or gender. In this assignment students incorporate research from a secondary source text into a literary analysis of one major novel, play, or travel narrative discussed thus far.

Students also must draft a short essay (six to eight pages) with a clearly stated argument as their thesis. Through this process students consider questions like these: What role does western geography play in character development? How do characters interact with each other? How is ethnic identity addressed in the text? What larger political questions or movements inform the literature? The essay instructions encourage students to use open-source text mining software (Voyant, Wordle) to assist in idea generation and research. Through CANVAS, students can embed images or video into the submitted essay to further illuminate an idea or support their argument.

Module 3: Early to Mid-twentieth Century (Weeks 8–11)

The twentieth century opens a wide range of discussion about what it means to read and reinscribe "blackness" onto western spaces, primarily because the earlier tensions, conflicts, possibilities, and promises we see in the multiethnic, multinational, and multicultural West are challenged by "closed border" policies of the late nineteenth century. Therefore, many of the writings chosen for module 3 work to legitimize black western experience in the face of romantic visions of a "white West" threatened by "fierce natives." Mainstream film and literature reflecting the early to mid-twentieth-century American West tend to disregard a black presence. Instead, the third module relies on films, fiction, and nonfiction that demonstrate the persistence of a black western presence.

We begin with chapter 5 of Taylor's *In Search of the Racial Frontier*, titled "Migration and Settlement, 1875–1920." This chapter provides important context, tables with settlement and census data, and a discussion of the locations where African Americans rooted themselves during the period. Also important to this chapter are the multiple stops emigrants made in an attempt to find permanent homes and why they chose these particular locations. This is where it is important to acknowledge how social and economic factors within the African American community became factors in western migrations. I introduce personal research and lectures on African American western identity politics, as well as the reality of exclusivity in all-black towns and communities in Oklahoma, where the largest number of black western towns existed during the period.

Toni Morrison's *Paradise* (1997) gives the historical fiction treatment to the "come prepared or not at all" rhetoric used by established African Americans to forewarn and often exclude poor black refugees from the American South after the Civil War. We examine how Morrison embeds a politics of exclusion throughout the novel. We also discuss the novel in terms of the physical characteristics of the plains community Morrison describes and what can be discovered through her rendering of African American residents on the Great Plains. Alongside *Paradise* I include newspaper columns published in Langston City, Oklahoma, in 1891 and 1892, describing the type of individual desired for settlement on the plains. I also assign readings from R. Bruce Shepard's *Deemed Unsuitable* (1997) that detail federal and local attempts to prevent African Americans who were leaving Oklahoma from settling on the western Canadian plains in the early twentieth century. I focus on chapters 4 and 5 ("The Politics of Racism" and "Racism on the

Northern Plains") as points of entry for discussing the controversial federal policies that allowed for the recruitment of European immigrants alongside the simultaneous rejection of African American migrants.

Jewell Parker Rhodes's *Magic City* (1997) and its nuanced depiction of the effects the Tulsa "race riots" had on the black victims of the massacre is important to this module. When introducing the Rhodes text, I show a History Channel documentary on the riots in Oklahoma, and we discuss the treatment of the events in fiction and journalism. Considerable attention is also paid to how the Great Plains is defined by racial violence in the aftermath of World War I.

In a different version of this module I assign Shepard's complete text and focus on how the federal immigration policies in Canada actively exclude "undesirable" African Americans. I also show a political cartoon depicting African Americans being physically stopped at the western Canadian border. For the Tulsa, Oklahoma, conversation I assign either Hannibal Johnson's *Black Wall Street* (1998) or Scott Ellsworth's *Death in a Promised Land: The Tulsa Race Riot of 1921* (1982) instead of the documentary.

Writing contemporary to the period is key to fully understanding the artistic and literary output. With this in mind, students read poetry, listen to music, and examine visual art produced by black western artists during the early to mid-twentieth century. Key to these discussions is a larger conversation about the postwar and modernist periods. Selections from the artwork of Aaron Douglas, the first twelve chapters of Langston Hughes's *Not without Laughter* (1930), and Wallace Thurman's novel *The Blacker the Berry* (1929) are introduced. Also, various excerpts from *Tuneful Tales* ([1925] 2002) highlighting the poetry of Bernice Love Wiggins (a Harlem Renaissance–era writer from El Paso, Texas) are assigned. Theoretical discussions on this period are framed with excerpts from Bruce Glasrud and Cary Wintz's *The Harlem Renaissance in the American West* (2012) and Emily Lutenski's *West of Harlem: African American Writers and the Borderlands* (2015).

This module also provides space in which to discuss black western "race films" of the 1930s. One of the black-cast feature films, such as *The Bronze Buckaroo* (1939), *Harlem Rides the Range* (1939), or *Harlem on the Prairie* (1937), is discussed with Julia Leyda's 2002 *Cinema Journal* article on black-audience westerns. Through the documentary film *Midnight Ramble*, students are also introduced to filmmaker, businessman, and author Oscar Micheaux in the context of a discussion of black western communities on the upper Great Plains.

For an additional extra-credit class activity, students have an opportunity to compile information from Ralph Ellison's essays on jazz, interviews (specifically in Robert Penn Warren's 1965 *Who Speaks for the Negro*), the "Battle Royal" section of *Invisible Man* (1952), and various articles (e.g., those posted at Blackpast.org) to create a composite picture of the large African American community in Oklahoma City during the period from the late 1910s through World War II (a community also known as Deep Deuce). Through this activity interested students have the opportunity to learn how Ellison's reflections on his formative years in the West and his inclusion of these experiences in his writings speak to the larger cultural impact of the region on all of African American literature.

Module 4: The Contemporary Moment and the Future (Weeks 12–14)

The final module brings us to more contemporary texts and topics. Students are introduced to the civil rights movement in the West through a chapter of the same name assigned from Taylor's *In Search of the Racial Frontier*. The discussion of African American western activism continues with video segments from "Power! 1966–1968" (a 1990 episode of *Eyes on the Prize*) and Stanley Nelson's more recent *The Black Panthers: Vanguard of the Revolution* (2016). I assign Ishmael Reed's *The Last Days of Louisiana Red* (1974) as a companion to the visual narratives. Set in the San Francisco Bay Area, it is a detective novel that delves into the underbelly of student activism in the 1960s.

The limitations of the fifteen-week course require a skillful glossing over of many important movements and moments that have come after the mid-twentieth century. For example, I briefly note how in the 1970s there is a nod to the 1930s-era black westerns with two very different depictions of the black cowboy, first in Sidney Poitier's *Buck and the Preacher* (1972) and then the casting of Cleavon Little in *Blazing Saddles* (1974). We discuss how the renowned Bill Pickett Invitational Rodeo honoring the famous "bulldogger" started in 1984, while the westerns *Silverado* (1985) on the big screen and *Lonesome Dove* (1989) on television also incorporated black characters into the main storylines. Rap and reggae music saw the mass appeal of songs like the Sugarhill Gang's popular (yet cartoonish and stereotypical) crowd pleaser "Apache (Jump on It)" (1981) and Kool Moe Dee's "Wild Wild West" (1987–88) among others. We discuss how in these songs the black male subject is positioned as the cowboy hero. This allows us to return to the problematic of *referencing*, this time in the form of a mythic, comic book West. Bob Marley's "Buffalo Soldier" (1983), however, is able to advance conversations about survival and double consciousness in western spaces in important ways.

African American women published a significant number of western texts during the 1990s and beyond. While students would have already read Toni Morrison's *Paradise*, Cleage's *Flyin' West*, and Rhodes's *Magic City* in earlier modules, I emphasize examples of many other noteworthy books that speak to both the popularity of black women writers and late twentieth-century western fiction. One example is Octavia Butler's oeuvre of futuristic texts that imagine the global effects of a discordant West. We discuss Butler as a western author who, like Ralph Ellison, was deeply aware of how she was shaped by her western origins—and what that meant for how she developed her characters. Students read chapters 1–5 of *Parable of the Sower* (1993) and discuss the relationship between California's present (and predicted) environmental challenges, as well as parallels to contemporary American society.

The final module also focuses on the music of the far West with discussions of West Coast rap based in California and a reading of Kendrick Lamar's song lyrics as poetic reprisals of major themes in African American literature (e.g., "The Blacker the Berry" from the album *To Pimp a Butterfly*). I suggest Ricardo Cortez Cruz's experimental novel *Straight Outta Compton* (1991), alongside the first chapters of Paul Beatty's *The Sellout* (2015) and *The Mothers* (2017), by Brit Bennett, as possible references for the final project. The module ends with a screening of *Dope*, written and directed by Rick Famuyiwa (2015). In this film Southern California contemporary youth culture is highlighted and explored in ways similar to what is found in the suggested readings. A necessary reflection on John Singleton's pioneering 1990s films focused on African American communities in Los Angeles is incorporated here as well.

The course concludes with a discussion of what it means to emphasize literatures and cultures of a multivalent Black West within the contemporary context of gentrification, racialized policing, and economic disenfranchisement (among many other social ills) facing most across the country. In other words, I challenge the class to explore the "point" of what could appear to be a romantic regional focus on western freedoms within the larger scheme of American nationalism, and I ask them to make a strong case for how reading the Black West over the centuries is relevant to understanding the nation in the present day.

Final Project Options and Presentations (Week 15)

Project Option 1. This final project allows students to demonstrate through reading, writing, discussion, technology, and visual presentation an understanding of the historical, social, political, and cultural contexts out of which western literature emerges and the social relations of power that govern identity and culture. Specifically, students can craft a research essay analyzing the ways one of the studied authors develops a consciousness of place and environment in his or her writing using a well-defined and theoretical definition of either term. They are required to use available open-source software to create a visual presentation that will accompany the essay and further illustrate the essay's main themes and argument. In the end students will (1) submit an argumentative research essay (ten to twelve pages) examining original ideas and (2) will create a narrative map of the chosen text. The research and design for the narrative map will include fictional representations of the geographical location, characters' travels, and communities that provide a foundation for the novel. Using basic mapping software (WorldMap, StoryMap Js, or Google Maps) and scholarly research, the students create visual presentations that will complement their essays.

Project Option 2. Separate student groups must create an engaging multimedia project relevant to class readings and discussions. The group will not answer a prompt per se but will (in close consultation with the professor) design an original, thesis-driven project in which students analyze and dramatically interpret (act out) a pivotal scene in one of the primary readings. The key is to connect the chosen section to one of the major themes discussed in the course. This final project requires the incorporation of a theoretical approach, library research, essay writing, and the use of digital media, presentation software, and video.

Final Presentations. Prior to the end of the semester, all students must present an outline or prospectus of the chosen final project to the class.

Conclusion

In *Imagining the African American West*, Blake Allmendinger writes, "I came to realize that there is no such thing as a 'representative' African American western experience."[8] Through our descriptions of two model black western studies courses, we hope we have demonstrated the wide range of materials available for illustrating multiple facets of African American western experiences. Although our teaching and research interests often overlap in our individual investigations of the Black West, our syllabus design has attempted to create two courses with a unique set of primary texts for each. Instructors interested in designing a black western studies course might usefully follow either model—or mix and match texts from each syllabus. And, when it comes to textual representations of the Black West, we've provided here only a sample of available materials, and we encourage anyone who wishes to embark on a Black West course to explore further. When it comes to the African American West, there is still much more yet to be discovered.

NOTES

1. Tompkins, *West of Everything*, 14.
2. Gates, "Criticism in the Jungle," 3–4.
3. See Watkins, *On the Real Side*, 70–79.
4. Tompkins, *West of Everything*, 81.
5. See hooks's essay "Homeplace."
6. Lutenski, *West of Harlem*, 75.
7. Nama, "Subverting the Genre," 160.
8. Allmendinger, *Imagining the African American West*, xvi.

BIBLIOGRAPHY

The Adventures of Brisco County, Jr. "Riverboat." Directed by Fred Gerber. Performances by Bruce Campbell and Julius Carry. Season 1, episode 6. Aired October 1, 1993, on Fox.
Alias Smith and Jones. "The Bounty Hunter." Directed by Barry Shear. Performances by Pete Duel, Ben Murphy, and Lou Gossett Jr. Season 2, episode 12. Aired December 9, 1971, on ABC.

Allmendinger, Blake. *Imagining the African American West*. Lincoln: University of Nebraska Press, 2005.

American Experience: Midnight Ramble. Directed by Pearl Bowser and Bestor Cram. Written by Clyde Taylor. Northern Light Productions (for) WGBH, 1994.

Beatty, Paul. *The Sellout*. 2015. New York: Picador, 2016.

Bederman, Gail. *Manliness and Civilization: A Cultural History of Gender and Race in the United States, 1880–1917*. Chicago: University of Chicago Press, 1995.

Behan, Barbara Carol. "Forgotten Heritage: African Americans in the Montana Territory, 1864–1889." *Journal of African American History* 91, no. 1 (2006): 23–40.

Behnken, Brian D. *The Struggle in Black and Brown: African American and Mexican American Relations during the Civil Rights Era*. Lincoln: University of Nebraska Press, 2012.

Bennett, Brit. *The Mothers*. New York: Riverhead, 2017.

Berardi, Gayle K., and Thomas W. Segady. "The Development of African-American Newspapers in the American West: A Sociohistorical Perspective." In *African Americans on the Western Frontier*, edited by Monroe Lee Billington and Roger D. Hardaway, 217–30. Niwot: University Press of Colorado, 1998.

The Black Panthers: Vanguard of the Revolution. Directed by Stanley Nelson. PBS, 2016. DVD.

Blazing Saddles. Directed by Mel Brooks. Performance by Cleavon Little. Warner Brothers, 1974. DVD.

Bowser, Pearl, and Louise Spence. *Writing Himself into History: Oscar Micheaux, His Silent Films, and His Audiences*. New Brunswick NJ: Rutgers University Press, 2000.

Buck and the Preacher. Directed by Sidney Poitier. Performances by Sidney Poitier and Harry Belafonte. Columbia Pictures, 1972. DVD.

Butler, Octavia. *Parable of the Sower*. 1993. New York: Grand Central Publishing, 2000.

Campney, Brent M. S. "'Light is bursting upon the world!': White Supremacy and Racist Violence against Blacks in Reconstruction Kansas." *Western Historical Quarterly* 41, no. 2 (2010): 171–94.

Cleage, Pearl. *Flyin' West*. New York: Dramatists Play Service, 1995.

Coleman, Robin Means. *Horror Noire: Blacks in American Horror Films from the 1890s to Present*. New York: Routledge, 2011.

Crane, Stephen. "The Bride Comes to Yellow Sky." *McClure's Magazine*, February 1898, 377–84.

Cruz, Ricardo Cortez. *Straight Outta Compton*. 1991. Boulder: Fiction Collective Two and the University of Colorado, 1992.

Davis, Cynthia, and Verner D. Mitchell. *Western Echoes of the Harlem Renaissance: The Life and Writings of Anita Scott Coleman*. Norman: University of Oklahoma Press, 2008.

Dewese, Mohandas, writer. "Wild Wild West." *Kool Moe Dee: Greatest Hits*. Legacy, 2008. Compact disc.

Django Unchained. Directed by Quentin Tarantino. Performances by Jamie Foxx, Christoph Waltz, Leonardo DiCaprio, and Kerry Washington. Columbia Pictures, 2012.

Dope. Directed by Rick Famuyiwa. Produced by Forest Whitaker and Nina Yang Bongiovi. Performances by Shameik Moore, Tony Revolori, Kiersey Clemons, Kimberly Elise et al. 2015. Film.

Douglass, Frederick. *Narrative of the Life of Frederick Douglass, an African Slave* (1845). In *The Classic Slave Narratives*, edited by Henry Louis Gates Jr., 243–331. New York: Penguin Books, 1987.

Douglass, Frederick, and R. T. Greener. "Reasons for and against the Negro Exodus." *New York Times*, September 13, 1879. https://www.nytimes.com/1879/09/13/archives/reasons-for-and-against-the-negro-exodus-frederick-douglass-gives.html.

Du Bois, William Edward Burghardt. *The Souls of Black Folk*. 1903. New York: Penguin, 1989.

Ellison, Ralph. *Invisible Man*. New York: Random House, 1952.

Ellsworth, Scott. *Death in a Promised Land: The Tulsa Race Riot of 1921*. Baton Rouge: Louisiana State University Press, 1992.

Erisman, Fred. "*Stagecoach* in Space: The Legacy of *Firefly*." *Extrapolation* 47, no. 2 (2006): 249–58.

Everett, Percival. *Watershed*. 1996. Boston: Beacon Press, 2003.

———. *Wounded*. St. Paul MN: Graywolf, 2005.

Eyes on the Prize: America's Civil Rights Years, 1954–1965. "Power!" Produced by James A. DeVinney and Henry Hampton. Narrated by Julian Bond. Season 2, episode 3. Aired January 20, 1990. Alexandria VA: PBS, 2010. DVD.

Firefly. "War Stories." Directed by James Contner. Performances by Nathan Fillion, Gina Torres, and Ron Glass. Season 1, episode 9. Aired December 6, 2002, on Fox.

Flamming, Douglas. *African Americans in the West*. Santa Barbara: ABC-CLIO, 2009.

Gates, Henry Louis, Jr. *The African Americans: Many Rivers to Cross*. PBS Distribution, 2013.

———. "Criticism in the Jungle." In *Black Literature and Literary Theory*, edited by Henry Louis Gates Jr., 1–24. New York: Methuen, 1984.

Glasrud, Bruce A. and Charles A. Braithwaite. *African Americans on the Great Plains: An Anthology*. Lincoln: University of Nebraska Press, 2009.

Glasrud, Bruce A., and Cary D. Wintz. *The Harlem Renaissance in the American West: The New Negro's Western Experience*. New York: Routledge, 2012.

Goin' to Chicago: A Documentary Film. Directed by George King. Atlanta: George King & Associates, 1994.

Griggs, Sutton E. *Imperium in Imperio: A Novel*. 1899. N.p.: Ayer, 1977.

Handley, William R. "Detecting the Real Fictions of History in Watershed." *Callaloo* 28, no. 2 (2005): 305–12.

The Harder They Come. Directed by Perry Henzell. Produced by Perry Henzell. Performance by Jimmy Cliff. 1972.

Hinger, Charlotte. *Nicodemus: Post-Reconstruction Politics and Racial Justice in Western Kansas*. Norman: University of Oklahoma Press, 2016.

hooks, bell. "Homeplace: A Site of Resistance." In *Yearning: Race, Gender, and Cultural Politics*, 41–91. Boston: South End, 1990.

Hughes, Langston. *Not without Laughter: With an Introduction*. New York: Collier Books, 1985.

In Motion: The African-American Migration Experience. New York Public Library, 2005. http://www.inmotionaame.org.

Ireland, Justina. *Dread Nation*. New York: HarperCollins, 2018.

Jacobs, Harriet. *Incidents in the Life of a Slave Girl*. 1861. New York: Penguin, 2000.

Jaji, Tsitsi. "Cassava Westerns: Ways of Watching Abderrahmane Sissako." *Black Camera* 6, no. 1 (2014): 154–77.

Johnson, Hannibal. *Black Wall Street: From Riot to Renaissance in Tulsa's Historic Greenwood District*. Woodway TX: Eakin Press, 1998.

Johnson, Michael K. *Black Masculinity and the Frontier Myth in American Literature*. Norman: University of Oklahoma Press, 2002.

———. *Hoo-Doo Cowboys and Bronze Buckaroos: Conceptions of the African American West*. Jackson: University Press of Mississippi, 2014.

———. "Sammy Davis Jr., Woody Strode, and the Black Westerner of the Civil Rights Era." In *Hoo-Doo Cowboys and Bronze Buckaroos*, 154–85. Jackson: University Press of Mississippi, 2014.

Lamar, Kendrick. "The Blacker the Berry." *To Pimp a Butterfly*. Santa Monica CA: Aftermath Entertainment, 2015. Sound recording.

Leyda, Julia. "Black-Audience Westerns and the Politics of Cultural Identification in the 1930s." *Cinema Journal* 42, no. 1 (2002): 46–70.

Love, Nat. *The Life and Adventures of Nat Love, Better Known in the Cattle Country as "Deadwood Dick."* 1907. Lincoln: University of Nebraska Press, 1995.

Lutenski, Emily. *West of Harlem: African American Writers and the Borderlands*. Lawrence: University Press of Kansas, 2015.

Mack, Dwayne A. *Black Spokane: The Civil Rights Struggle in the Inland Northwest*. Norman: University of Oklahoma Press, 2014.

Martin, S. R., Jr. *On the Move: A Black Family's Western Saga*. College Station: Texas A&M University Press, 2009.

Matthieu, Sarah-Jane. *North of the Color Line: Migration and Black Resistance in Canada, 1870–1955*. Chapel Hill: University of North Carolina Press, 2010.

Micheaux, Oscar. *The Homesteader*. 1917. Lincoln: University of Nebraska Press, 1994.

Morrison, Toni. *Paradise*. 1997. New York: Knopf, 1998.

Nama, Adilifu. "Subverting the Genre: The Mothership Connection." In *Black Space: Imagining Race in Science Fiction Film*, 148–70. Austin: University of Texas Press, 2008.

Old Town Road (Official Movie). Directed by Calmatic. Performances by Lil Nas X and Billy Ray Cyrus. 2019.

Painter, Nell Irvin. *Exodusters: Black Migration to Kansas after Reconstruction*. With a new introduction. New York: Norton, 1992.

Poetic Justice. Directed by John Singleton. Written by John Singleton and Maya Angelou. Produced by John Singleton and Steve Nicolaides. Performances by Janet Jackson and Tupac Shakur. Columbia Pictures, 1993.

Reed, Ishmael. *The Last Days of Louisiana Red*. 1974. Normal IL: Dalkey Archive Press, 2000.

Rhodes, Jewell Parker. *Magic City*. New York: HarperCollins, 1998.

Rodríguez de Montalvo, Garci. *Las Sergas de Esplandián*. Translated by Salvador Bernabéu Albert. Madrid: Doce Calles, 1998.

Royster, Jacqueline Jones, ed. *Southern Horrors and Other Writings: The Anti-Lynching Campaign of Ida B. Wells, 1892–1900*. Boston: Bedford Books, 1997.

Ruffin, Herbert G., II, and Dwayne A. Mack, eds. *Freedom's Racial Frontier: African Americans in the Twentieth-Century West*. Norman: University of Oklahoma Press, 2018.

Rutkoff, Peter M., and William B. Scott. *Fly Away: The Great African American Cultural Migrations*. Baltimore: Johns Hopkins University Press, 2016.

Safundi: The Journal of South African American Studies 16, no. 3 (2015). Special issue on *Django Unchained*.

Scheckel, Susan. "Home on the Train: Race and Mobility in the Life and Adventures of Nat Love." *American Literature* 74, no. 2 (2002): 219–50.

Shepard, R. Bruce. *Deemed Unsuitable: Blacks from Oklahoma Move to the Canadian Prairies in Search of Equality in the Early 20th Century, Only to Find Racism in Their New Home*. Toronto: Umbrella Press, 1997.

Slotkin, Richard. "Regeneration through Violence: The Language of Myth." In *Gunfighter Nation: The Myth of the Frontier in Twentieth-Century America*, 10–16. New York: HarperPerennial, 1993.

Smith, Jimmy Dean. "Wrighting the West: Leaving Marks in Frank X Walker's York Poems." *Western American Literature* 52, no. 4 (2018): 435–51.

Smith, Stephen Drury, and Catherine Ellis, eds. *Free All Along: The Robert Penn Warren Civil Rights Interviews*. New York: New Press, 2019.

Sorry to Bother You. Directed by Boots Riley. Performances by LaKeith Stanfield and Tessa Thompson. 2018.

The Symbol of the Unconquered. Directed by Oscar Micheaux. Performances by Iris Hall, Walker Thompson, and Lawrence Chenault. 1920.

Taylor, Quintard. *In Search of the Racial Frontier: African Americans in the American West, 1528–1990*. New York: Norton, 1998.

Thompson, Era Bell. *American Daughter*. 1946. St. Paul: Minnesota Historical Society Press, 1986.

Thurman, Wallace. *The Blacker the Berry*. 1929. Introduction by Allyson Vanessa Hobbs. New York: Penguin Books, 2018.

Timeless. "The Murder of Jesse James." Directed by John F. Showalter. Performances by Malcolm Barrett, Abigail Spencer, Matt Lanter, Goran Visnjic, Colman Domingo, and Zahn McClarnon. Season 1, episode 12. Aired January 23, 2017, on NBC.

Tompkins, Jane. *West of Everything: The Inner Life of Westerns*. New York: Oxford University Press, 1992.

To Sleep with Anger. Directed by Charles Burnett. Performances by Danny Glover and Paul Butler. 1990.

Walker, Frank X. *Buffalo Dance: The Journey of York*. Lexington: University Press of Kentucky, 2004.

Washington, Booker T. *Up from Slavery*. 1901. Edited by William L. Andrews. Oxford: Oxford University Press, 1995.

Warren, Robert Penn. *Who Speaks for the Negro? The Robert Penn Warren Interviews*. 1965. New Haven: Yale University Press, 2014.

Watkins, Mel. *On the Real Side: Laughing Lying and Signifying; The Underground Tradition of African-American Humor.* New York: Simon and Schuster, 1994.

Widener, Daniel. "How to Survive in South Central: Black Film as Class Critique." In *Black Arts West: Culture and Struggle in Postwar Los Angeles*, 250–82. Durham: Duke University Press, 2010.

Wiggins, Bernice Love. *Tuneful Tales.* 1925. Lubbock: Texas Tech University Press, 2002.

Wilcox, Rhonda V., and Tanya R. Cochran. *Investigating "Firefly" and "Serenity": Science Fiction on the Frontier.* London: I. B. Tauris, 2008.

Yarbrough, Fay A. *Race and the Cherokee Nation: Sovereignty in the Nineteenth Century.* 2008. Philadelphia: University of Pennsylvania Press, 2013.

Young, Kenneth M. *As Some Things Appear on the Plains and among the Rockies in Mid-Summer.* Spartanburg SC: Press of W. Al. Fowler, Lessee, Herald Printing Establishment, 1890. https://www.loc.gov/item/91898500/.

Zane Grey Theatre. "The Mission." Directed by William D. Faralla. Performances by Sammy Davis Jr. and James Edwards. Season 4, episode 7. Aired November 12, 1959, on CBS.

PART 2

Affect, Indigeneity, Gender

4

Gender, Affect, Environmental Justice, and Indigeneity in the Classroom

AMY T. HAMILTON

April in Marquette, Michigan, is icebound. Lake Superior pushes frozen slabs of lake water onto the beaches that trace the edge of town. Pedestrians pick their way slowly over slick sidewalks, and even the dogs are wearing booties. When I'm in a more contemplative frame of mind I often find myself thinking of Bashō's haiku:

> Winder solitude:
> In a world of one color
> the sound of wind.[1]

April in Marquette will break your heart a dozen times over. By April we have been deep in snow and ice for nearly six months, and while there are signs of hope (the sun rises earlier and sets later, the birds show up at feeders a little more often, and the rare crocus nestles in a gap in the mantle of snow), we are not yet out of winter's grip. Just as we dare to dream of summer afternoons kayaking and hiking, we are hit with another blizzard that covers up the crocuses and sends the birds deep into tree cover and under shrubs, asserting more vehemently than Punxsutawney Phil ever could that those summer days are a long way off.

On one such blustery evening I arrived at my class grousing as I stamped snow off my boots, unwound my enveloping scarf, and pulled off my mittens.

I dug our text for the night out of my bag and turned to face my students. Creative writers and English majors, these students were all from the upper Midwest. Used to long winters and landscapes covered by forests punctuated with rivers and lakes, they were at home in the snow. But when they entered that classroom, a course on western American literature and ecocriticism, we ventured out of the woods and into the deserts and mountains of the American Southwest. The sun was hot, the plants were covered in spines, and the sky was a deep, deep blue. A desert rat at heart, I brought them home with me.

That evening we were discussing Luis Alberto Urrea's masterful text *The Devil's Highway*. Chronicling the journey of a group of Mexican men who crossed the border with the help of a shady smuggling operation in May 2001, the text blends creative narrative with regional history, cultural and religious stories, and scientific information. The particular passage we were discussing detailed the final minutes of several of the men who died from dehydration and exposure. Urrea writes of their deaths in prose both factual and compassionate. I pointed my students to a passage and read aloud: "'When we got sick,' José Bautista says, 'there was no shade. So I crawled up to hide in the rocks. One of the boys went crazy and started jumping up and down. He started screaming, 'Mama! Mama! I don't want to die!' He ran up to a big cactus and started smashing his face against it. I don't know what his name was.' . . . A voice carried on the still air, crying, 'Mother, save me!'"[2]

As I read this passage—words I had read many times before—my voice caught and my eyes blurred with tears. I looked up. The room was completely still and silent. It felt as though the students were collectively holding their breath; we were suspended in balance. Initially I attempted to control or minimize my reaction to the passage; I cleared my throat and laughed nervously. I was embarrassed by my emotional response and worried about the vulnerability I felt as the words cracked my heart open. I looked at the faces of my students, these Michiganders and Wisconsinites, their eyes round. The book was introducing them to both a story of border crossing and to the stark and potentially deadly desert. They were outside of their familiar landscapes and their professor was crying. Were they adrift? Did they feel uncomfortably alienated? Was I losing them? But then I realized that my response was rooted in empathy as well as my own life experiences—it was honest. The breathless silence between my tears and my students' reaction was not evidence of a pedagogical error; rather, it signaled a powerful energy. Something was happening.

To Emote or Not to Emote: Affect and Emotion in the Classroom

I often find myself attempting to steer students away from their emotional responses to a place that is more intellectually objective, a rational place from which I have imagined scholarship emerges. I can feel uncomfortable with the thought that I am somehow responsible for helping students navigate their emotions and concerned that their emotional responses hinder their ability to analyze rationally. "Ground your discussion in the text" has been my mantra. If I have encouraged emotion at all, it has usually been in service of selecting a text to write about: "Which text did you feel drawn to or repelled by? Look there for a potential topic that will keep you invested in your essay." I've been getting it wrong.

Emotion *is always* present in literature classrooms, inseparable from the texts we read and our responses to them. It can't quite be controlled in the way I had attempted. bell hooks suggests that "refusing to make a place for emotional feelings in the classroom does not change the reality that their presence overdetermines the conditions where learning can occur."[3] Ignoring or even actively attempting to deny emotional responses to literature does not create an environment of rational or subjective learning, as I had hoped; rather, such suppression curbs engagement and potentially limits intellectual exploration. In my anxiety about my students' emotions and my responsibility to both students and texts, I was creating a falsity in the classroom that, if not actually hindering student learning, was certainly limiting their options. Sara Ahmed maintains that emotion is always part of the classroom; indeed, "affect is what sticks, or what sustains or preserves the connection between ideas, values, and objects."[4] Affect (emotion as it is expressed and embedded in social/material/political contexts) and reason do not exist as opposites in an imaginary continuation of readers' interactions with texts. However, that does not mean that the ways affects are experienced are free from problems or complications. Clare Hemmings critiques the tendency among affect theorists to imagine "affect as outside social meaning, as providing a break in both the social and in critics' engagements with the nature of the social."[5] Affect is often framed as prepersonal forces that all beings share.[6] However, Hemmings points out that social and personal contexts cannot be dismissed but instead are an integral part of affects and emotions. How affect is experienced and interpreted is intimately entangled with issues of gender, sexuality, race, ethnicity, and ability.

Since I was hired by Northern Michigan University (NMU) in 2008, approximately 70 percent of the courses I have taught have been upper division undergraduate courses in Native American literature. As of the spring 2019 semester, I have taught thirty-two sections of these courses at NMU, or roughly eight hundred students. As a white woman teaching Native American literature to a largely white student population, I am acutely aware that I have—and will always have—a lot to learn. Further, as a non-Native ally scholar and teacher, I have been wary about infringing on areas of cultural knowledge that are not—and should not be—available to me. This positioning has further complicated how I have thought about emotion in the classroom. How can non-Native students and I interrogate our affective responses to course readings without appropriating stories and experiences that belong to someone else? How can I make room in the classroom for multiple emotional responses from Native and non-Native students? How can I be an ethical ally when it comes to emotion?

Theoretical Perspectives

To help me navigate the complex terrain of affect in my classroom, I have found feminist studies, environmental justice studies, and Indigenous studies particularly useful. All three areas engage questions of ethics and offer useful frameworks for thinking through the relationships among texts, readers, cultural and historical contexts, and the more-than-human world.

Discussions of the relationship between emotion and critical reading practices have been particularly complicated in women's and gender studies classrooms. As Naomi Greyser argues, this problem arises from "the history of femininity's overassociation with emotions as well as the history of psychoanalysis's complex entanglements with both sexism and feminism." She continues, "One response to these problems for many feminized subjects has been to clamp down on the personal in academic or public arenas because it threatens to undermine or delegitimate scholarly pursuits."[7] The traditional western binary that places men and reason on one side and women and emotion on the other has created a situation in which women have felt that in order to be taken seriously as scholars they have to jettison emotion. Thus, in university classrooms issues of gender continue to be entangled with a persistent prejudice that attempts to fuse gender expression with emotional states. An instructor expressing emotion in the classroom risks being dismissed as irrational and less intellectually rigorous.

Feminist scholars, however, insist on the possibility of an analysis of affective response that avoids getting bogged down in solipsistic reminiscences and navel gazing. Such an approach, Greyser argues, "understands the subject in terms of socio-structural forces, and it understands materiality as never divorced from how we feel, whom we relate to, and the histories of emotion that shape us."[8] Within feminist studies affect provides a method for employing the personal through emotion in thinking through "relations of identification and disidentification, privilege and oppression, comfort and discomfort, affect and intellect, and academia and activism in complex ways."[9] Affective response is not only *linked* to critical engagement, it helps to *direct* that engagement, encouraging students to attend to the ways affect (both within the text and within the reader) is linked to historical, cultural, material, and ethical questions. bell hooks calls on feminist educators to "make the classroom a place that is life-sustaining and mind-expanding."[10] She insists that "radical openness" is paired with "devotion to critical thinking."[11] Therefore, within this framework, it is the denial or minimizing of emotion—rather than emotion itself—that threatens to limit critical rigor.

Indeed, feminist scholars remind us that mistaking the denial of emotion as the more rigorous or "academic" approach erases minority voices and experiences. hooks argues that "objectivism," which is too often understood as an "unbiased standpoint," should not be a goal in critical thought. She quotes Parker Palmer, who explains, "The oppression of cultural minorities by a white, middle-class, male version of 'truth' comes in part from the domineering mentality of objectivism. Once the objectivist has 'the facts,' no listening is required, no other points of view are needed."[12] Paula Moya echoes this concern: "Different worlds of sense are never equal."[13] Thus, when educators attempt to drain emotion from discussions of literary studies, they risk reinstituting a particular set of social hierarchies that are mistaken as rational—and therefore valid—thought.

In its consideration of how environmental burdens and risks are disproportionately visited on poor people, women, and communities of color, environmental justice similarly critiques the conception that there is one rational, and therefore correct, method of interpretation. Finding a way into an environmental justice framework requires a sense of empathy. Kristie Dotson and Kyle Whyte argue that "unknowability with respect to struggles for environmental justice concerns whether the moral knowledge of members of dominant societies can detect certain wrongs."[14] In other words, affect in the form of "moral knowledge" is linked to the ability of members of dominant societies to even *discern* certain injustices. Attending to environmental justice requires that "one at least retains an openness to what one is not detecting and, at most, aggressively search for what one is not detecting."[15] Affect both assists in "knowability," which in turn encourages ethical engagement, and opens space for a recognition of what one does not know and therefore what one can seek out.

Sarah Jaquette Ray traces the affective experiences her students have in her environmental justice classrooms: "As they learn more about the seriousness of the climate change crisis, students gain new insights: they are complicit in the crises; their moral and political energies are often misguided, even oppressive; environmental problems are too entrenched, structural, and complicated to be addressed by their green lifestyle choices; and the experts in technology and science may not have all the answers."[16] She describes the students' experiences in terms of deeply emotional crises: not only is the environment in worse shape than they thought, they are complicit in its destruction and *there is little they can do about it*. Worse, Ray reports, "many students who are not Native American are appalled when they realize that their love of national parks, for instance, is shaped by a privilege that makes it possible for them to be unaware of the history of genocide in these landscapes. These students reel from becoming aware of their myriad cognitive dissonances, and they struggle to reconcile their love of nature with their ostensibly progressive social ideals."[17] Ray describes her students' engagement with environmental and social justice realities in terms of despair and disillusionment. Yet, she argues, these very emotional reactions are an important part of the students' learning process. "Working through their emotional responses, considering and responding to the emotions of others, and conversing, thinking, and reflecting," Ray argues, "all build community and cultivate the ecological imagination."[18]

The emotions Ray describes are largely negative: despair, helplessness, anger, frustration, betrayal, and so on. As such, they are responses that students may shy away from and that instructors may feel reluctant to confront. Yet, in experiencing, discussing, and interrogating these responses, students can find their way to a place of deeper engagement. In the article "Our Story Begins Here: Constellating Cultural Rhetorics," Indigenous studies scholar Malea Powell and her coauthors cite a presentation by Jay Dolmage: "It wasn't enough, he said, to change things, to 'find new stories.' We needed new ways of *doing*."[19] The authors go on to argue that "an indigenous research paradigm us[es] indigenous practices such as relationality and relational accountability. . . . To enact relationality means to understand one's relationship: to land, people, space, ideas, and the universe as interconnected and fluid."[20] In Indigenous studies, questions of cosmology—of how humans place themselves within and among the more-than-human and the nature of their responsibilities—are at heart questions of kinship, of connection. Of *emotion*.

I have taught students about Indigenous cosmologies and kinship systems for years. But I have focused on introducing and emphasizing these ideas as theoretical lenses, something that exists *outside* the classroom, rather than something that informs the work *inside* the classroom. Potawatomi botanist Robin Wall Kimmerer recounts an interaction she had with her academic advisor, a botany professor, when she was a young undergrad. He asked her why she was interested in majoring in botany. Kimmerer told him she wanted to know "why asters and goldenrod look so beautiful together."[21] Kimmerer explains that her interest in this question is something she's held for a long time: "I like to imagine [asters and goldenrod] were the first flowers I saw, over my mother's shoulder, as the pink blanket slipped away from my face and their colors flooded my consciousness. . . . Love at first sight."[22]

Her professor told her that her question was "not science" and "not at all the sort of thing that botanists concern themselves with."[23] Kimmerer's professor attempted to draw a clear line: on the one side were aesthetic and emotional questions about beauty and love and on the other was the "objective" work of botany. Kimmerer tells us that she set her question about beauty aside and completed her degree. But she had not forgotten that question or her professor's response. Years later she came back to the puzzle of flowers and beauty. She talked with artists and biologists about color theory, human and bee eye anatomy, and pollination. She discovered that goldenrods and asters are beautiful together not only for humans but also, and more importantly, for bees. "Growing together," she writes, asters and goldenrod "both receive more pollinator visits than they would if they were growing alone. It's a testable hypothesis; it's a question of science, a question of art, and a question of beauty."[24] I would add that it is also a question of affect. By following a line of inquiry her botany professor dismissed as nonscientific and nonrational, Kimmerer demonstrates the interconnections between analysis and perception, emotion and reason. In steering my students away from emotion in the classroom, have I been making the same mistake as Kimmerer's botany professor? Have I been communicating to my students that questions of their own affective responses are incidental and not worth investigating? I need to find a new way of "doing," and I know that in academe I am not the only one.

We Laugh, We Cry, We Analyze

Now to return to the questions that this chapter engages: How can the affective responses students have to course texts be interrogated as places to deepen critical inquiries? How can gender studies, environmental justice, and Indigenous studies frameworks help us make room for emotion in the classroom in a productive way? For the remainder of the chapter I tackle these questions by looking at how two stories of Indigenous removal can be engaged in the classroom through attention to affect as a method for deepening analysis. The first is Diane Glancy's *Pushing the Bear: A Novel of the Trail of Tears*, and the second is Luci Tapahonso's poem "In 1864," which is about the Navajo Long Walk. Both of these texts engage events from the fraught histories of contact between Indigenous cultures and settler-colonists in what is currently the United States, histories that are punctuated with U.S. aggression and violence and the forcible removal of Indigenous peoples from their ancestral lands. Students find both texts emotionally and intellectually engaging in complex ways that provide opportunities for exploring ethical analysis.

I have taught Diane Glancy's *Pushing the Bear* in several undergraduate and graduate classrooms. The novel tells the story of the third detachment of Cherokee forced along the approximately nine-hundred-mile northern route of the Trail of Tears to the land west of the Mississippi River designated as Indian

Territory. Readers encounter more than forty narrative voices, but the central story revolves around the Cherokee woman Maritole, who loses both her mother and her baby to the trail and nearly sees the dissolution of her marriage.

Students respond well to the text—they are intrigued by its multiple voices and have strong opinions about Maritole and Knobowtee's marriage and fidelity (or lack thereof). Most students have not engaged with stories or histories of the Trail of Tears beyond a perfunctory treatment in a high school American history course. Their response to the novel is often extremely emotional, ranging from disdain to sympathy, grief to anger, laughter to disbelief. In particular, students are often distressed because of conflicting emotions they experience toward the main character: they grieve with Maritole after the death of her mother and baby, but they judge her harshly for the affair she has with a white soldier. The students' emotional responses to the novel can be overwhelming to them and can loom over classroom discussions. Rather than attempting to move students away from these complicated and difficult emotions precisely *because* they cause both students and instructor discomfort, what if I encourage students to follow these emotions as their path into analysis, heeding Dotson and Whyte's call to "retain openness"?

Students initially respond with sympathy to Maritole when she describes her experience of forcible removal from her home as both emotionally and physically traumatic. "My feet would not walk," she recalls, "and the soldier held me up by my arm. I walked sideways and fell into the cornstalks at the side of the road. . . . I walked like my grandmother before she died, when her knees wouldn't hold."[25] As Maritole falls into the cornstalks she reasons, "They couldn't remove us. Didn't the soldiers know we were the land? The cornstalks were our grandmothers. . . . The cornstalks waved their arms trying to hold us. Their voices were the long tassels reaching the air. Our spirits clung to them. Our roots entwined."[26] Students often point to this passage as one that impacts them deeply. Maritole's fear and grief resonate with them, and they are interested in the intensity of reading about the physical response she has to trauma. Further, they are interested in the powerful links that Maritole draws to the corn as grandmothers, links that underscore what Maritole is leaving behind—her home, yes, and also her more-than-human relatives.

Because students respond to Maritole's story in powerful ways here— identifying with her grief and her loss of family—an opportunity is created for pushing their analysis into new places. Rather than using identification merely to mark an important passage and then bracketing it so that the "real" work of analysis can be done, I might encourage students to pursue their own emotions deeper into Maritole's story while simultaneously interrogating her physical affective response to grief. In so doing, students can complicate their analysis of the text by following affect and emotion into investigations of how U.S. government policies and Cherokee belief systems inform Maritole's experience, how gender weaves through the scene as Maritole's body is cradled by her cornstalk grandmothers, how their own placement in history and in the university classroom informs their response to Maritole's story, and how the passage encourages readers to consider the complex relationship between people and place and the ways in which colonialism and imperialism act upon human and more-than-human bodies.

Students' initially sympathetic response to Maritole is challenged by the developing story of Maritole's affair with one of the white soldiers who is facilitating the removal of her community from their traditional homelands. Following the deaths of her mother and baby and her near-abandonment by her husband, Maritole finds solace in her increasingly intimate relationship with Sergeant Williams. As their relationship grows on the trail, the rest of the Cherokee walkers ostracize Maritole and condemn her. "You deserve the trail," her friend Quaty tells her.[27] Maritole's affair is very clearly tied to her grief, as well as a larger history of colonialism and loss. Students, however, often connect more to the emotional impact her actions have on her husband and community and thus lose sympathy for Maritole. They view her through a moral lens that is fraught with judgment and emotion. Further, because they often initially recognize Maritole as the protagonist, as the character who will act as their logical and moral guide through the text, their feelings about her behavior can be tinged with a sense of personal betrayal. In betraying her husband, she betrays the students.

Encouraging students to pay attention to affect in this part of the novel requires them to track both their own responses to plot and character, as well as the emotional responses the Cherokee experience. If attention to affect requires, as Dotson and Whyte suggest, at least "an openness to what one is not detecting and, at most, [an] aggressive[e] search for what one is not detecting," the shifting emotions within *Pushing the Bear* paired with the conflicted responses of the reader provide multiple paths into a deep engagement with the text through attention to both identification and disidentification.[28] By engaging seriously with the emotional responses the students have to the novel, we can create space in the classroom to explore moments such these, moments that can open out into a broader discussion of how the characters in the novel view Maritole and how those judgments are linked to the politics of removal. As Greyser reminds us, "affect entails politicized relations to temporality, such as melancholy/loss/nostalgia, or self-satisfaction/celebration/progressivism."[29]

Like *Pushing the Bear*, Luci Tapahonso's poem "In 1864" also centers on a removal trail and creates strong emotions in students. In this case the removal story is the Navajo Long Walk—the forced displacement of thousands of Diné people from their traditional homelands in the Four Corners region to a small reservation in New Mexico. Tapahonso's poem is told through nested perspectives. The main part of the poem follows the speaker, who is driving across New Mexico with her daughter. The speaker recounts the story of the Long Walk, moving from her own voice to the voice of her aunt and finally transitioning to her grandmother's voice, aligning the perspective of multiple generations of women. The poem is filled with heartbreaking images recounted in spare, direct language. Readers encounter stories of loss of land and livestock and the brutality of the forced march. A particularly devastating stanza tells of the drowning deaths of those forced to cross the Rio Grande:

> Some babies, children, and some of the older men
> and women were swept away by the river current.
> We must not ever forget their screams and the last we saw of them—
> hands, a leg, or strands of hair floating.[30]

At the end of the poem, the perspectives telescope back out from grand-mother, to aunt, to mother and finally focus on the daughter, who, in listening to her mother tell the story, functions as a stand-in for the reader. When the speaker finishes her story, her daughter is in tears: "Tears stream down her face. She cannot speak."[31]

The poem is filled with emotion, from the anguish and fear of the walkers to the grief of the daughter. The emotion is linked clearly and unambiguously to bodily experience and the land itself (the occasion of the storytelling is the car moving over the land the walkers crossed). Students cite the image of the floating strands of hair as one that is particularly arresting. They say there is something—an immediacy or perhaps an intimacy—about that hair that shocks them and draws them into the tragedy of the Long Walk. Their tears and the daughter's tears are mingled; both audiences are positioned alongside the walkers, and that sense of emotional entwinement is overwhelming.

The poem's speaker recognizes the intensity of the daughter's emotional response (and by association, the reader's). She tells us that there are good things that can be traced to the Long Walk: coffee, fry bread, "traditional" Diné clothing like velvet shirts and calico skirts, jewelry made from silver coins. The ending image captures that jewelry: "It is always something to see—silver flashing in the sun / against dark velvet and black, black hair."[32] Both daughter and reader emerge from the poem not with the haunting image of the hair of drowned victims but the hair of living Diné people, representing survival, adaptability, and flashing defiance.

With the daughter as a kind of affect guide, students can engage their own responses to trace the ways the poem draws trauma through generations, linking it not only to place and time but also to survival. If, as Janet Fiskio has argued, "the lack of attention to affectivity closes off entire dimensions of cultural citizenship that are not reducible to managerial and expert discourses and problem-solving frameworks," then attention to affectivity (emotional quality or capacity) can function to *open* "dimensions of cultural citizenship" and deepen our understanding of texts, cultures, peoples, and histories in productive ways.[33]

The students' affective responses are driven by a sense of identification with the speaker and her daughter. But as classroom discussions quickly demonstrate, that identification is complicated by a sense of guilt or complicity. They recognize that the suffering of the Diné is brought about by settler-colonialism's land greed, a greed that has directly benefited most of them. Here at Northern Michigan University our classrooms sit on the traditional homelands of the Anishinaabe people. Our presence here is a direct result of the U.S. government's forced displacement of the Anishinaabeg. For my Indigenous students, their affective response is even further complicated by their historical and cultural identification with the speaker and her daughter and their experience in a classroom of largely non-Native students who may be confronting these ideas for the first time. Their emotional burden can be intense.

Christina Katopodis's article "Addressing Despair in the Classroom: An Ecocritical Approach to Non-Canonical American Writers" advocates replacing "despair" with activism. "Empathy and anger," she writes, "are only preliminary, limited responses to literature. Literature leads to activism, which is the *best* way to argue for its relevance today."[34] I find myself conflicted about this sentiment. On the one hand, yes, it doesn't do to dwell in sadness if it leads to inaction. But on the other hand, are emotion and action opposites? Can one only do one or the other? Is emotion somehow a self-indulgent or nonserious response to literature? What if we refuse to relegate emotion to a "preliminary" or starting position and instead treat it as an opportunity to deepen our engagement? Not because it represents a first step or an initial reaction, but because circulating within a text and among a text, its contexts, and its readers are affects and emotions that help create access to what Dotson and Whyte call "moral terrains," where values, practices, and emotions are located in space, linking peoples and lands in a complex system that moves well beyond a personal reaction.[35] It is in affective response that we can actually encourage students to craft the deepest and most rigorous, as well as the most meaningful, analytical interventions.

I'd like to end by returning to that moment of suspension in my western American literature classroom, that breathless space when emotions—my emotions—were suddenly made visible. My initial interpretation of the students' response was that they were uncomfortable and worried; my instinct was to retreat to dry, critical inquiry. But in retrospect I think that their response wasn't fear and discomfort so much as it was *hunger*. Students, like all readers, know that what brings us back to literature again and again—the good stuff—is the emotion, the connection. The true pleasure of reading lies in our emotional engagement. As Moya suggests, readers connect to texts intellectually and emotionally, and it is that relationship between heart and head where space is created for interpretation.[36]

As I sat in my office working on the introduction to this chapter, there was a knock on my office door. A former student wanted to talk about a recent visit Luis Alberto Urrea had made to NMU's campus. His talk had made a deep impression on her, and she described the way her eyes filled with tears when he spoke of the night Mexican *federales* murdered his father. She wanted to thank me for assigning *The Devil's Highway* in our western American literature and ecocriticism class. She told me that before reading the book she had had little understanding of the U.S.-Mexico border and no empathetic connection to border crossers. She called the text a "paradigm shift" and said that it helped open her eyes—and her heart—to stories and histories that had previously seemed so removed. When I mentioned the topic of this chapter and that I had written about our class, she remarked, "Well, yes! We *are* in the humanities after all—knowledge and emotion go together!" Ultimately, her response gets to the very core of the question of whether affect and emotion belong in the literature classroom: they have always been there. Perhaps this is particularly true of the western American literature classroom, where stories of contact, conflict, removal, and violence are common. A pedagogy that draws on feminism, environmental justice, and affect theory acknowledges the complex emotions that swirl around the classroom and also encourages students to follow the trail of those emotions into a deeper consideration of texts and the peoples and cultures from which the texts emerge. Far from self-indulgent, affective responses offer us an opportunity for an ethically engaged criticism, what Ray calls "critique as a form of active care."[37] This is not to suggest that I now regularly cry in class but that I consciously make room for the possibility of emotion.

When my student left my office, I gazed out of the window into another frigid April day. I could just see Lake Superior over the tops of the trees. Even from a distance the sight of her steel-gray water made me shiver. As I looked, a watery ray of sunlight broke through the clouds, spotlighting the waves as they neared shore. April may be winter in Michigan, but it's summer in the Sonoran Desert. That weak sunbeam that wavered over the lake was from the same hot sun that bakes the borderlands. Winter is not separate from the sun, not separate from summer, just as critical reading and writing are not separate from affect and emotion. As the sun links me to my desert homeland even in the Marquette deep freeze, so too can our affective responses connect us more deeply to literature, allowing us to enter into the work of the classroom with the intention of reconnecting head and heart in an ethical practice of reading, writing, and teaching.

NOTES

1. Bashō, "Winter Solitude," 33.
2. Urrea, *Devil's Highway*, 166.
3. hooks, *Teaching Community*, 133.
4. Ahmed, "Happy Objects," 29.
5. Hemmings, "Invoking Affect," 565.
6. Bertelsen and Murphie, "Ethics of Everyday," 140.
7. Greyser, "Beyond the 'Feeling Woman,'" 85.
8. Greyser, "Beyond the 'Feeling Woman,'" 86.
9. Greyser, "Beyond the 'Feeling Woman,'" 103.
10. hooks, *Teaching Community*, xv.
11. hooks, *Teaching Community*, 22.
12. hooks, *Teaching Community*, 128.
13. Moya, *Social Imperative*, 151.
14. Dotson and Whyte, "Environmental Justice," 56.
15. Dotson and Whyte, "Environmental Justice," 75.
16. Ray, "Coming of Age," 303.
17. Ray, "Coming of Age," 304.
18. Ray, "Coming of Age," 312.
19. Powell et al., "Our Story Begins Here," act 2, scene 3.
20. Powell et al., "Our Story Begins Here," act 2, scene 3.
21. Kimmerer, *Braiding Sweetgrass*, 39.
22. Kimmerer, *Braiding Sweetgrass*, 40.
23. Kimmerer, *Braiding Sweetgrass*, 40.
24. Kimmerer, *Braiding Sweetgrass*, 46.
25. Glancy, *Pushing the Bear*, 4–5.
26. Glancy, *Pushing the Bear*, 4.
27. Glancy, *Pushing the Bear*, 167.
28. Dotson and Whyte, "Environmental Justice," 75.
29. Greyser, "Beyond the 'Feeling Woman,'" 103.
30. Tapahonso, "In 1864," 10.
31. Tapahonso, "In 1864," 10.
32. Tapahonso, "In 1864," 10.
33. Quoted in Dotson and Whyte, "Environmental Justice," 60.
34. Katapodis, "Addressing Despair" (emphasis added).
35. Dotson and Whyte, "Environmental Justice," 57.
36. Moya, *Social Imperative*, 53.
37. Ray, "Coming of Age," 313.

BIBLIOGRAPHY

Ahmed, Sara. "Happy Objects." In *The Affect Theory Reader*, edited by Melissa Gregg and Gregory J. Seigworth, 29–51. Durham NC: Duke University Press, 2010.

Bashō. "Winter Solitude." In *The Essential Haiku: Versions of Bashō, Buson, and Issa*, edited and translated by Robert Haas, 33. New York: HarperCollins, 1994.

Bertelsen, Lone, and Andrew Murphie. "The Ethics of Everyday Infinities and Powers: Félix Guattari on Affect and the Refrain." In *The Affect Theory Reader*, edited by Melissa Gregg and Gregory J. Seigworth, 138–57. Durham NC: Duke University Press, 2010.

Dotson, Kristie, and Kyle Whyte. "Environmental Justice, Unknowability and Unqualified Affectability." *Ethics and Environment* 18, no. 2 (2013): 55–79.

Glancy, Diane. *Pushing the Bear: A Novel of the Trail of Tears*. New York: Harcourt, 1996.

Greyser, Naomi. "Beyond the 'Feeling Woman': Feminist Implications of Affect Studies." *Feminist Studies* 38, no. 1 (2012): 84–112.

Hemmings, Clare. "Invoking Affect: Cultural Theory and the Ontological Turn." *Cultural Studies* 19, no. 5 (2005): 548–67.

hooks, bell. *Teaching Community: A Pedagogy of Hope*. London: Routledge, 2003.

Katopodis, Christina. "Addressing Despair in the Classroom: An Ecocritical Approach to Non-Canonical American Writers." *Pedagogy and American Literary Studies*, May 18, 2016. https://teachingpals.wordpress.com/2016/05/18/addressing-despair-in-the -classroom-an-ecocritical-approach-to-non-canonical-american-writers/.

Kimmerer, Robin Wall. *Braiding Sweetgrass: Indigenous Wisdom, Scientific Knowledge, and the Teachings of Plants*. Minneapolis: Milkweed Editions, 2015.

Moya, Paula. *The Social Imperative: Race, Close Reading, and Contemporary Literary Criticism*. Stanford: Stanford University Press, 2016.

Powell, Malea, et al. "Our Story Begins Here: Constellating Cultural Rhetorics." *Enculturation: A Journal of Rhetoric, Writing, and Culture*, October 25, 2014. http://www .enculturation.net/our-story-begins-here.

Ray, Sarah Jaquette. "Coming of Age at the End of the World: The Affective Arc of Undergraduate Environmental Studies Curricula." In *Affective Ecocriticism: Emotion, Embodiment, Environment*, edited by Kyle Bladow and Jennifer Ladino, 299–319. Lincoln: University of Nebraska Press, 2018.

Tapahonso, Luci. "In 1864." In *Sáani Dahataał: The Women Are Singing*, 7–10. Tucson: University of Arizona Press, 1993.

Urrea, Luis Alberto. *The Devil's Highway: A True Story*. New York: Back Bay Books, 2004.

5

Teaching Queer and Two-Spirit Indigenous Literatures, or The West Has Always Been Queer

LISA TATONETTI

As of 2019 I've been teaching queer Indigenous texts at the college level for eighteen years, including poetry and fiction in American and Native American literature surveys, and teaching seminars that focus on queer Indigenous studies. I've taught at two large midwestern universities, the first of which is on the ancestral lands of the Menominee and Anishinaabe and the second, on the ancestral lands of the Kaw, Osage, and Pawnee. The latter, Kansas State University, a land-grant institution founded in 1863, was only the second school in the United States to admit both men and women equally, and it had graduates of color by the late 1800s. However, despite the university's relatively progressive past, the complex Indigenous histories of this area and the fact that there are four federally recognized Indigenous nations here today—Iowa, Kickapoo, Prairie Band Potawatomi, and Sac and Fox—are largely unknown to the vast majority of students who enroll in my classes.

To most of my students Kansas is part of a white heteronormative narrative of western progress that involves a celebration of pioneers who bravely came to the newly created Kansas Territory in the wake of its official 1854 opening for non-Indian settlement under the Kansas-Nebraska Act. In many cases my Kansas-raised students know stories of "bleeding Kansas," the years between 1854 and 1861 when Kansas was at the center of a controversy over whether the territory should enter the union as a free or slave state. As of yet, though, not a single student has come to my classes knowing the painful history of Kanza (Kaw) removal that occurred during and after these same events on the land K-State now claims as its own. As these realities suggest, then, teaching queer Indigenous literature is necessarily intersectional, as we must make visible not only Two-Spirit histories and presents but also the narratives of sovereignty and indigeneity that create and sustain them.

Scene One: Tales of Queer Invisibility

Although iterations of queerness—what scholars and creative writers Craig Womack (Creek/Cherokee) and Daniel Heath Justice (Cherokee Nation) refer to in Indigenous contexts as "anomaly"—have always been with us, the connection of queerness to the U.S. West has not always been visible in literature, scholarship, and public perception.[1] Nowhere is this truer than in students' responses to the geospatial and psychological imaginary of the region. The simple introductory exercises with which I begin my courses reveal not only how students' understandings of the American West have deep-seated heteronormative foundations but also how they elide the very Indigenous peoples and histories on which this common imaginary depends. To be clear, this is not an indictment of student naïveté but rather a commentary about how classroom experiences illuminate the persistence of certain ideologies in contemporary U.S. cultures.

I frequently start both my Indigenous literature classes and my Imagining the West course by asking my students to free-write and then pair-and-share as they brainstorm (1) all the names of Indigenous persons they can list and (2) what images define the West for them. The responses invariably include Pocahontas, Sacagawea, Geronimo, and Sitting Bull, and cowboys, Indians, and wagon trains. None of this is surprising to folks who teach the West, as these iconic names and common tropes continue to circulate in popular movies, TV series, documentaries, and social studies lessons taught in the United States. Even in Manhattan, Kansas, located just down the road from the iconic western city of Abilene, my students, as the savvy consumers of pop culture they are, often recognize and joke about the fact that their ideas about the West come from mid-twentieth-century movies that, even if they themselves don't watch them, still pervade both their sense of the West as concept/geographical space and also their knowledge of Indigenous peoples.

Our ensuing discussions serve as a springboard from which to introduce settler colonialism and its ongoing attempts to camouflage its own existence. As Lorenzo Veracini explains in "Introducing Settler Colonial Studies," a favorite read of my classes, "Settler colonialism . . . covers its tracks and operates towards its self-supersession."[2] With this systemic erasure in mind, we question how this land could have been seized and entire communities decimated and relocated in the very spot on which we stand without a single student in our class knowing a thing about it. This eradication of historical memory resonates deeply by the end of these introductory conversations. Thus, students come to see the unseen when they recognize the complete absence of information they've received about their current locale.

Students are therefore quick to recognize the limits of their knowledge. In fact there's often some squirming when folks realize that even on a larger, less local scale they can name very few Native people, which is a dismaying but common student dilemma in the midwestern context in which I run this exercise. A key caveat that turns this into an engaging conversation rather then a lesson in public shaming is that I'm overt about the fact that the students themselves are not being called into question; instead, our discussions reveal educational gaps that enable the continuing prevalence of dominant cultural narratives about indigeneity, western expansion, and gender and sexuality. These gaps offer a clear example of the success of settler ideologies into which they didn't even know they had been inculcated.

In the early stages of this class conversation I'll often ask (after maybe five to ten minutes of brainstorming and the further free-associating that occurs when folks begin to share) why the images we're putting on the board are so limited. So why, for example, does the list of Indigenous people we compile end—as it nearly always does—in the nineteenth century, more than a hundred years before the time of our present discussion? Moreover, the fact that very few can answer the questions I pepper into our discussion—such as "Whose land are we on?" or "What Indigenous nations are in Kansas today?"—serves to illustrate the point about how settler colonialism "covers its tracks." Furthermore, in terms of thinking of the goals of an introductory class, the answers students share individually or write on the board in pairs in response to these introductory questions usually get them talking, laughing, and sharing memories as they recall the origin of their own indoctrination into these foundational U.S. myths (e.g., grade-school Thanksgiving pageants, school trips to various types of historical sites, racialized Boy Scout activities, or social studies dioramas). These conversations thus introduce settler colonialism, demonstrate the real imperative for education on Indigenous nations, lands, and peoples, and also build community between and among students.

What is not as readily apparent, however, even for students who may already be fairly critical of tales of U.S. exceptionalism, is how these popular western imaginaries rest on a limited narrative of gender and sexuality. For example, in the still much-beloved Disney film that continues to ground my students' knowledge of Pocahontas even twelve years after its release, the heroine offers to sacrifice herself for John Smith, thereby turning a tale of colonial incursion into Powhatan territory into a sanitary and, in most of their experiences, pleasurable romance narrative rooted in Eurocentric norms of monogamous heterocouplehood. Meanwhile, the most commonly referenced male-identified counterpoints among the Indigenous peoples my students are able to recall—Geronimo and Sitting Bull—are marked by a hypermasculinity indexed in student descriptions of plains war paint, bare chests, loincloths, impressive horsemanship, and the various accoutrements (bows, arrows, spears, etc.) of what Richard Slotkin would deem "savage war."[3]

Once these images and names are on the board, I often group the data chronologically, which helps highlight the fact that the nineteenth-century names are all male and, in contrast to their imagined settlers, sans family. These groupings prompt students (or I prompt students) to consider what disappears: there are no more Sacagawea figures—mothers with babies—and in fact no women at all in the amalgamation of images that signify western expansion. These erasures point to the ways this narrative of the West elides Indigenous family and kinship networks and substitutes the specter of a violent masculinity that continues to be perpetuated (perhaps most ubiquitously in Hollywood film and Indian mascots). Such nineteenth-century "masculindians," to borrow a term from Sam McKegney, threaten white nuclear families—like Ma, Pa, and Laura Ingalls et al.—who innocently arrive in Kansas on wagons in stories that Dakota theorist Philip Deloria has famously deemed tales of "defensive conquest."[4] My students, who help me cover the whiteboard with these names and images, quickly come to see the patterns and absences in the depictions of gender that arise from their collective brainstorming.

In the end, spending the first day of the term discussing how hegemonic images of the West are constructed by and reflect Eurocentric cosmologies ultimately sets the stage for our semester-long deconstruction of such long-standing myths. Importantly, this approach also allows me to begin to tease out how dominant versions of the West are deeply and problematically gendered and sexualized and to introduce students to what they still often encounter as a surprising fact: the West has always been queer.

Scene Two: The Textual Politics of Queering John Wayne

The question becomes, then, how to bring students to recognize that queer indigeneity, rather than white masculinity, monogamous heterocouplehood, and/or the heteropatriarchal nation-state, has long grounded public and intimate relations on Turtle Island. While I have approached this question from any number of angles, I turn here to the rich possibilities represented by Maurice Kenny's (Mohawk) landmark poem "Winkte," Beth Brant's (Bay of Quinte Mohawk) "Coyote Learns a New Trick" and "A Long Story," and Deborah Miranda's (Ohlone Costanoan Esselen Nation) *Bad Indians: A Tribal Memoir*. Having taught each of these texts in multiple contexts—including to first-year students in introductory literature classes for humanities requirements, mid-degree students taking Native literature survey classes for a diversity requirement, and upper-level undergraduates and graduate students who freely chose special topics like Twenty-First Century Native Literature, Race, Sexuality, and Nation in the U.S., and/or Sovereign Erotics: Two-Spirit Literatures and Theory—I believe they present an array of rich pedagogical opportunities that help students expand their grasp of gender, sexuality, indigeneity, and the focus of this particular collection, the North American West.

Like most of us, I entwine the literature I teach with historical documents, sociological data, videos, music, and various forms of scholarly criticism. In classes that offer the time and have a particular focus—such as queer studies, queer Indigenous literature and theory, or Native literature surveys—I'll precede these literary texts with the introduction to Sue-Ellen Jacobs, Wesley Thomas, and Sabine Lang's *Two-Spirit People: Native American Gender Identity, Sexuality, and Spirituality*. For upper-level classes that landmark book is paired with the introductions to two more recent collections: *Sovereign Erotics: A Collection of Two-Spirit Literature* and *Queer Indigenous Studies: Critical Interventions in Theory, Politics, and Literature*. As we'll see, these selections introduce students to the histories and literatures of queer Indigenous peoples, to the inception of the term "Two-Spirit" as a political statement, and to the rise of Two-Spirit critiques.

Each of these edited collections offers valuable information that frames students' understandings of the complex histories of genders and sexualities in Indigenous traditions. The first, the landmark *Two-Spirit People*, offers a quick overview of gender, sex, and sexuality as terms, as well as briefly explaining why "Two-Spirit" was chosen by Indigenous activists in the late 1980s and early 1990s to replace the pejorative term "berdache." At the same time, *Two-Spirit People* addresses the incompatibility of "Two-Spirit" with some Indigenous cosmologies and linguistic traditions, thereby highlighting the vast distinctions between and among Indigenous belief systems. Basically, from a pedagogical perspective this piece lays some solid groundwork while still leaving time for other readings.

I teach this text by using a worksheet that asks students to pick out key definitions and concepts in groups. This includes basic questions: What are sex, gender, and sexuality? How would you define Two-Spirit? Why did the term arise? What might be the problems with its use? My goal here is to get the students talking and working through the text, as well as to have them take away key information that they can return to and expand on as we move on to more contemporary sources. To that end, although they answer the worksheet questions in groups, they each fill in their own copy, which I have them pull out and use in the next class.

The introductions to *Sovereign Erotics* and *Queer Indigenous Studies*, which were published as companion texts, can be taught together or separately, depending on the class and available time. *Sovereign Erotics* presents an overview of the rise of queer Indigenous literatures in the United States, which is helpful in literature surveys or Indigenous studies classes. *Queer Indigenous Studies*, like the other two texts, further discusses the term "Two-Spirit" and also offers a valuable overview of Indigenous methodologies, contending that "the full complexity of Indigenous thought in the past and present should set a first frame for interpreting Indigenous knowledges."[5] I most often teach these introductions in large group discussions, stopping to read essential passages that relate to the ideas I most want to emphasize. So, for example, I stop to ask, "What is Indigenous methodology as framed by Driskill, Finley, Gilley, and Morgensen, and why is it important to start there?"

I continue to emphasize the absences we discussed on the first day by asking, for instance, when students read *Sovereign Erotics'* history of queer Indigenous literature, which of the authors they've read. I ask the same question of *Queer Indigenous Studies'* list of Indigenous theorists. This repeated reminder of the gaps in their education tends to encourage students to be vocal advocates for educational change. They often tell me during or after the term of speaking with parents and past and present teachers, which is exactly what needs to happen to encourage curricular revision and development.

After we discuss *Sovereign Erotics* and *Queer Indigenous Studies*, students pair up (ideally with their notes from this discussion and their answers from the previous class meeting's exercise) to talk about how exactly these two texts expand our knowledge base. These readings offer students different pieces of the puzzle, then, as we begin to build a preliminary understanding of the queer Indigenous histories of the land on which they stand as well as present them with an array of contemporary Native writers and theorists that few had previously encountered.

Before turning to literature, I want to offer one more layer to the potential critical readings for this segment of the class—scholarly essays that, like the previous introductions, each add depth to the engaged conversations that should at this point be occurring as students develop knowledge about the queer West. Qwo-Li Driskill's essay "Stolen from Our Bodies: First Nations Two-Spirits/Queers and the Journey to a Sovereign Erotic," which stimulates lively student discussions, provides an invaluable understanding of the tightly entwined nature of sexual trauma and colonialism, as well as how what many students see as the realm of the personal—sexuality, desire, and the erotic—directly impacts Native communities.

Additionally, Driskill's piece adds another layer to the previous discussions of terminology by considering the efficacy of the term "Two-Spirit" alongside that of "gay," "trans," and "queer." Since we by now have covered quite a bit of information, I often have students stand in a semicircle as we begin this piece and ask quick factual questions about what the previous readings taught us about the queer West: What is settler colonialism? How do we see it in common images of the West? What is the difference between gender and sexuality? How are dominant images of the West gendered? How would you define "Two-Spirit"? Who can add to this definition? Why was "Two-Spirit" coined? What are potential problems with the term? When did we begin to see the rise of queer Indigenous literature? Name one queer Indigenous writer, two theorists, and so on.

I might direct these questions to two students at a time in the group, allow them to "save" each other, and ask that they repeat and build on previous answers so that (1) they listen to one another carefully and (2) they verbally and collectively reinforce the ideas we've learned. Basically it's a rapid-fire run through our previous readings and conversations. I encourage students to review their notes before class begins, laughingly warning them a "pop quiz" will soon be upon them. My teasing throughout these type of exercises emphasizes that such reviews, like the first-day exercises, are fun, not punitive, which encourages shy students to willingly participate. (I call on everyone at some point, so they can't really duck out of participation.) There is usually a lot of laughter in this exercise, as I move quickly and do a lot of joking—for example, humming the *Jeopardy* song if someone draws a blank or asking if someone wants to "phone a friend," just to relieve any pressure they might feel. The point I overtly make as we review is that we're building an interconnected scaffold rather than studying individual writers, theorists, or ideas.

Once we have a set of definitions or theories from our review, I ask students to open their texts and sit in pairs or trios to consider, and find specific evidence about, how Driskill expands the concepts we just reviewed (for better paired discussions, choose a few students to record ideas and conversation on the board during the review). After maybe five to ten minutes of paired discussion, I ask folks to share the ideas they developed with the large group. Together we build a definition of what Driskill has notably termed a "sovereign erotic," considering how it "relates to [Indigenous] bodies . . . nations, traditions, and histories."[6] Driskill's piece provides numerous references that help to expand our growing body of knowledge about queer Indigenous writers and histories and also brings us back to those opening-day conversations by alluding to colonized masculinities such as those that arose in the class brainstorming. In the process, these Indigenous knowledges actively disrupt the versions of the West most students had as they entered our class. This is an especially fruitful piece to spend writing time on, and I often ask students—either in the last fifteen minutes or so of class or as a take-home "knowledge application quiz"—to read dominant versions of the West (movies, books, school projects, toys, club activities, etc.) through the lens of a sovereign erotic. The writing assignment makes for a great opener for the next class, and I let students know that we'll be returning to it.

Three essays have become important pieces to ground queer Indigenous critiques in literary studies: Koyangk'auwi Maidu poet/theorist Janice Gould's "Disobedience (in Language) in Text by Lesbian Native Americans"; Anishinaabe writer/theorist Kateri Akiwenzie-Damm's "Erotica, Indigenous Style"; and Deborah Miranda's "Dildos, Hummingbirds, and Driving Her Crazy: Searching for Native American Women's Erotics." These writers help students grasp how important the turn toward queer Indigenous literature is by highlighting how these queer and gender-expansive Indigenous histories and socialities have been silenced even in classes on the literary erotic, feminisms, or Indigenous literature more broadly. To stake this critique, they engage the absence of and need for queer Indigenous writers and particularly, in the case of Gould and Miranda, women's writing and lesbian writing. Their arguments thus bring the production and distribution of literature into question, detailing troubling patterns in the publishing industry, in academia, and in the popular imagination. Collectively, Gould, Akiwenzie-Damm, and Miranda approach representations (and the lack thereof) of what Miranda later terms "the Indigenous erotic" in literature.[7] It's important to note that Gould is among the first generation of queer Native writers whose creative and scholarly work engages these questions, that Akiwenzie-Damm offers a First Nations perspective, and that both Gould and Miranda are themselves queer Indigenous creative writers and scholars.[8] Whether an instructor picks one or all of these pieces to frame the move to the queer Indigenous literature, each article insists on the significance of this body of work and on the necessity for queer Indigenous voices in discussions of land, colonialism, and/or gender and sexuality in the West.

By this time in a class, whether I have taught all of the above readings or perhaps just the introduction to *Two-Spirit People* alongside Driskill's and/ or Gould's essays, students are primed to move on to the rich body of memoir, poetry, drama, and fiction that makes up queer Indigenous literature. I emphasize to students that Gould's, Akiwenzie-Damm's, and Miranda's calls have been answered because, for those who know where to look, the abundance of contemporary queer Indigenous literature is marvelously overwhelming. In fact in late 2016 Qwo-Li Driskill, Daniel Heath Justice, myself, and many writers, students, and friends collaboratively expanded a bibliography of creative and critical work in queer Indigenous studies to more than sixty single-spaced pages. As this length suggests, the texts I discuss here are just a handful of the many potential options.

Now that students have gained a measure of knowledge about how the braided threads of sovereignty and sexuality undergird the places, images, peoples, and histories of the West, I bring literature to bear on our conversations, reminding them of the queer Indigenous literary history set up in *Sovereign Erotics*. We begin in the 1970s and 1980s, when gay and lesbian Native writers were (re)claiming their place in their literature and nations; to do this, I often pair Maurice Kenny's poem "Winkte" with Beth Brant's short story "Coyote Learns a New Trick," which were both in the first collection of queer Indigenous literature, *Living the Spirit*, published in 1988.[9] Kenny's poem invokes the history of multiple gender traditions among Indigenous nations while also claiming the significance of queer Indigenous peoples to their contemporary nations. Brant highlights the gender malleability of many trickster figures in Indigenous traditions when a female-identified Coyote pretends to be male in a trick played on her female friend—a trick with a conclusion that's clearly pleasurable to all involved.

While Kenny's poem alludes to a history to which students have since been introduced, Brant's piece presents openings for new conversations, including the importance of humor in Indigenous cultures and the ways sexuality, often cast as shameful in settler traditions, was and is engaged with openness among Native peoples and in written and oral Indigenous literatures. This is another teaching moment in which returning to or contrasting the images that arise from Kenny's and Brant's writing with dominant ideologies of the West is particularly fruitful since, in classic westerns, white women are cast as chaste damsels in distress barreling toward monogamous heterocouplehood, as prostitutes (with or without a heart of gold), or, in the case of the bonneted pioneer woman, as markedly asexual. The overt embrace of the erotic found in this and many other of Brant's texts stands in stark contrast to such narratives, a fact that speaks to the alternate and decidedly complex understandings of genders and sexualities common in Indigenous traditions.

Brant's short fiction "A Long Story," which was also in *Living the Spirit*, provides a beautiful bridge to move conversations about the queer West further into the late twentieth century. Brant's narrative parallels two scenarios—one in 1890–91, in which a Lakota woman's children are taken from her and sent to a government boarding school, and another in 1978–79, in which a contemporary Native woman loses her children to her former husband because of the state's negative view of her lesbianism. The structure of the story—three paired segments headed by dates (1890/1978, 1890/1978, and 1891/1979)—encourages readers to compare each set of paired sections; I therefore split students into three or six groups, depending on class numbers, asking each group (or pair of groups if there are six) to carefully analyze one of the paired sections. When we come back to large group discussion, we follow Brant's argument through the arc of these two characters' lives and are thus brought to see how the concept of queerness can apply to multiple aspects of identity. The 1890 mother, Annie, though married, is cast as just as queer as the unnamed lesbian mother in the later sections of the piece; both characters are penalized for resisting hegemonic norms of the period. In each section Christian beliefs are employed like weapons to mark a certain segment of the population as "uncivilized" or, as in the case of Brant's nineteenth-century protagonist, as "crazy." The story also allows for rich discussion of intersectionality, since both protagonists confront legal barriers and experience psychological trauma based on multiple aspects of their identities (as Native Americans, as socioeconomically disadvantaged peoples [in the first narrative], as women, as queers, etc.).

This short story is a favorite, and, with their new understanding of the history of the West, students are quick to see how state-enforced mandates arise from settler ideologies. Furthermore, depending on an instructor's or class's focus and interests, "A Long Story" may offer an opening for discussions about representations of disability and the deployment of insanity charges as a containment mechanism in institutions like the so-called Hiawatha Asylum for Insane Indians, or about contemporary Defense of Marriage Act laws within the Navajo and Cherokee Nations alongside the growing number of Indigenous nations that have enacted same-sex marriage provisions. There is also an array of short- and full-length videos to augment this section of the course.[10] Finally, in an upper-level course, Mark Rifkin's work effectively points to the ways the U.S. nation-state was built on the promotion of monogamous heterocouplehood at the expense of more expansive networks of Indigenous kinship. Thus, the boarding schools, as Brant shows, were intended to inculcate, and at the same time legitimate, settler logics of sexuality, gender, and nation. Understanding these realities helps make visible how the highly romanticized versions of the West that still circulate with infectious power intentionally and violently suppress alternate histories of the land on which we stand (thereby returning us to our previous discussions of how settler colonialism aims to make itself and its violent histories invisible).

While there are innumerable texts to include here, due to space constraints I end this section with one of the most powerful recent texts to engage the topics under discussion—Deborah Miranda's tribal memoir, *Bad Indians*. I've had success teaching this challenging text at both the first-year and graduate levels. Miranda's brilliant book—a mosaic of memoir, satire, poetry, fiction, and historical documents such as charts, letters, mission records, newspaper clippings, and archival documents—is invaluable in any context and especially worthwhile for those interested in queer Indigenous studies and the queer West. *Bad Indians* is particularly effective with students, as it begins with a return to the elementary- and middle-school classroom (again reminding us of the stories shared on the first day). Addressing the way California settler narratives describe histories of conquest in the elementary education classroom, Miranda directly challenges heteronormative, sanitized versions of contact, colonization, and the West forwarded in contemporary K–12 curriculums. Speaking of California, where fourth-grade classes still build Catholic mission dioramas, she argues that now is the "time for the Mission Fantasy Fairy Tale to end."[11] In its stead Miranda creates an alternate "mission history" that foregrounds both the genealogy of settler violence and the survivance stories of California Indian people. In the process Miranda queers the settler version of the missions by revealing their brutal realities, and she brings into these conversations references to sexual violence against Indigenous women, the padres' oppression of Two-Spirit peoples, and the missions' direct attacks on nonbinary understandings of sexuality.

Overall, the palimpsest of critical and creative texts I touch on in this section provides the basis for a reenvisioning of the U.S. West, one that shows, through the interweaving of the histories and contemporary imaginations of queer Indigenous peoples, that the foundation of this geographical and ideological space rests on a radically different reality than that most students carry with them to the first day of class. Importantly, students often experience this new perspective on the West as radically transformative.

Scene Three: Queering Removal

As scholars of the West know, geographical location is a moving target—the West as a place and an ideological concept expanded with each successive wave of contact and colonization. Thus this final section suggests another way we might queer the West, which is to grow our pedagogical approaches to the most frequently taught historical moment of nineteenth-century U.S. western expansion: the migrations forced by the Indian Removal Act of 1830. To destabilize and expand student understandings of this key historical moment, I turn to Diane Glancy's poem "The Abandoned Wife Gives Herself to the Lord" and Daniel Heath Justice's fantasy trilogy *The Way of Thorn and Thunder*. In doing so, this section demonstrates how employing a queer Indigenous critical lens to teach the West enriches classroom conversations about key events in western history while simultaneously de-suturing the West from heteropatriarchal settler narratives about U.S. history and Indigenous identities.

Although Glancy is a heterosexually rather than queer-identified Cherokee writer, her brief poem "The Abandoned Wife Gives Herself to the Lord" effectively queers the U.S. demand for monogamous heterocouplehood. Glancy's piece begins with an 1871 quote from Chief Mark as he "considers monogamy at the Warm Springs Agency." He states, "I love all my women. My old wife is a mother to the others; I can't do without her, but she is old and cannot work very much; I cannot send her away to die."[12] In the poem that follows, an omniscient narrator depicts a nineteenth-century Indigenous woman who has been cast aside by her husband because of the U.S. government's insistence on monogamous marriage. "Dizzy with hunger," the protagonist sits on a rock as she waits for a Judeo-Christian God—"a man who took more than one wife"—to come to her. The juxtaposition of the quote, the abandoned wife's hunger, and my students' collective belief that God is a no-show in this scenario all suggest an imminent death. This poem therefore allows for a fruitful discussion of how dominant beliefs about kinship are forced onto Indigenous polities, with disastrous consequences.

While the poem is not about the Cherokee specifically, I employ it to introduce conversations about how the demands of the U.S. nation-state forced Indigenous peoples to change, or at least appear to change, long-standing cultural practices, including those tied to gender and sexuality. Its effectiveness lies in the fact that I find few students enter my classrooms having ever questioned the primacy of monogamous couplehood. This poem usually launches an animated conversation about why multiple marriage practices are considered some sort of inherent problem. In most cases, supporting claims for such beliefs stem from a heteropatriarchal ideology that envisions gender as a binary within which women inevitably have less power than men. Such a reading suggests that Indigenous women in what, to dominant culture, were "illegal" polygamous marriages were forced into these unequal relationships to their detriment. When we consider the efficacy of multiple partners in eighteenth- or nineteenth-century contexts, in which a great deal of labor was needed for daily survival, or the possibility of a woman choosing to invite a sister or friend into her household for companionship and psychological and physical support, a paradigm shift ensues. These discussions directly relate to the demands being made on the Cherokee Nation in the late eighteenth and early twentieth centuries and the subsequent changes in property rights and leadership that, at least on paper, took the right of inheritance from women and gave it to men. As we then compare Cherokee clan law to the evolving iterations of the Cherokee constitution, students are able to see how the move toward Indian removal demands consideration of the intimately entwined nature of gender, sexuality, and nation.

After teaching the Cherokee Nation constitution, excerpts from President Andrew Jackson's speeches, and Elias Boudinot's "An Address to the Whites," I turn to Daniel Heath Justice's fantasy trilogy *The Way of Thorn and Thunder*, which is an allegory for Cherokee removal. Importantly, Justice's alternate reality demands that readers see Cherokee Nation writers as part of the historical present in which science fiction and fantasy are ubiquitous. The hero of Justice's novel is a kick-ass, polyamorous she-Kyn warrior, Tarsa'deshae. Arising from both the actual Indigenous histories of warrior women, the history of Cherokee removal, and the long-standing literary tradition of high-fantasy fiction, Justice's hero expands the body of removal literature and allows for incredibly productive conversations about how expansive genders and sexualities can be vehicles for Indigenous resistance and change.

In this segment of the course I assign students a comparative project: they research aspects of Cherokee Nation history, create an eight-entry annotated bibliography, and then write a paper or create a short film that engages how Justice, a queer Cherokee Nation writer, employs and revises that history as he imagines alternate realities and Indigenous futurities. The eight-entry annotated bibliography usually runs four to five single-spaced pages, as I require detailed entries that mix primary sources with contemporary theory and an abstract for the paper. Subsequent student papers have ranged from explorations of Indigenous science fiction to the function of Two-Spirit erotics to a literary mapping of Justice's alternate universe.

These assignments function in a number of ways. The annotated bibliography on some aspect of removal history is a common assignment that many of the readers of this book likely use to augment students' knowledge of this historical event. However, using Justice's fantasy trilogy as the point of comparison rather than something more conventional, such as Glancy's *Pushing the Bear* (which I sometimes teach before Justice), forces students to move beyond a narrative of tragic victimry that turns on a sad sense of inevitability and loss. So, for example, in Justice's novel the betrayal of the nation is led not by Boudinot and the Ridges but by a female-identified character, Neranda Ak'shaar, who signs "The Oath of Western Sanctuary," the document that formalizes the Kyn removal from Everland in much the same way the 1835 Treaty of New Echota did for the Cherokee. Neranda's complex motives and ultimate integration into the revitalization of the Kyn nation allow students imaginative access to some of the struggles that the signers of the treaty may have undergone. This fictional reenvisioning thus challenges histories that too easily brand the members of the Treaty Party as one-dimensional traitors. While it's possible to assign only the first section of the trilogy as the basis of comparison, given that the entire book is more than five hundred pages, the conclusion of the book(s) is especially valuable because of its focus on renewal and cultural continuity.[13]

Moreover, the world of Justice's Kyn privileges the Indigenous erotic and offers it as a place of power, thereby demanding nuanced readings of gender and sexuality. In this way Justice follows a path forged by queer Indigenous feminists like Brant, who, as we have seen, explicitly engages the lived experience of the erotic in her fiction and also addresses the erotic as a formative theory in her nonfiction collection *Writing as Witness* (where she situates the erotic at the center of growth and productivity for Indigenous nations). Bringing such considerations to bear on the literature of removal puts these significant historical events into conversation with a living, breathing, embodied present in which Native peoples not only continue to exist but also make love, make art, and extend Indigenous knowledges into the future. As my enthusiastic student responses have repeatedly demonstrated, teaching through a Two-Spirit Indigenous lens can queer the past, present, and future of the West in productive and pleasurable ways.

Epilogue: Queer Indigenous Potentials

As I hope these examples have shown, reading the West through a queer Indigenous lens can unsettle the obfuscating—and inevitably more comfortable—ideologies of the West our students all too often carry into the classroom. Introducing the fact that queer images, texts, and peoples in Native American and Aboriginal contexts have existed since time immemorial in the land on which we currently stand makes visible and also radically challenges gender narratives of contact and colonization. In light of these long-standing realities, to teach the literature and history of the U.S. West responsibly, instructors must introduce students to this important fact: whether we are talking about literature or history, the West has always been queer. In the end, teaching the queer West is thus not a new pedagogical approach to the field but instead a way to allow students to more effectively see the West that always was.

NOTES

1. Womack contends that "rather than disrupting society, anomalies actually reify the existing social order. Anomalous beings can also be powerful; queerness has an important place. Phenomena that do not fit 'normal' categories are ascribed special powers." Womack, *Red on Red*, 244. Justice explains that "we can draw on a more expansive understanding of tradition to the significance of same-sex desire as a tribal good. As one of many evocative possibilities, we might look to the iconographic archive of a significant ancestral stream of the Cherokees and other Southeastern nations—the Mississippians—and the powerful Mississippian category of 'anomaly.'" Justice, "Notes toward a Theory of Anomaly," 216.
2. Veracini, "Introducing Settler Colonial Studies," 3.
3. As Slotkin famously argues, "The symbol of 'savage war' [is] both a mythic trope and an operative category of military doctrine. The premise of 'savage war' is that ineluctable political and social differences—rooted in some combination of 'blood' and culture—make coexistence between primitive natives and civilized Europeans impossible on any basis other than that of subjugation." Slotkin, *Gunfighter Nation*, 12.

4. See McKegney, *Masculindians*; and Deloria, *Playing Indian*.
5. Driskill et al., *Queer Indigenous Studies*, 5.
6. Driskill, "Stolen from Our Bodies," 52.
7. Miranda, *Zen of La Llorona*, 4.
8. For more on the rise of queer Native literature, including where these authors fit into queer Indigenous literary history, see Tatonetti, *Queerness of Native American Literature*, chapter 1.
9. "Winkte" was first published in *ManRoot* 11 (Spring–Summer 1977), while both "Coyote Learns a New Trick" and "A Long Story" were published in Brant's *Mohawk Trail* before their inclusion in *Living the Spirit*.
10. To extend conversations about disability studies, one might show Cree filmmaker Thirza Cuthand's *Love & Numbers* or *Madness in Four Actions* (currently available on Vimeo). For videos to include in conversations about queer indigeneity, to name just a few, Diné filmmaker Sydney Freeland's *Drunktown's Finest* and Cree writer and director Adam Garnet Jones's *Fire Song* can be taught alongside Cuthand. Among these films, Cuthand's are student favorites and, given their status as shorts, are most easily integrated into often packed curricula.
11. Miranda, *Bad Indians*, xix.
12. Glancy, "Abandoned Wife Gives Herself to the Lord," 3.
13. Justice's text was first published in three separate books by Kegedonce Press and was later republished in an omnibus edition by the University of New Mexico Press. (Justice prefers the latter version, as he wrote the text as a single book; the former have fantastic covers based on his illustrations.)

BIBLIOGRAPHY

Akiwenzie-Damm, Kateri. "Erotica, Indigenous Style." In *Without Reservation: Indigenous Erotica*, edited by Kateri Akiwenzie-Damm, xi–xii. Wharton ON: Kegedonce, 2003.

Boudinot, Elias. "An Address to the Whites." 1826. National Humanities Center. Accessed February 15, 2020. https://courses.lumenlearning.com/ushistory1os/chapter/primary-source-elias-boudinot-an-address-to-the-whites-1826/.

Brant, Beth (Degonwadonti). "Coyote Learns a New Trick." In *Living the Spirit: A Gay American Indian Anthology*, edited by Gay American Indians and Will Roscoe, 163–66. New York: St. Martin's Press, 1988.

———. "A Long Story." In *Mohawk Trail*, 77–85. Ithaca NY: Firebrand Books, 1985.

———. *Writing as Witness: Essay and Talk*. Toronto: Women's Press, 1994.

Cuthand, Thirza Jean, dir. and writer. *Love & Numbers*. Toronto: Vtape, 2004.

———. *Madness in Four Actions*. Toronto: Vtape, 2008.

Deloria, Philip J. *Playing Indian*. New Haven CT: Yale University Press, 1999.

Driskill, Qwo-Li. "Stolen from Our Bodies: First Nations Two-Spirits/Queers and the Journey to a Sovereign Erotic." *Studies in American Indian Literatures* 16, no. 2 (2004): 50–64.

Driskill, Qwo-Li, Chris Finley, Brian Joseph Gilley, and Scott Lauria Morgensen, eds. *Queer Indigenous Studies: Critical Interventions in Theory, Politics, and Literature*. Tucson: University of Arizona Press, 2011.

————. "The Revolution Is for Everyone: Imagining an Emancipatory Future through Queer Indigenous Critical Theories." In *Queer Indigenous Studies: Critical Interventions in Theory, Politics, and Literature*, edited by Qwo-Li Driskill, Chris Finley, Brian Joseph Gilley, and Scott Lauria Morgensen, 211–21. Tucson: University of Arizona Press, 2011.

Driskill, Qwo-Li, Daniel Heath Justice, Deborah Miranda, and Lisa Tatonetti, eds. *Sovereign Erotics: A Collection of Two-Spirit Literature*. Tucson: University of Arizona Press, 2011.

Freeland, Sydney, dir. and writer. *Drunktown's Finest*. Provo UT: Wildwood Enterprises, 2014.

Gay American Indians and Will Roscoe, eds. *Living the Spirit: A Gay American Indian Anthology*. New York: St. Martin's Press, 1988.

Glancy, Diane. "The Abandoned Wife Gives Herself to the Lord." In *Primer of the Obsolete*, 3. Amherst: University of Massachusetts Press, 2004.

————. *Pushing the Bear: A Novel of the Trail of Tears*. New York: Harcourt & Brace, 1996.

Gould, Janice. "Disobedience (in Language) in Text by Lesbian Native Americans." *ARIEL: A Review of International English Literature* 25, no. 1 (1994): 32–44.

Jacobs, Sue-Ellen, Wesley Thomas, and Sabine Lang, eds. *Two-Spirit People: Native American Gender Identity, Sexuality, and Spirituality*. Urbana: University of Illinois Press, 1997.

Jones, Adam Garnet, dir. and writer. *Fire Song: Refuse to Be Broken*. New Almaden CA: Wolfe Video, 2015.

Justice, Daniel Heath. *Dreyd: The Way of Thorn and Thunder, Book 3*. Wharton ON: Kegedonce, 2007.

————. *Kynship: The Way of Thorn and Thunder*. Wharton ON: Kegedonce, 2005.

————. "Notes toward a Theory of Anomaly." In "Sexuality, Nationality, and Indigeneity." Special issue, *GLQ: A Journal of Lesbian and Gay Studies* 16, no. 1–2 (2010): 207–42.

————. *The Way of Thorn and Thunder: The Kynship Chronicles*. Albuquerque: University of New Mexico Press, 2011.

————. *Wyrwood: The Way of Thorn and Thunder, Book 2*. Wharton ON: Kegedonce, 2006.

Kenny, Maurice. "Winkte." *ManRoot* 11 (1977): 26. Reprinted in *Only as Far as Brooklyn: Poems*, 10–11. Boston: Good Gay Poets, 1979. Also reprinted in *Living the Spirit: A Gay American Indian Anthology*, edited by Gay American Indians and Will Roscoe, 153–54. New York: St. Martin's Press, 1988.

McKegney, Sam, ed. *Masculindians: Conversations about Indigenous Manhood*. East Lansing: Michigan State University Press, 2014.

Miranda, Deborah. *Bad Indians: A Tribal Memoir*. Berkeley CA: Heyday Press, 2013.

————. "Dildos, Hummingbirds, and Driving Her Crazy: Searching for Native American Women's Erotics." *Frontiers* 23, no. 2 (2002): 135–49.

————. *The Zen of La Llorona*. Cambridge: Salt Publishing, 2005.

Slotkin, Richard. *Gunfighter Nation: The Myth of the Frontier in Twentieth-Century America*. New York: Atheneum, 1992.

Tatonetti, Lisa. *The Queerness of Native American Literature*. Minneapolis: University Minnesota Press, 2016.

Veracini, Lorenzo. "Introducing Settler Colonial Studies." *Settler Colonial Studies* 1, no. 1 (2011): 1–12.

Womack, Craig. *Red on Red: Native American Literary Separatism*. Minneapolis: University of Minnesota Press, 1999.

6

An Interdisciplinary Approach to Teaching Gender in Western American Literature

AMANDA R. GRADISEK AND MARK C. ROGERS

As we all know, there are many different ways to be a professor, and many of the factors affecting our teaching come from without; where we teach and who we teach generally, inevitably, influence how we teach, and even what we teach, whether we like it or not. Many of the contributors to this volume work at larger research institutions, meaning they are likely to have more classes for majors and therefore more students choosing an elective or major course. But we know that humanities majors are on the decline nationwide. For example, in 2015 the University of Maryland reported a 40 percent decline over just the previous three years.[1] Another study finds an 8.7 percent drop in humanities majors nationwide from 2012 to 2014.[2] For those of us who teach at small liberal arts colleges and universities, these shrinking numbers affect us daily, changing the numbers in our classes, the types and numbers of students who enroll, and the pressure we may experience from our administration.

At our institution, one way we try to protect the role of the liberal arts in the face of increasing focus on job-focused educational paths is by having students in some programs take liberal arts courses that prioritize reading and writing and encourage critical thinking. Our honors and global scholar students take a variety of courses primarily taught by humanities and social sciences faculty who are willing and able to collaborate on special topics courses. While we don't have enough students to allow us to offer a course on the West in the American imagination very often, we are able to offer a course for honors students to provide an interdisciplinary approach to western American literature and film. Our contribution to this conversation about approaches to teaching western literature is fundamentally grounded in the reality of our institutional situation, which enrolls many excellent students but seems to foster a culture that sometimes fails to support the intrinsic value of the liberal arts. As such, when we were given the opportunity to teach a junior honors seminar, we—an English professor with a focus in American literature and gender and a communications professor with a background in American studies and film genres—chose to work within existing curricular structures to present students with a dynamic aesthetic representation of the American West and the western as genre. Rather than being a course in which students with an interest in the West or western films elect to enroll, this honors course required us to build a syllabus with a theoretical framework that encourages intellectual curiosity in students with limited interest in the subject and almost no prior knowledge. For honors students, who are often hyperfocused on preprofessional majors, the biological sciences, and job training, gender was an accessible lens with which to introduce students to the complex idea of the West in literature and film, while simultaneously subverting traditional approaches to a field historically dominated by white male perspectives and representations.

While most students have experience analyzing gender as a social construct related to power structures, we wanted to ensure that students were pushed beyond traditional understandings of binary gender representation. Feminist scholars have in recent years reframed the conversation about the western genre to challenge the dominance of masculinist settler colonialism. Krista Comer calls for more focus on methodologies such as critical regionalism, which focuses on the American West rather than the western genre, arguing that the West's "borders and outsides [are] positioned for mutuality across fields like feminist studies, globalization studies, Western and Latin American studies, comparative indigeneity, and so on."[3] Here Comer emphasizes the need for attention to ambiguity and liminal spaces, paradoxes and interdisciplinarity. As such, we decided to close our course by modeling this sort of practice, drawing out contradictions that are nonetheless real. As Christine Bold explains in *The Frontier Club*, inclusions and exclusions work paradoxically, and the recurrent showdowns between white men acting out Richard Slotkin's "regenerative violence" make invisible the claims of Indigenous peoples; "alliance and exclusion," she writes, "go violently hand in hand."[4] Her characterization here moves academic and pedagogical discourse into a more inclusive methodology that makes room for a variety of voices rarely heard in traditional understandings of the West. Bold suggests that the primary narrative elements of the traditional western genre—the shootout between aggressive white men—is situated in the simultaneous exclusions and alliances that structure power relationships in the literal West.[5] In her 2016 book *Westerns: A Women's History*, Victoria Lamont challenges the traditional view of the birth of the western genre by addressing the role of women who were foundational to its inception. She argues that "the popular western, widely considered a male-authored tradition, was founded as much by women writers as by men and played a significant role in American women's literary history at the turn of the twentieth century."[6] Modeling an intersectional approach, contemporary feminist and revisionist scholarship provides a dynamic and evolving view of western literature and film.[7]

Incorporating these complex theoretical concepts into our course was a challenge. In order to engage the twenty-nine students who had enrolled in this class—which was nominally a seminar—we foregrounded theoretical concepts that helped students relate to large-scale ideas of American identity and history. Our course focused on introducing students to generic conventions of the western, complicating their perspectives by then presenting them with texts that challenged these norms of genre, and exposing the role these kinds of foundational narratives play even in the contemporary American mythology of the West. Situating each unit of the course in scholarship that encouraged students to reconsider their own understanding of the idea of the West, we tried to explain to students who may never have been west of the Mississippi why these ideas matter—both to their own lives and the way in which the West figures in the collective American consciousness. To situate our critical inquiry into gender, we used Annette Kolodny's pioneering feminist ecocritical perspective as a theoretical touchstone. These gendered stories advance the narrative of Anglo, settler-colonist mythology on the frontier.

We wanted to teach students to think about gender as a larger-scale construct that includes masculinity, rather than just associating it with women, so we began by presenting the conflict between wilderness and civilization that is narratively at the center of the western genre. At our Catholic institution, which can lean toward the conservative in its student body and administration, gender studies is often dismissed by those who see no need for feminist or critical gender discourse. As a result, foregrounding masculinity studies not only demonstrates the importance of better understanding this construct but also lends credibility to the field. This contrast is often mapped onto a conflict between what is portrayed as lawless masculine violence of the wilderness, justified by the initial expansion, and the more traditionally feminine values that civilization brings with it, often coded as law, religion, and domesticity. This classic approach to theorizing representations of the American West, when coupled with Kolodny's revisionist approach to the frontier myth, introduced students unfamiliar with studying genre to key structural elements before destabilizing these narrative forms.[8] In the classic structure, the western hero is usually a liminal figure, associated with the wilderness both narratively and visually (in films), who uses his (almost always his) masculine violence to assist the progress of civilization, though generally without being able to be a part of the new civilization. As John Cawelti writes, America is anxious about a "sense of eroding masculinity" despite the fact that one of its central origin stories is "a great history of men against the wilderness." This leads to a "need for a means of symbolic expression of masculine potency."[9] As Leslie Fiedler puts it, "the typical male protagonist has been a man on the run, harried into the forest and out to sea, down the river or into combat—anywhere to avoid 'civilization,' which is to say, the confrontation between a man and a woman which leads to the fall to sex, marriage and responsibility."[10] In order to avoid this clash with civilization and women, the typical masculine protagonist in western stories has "marginal connections to the Metropolis and its culture. He is a poor and uneducated borderer or an orphan lacking the parental tie to anchor him to the Metropolis and is generally disinclined to learn from book culture when the book of nature is free to be read before him."[11] As the space closes in on men in the West, whether it is because they enter towns, homes, or relationships with potential dependents, this crisis of masculinity emerges.

To begin the students' exploration of the West, we start with an interdisciplinary framework for both the western (as genre) and the West (as ideal or reality). The course starts with John O'Sullivan's 1839 essay "Manifest Destiny," which articulates the edict that guided the American push westward. As "the nation of human progress," he writes, "who will, what can, set limits to our onward march?" This well-known concept, and the concept that Providence guided and backed this ambitious and in fact moral quest, serves as an underlying principle to American history and to the material of our course.[12] To examine further the crumbling of the American moral imperative to move into virgin and empty western lands, we frame the course with Loren Baritz's "The Idea of the West," reminding students that throughout centuries, and not just in America, "the West" has been a "mere direction" rather than a geographic or physical location, inspiring the imperial and colonial march.[13] We then move to Kolodny's path-breaking essay "Letting Go Our Grand Obsessions" to clarify for students the lasting effects of some of these ideas about western spaces. Expanding the definition of the "frontier" to include multiple locales, as well as moments in time—that is, the moment of first contact between groups—Kolodny illustrates the possibilities for reimagining the West through a methodological practice that includes multiple perspectives. As she reminds us, the prevailing narratives of the frontier presumed a "population scarcity and either primitive technology or a site where a more developed or superior technology overwhelms an inferior one. Both are willfully ahistorical."[14] From this perspective of the "willfully ahistorical," we begin our conversation about the many ideas Americans willfully choose to maintain about America and its attitudes about the West. By working from the wilderness and civilization binary and the larger idea of gender, we hope to provide an engaging framework from which to begin our interrogation of the way in which the West figures in the collective American consciousness.

While our course has four units—covering the traditional western, gender and the West, the environment and the West, and revisionist westerns—gender serves as a focus throughout the course. This is in some ways a deliberate choice, as gender is a construct that all students have experienced in some way, but in other ways this underlying theme is the product of a variety of theoretical and critical perspectives that inform our work and reading on western literature and film. We have already mentioned the importance of Kolodny's pioneering feminist ecocritical perspective to our understanding of the topic, but her work is obviously a critical touchstone when considering gendered narratives of western experience. As she writes in *The Land Before Her*, woman as constructed and represented by the genre has always been the "unwilling inhabitant of a metaphorical landscape she had no part in creating—captive, as it were, in the garden of someone else's imagination."[15] The vision of the West as an idyllic playground waiting to be conquered by man, she suggests, is written by and for men, and the women who inhabit it advance the men's stories as stock characters hemmed in by the tropes of genre. In this imagined West, women can occupy only a supporting role. Despite the ideas that the West was a place for roaming open territories, Kolodny points out that most white, settler-colonist women, relegated to the civilized space of tiny, underdeveloped towns and primitive, unfinished home, experienced life on the frontier more like "domestic captivity." In "Letting Go Our Grand Obsessions" Kolodny frames the frontier as a point of contact that brings together two groups, rather than as the advancement of one group into empty space.[16] This construct helps students to understand the limitations of the gendered space of the West, especially as it is often represented in classic generic texts.

Because our students have little prior understanding of genre, we begin with ideas such as Cawelti's early emphasis on the conflict between wilderness and civilization in the structure of the western genre.[17] In Cawelti's analysis, western genre stories largely take place at the location of the encounter between westward expansion and the wild frontier of the open West. This narrative structure is common in the western genre and provides a lens with which to analyze how gender is represented in films and other narratives set in the West. Considering how this structure is reinforced or complicated provided a way for us to have the students examine both the portrayal of gender in the generic texts (Charles Portis's novel *True Grit* and the films *Stagecoach*, *Shane*, *The Searchers*, and *Unforgiven*) and the ways that gender is represented differently in the other texts in the course (Willa Cather's *The Professor's House*, Edward Abbey's *Desert Solitaire*, and Leslie Marmon Silko's *Ceremony*). Our choice of novels is designed to assist students in understanding the ways in which different writers make use of the conventions of genre, even as they challenge, modify, and reinvigorate them. This conceptual model is essential to our pedagogical approach, as we continue to foreground the construction of separately gendered narratives in western texts and texts about the West.

Scholars such as Cawelti, Slotkin, and Joe Dubbert informed our consideration of masculinity in the western genre and in relation to ideas of the space of the West. As the aesthetic of the represented West evolved, so too did our theoretical approach; our pedagogical methodology is designed to engage with this ideological shift. While once the western-as-genre assumed certain stock characters and stereotypes almost as fact, more recent critics and theorists have brought evolving trends in the field to the genre. As Cawelti writes in *The Six-Gun Mystique Sequel*, if classic American masculinity is truly disintegrating before our eyes, most likely because of the changes in how men live and the change in their relationships to women, then it's not surprising that this evolving lack has led to the use of "the gun, particularly the six-gun."[18] Here Cawelti makes it clear that the gun represents the masculine capacity for violence in the wide-open spaces of the western wilderness. Motivated by the threat to what Joe Dubbert calls the "space paradigm," many men saw the move westward as an answer to the crisis in masculinity they were experiencing in the rapidly growing population centers of the East.[19] As urban development spread farther westward, many men clung to the expressions of violence still marginally permissible in what they saw as a less civilized environment.

Particularly salient for discussions of gender in the West is Jane Tompkins's landmark book *West of Everything*. Tompkins argues that the overwhelmingly masculinized violence of the western genre is not only about conquering the savage wilderness of the western frontier but is also really about the rejection of the feminine values of civilization and religion: "Time after time, the Western hero commits murder, usually multiple murders, in the name of making his town/ranch/mining claim safe for women and children. But the discourse of love and peace which women articulate is never listened to (sometimes the woman who represents it is actually a Quaker, as in *High Noon* and *Cheyenne Autumn*), for it belongs to the Christian worldview the Western is at pains to eradicate. Indeed, the viewpoint women represent is introduced in order to be swept aside, crushed, or dramatically invalidated."[20] Women and children are narratively necessary in the western genre to provide motivation for masculine violence, but they are almost always relegated to secondary roles in the stories. Rarely do they participate in violence other than as hapless victims or stock figures in need of rescuing by violent men. Lamont expands the feminist consideration of the West when she challenges "both Tompkins's account of the popular western as masculine backlash against a female-dominated sentimental culture, and [Norris] Yates's characterization of women's westerns as domestic texts. Instead of reifying the centrality of the male-authored tradition, [Lamont offers] an account of the western as a complex cultural field in which both men and women participated, although not always on equal footing."[21] While the field of western studies is evolving and new scholarship is published every year, our plan was to ground the course in the current feminist and intersectional methodologies in the field.

Unit Case Study: *The Professor's House* and *Shane*

The primary novel for the Gender and the West unit is *The Professor's House*. We couple the book with the classic film *Shane* to contrast traditional representations of gender in the western genre against a destabilizing view of masculinity. While not as well known as some of Willa Cather's other novels, *The Professor's House* provides a clear foundation for our conversation about gender. Especially because of some students' tendencies to resist discussion of gender, we intentionally chose to focus on masculinity in this novel. A key theme in it is Prof. Godfrey St. Peter's nostalgia for his long-gone, ideal student Tom Outland and his longing for a more traditionally masculine existence. Idealizing Tom's "discovery" of a long-abandoned cliff dwelling, St. Peter's own issues with his waning masculinity are mapped onto his memories of Tom.

Students engage easily and well with the sense of the professor's stifled masculinity in the context of the wilderness-and-civilization binary we use to frame our approach. They find it engaging to juxtapose St. Peter's stifling domestic and professional life with Tom's strikingly physical presence and adventures in the West. Unlike Tom's adventures, the professor's life, at least in his view, is something out of his control: "[h]is career, his wife, his family, were not his life at all, but a chain of events that happened to him."[22] Meanwhile, Tom's "reverence" for the New Mexico cliff dwelling comes from his belief that wherever "humanity has made the hardest of all starts and lifted itself out of brutality" is a "sacred spot."[23] The isolated nature of the mesa dwellers in the wilderness seems to be part of their appeal, and St. Peter longs for a similar adventure. Instead, while he did travel to Europe when he was younger, he was left with only daughters (who no longer carry his name) and imagined sons, in the form of Tom and the "splendid Spanish-adventurer sons" who were the subject of his historical research.[24] Seemingly more important than his real-life daughters, the Spanish explorers are still only secondhand adventures, and they signify St. Peter's fear that he has failed to live his own life. This critique is inherently gendered, and our students found it easy to follow. However, it was difficult to get them to think more sympathetically about a character such as St. Peter, likely due to the difference between their age and his.

While we focus primarily on masculinity in our consideration of the novel, many students also want to focus on the women. St. Peter's wife, Lillian, is far from sympathetic (at least from his perspective), as he judges her for beginning "the game of being a woman" all over again for her sons-in-law.[25] She pushes for a fashionable new house, and she could never "forgive Outland for the angle at which he sometimes held a cigar in his mouth, or for the fact that he never learned to eat a salad with ease."[26] Focused here on manners and other trivialities, Lillian remains associated with a superficial and vapid civilization. In her condemnation of Tom, Lillian becomes, at least in the professor's eyes, the weight dragging him down, domesticating him, and preventing him from living the masculine existence he covets. While St. Peter has some grudging respect for his daughters, he is likely crushed by the fact that Rosamond never married Tom and thus did not provide him with a legitimate connection to the young man he loved so much. Students are able to grasp the superficial nature of the female family, although they initially have some difficulty realizing that this was not necessarily Cather's feeling about women but her crafting a vision of a disenchanted man's perspective.[27]

Our class spends considerable time on the fact that there are only two women in the novel who are treated favorably. One is Augusta, a working-class woman who has labored for the St. Peter family for years. She receives both praise and condescension from St. Peter, who admires her physical labor but seems incapable of imagining that she could have desired something else for her life. Most notably, St. Peter shares his working space in the attic with her sewing forms, which he finds "the most unsympathetic surface imaginable. . . . It was dead opaque lumpy solidity."[28] Our students quickly grasp the way in which St. Peter projected his dissatisfaction with the women in his life onto these forms, and they were quick to wonder why it is Augusta who wakes the professor when he nearly dies after falling asleep in the attic filled with fumes from the stove. They wonder if this is St. Peter coming to terms with his own life. The only other praiseworthy woman in the novel is one who has been dead, likely for hundreds of years, as she is found mummified on the mesa. This mummy, Mother Eve, is more valuable than "any living woman," according to Tom, and she is most notably dead and named after the stigmatized first woman in the biblical tale of the Garden of Eden.[29] Students are quick to wonder what this suggests about St. Peter's understanding of women—the idea that they could never escape the stigmas placed on them by a society that considers them tied, whether they like it or not, to the domestic sphere.

It becomes clear in the novel and in class, after much discussion, that it was the very idea of a life in the West—which is to say, an idealized masculine life away from women and civilization—that St. Peter feels he has missed. We discuss what might have happened to Tom if he had lived—that he most likely would have married the professor's daughter, had children, been burdened by domesticity, and had his ideas commodified for profit, which is to say, he would have been corrupted. While St. Peter is an educated, relatively privileged, and successful man, he is still assessing himself by an old-fashioned rubric. What St. Peter longs for is a simpler world, one in which he might espouse a traditional, white, American masculinity, but what he also yearns for is his youth.

Another point of entry for thinking about gender, and specifically masculinity and the privilege it has traditionally enjoyed and that men have perhaps come to expect, is the way in which Tom, despite St. Peter's feelings about him, fails in his goals. While Tom was able to truly explore, the land he discovered was still corrupted in the end by his meddling. This is where Cather is at her most nuanced. It might be easy to assume that she, like Tom, imagines this as a scene of discovery that fails to consider the relatively advanced civilization that once lived on the mesa. But when Tom's encounter with this relatively untouched site ends up destroying it, it becomes clear that Cather is aware of the naïveté of Tom's manifest destiny when it is put into action.[30] While students are able to imagine that Tom may "mean well," this point also allows for nuanced conversations about preservation, intervention, and archiving. We are able to discuss what *should* have happened to the mesa and what problems might stem from preserving artifacts in museums. With some pushing through the students' resistance to the fact that the novel is certainly not a western in the traditional sense, it nonetheless allows us to access crucial conversations about the effects of the western genre on the American psyche, what false histories it provides, and what fictions about masculinity it perpetuates.

Shane is the key film for the gender unit. The 1953 film, directed by George Stevens, tells the story of a gunfighter who tries to transition to a role as a farmhand but is drawn into the violent conflict between ranchers and the community of farmer-settlers. While all the films in the course portray gender roles in ways that are common to the genre, *Shane* most clearly maps masculinity and femininity onto the opposition between wilderness and civilization that is the animating principle of the classic western. Civilization, embodied by the domesticity of the settlers led by Joe Starrett, is the new and inevitable West, contrasted with the wilderness of the open-range cattle ranching of the villainous Stryker clan. Starrett makes this clear:

> These old-timers, they just can't see it yet, but runnin' cattle on an open range just can't go on forever. It takes too much space for too little results. Those herds aren't any good, they're all horns and bone. Now, cattle that is bred for meat and fenced in and fed right—that's the thing. You gotta pick your spot, get your land, your own land. Now a homesteader, he can't run but a few beef. But he can sure grow grain and cut hay. And then what with his garden and the hogs and milk, well, he'll make out all right.

What is often presented narratively in western films, particularly those of the classic genre iteration, is the idea that civilization, though inevitable, is often unable to protect itself against the lawless violence of the West, whether represented by Native Americans, outlaws, or open-range ranchers. The social and sanctioned violence of civilization, represented by the law or the military, is either unavailable (the late-arriving cavalry in *Stagecoach* or the posse members who leave the house unprotected in *The Searchers*) or ineffective (the token punishment meted out by Little Bill in *Unforgiven*). The preservation of civilization falls to the western hero, who, unencumbered by domesticity, has access to effective if unsanctioned violence that he uses to restore civilization. This is a common plot in western films; Slotkin notes that in the decade after *Shane*'s release, a number of films mirrored its plot formula of a gunfighter who is marked as an outsider but uses his skills to save civilization from criminals and corruption.[31]

The character Shane is narratively (with his past as a gunfighter) and visually (with his buckskin clothing) presented as a part of the wilderness. But it is only Shane who can help the Starretts conquer the wilderness. This point is emphasized both visually and narratively when Shane helps to remove a massive tree stump that Joe Starrett has been unable to conquer himself. While triumphant music plays and the men celebrate, Shane is shirtless and in his buckskins, and Marian Starrett looks on approvingly at this masculine display. The removal of the tree stump, enabled by Shane's superior masculinity, underscores the fact that the Starretts need Shane's mastery of the wilderness to establish civilization fully in the Wild West. Narratively, the Starretts and the other homesteaders need Shane's violent competence to preserve civilization, but as is inevitable in the genre, Shane's violence must ultimately exclude him from taking part in civilization. This is foreshadowed by Marian Starrett's line, "We'd all be much better off if there wasn't a single gun left in this valley—including yours." This quotation underscores the putatively feminine view of the future of the West as a less violent and more civilized environment.

As is probably clear, *Shane* is a not an especially subtle film in terms of gender. Masculine and feminine traits are explicitly presented both narratively and visually. Once prompted to look for them, students are able to make connections between gender and the wilderness/civilization dichotomy. One of the student group presentations effectively considered the link between marriage (and domesticity, though they did not use the term) and civilization in both *Shane* and *The Professor's House*. Another was able to use *Shane* to discuss how masculinity in western films is often defined by what it is not—the home and the family. But the film also makes clear an ongoing issue in the class. While the students have some experience with close reading of books and are generally able to support their points with quotes and specific references to the texts, they struggle with engaging films beyond the narrative level and at times are somewhat resentful of being asked to actually pay attention to what was presented visually in the film. While we have been able to address this somewhat as the class evolves and prompt the students to consider more carefully what they see, studying *Shane* as the second unit means the students are for the most part not effectively analyzing the rich visual presentation of gender in *Shane* in developing their arguments about gender and the West. In the opening sequence, for example, Shane's relationship to the wilderness is clearly established visually. He enters the film riding down from the mountain, descending directly from the wilderness. This connection is reinforced by his buckskin clothing. As he approaches the Starrett homestead, a few fleeting frames capture his image positioned between the antlers of a deer. Marian Starrett's representation of domesticity is also underscored during this sequence—when we first see her, she is inside the Starretts' house and framed by a window. In general, students can appreciate these types of visual connections in the films when they are pointed out but have difficulty making these connections independently.

Gender as an Interdisciplinary Link: *True Grit*, *Stagecoach*, and *The Searchers*

While our focus in this chapter has largely been on gender, which was explicitly the topic of the second unit of our course, this thematic approach was a foundational aspect of each of the four units. As the civilization-and-wilderness binary reflects themes of gender quite well, this overall structure for the course helped create connections in other units. For example, our first unit, on the traditional western, features Charles Portis's *True Grit* and the John Ford film *Stagecoach*. *True Grit* is nearly impossible to discuss without considering the gender of the heroine, who, despite the best efforts of those around her, refuses to be confined to the domestic sphere. A young girl seeking to avenge the death of her father and trekking into the wilderness in the company of various outlaws, Mattie challenges gendered stereotypes of genre while reinforcing narrative structures. *Stagecoach*, one of the key texts of the classical western film genre, is about a disparate group of individuals who try to travel from Arizona to New Mexico by stagecoach while under threat by Apaches. The film makes use of a variety of stock male and female characters—Mrs. Mallory, who is nearly shot by a disgraced antebellum gentleman hoping to save her from barbarous Indians; Dallas, the prostitute with the heart of gold; the loner, Ringo Kid; the law-and-order marshal, Curley Wilcox; and the villainous Plummer brothers. We pair *Stagecoach* with *True Grit* to establish norms of the genre and thus help the students understand the ways in which later texts present a more complicated idea of the West. However, while this model works theoretically, our students often resist understanding later texts as stories about the West rather than as part of the western genre. It may be that the ubiquity of the western genre, especially once we have discussed it in class, causes students to have difficulty understanding why we moved away from strictly genre texts. This experience underscores the importance of emphasizing that the course topic is the West in the American imagination, rather than simply a class about the western genre. It was and is our goal to analyze the role of the West and the western genre in the evolving American consciousness.

Our third unit stretches our interdisciplinary methodology as we focus on the West and the environment. Our texts, Edward Abbey's *Desert Solitaire* and another John Ford film, *The Searchers*, initially seem the least obvious pairing, but as we begin the unit the match generally begins to work to our advantage. In the case of Abbey, the theme of the environment is obvious, but *The Searchers* has a less explicit connection. However, the film exemplifies the wilderness and civilization divide through its cinematography. Although narratively set in Texas, most of the location shooting was done in Monument Valley, in Arizona and Utah. Ethan Edwards (played by John Wayne) and Martin Pawley travel the wilderness for three years seeking Ethan's niece, Debbie, who has been abducted by Native Americans. John Ford and his cinematographer Winton Hoch paint the West on the vast canvas provided by the new technologies of Technicolor film processing and the widescreen Vistavision format (Paramount's version of CinemaScope). The lushness of the cinematography effectively conveys the beauty and enormity of the western landscape, making the rugged natural environment a more central component of the genre narrative. These aesthetic choices, while not always easy for students to grasp, were an essential part of our approach to the genre, as the West is an idea that is intensely iconographic and visual.

From its framing of Martha Edwards in the domestic space, to Ethan's determined, dark quest to find Debbie, the film divides its characters clearly by gender. In the case of the film, we present the environment as manifested by Native Americans, whose presence is characterized as more like that of aggressive wild animals than as people. Abbey's work also presents such a divide; it is known for its focus on masculinity and its marginalization of femininity—the text barely mentions women—and it idealizes, even in the 1950s, a man alone in the wilderness, free from the burdens of femininity and civilization. One challenge of teaching *Desert Solitaire* in relation to gender is helping students to understand the inherently gendered nature of a text that rarely mentions women. While the story is clearly a masculine wilderness fantasy, lining up neatly with our framing concept of the wilderness-and-civilization binary, many students associate the concept of gender with femininity.[32] The text's lack of female characters challenges them to think more critically about the default masculine subject, as well as the author's clear preference for spaces free of feminine influence. Because the class considers these texts through the unit theme of the environment, our study of gender is less explicit, but it nonetheless guides our continued inquiry into the tropes of identity and wilderness in stories about the West.

Revisionist Western Unit: *Ceremony* and *Unforgiven*

Our last unit, on the revisionist western, allows students to consider the ways in which the western genre has evolved in relation to the classic aesthetic. It also allows us to include the perspectives of various groups traditionally underrepresented in the genre, despite their integral roles. In this unit the novel is Leslie Marmon Silko's *Ceremony*, a text that features Laguna Pueblo Tayo's attempts to deal with his posttraumatic stress disorder after World War II and his return to the land-centered practice of his tribal heritage. We pair this with the Clint Eastwood–directed film *Unforgiven*, a more obvious engagement with the western as genre and a film that brings to light (some of) the realities of women's experiences in western spaces. The film opens with a violent attack on a prostitute, followed by the quest for revenge inspired by that event. As the story of a retired outlaw hired by a group of prostitutes to avenge the attack, the film provides an unapologetically revisionist perspective on the traditional western that complicates the role of violence in the genre. While *Unforgiven* presents alternatives to the highly stylized death scenes in earlier westerns, the class discusses the variety of ways in which the women were still simply a plot device to advance the action in which men participate in more stereotypical storylines. This pairing also allows for a conversation about race, particularly with the inclusion of Ned Logan, a black cowboy. Ned's race is not mentioned by any character in the film; as director, Eastwood may have been trying to mirror the historical reality of black cowboys or just making a "color-blind" casting choice. Nonetheless, the visual presentation of Ned's blackness gives extra resonance to the scene in which he is whipped to death by Little Bill, and the display of his body outside the saloon is reminiscent of lynching and the punishment of slaves.[33]

Silko's work in particular is an example of those stories that had been previously excluded from canonical and generic representations. While she is a Native writer who tells the story of the half-white, half–Laguna Pueblo Tayo, her story is also deeply invested in the study of gender. Her protagonist is a World War II veteran who suffers from battle fatigue, or posttraumatic stress disorder, a diagnosis that brings to life the vibrant conflicts with discourses of masculinity both in his Laguna Pueblo community and in the larger sense. Returning to his native lands, Tayo focuses on his tribal stories and ceremony to recenter himself after the violent treatment of the hospital. While suffering mentally and emotionally after the war conflicts with dominant American stories of masculinity, Tayo's grounding in Native lands aligns with his home community and also, almost paradoxically, with western traditions of masculinity. The man in these stories is grounded in wilderness and the land, having escaped the feminizing—and, here, also sterilizing, dominating cultural—effects of civilization; more to the point, the Native perspective understands the natural world and its landscape as not distinct from culture. Tayo's exploration of his masculinity is grounded in different conceptualizations of power and marginalization. In class we were able to consider the ways in which Tayo was both masculine and feminine but, more importantly, existing perhaps on a gender spectrum that rejects traditional colonist and European concepts of gender as binary even as it maintains some of its key tenets. Students were able to see the ways in which gender may evolve but still remains a real force in people's lives, intersecting, like the field of western literature, with various other methods, cultural forces, and discourses.

In designing a course that includes traditional texts and films of the western genre, literature about the West, and contemporary, intersectional approaches to understanding the West, we took on a large task. While we feel confident in the effectiveness of using gender as a lens for beginning our interdisciplinary study of the West in the American imagination, we have experienced some resistance from students puzzled that not everything fit into the western genre mold that we had presented at the beginning of the term. Despite the fact that we never tell students that the class will focus on the western-as-genre, it becomes clear that many students have internalized key aspects of it, even though many claim never to have seen any western films. While we have occasionally wondered if we should avoid beginning the course with the classical genre pieces, we have discussed the issue and feel certain that it would be impossible to teach a course of this kind without this sort of aesthetic background. However, it does reinforce the generic conventions and can make it harder for some of the students to engage with texts that consider the West in nontraditional ways. *The Professor's House*, for example, is clearly not a western in genre—rather, it is a modernist novel that is about the anxiety a modernist man has in relation to the lost image and story of the West—and the students struggle with this difference. Abbey's *Desert Solitaire* may be more clearly a different kind of text, as it is explicitly political, ecocritical, and nonfiction. *Ceremony* and *The Professor's House* challenge students to consider the ways in which the genre relates to other texts.

Our experiences with this course leave us to conclude that its unique challenges as an interdisciplinary honors program course for nonmajors at a small university are best met by the application of the lens of gender. This focus helps bridge many gaps that are beyond our control and provides a point of entry with which students are at least somewhat familiar. The somewhat focused attention to majors (and subsequent resistance to liberal arts inquiry) on the part of our students, as well as their general inexperience with the study of genre, does present us with some pedagogical challenges. The approach, however, facilitates some progress toward our goal, which is a fuller understanding of the ideas of the West in the American imagination, as well as an improved comfort with challenging conventions of genre through close textual analysis. Despite some of our limitations, our greatest issue is attempting to translate a classroom of twenty-nine students into a seminar format that prioritizes student-centered discussion and active learning. While working within the given framework our institution requires and building thematic units in support of an interdisciplinary experience, the lens of gender allows us to engage students initially in order to build a better practice of thinking critically and intersectionally about texts, films, and theoretical materials about the West.

1. Flaherty, "Mass Exodus."
2. Jaschik, "Shrinking Humanities Major." Flaherty's and Jaschik's articles, both published by *Inside Higher Ed*, suggest that some of the problem comes from pressure to cut general-education curriculum and the resulting loss of exposure to less directly career-focused fields. Of course, as the article suggests, humanities degrees actually are marketable, but students—and parents—fear they are not. Both authors cite research that indicates colleges' programmatic and curricular changes are driving the shift away from the humanities, not the desires of students themselves.
3. Comer, "Exceptionalism, Other Wests, Critical Regionalism," 163. Krista Comer argues for the importance of critical regionalism as a methodology, specifically in terms of better understanding the ways in which Wallace Stegner appropriated the life story of Mary Hallock Foote.
4. Bold, *Frontier Club*, 13.
5. In the introduction to *The Frontier Club* Bold argues that clubs, cattle rights, and print culture created networks of inclusion in the West that often disenfranchised anyone other than white men.
6. Lamont, *Westerns*, 13.
7. Lamont makes this project explicit: "I do not judge the authenticity of western texts; rather, I analyze the ways in which this concept was defined and deployed by authors, publishers, and other cultural agents." Lamont, *Westerns*, 7.
8. Kolodny articulates the ways in which the characterization of land as gendered female, including language such as "virgin land," frames the expansion of colonial white America in terms of the violent conquest of women's bodies.
9. Cawelti, *Six-Gun Mystique Sequel*, 39.
10. Fiedler, *Love and Death in the American Novel*, 26. Fiedler's path-breaking text considers the foundational American historical narrative in terms of literary history, here in relation to our foundational concept of the civilization and wilderness binary. The male is always at risk of being civilized—sterilized, emasculated, domesticated, etc.—by the feminizing influence of civilization.
11. Fiedler, *Love and Death in the American Novel*, 374.
12. O'Sullivan, "Manifest Destiny," 5. O'Sullivan's well-known piece makes clear the prevailing notion that the right to expand was God-given.
13. Baritz, "Idea of the West," 629.
14. Kolodny, "Letting Go Our Grand Obsessions," 10.
15. Kolodny, *Land Before Her*, 6.
16. Kolodny, *Land Before Her*, 9.
17. Cawelti's *Six-Gun Mystique* was originally published in 1970 and revised and updated in 1984 and 1999. The references in this essay come from the 1999 edition, titled *The Six-Gun Mystique Sequel*.
18. Cawelti, *Six-Gun Mystique Sequel*, 39.

19. Dubbert, *Man's Place*, 10.
20. Tompkins, *West of Everything*, 41.
21. Lamont, *Westerns*, 4. Lamont goes on to write, "The fact that these women did not always reach vast readerships (although they often did) should not exclude them from discussion of the genre: To do so would be to reconstitute the power relations that marginalized them in the first place. In this regard I am particularly indebted to the methods of Pierre Bourdieu, which take marginal texts seriously for what they tell us about both the structure of a field as a whole and the perspectives that have been sidelined by more powerful cultural agents" (4).
22. Cather, *Professor's House*, 240.
23. Cather, *Professor's House*, 199.
24. Cather, *Professor's House*, 144.
25. Cather, *Professor's House*, 64.
26. Cather, *Professor's House*, 64.
27. The house figures consistently in characterizations Cather creates; it is an ambiguous site of domestication, personal space, and family identity. Eudora Welty has reflected on the significance of a physical house. "The house is the physical form, the evidence that we have lived, are alive now," she writes. "It will be evidence someday that we were alive once, evidence against the arguments of time and the tricks of history." Welty, "House of Willa Cather," 56.
28. Cather, *Professor's House*, 9.
29. Cather, *Professor's House*, 221.
30. As Deborah Karush puts it, this depiction, of "a young cowboy's exploration and domestication of a conveniently uninhabited southwestern landscape, is filled with allusions to frontier mythology." Karush, "Bringing Outland Inland," 146. This analysis connects to other conceptualizations of frontier representations.
31. Slotkin, *Gunfighter Nation*, 402.
32. *Desert Solitaire* is Edward Abbey's narrative of his time spent as a park ranger in Arches National Park in the 1950s. Largely lamenting the development of the park (in the form of paved roads and dams), Abbey's text angers students with its sexism and extremism but often astounds them with its sharp critique of environmental destruction.
33. Rather than focus an entire unit on race, the course provided discursive space to discuss race across units, especially in the unit on revisionist westerns, in which we discussed the many ways the traditional versions of the genre diluted western representation, leaving a mostly masculinist, settler-colonist perspective.

BIBLIOGRAPHY

Abbey, Edward. *Desert Solitaire: A Season in the Wilderness*. 1968. New York: Touchstone, 1990.
Baritz, Loren. "The Idea of the West." *American Historical Review* 66, no. 3 (1961): 618–40.
Bold, Christine. *The Frontier Club: Popular Westerns and Cultural Power, 1880–1924*. Oxford: Oxford University Press, 2013.
Cather, Willa. *The Professor's House*. 1925. New York: Vintage, 1990.

Cawelti, John. *The Six-Gun Mystique Sequel.* Bowling Green OH: Bowling Green State University Popular Press, 1999.

Comer, Krista. "Exceptionalism, Other Wests, Critical Regionalism." *American Literary History* 23, no. 1 (2011): 159–73.

Dubbert, Joe L. *A Man's Place.* Englewood Cliffs NJ: Prentice-Hall, 1979.

Fiedler, Leslie A. *Love and Death in the American Novel.* 1960. Normal IL: Dalkey Archive Press, 2003.

Flaherty, Colleen. "Mass Exodus." *Inside Higher Ed*, January 26, 2015. https://www.insidehighered.com/news/2015/01/26/where-have-all-english-majors-gone.

Jaschik, Scott. "The Shrinking Humanities Major." *Inside Higher Ed*, March 14, 2016. https://www.insidehighered.com/news/2016/03/14/study-shows-87-decline-humanities-bachelors-degrees-2-years.

Karush, Deborah. "Bringing Outland Inland in *The Professor's House*: Willa Cather's Domestication of Empire." In *Willa Cather's Canadian and Old World Connections*, edited by Robert Thacker and Michael A. Peterman, 144–71. Lincoln: University of Nebraska Press, 1999.

Kolodny, Annette. *The Land Before Her: Fantasy and Experience of the American Frontiers, 1630–1860.* Chapel Hill: University of North Carolina Press, 1984.

———. *The Lay of the Land: Metaphor as Experience and History in American Life and Letters.* Chapel Hill: University of North Carolina Press, 1975.

———. "Letting Go Our Grand Obsessions: Notes toward a New Literary History of the American Frontiers." *American Literature* 64, no. 1 (1992): 1–18.

Lamont, Victoria. *Westerns: A Women's History.* Lincoln: University of Nebraska Press, 2016.

O'Sullivan, John. "Manifest Destiny." Excerpted from "Annexation," *United States Magazine and Democratic Review* 17 (July 1845): 5–10.

The Searchers. Directed by John Ford. Performances by John Wayne, Jeffrey Hunter, and Natalie Wood. Warner Brothers, 1956.

Silko, Leslie Marmon. *Ceremony.* New York: Penguin Books, 2006.

Slotkin, Richard. *The Fatal Environment: The Myth of the Frontier in the Age of Industrialization, 1800–1890.* Norman: University of Oklahoma Press, 1985.

———. *Gunfighter Nation: The Myth of the Frontier in Twentieth-Century America.* Norman: University of Oklahoma Press, 2008.

Stagecoach. Directed by John Ford. Performances by John Wayne, Claire Trevor, and John Carradine. United Artists, 1939.

Tompkins, Jane P. *West of Everything: The Inner Life of Westerns.* New York: Oxford University Press, 1993.

Unforgiven. Directed by Clint Eastwood. Performances by Clint Eastwood, Frances Fisher, and Morgan Freeman. Warner Brothers, 1992.

Welty, Eudora. "The House of Willa Cather." In *The Eye of the Story: Selected Essays and Reviews*, 41–60. New York: Random House, 1977.

Wright, Will. *Six Guns and Society: A Structural Study of the Western.* Berkeley: University of California Press, 1977.

PART 3

Place and Regionality

7

Moving Beyond the Traditional Classroom and *So Far from God*

Place-Based Learning in the U.S. Southwest

KAREN R. ROYBAL

In *A Voice of My Own: Essays and Stories* (2010), Rolando Hinojosa-Smith describes how he learned what was meant by the idiom "sense of place": "I had a sense of it, and by that I mean that I was not learning about the culture of the [Rio Grande] Valley, but living it, forming part of it, and thus, contributing to it."[1] The late Juan Estevan Arellano, author and respected scholar of *acequia* culture and traditions, echoes many of the same sentiments as Hinojosa-Smith when he states that knowledge of place is "based on the information stored in my mind and experienced through the senses, that repository of personal and collective memory."[2] In their descriptions Hinojosa-Smith and Arellano underscore the importance of embodying place in order to truly understand it. Place grounds us. Place teaches us. Place reveals our connections to the environment. Place invites us be part of it. Sense of place, in other words, is not something one learns *only* by reading about it in a book; it is also a lived experience realized only when we encounter it for ourselves and come to terms with our own relationship to the environment.

As professors in literary studies, we face the challenge of teaching our students about sense of place in ways that matter to them. It is increasingly difficult for students to imagine the type of material connection to place described by Hinojosa-Smith and Arellano because we are tied to technology and the virtual realities created by it; we are also far removed from the privileged experience of "life in the woods," as a mode of moral and "environmental" living—a different sense of place documented by Henry David Thoreau in *Walden* (1854). So how do we negotiate this potential disconnect in courses in which we seek to provide students with a holistic conception of and encounter with place that allows them to truly experience the sentiments articulated by Hinojosa-Smith and Arellano in meaningful ways and perhaps in ways that they have not experienced before?

In my Environmental Justice in the Southwest (EJSW) course, one way in which I've addressed this conundrum is by assigning Ana Castillo's novel *So Far from God* (1993), as it offers the type of setting, subject matter, characters, and literary devices that allow for discussions and real-world experiences that also provide students with a deep understanding of the connections linking place, identity, literature, and the environment. This novel is not typically considered western American literature—it is Chicana literature; however, I also read it as a story that centers the Southwest and its inhabitants in important ways that draw attention to environmental (in)justice. Since EJSW is not a literature course, I employ some of the pedagogical strategies from my Interdisciplinary Approaches to Chicana/o Literature course, which enables me to bring into EJSW a "crash course" on literary studies and couple it with an environmental justice (EJ) framework that places at its center interdisciplinary, place-based learning. In this chapter I contend that we cannot rule out literature as a tool through which students learn about sense of place; it offers the possibility for them to transport themselves to a time and place they might not otherwise experience—a different form of virtual reality than that offered through technology.[3] However, when we combine that "fictional" experience with interdisciplinary, place-based learning, we can create innovative classrooms that situate students within the particular social, political, gendered, and environmental realities of the communities on whom these fictional stories are based.[4]

Course Description

My EJSW course is designed to provide students with an interdisciplinary approach to understanding environmental issues through an EJ lens. The course's main objective is to help students develop skills to critically analyze examples of EJ cases and to develop an understanding of the complex relationships among actors and the social, political, and economic processes that lead to environmental injustices. We attempt to meet this objective as students learn key concepts, the foundational principles, and the history of the EJ movement and how this history intersects with race, class, and gender. We explore case studies related to this history; we read and analyze literature that focuses on EJ, race, class, gender, and the significance of place; and we embark on a fieldwork project in New Mexico to see firsthand how activities related to EJ materialize in communities in the Southwest. In the course we address questions such as the following:

1. What is environmental (in)justice?
2. What are the causes of environmental (in)justice and how is it being addressed?
3. Why and through what social, economic, and political processes are some groups denied access to a clean environment?
4. What might fairer, more equitable, and more just human-environment relations look like?
5. What methods and texts (nonfiction and literary) are used to discuss, call attention to, and render visible environmental (in)justice issues?

These questions provide a teaser of sorts that signals to students that we will examine literary texts and discuss how literature (Chicana literature in particular) is one way through which we will interrogate EJ issues.

The fieldwork is what allows students to see firsthand the ways in which activities related to EJ materialize in communities in an area of the Southwest that has historically been exposed to environmental injustices. Fieldwork allows us to engage in interdisciplinary, place-based learning through which students gain a better understanding of the ways EJ is about the relationship between scholarship and theory, as well as about action, organizing, and raising awareness (in other words, nonscholarly activities). They see firsthand what it takes to build and participate in the EJ movement and see in practice what is at stake when we focus solely on "environmental privilege."

I teach at a predominantly white institution (PWI). Courses at my college last only three and a half weeks, which means I have to be selective about what framework and pedagogical strategies I use. The majority of students who enroll in this course are generally not English majors, which presents its own set of unique challenges when we get to the section of the course on Chicana literature. To mitigate the potential uneasiness students might feel in shifting from reading and discussing environmental essays and book chapters to literature, I use our fieldwork to build their experience with what they will read in literary criticism, a play, and a novel the following week. In many ways I work backward, by using their place-based field experience to ground them in the literature and the plots guiding the stories. I have found that this organization and combination provide the most robust example of theory and praxis.

Interdisciplinary, Place-Based Learning

Place is commonly discussed in fields like environmental studies and geography, in which place, space, and landscape intersect with people's relationships to them. Anthropologists also consider place and typically investigate it in relation to culture; they explore how we learn about culture *through* place. Here I focus on how Chicana literature, environmental justice studies, and feminist activism are also areas of inquiry through which place is central to understanding the real, lived experiences of communities of color that often experience significantly more injustice regarding environmental issues. Placing women at the center of our discussion is imperative for foregrounding who performs the grassroots work we read during the first week of class, and it prepares students for what we will see and who we work with in the field—all women of color engaged in activism that is also rooted in place. Peter McInerney, John Smyth, and Barry Down, citing a number of scholars, note that place-based pedagogy "invests young people with a sense of agency . . . , acknowledges them as producers rather than consumers of knowledge . . . , enriches their education through hands-on, community-engaged learning, and provides them with relevant knowledge and experiences to participate actively in democratic processes and devise solutions to social and environmental problems."[5]

Students are generally comfortable with reading about environmental (in)justices; however, visiting the communities and talking with residents typically shifts their understanding of the reality of these issues and provides them with completely different perspectives that help them fill in the gaps left by their readings. This combination of readings and discussions with place-based fieldwork is a way in which we deal with comfort *and* discomfort for students who have not confronted their own material and social realities. Throughout the first week of the course we discuss the most vulnerable populations exposed to environmental injustices: women and young children. To put into practice what we are reading, during our fieldwork I engage organizations and cultural institutes run by women of color. In doing this, students better understand the material we read prior to embarking on fieldwork, which details how grassroots movements are most commonly started and sustained by women, whose actions are modeled for them in the field. Because we begin to consider the importance of sense of place prior to our fieldwork, students become attuned to listening to how the women (especially women of color) we work with embody and discuss sense of place; we also discuss how displacement can and has historically ruptured that sense of place, especially for communities of color, a point made most evident during our fieldwork. Considered in this way, place-based learning is developmental *and* dynamic.

To further ground students' understanding of these intersections of theory and praxis, during our fieldwork I assign essays written by the women with whom we work: Dr. Sofía Martínez, co-director of Los Jardines Institute in Albuquerque, New Mexico, and Dr. Jaelyn deMaría, professor of communication and journalism at the University of New Mexico (UNM), a large research and Hispanic-serving institution.[6] DeMaría and I schedule course convergences that allow us to bring my EJSW students together with her ecocritical communication students. Our classes meet at women of color–run cultural institutes committed to combating racial, social, and EJ issues in their communities, which gives deMaría's and my students opportunities to get to know each other and share what they have been learning in their respective classes. This step is important because many of deMaría's students are from the region, which means they have additional insight and sometimes different relationships to the place(s) about which my students are reading. The college where I teach is a PWI; UNM is a Hispanic-serving institution. This point is important because the student demographics are distinctly different and provide another way in which instructors can emphasize the importance of understanding place and position from a different angle. After deMaría and I introduce our students, we go into the field and work with women of color–run organizations like Los Jardines, an "agricultural literacy community" committed to "social, environmental and economic justice organizing, education and building a multi-generational movement."[7] Students work at the Los Jardines farm and participate in activities such as preparing agricultural beds for planting, learning about herbs and flowers used for healing, and observing how this agricultural classroom allows Los Jardines to engage in food justice initiatives in the South Valley of Albuquerque and other neighboring communities.

This type of place-based pedagogy creates an active learning environment for my students. Sean P. MacDonald attests that place-based learning allows instructors to introduce students to interdisciplinary methods for, in my case, understanding real-world EJ issues and their direct impacts on communities, especially communities of color. He states, "This active research of place encourages the process of . . . making connections between these observations and secondary research sources." He goes on to say that "interdisciplinary, place-based research further encourages the development of a multidimensional understanding that integrates the perspectives of other disciplines into the research topic."[8] To further underscore the multidimensional understanding MacDonald describes, I have students compile a field research journal. In it they are asked to make observations and then to *reflect* on those observations. Students bring their journals to class the week we discuss Chicana literature so that we can connect their reflections to the literary texts. This pedagogical framework allows me to introduce students to a literary perspective on EJ in a way that makes them feel more at ease because they use their own reflections as a jumping-off point to address the symbols, themes, and ideas they see in the literature.

When we return from the field, I scaffold readings to ease students who have not been exposed to literature in their other coursework into that section of the course. I begin our week by assigning pieces that facilitate the shift in texts and with which they are fairly comfortable—work from ecofeminists who situate the impacts of environmental (in)justice on women of color in material ways, which is similar to what they have already seen in the field. Then I shift the readings again when I assign the work of *literary* and environmental studies scholars, like Priscilla Solis Ybarra.[9] I have also invited Dr. Ybarra to Skype into our class when we discuss her work, which my students love because they can ask questions about her scholarship and how she employs an intersectional and interdisciplinary approach to literature and environmental studies. Scholarship like Ybarra's helps to introduce and bridge the divide between the literal and the literary in our studies of EJ. For instance, in one chapter of her text that I assign, Ybarra discusses how Cherríe Moraga's work "engage[s] with transnational dynamics and the global currents of neoliberal politics of capital that put Chicanas/os and other peoples of color in the Global South in the position of paying the world's ecological debt"—larger themes we have discussed in class and in the field.[10] I couple Ybarra's literary and environmental work with Moraga's play, *Heroes and Saints* (1994), which is set in California's Central Valley and depicts the impacts of pesticide poisoning on Mexican migrants working the fields there.[11] My approach to incorporating Chicana literature at this point in the course is to introduce students to multiple genres and forms; in this case I incorporate literary criticism and a play. Students find similarities between what Ybarra and Moraga identify as environmental injustices and what students have seen and learned in the field. Over the next three class meetings I introduce another genre, the novel, specifically Castillo's *So Far from God* (1993). The novel serves as a way to bookend the course by further demonstrating to students how cultural production like literature can be used to address and critique the social and environmental injustices they have witnessed firsthand.

So Far from Justice

So Far from God tells the story of Sofi and her four daughters—La Loca, Caridad, Fe, and Esperanza—all of whom reside in Tomé, New Mexico. Sofi's husband, Domingo, has left the family, and she must raise the girls on her own in a small community that is rich in history and gossip and that is on the eve of change. The novel begins with what might be read as an atypical scene, in which Sofi's youngest daughter, La Loca, has passed away and the family and *vecinos*, or neighbors, attend her funeral. Building on Spanish legend and folklore, Castillo depicts three-year-old La Loca sitting up in her casket and then lifting herself into the air and landing on the church roof to avoid the crowd and Father Jerome, who attempts to sprinkle her with holy water because he isn't quite sure if her resurrection is a sign of the devil or a miracle of God. This opening scene often shocks students (especially those unfamiliar with Mexican or Spanish legends).[12] We discuss how the scene and the novel have been read as "magical realist" because of the seemingly surreal scenarios experienced by the Tomé residents.[13] Magical realism was first introduced to the broader American reading public by Gabriel García Márquez in his landmark novel *One Hundred Years of Solitude* (1967). The novel allows the reader to believe that anything is possible, especially "magical" and "fantastical" events like La Loca's resurrection in *So Far from God*. Students are quick to identify this opening scene as magical realist; many of them are familiar with the concept and/or have read Márquez's novel. Establishing this familiarity with students is a great way to begin our discussion about *why* I would assign *So Far from God* in an EJ course.

As one might expect, most of the students who enroll in the course are unfamiliar with Chicana literature and with the work of Ana Castillo. They are even less aware of the ways in which she has been labeled a renowned Chicana author, Xicana feminist, and artist. They surely do not characterize her as an EJ activist. However, I begin our analysis by discussing how she has used her literary work to address social and environmental injustices that continue to affect communities of color, especially those in the U.S. West and Southwest, and we discuss how she connects these issues to those experienced by subaltern communities globally. I inform students that, as they read the first half of the novel, my reason for assigning it still might be unclear to them. I ask them to be patient, and I explain that we will examine the novel in combination with their fieldwork and reflect on community projects and sense of place depicted in the novel that parallel what they have experienced. This intersection of fact and fiction provides students with tangible ways to apply the theories we learn in class, to learn firsthand from the women in the field who shared their experiences with them, and to see how literature can be used to expand the discussion of environmental (in)justice. We also address the idea that magical realism is itself place-based, as in Márquez's Macondo and Castillo's Tomé. Place-based learning and literature also allow students to understand environmental issues (and specifically EJ) from a decolonial framework, similar to what

Ybarra describes when she advocates for a decolonial understanding of ecocriticism. She states, "The decolonial prioritizes a non-Western theoretical basis and puts the body, a body politics of knowing, at its center."[14] Students see this body politic in practice in the field and can then transfer that experience and reading to their examination of Sofi, her daughters, and the Tomé community in *So Far from God*.

When we are in the field, I take students on a brief tour of nearby Tomé, the small town in which *So Far from God* is set, to help them generate a sense of place. This visit is another dimension of the scaffold approach I apply in the course. I take students to Tomé Hill, where they witness the landscape and agricultural areas of the town and read signs that offer historical information (which I supplement with further detail). For instructors who are not able to drive there, images of the town also work well, along with a discussion of the town's history, which I introduce before our discussion of the novel. Tomé is part of the Town of Tomé Land Grant, a settlement dating back to 1739, when the grant was issued by the Spanish Crown to early settlers who sought to "build and cultivate an agricultural community that afforded them a way of life that is still part of the rich and lasting history of the area."[15] Much of Tomé remains an agricultural community in which residents rely on the land for their livelihoods. My past research focuses on land grants in the Southwest, so I also explain how women in the community started and maintain the Tomé Dominguez Community Center Museum, which houses important historical documents about the town's history. I also describe how female residents of Tomé have continuously advocated for justice in their community and have worked tirelessly to preserve their sense of place and history.

The field experience offers a way for students to feel more connected to the material we read and to further develop their own sense of place. During the course of our visits to field sites, students participate in the physical work performed in the gardens at Los Jardines, while at the same time networking with students from another institution also interested in EJ. My students also get to meet one-on-one with the women with whom we work as they interview them for their research papers and ask questions about the work done through their respective organizations. In course feedback and evaluations, students most often comment on the impacts of the fieldwork. One student said, "[The fieldwork] really created a bridge between us and the community." Another student said, "Without taking this class, I'm not sure that I would have recognized that as a community of color, the town of Tomé was disproportionately subject to toxins and pollution."[16] This second comment emphasizes the importance of discussing place, displacement, and history with students before, during, *and* after our fieldwork and as we move into our examination of *So Far From God*.

Sample Activity: Visual Map

Following the discussion of place and history, we proceed to an activity in which I ask students to identify the themes and symbols they have noted in the first section of Castillo's novel. I write the themes and symbols on the board so they can all work with identified themes. I then ask students to work in groups of three and task each group with drawing a visual map for the class. This small group structure allows those students who might not feel comfortable commenting in the large group discussion an opportunity to share their ideas and contribute to the analysis of the novel in this more intimate setting. Groups are each assigned one character on whom they will base their visual map. They are asked to link that character to at least two themes and to select three scenes in the first half of the novel that most distinctly depict that character's attributes and place in the narrative. As a group, they present their characters and scenes to the class and describe the significance of the scenes, themes, and character, which also helps to alleviate the nerves of students having to present individually. This activity also helps students learn close reading skills through their scene selection and analysis of that scene; it encourages them to make connections between characters, their role(s) in the novel, and their connections to larger themes, as well as to better understand the importance of symbolism. The visual mapping exercise also allows them to see the connections between the novel and EJ studies. For example, in one group's visual map students identified connections between two of the sisters, La Loca and Esperanza, both of whom "challenge the patriarchy," as they defy common conceptions of what Chicanas should do and how they should act.[17] The visual map also demonstrated how students emphasized the ways Castillo's character Esperanza is crafted to invite the reader to reflect on national and global links to Tomé, Washington DC, and Saudi Arabia—locations tied to other social and political issues. Students linked these key sections of the novel to other topics, such as the military industrial complex, and in their presentation described how actions at the national level affect the local and global, as brown bodies feel the direct repercussions of war. Through this activity students not only create their own visual map but can better identify "Castillo's techniques of mapmaking."[18]

By situating the text in a national and global context, students are better prepared to identify the potential issues of positioning texts like *So Far from God* as strictly magical realist, a common way in which this novel has been read. We discuss as a class how there is nothing magical about environmental injustices that harm the brown female bodies on which this novel is based. To encourage students to think more critically about how to engage with this idea, I refer to Frederick Luis Aldama's view of "magicorealism," as laid out in an essay originally published in 2000.[19] In a revised version of that essay he argues that "magicorealist texts amplify reality to reveal the cultural, economic, political, biological, sexual, and racial polyphonies at work in the world; in form and content, the mode questions the 'pure' divisions set up between metropolis and country, mestizo and pure blood, Western and indigenous, and reveals such divisions to be artificial constructs used to control, contain, and even erase the Other."[20]

It isn't difficult to convince students that Aldama's points have significant validity, especially after what they have experienced in the field through interdisciplinary place-based learning—a point to which the second student, quoted above, refers. Students also better understand how Castillo's novel is "a new form of representational mode that bridges the chasm between different ontological and epistemological terrains," as described by Aldama.[21] In our reading of the second half the novel, students are especially quick to identify the politico-cultural and historically specific experiences of Chicanas within the larger context of EJ studies *and* Chicana literature. As one student noted, "This portion of the novel really reminded me of the network of activism we saw throughout New Mexico . . . to address food insecurity and reclaim traditional farming practices and how their work intersected with other cultural and community initiatives."[22]

To further situate the story line in *So Far from God* within an EJ framework, I show students a clip from the film *Tierra o Muerte* (1992). The film includes a section on Ganados del Valle, a cooperative started in 1983 in Los Ojos, New Mexico, that mirrors the major tenets of Sofi's fictional co-op, Los Ganados y Lana Cooperative. Sofi nods to Ganados del Valle when she states that the Tomé co-op is "modeled after the one started by the group up north that had also saved its community from destruction."[23] Along with a discussion of this connection, I call my students' attention to Castillo's acknowledgments page, where she says, "I am indebted to the members of the Southwest Organizing Project [SWOP] who assisted in my research; above all, for the inspiration I received from their consciousness, ongoing commitment, and hope."[24] I discuss with students the connections and networks between the long-term work SWOP has performed to combat environmental and social injustices in the Southwest and how that work is similar to the initiatives of Los Jardines Institute. To further reinforce the idea of the importance of EJ networks, we also discuss the fact that the directors of Los Jardines Institute were co-founders of SWOP in Albuquerque. Understanding this time line and network helps students see the longevity of EJ activism in the West and Southwest, as well as the ways in which Castillo's literary work contributes to that activism. Moreover, students feel a stronger connection to the book after having had the opportunity to meet the activists and community organizers whose experiences reflect Sofi's experiences in Tomé.

At this point in the class, I introduce students to theoretical approaches outside of environmental studies that are useful for articulating *what* Castillo attempts to do through *So Far from God*. I explain how in much of her work Castillo employs Paulo Freire's concept of *concientización*, or consciousness raising, as a dominant framework.[25] I also introduce Chicana feminist Chela Sandoval's theoretical concept of oppositional or differential consciousness, which "permits functioning within yet beyond the demands of dominant ideology."[26]

Sample Activity: Identifying Literary Devices and Theoretical Approaches

After a dialogue with students about these theoretical approaches and their genealogies, I give students approximately thirty to forty minutes to work in groups of three on a guided activity I provide them that includes five prompts.[27]

1. As a group, select one scene/section in the novel in which Castillo most clearly comments on environmental (in)justice and/or social (in) justice.
2. Discuss and record the rhetorical strategies Castillo employs in the selected scene. In other words, what devices does she use to convey her intended message?
3. Discuss and record how Castillo's characters connect to Freire's and Sandoval's concepts of *concientización* and oppositional, or differential, consciousness.
4. Discuss and record how Castillo politicizes the impacts of environmental and social ills experienced by the members of Sofi's family.
5. Discuss and record the interconnections your group establishes between what you learned in the field and the SFFG characters' experiences (use your field journals to reflect).

When we come back together as a larger group to discuss their reflections, students have generally selected the same key section of the text, one in which Sofi's daughter, Fe, lands her "dream job," at Acme International, a corporation that produces weapons parts and where she works as a weapons assembler. The discussion is organic, though they typically tend to note that Fe's exposure to toxins, which caused "nausea and headaches that increased in severity by the day," and her subsequent diagnosis with terminal cancer, combined with the fact that she worked with women who "spoke Spanish, Tewa, Tiwa or some other pueblo dialect" (read: Native women), is evidence of the type of "body politics" to which Ybarra refers in her work.[28] This means they are noting that women of color bear the greatest impact of environmental pollution in *So Far from God*, a reality that is far from magical. Students also describe how the conditions under which Fe works are not very different from those that minority communities experience in the neighborhoods we visited while in the field or those we read about and/or discussed during our coursework, especially those where environmental toxins primarily affect women of color. Other students have selected the section of the novel in which Sofi starts MOMAS (Mothers of Martyrs and Saints), a woman-run organization that, "by its very nature, excludes men" and in which she "empowers women like herself who have long suffered, and with their help she sets out to redefine society."[29]

Students' discussions also generally center on sense of place. When I ask them to consider what they experienced in the field versus what they read in the novel, they describe how the experiences shared by the women with whom we worked in the field shaped their understandings of the environmental injustices faced by communities of color. Their descriptions are reflective of Hinojosa-Smith's account of his own awareness of sense place when he says part of that "sense of the Border came from sharing: the sharing of names, of places, of a common history and of belonging to the place."[30] For Hinojosa-Smith, this sense of place is very personal, and my intention is not for students to connect to the places we visited as homelands; rather, I am interested in helping them establish a sense of place that "eschew[ed] the romanticism" of the people and landscapes of the Southwest typically associated with this region.[31] I also want to encourage them to think about how long-standing issues due to modernity, displacement, and lack of care for the environment and its stewards continue to affect these communities. The visual map and their discussions about the fieldwork get at these points.

Sample Activity: Final Online Discussion

In a final individual assignment centered on *So Far from God*, I ask students to write one to two pages in response to an online discussion prompt: "In her novel *So Far from God*, Ana Castillo presents many moments of social and political commentary that tie directly to the environmental justice issues we've been discussing in this block. In what ways do you see the intersections between our course readings, fieldwork, and in-class exercises related to the novel? How has your understanding of Chicana literature changed? When applicable, use direct citations from our readings and fieldwork to support your ideas and theories." This individual prompt allows students to think independently about topics, ideas, and methodologies we interrogate throughout the course. Because our courses are short, I find that having students reflect on what they have learned helps them carry those ideas into other courses and into their work when they leave the college. It also gives students who are more comfortable writing their ideas before discussing them an opportunity to structure their responses without having to be the first to raise their hand in class. Finally, it invites them to articulate on their own the intersectionalities of environmental (justice) studies, literature, and place-based learning, as they describe what they gained through their experiences.

So Far from Over

In *So Far from God*, Castillo illuminates links between women of color, place, identity, literature, and the environment. The combination of interdisciplinary place-based learning and Chicana literature that confronts EJ issues in the Southwest described in this chapter offers approaches through which instructors can create innovative classrooms and pedagogical strategies that help students ground themselves in the regions in which they reside for the better part of their college careers. The assignments described in this chapter are designed to encourage students to gain firsthand knowledge that they can then transfer to their "reading" of critical essays and literature that depict the unjust conditions within which many subaltern communities in the Southwest live. By experiencing for themselves (even at a cursory level) the types of grassroots projects that women of color activists in the Southwest engage in on a daily basis, the deep sense of place they feel, and the ways displacement affects their communities, students can better understand the depth of this work.[32] Further, by structuring a course such as this one with a blend of place-based methodologies and critical reading and discussion of the Southwest as a region bearing a significant impact from environmental injustices, I help my students become more aware of how place is tied to body politics characterized on the basis of race, gender, class, and social status. They also see that the EJ movement and environmental issues are far from reaching an end or a solution. My hope is that students finish the course with a solid understanding of how literature—and Chicana literature in particular—provides a venue in which these critically significant issues can be addressed and that they see how authors like Castillo use magical realism to get to the political realisms of minority communities. The course's heavy emphasis on place-based learning is also designed to encourage students to continue engaging with organizations committed to combating environmental injustices when they leave the college.

Special thanks to Katrina Bell for reviewing a draft of this chapter and offering invaluable feedback. Thanks also to my sw220: Environmental Justice in the Southwest (fall 2018) students for allowing me to use their comments, discussion points, and in-class exercise examples.

1. Hinojosa-Smith, "This Writer's Sense of Place," 10.
2. Arellano, *Enduring Acequias*, 19.
3. Platt, "Ecocritical Chicana Literature" (assigned course reading), similarly references the significance of experiencing the "virtual realities" of ej issues.
4. Platt also advocates for this type of interdisciplinary approach: "An investigation of literature conjoined with the study of less 'traditional' genres of cultural texts contributes to the theoretical, artistic, and practical bases of oppositional consciousness; thus these texts act in alliance to resist environmental racism." Platt, "Ecocritical Chicana Literature," 76.
5. McInerney, Smyth, and Down, "'Coming to a *place* near you?,'" 4.
6. I have assigned Martínez, "Learn from Our Past"; Martínez, "Color-Blind, Color-Mute"; deMaría, "Seeds of Resistance, Harvesting Justice," chapter 5; and deMaría with Collier, "Dances of Neoliberal Resistance and Activism for Land Reclamation."

   Dr. Tessa J. Córdova, Bianca Encinias, and Sheryl Romero are integral to this place-based work; they have shared their knowledge with students and opened their community spaces to them.
7. "About," Los Jardines Institute, accessed 2018, https://www.losjardines.org/about.
8. MacDonald, "From Local to Global," 92.
9. I have assigned different chapters from Ybarra's *Writing the Goodlife*, but chapter 5, "Ecology and Chicana/o Cultural Nationalism: Humility before Death in Cherríe Moraga's Millennial Writings" (13–168), is particularly relevant to examining Moraga's work and its relationship to environmentalism.
10. Ybarra, *Writing the Goodlife*, 142.
11. In *Heroes and Saints*, Moraga addresses topics like cancer, birth defects, and other illnesses caused by long-term exposure to toxic substances.
12. See Nogar, *Quill and Cross in the Borderlands*, for more on the legend on which Ana Castillo most likely based La Loca's resurrection: "Sor María de Jesús de Ágreda [the 'flying nun'], identified as the legendary 'Lady in Blue' who miraculously appeared to tribes in colonial-era New Mexico and taught them the rudiments of the Catholic faith" (book description posted on Amazon.com).
13. On magical realism, see Stavans, "And So Close to the United States"; Caminero-Santangelo, "'Pleas of the Desperate'"; and Aldama, *Postethnic Narrative Criticism*, among others.
14. Ybarra, *Writing the Good Life*, 12.
15. Town of Tomé Land Grant, accessed August 15, 2019, https://townoftomelandgrant.com/.
16. Anonymous evaluation comments provided by sw220: ejsw students, fall 2018.
17. Visual map crafted by sw220: ejsw students, fall 2018.
18. Platt, "Ecocritical Chicana Literature," 88.

19. See Aldama, "Oscar 'Zeta' Acosta," 199, where he discusses his reinterpretation of magical realism, or what he labels "magicorealism."
20. Aldama, *Postethnic Narrative Criticism*, 200.
21. Aldama, *Postethnic Narrative Criticism*, 200.
22. Discussion comment provided by a SW220: EJSW student, fall 2018.
23. Castillo, *So Far from God*, 146.
24. Castillo, *So Far from God*, n.p. I have also taken students to SWOP in Albuquerque, where we visited communities of color bearing the direct impact of pollution and other environmental injustices.
25. On *concientización*, see Freire, *Pedagogy of the Oppressed*.
26. Sandoval, *Methodology of the Oppressed*, 3.
27. My classes are three hours, five days per week, which allows this significant amount of time for discussion. The exercise could be truncated to twenty minutes in a fifty-minute class or a seventy-five-minute class. This exercise could also be done over two class periods.
28. Castillo, *So Far from God*, 178, 179.
29. Sirias and McGarry, "Rebellion and Tradition," 87.
30. Hinojosa-Smith, "This Writer's Sense of Place," 11.
31. Hinojosa-Smith, "This Writer's Sense of Place," 11.
32. These components are especially important for students at a private PWI, as such students generally do not have a "sense of place" that centers on the Southwest.

BIBLIOGRAPHY

Aldama, Frederick Luis. "Oscar 'Zeta' Acosta: Magicorealism and Chicano Auto-bio-graphe." *Lit: Literature Interpretation Theory* 11, no. 2 (2000): 199–218.

———. *Postethnic Narrative Criticism: Magicorealism in Oscar "Zeta" Acosta, Ana Castillo, Julie Dash, Hanif Kureishi, and Salman Rushdie*. Austin: University of Texas Press, 2003.

Arellano, Juan Estevan. *Enduring Acequias*. Albuquerque: University of New Mexico Press, 2014.

Caminero-Santangelo, Marta. "'The Pleas of the Desperate': Collective Agency versus Magical Realism in Ana Castillo's *So Far from God*." *Tulsa Studies in Women's Literature* 24, no. 1 (2005): 81–103.

Castillo, Ana. *So Far from God*. New York: Norton, 1993.

deMaría, Jaelyn. "Seeds of Resistance, Harvesting Justice: An Exploration of Spaces Where Native Seeds Grow—La Plazita Gardens at the Sanchez Farm." PhD diss., University of New Mexico, 2012.

deMaría, Jaelyn, with Mary Jane Collier. "Dances of Neoliberal Resistance and Activism for Land Reclamation: Strategic Community Landscapes in New Mexico." In *Community Engagement and Intercultural Practices*, edited by Mary Jane Collier, 164–85. New York: Peter J. Lang, 2014.

Freire, Paolo. *Pedagogy of the Oppressed*. New York: Seabury Press, 1968.

García Márquez, Gabriel. *Cien años de soledad* (*One Hundred Years of Solitude*). Buenos Aires: Editorial Sudamericana, 1967.

Hinojosa-Smith, Rolando. "This Writer's Sense of Place." In *A Voice of My Own: Essays and Stories*. Houston TX: Arte Público Press, 2010.

MacDonald, Sean P. "From Local to Global: The Role of Interdisciplinary Place-Based Research in Teaching Environmental Economics." In *Interdisciplinary Place-Based Learning in Urban Education: Exploring Virtual Worlds*, edited by Reneta D. Lansiquot and Sean P. MacDonald, 89–110. New York: Palgrave Macmillan, 2018.

Martínez, Sofía. "Color-Blind, Color-Mute, and Color-Deaf: Race and Expertise in Environmental Justice Rule Making." *Environmental Justice* 1, no. 2 (2008): 93–99.

———. "Learning from Our Past: EJ's Strengths and Missed Opportunities." *Race, Poverty, and the Environment* 10, no. 1 (2003): 11.

McInerney, Peter, John Smyth, and Barry Down, eds. "'Coming to a *place* near you?' The Politics and Possibilities of a Critical Pedagogy of Place-Based Education." *Asia-Pacific Journal of Teacher Education* 39, no. 1 (2011): 3–16.

Moraga, Cherríe. *Heroes and Saints and Other Plays*. Albuquerque NM: West End Press, 1994.

Nogar, Anna M. *Quill and Cross in the Borderlands: Sor María de Ágreda and the Lady in Blue, 1628 to the Present*. Notre Dame IN: University of Notre Dame Press, 2018.

Platt, Kamala. "Ecocritical Chicana Literature: Ana Castillo's 'Virtual Realism.'" *ISLE: Interdisciplinary Studies in Literature and Environment* 3, no. 1 (1996): 67–96.

Pulido, Laura. "Ganados del Valle: Resource Management as Contested Terrain." In *Environmentalism and Economic Justice: Two Chicano Struggles in the Southwest*, 125–90. Tucson: University of Arizona Press, 1996.

Sandoval, Chela. *Methodology of the Oppressed*. Minneapolis: University of Minnesota Press, 2000.

Sirias, Silvio, and Richard McGarry. "Rebellion and Tradition in Ana Castillo's *So Far from God* and Sylvia López-Medina's *Cantora*." *MELUS* 25, no. 2 (2000): 83–100.

Stavans, Ilan. "And So Close to the United States." Review of *So Far from God*, by Ana Castillo. *Commonweal*, January 1994, 37–38.

Thoreau, Henry David. *Walden*. New York: Thomas Y. Crowell & Co., 1854.

Tierra o Muerte: Land or Death. Produced by Luis Valdez, Carolyn Hales, and Amy J. Armstrong for KBDI-TV. Berkeley: University of California Extension Center for Media and Independent Learning, 1991.

Tierra Wools. "Our Story." Accessed February 8, 2019. https://www.handweavers.com/our -story-1/.

Ybarra, Priscilla Solis. *Writing the Goodlife: Mexican American Literature and the Environment*. Tucson: University of Arizona Press, 2016.

8

Quotidian Wests

Exploring Regionality through the Everyday

NANCY S. COOK

Context

At my public university in the American West, for years it went without saying that courses on western American literature occupied a legitimate place in the curriculum. Courses with titles such as Montana Writers routinely had high enrollment, as did others in western literary studies. But after years of full classes on the West, I found that the ground was shifting under our feet. Our enrollment numbers were down, our TA stipends hadn't increased since the 1980s, and students no longer assumed the value of studying the creative production of places such as ours in the West. In the classroom the balance shifted as my graduate courses enrolled more creative writing students than literature students, and I therefore needed to address both their presence and their goals. At the same time, as a researcher I began to read more deeply in areas such as bioregionalism and critical regionalism. Also, following some of my western studies colleagues, I began to read in studies of the everyday and affect theory, particularly the work of the anthropologist Kathleen Stewart.[1]

My goals are basic and lofty, myriad. I am searching for ways to engage students who aren't certain the West is important as a region, as a political or economic force, or as a center of cultural production. I want to mentally shake those who think of the West only in terms of myths or a dramatic (heroic or shameful) past. I want them to engage representations of place as embodied, environmental, social, and political. I want to provide them with theoretical tools that make place important, give them a vocabulary to articulate that importance, and delight them with the pleasures and dangers of multidisciplinary work. I want to offer a canvas and the tools to practice new modes of reading, ones that engage race, class, and gender in places they might think of as white, male, and classless. I want to complicate rurality, to both link and disrupt relations between rural and urban, to connect the West and western American studies outward. This is a multivalent, multivocal West. It is neither the "fit in or get out" notion of region nor a concept of region that ascribes to the inside/outside classifications of much genre criticism. Stuff happens here—complicated, interesting stuff performed and represented by all sorts of different people.

My courses changed accordingly. By design, this course, Quotidian Wests, undercuts the "outback" biases of so much material in the field, biases that render the less-populated West as the home of rednecks and Republicans or, less frequently, as principally the "native home of hope." The course instead triangulates between the lonesome places, towns, and cities. But that doesn't go far enough. How do writers express lived experience in the North American West? More than a type of emplotment or story, western literature at its best reveals how it feels to be in a western place or to move through western spaces. Such an approach doesn't take the value of western writing a priori; it shows both critics and producers of texts—the literature students as well as the creative writing students—how westernness gets under a text's skin.[2] Yet the regional perspective often seems largely to be one promoted *within* a region, a kind of literary boosterism that is disparaged outside the region, a geographical snobbery. Michael Kowalewski offers another reason: "region may be condescended to by critics or simply ignored as a category because many of them simply lack a vocabulary with which to ask engaging philosophical, psychological, or aesthetic questions about what it means to dwell in a place."[3] Moreover, region, while politically valuable in some circumstances, now carries more baggage than it once did. For parts of the West, it is really the microregion that has currency—constituencies of writers and artists bound together by training or mission or politics or influences of the place on their work.[4] While cultural geographers address concepts of region, micro and macro, and bioregionalism provides both ethos and tactics, for this class I want to give readers and writers some tools that would take them beyond plot and setting and into representational strategies that have affective force, that can help us become aware of our bodies in place, our socialities of place, our cultures. Stewart's work shows the importance of the quotidian in reexamining and reclaiming a place-based approach to course design and topic. For Stewart,

> the ordinary is a thing that has to be imagined and inhabited.
> It's also a sensory connection. A jump.
> And a world of affinities and impacts that take place in the moves of intensity across things that seem solid and dead.[5]

A focus on western American texts offers opportunities to make connections rather than cordon off this literature in a regional ghetto. Conversely, as Kowalewski has observed, "when certain works of western literature are taken seriously in the academy, they tend to be thought of in nonregional terms; they tend to be legitimized under the aegis of, say Chicano Studies, Native American Studies, or, more broadly, Environmental Studies."[6] What might we discover in some of these books that are best known in area studies if we reterritorialized them, put them back in place? What new readings might we find for James Welch's *Winter in the Blood*, with its careful distinctions between towns on Montana's Hi-Line? If we attend to the kinds of work the characters do or don't do, or what they eat? What if we think regionally about Jeanne Wakatsuki Houston's *Farewell to Manzanar*, with its careful attention to the different public school communities within California's cities? Below I will sketch the course, how the readings and assignments bring place and the everyday together, offering students some strategies for recognizing, analyzing, and producing texts that engage what it can mean to inhabit a place. With an emphasis on the work of Ben Highmore's everyday and Kathleen Stewart's concepts of ordinary affects and regionality, we have the tools to "displace and flatten hierarchies between the big (important) and small (off-register, invisible) or between notions of an official system in a distance and the lived affects of everyday life."[7]

The first day of class affords the time to raise some of these issues and to begin the process of locating each class member in terms of ideas and expectations about the West in literature. But first it is critical to locate ourselves in place. After outlining the course, I ask a series of questions, including some that work to locate us, our histories, and our goals. Students in turn introduce themselves and share the information they have written on notecards that respond to my prompts: Do you have ideas for your thesis? Where did you study as an undergraduate? What is your undergraduate degree in? What is your hometown? How do you reply when someone asks you where you are from? How many times have you moved? How does it feel to be in Missoula? The last prompt asks them to complete a sentence: "I know I am in _____ because _____." My example for them: "I know I am in Rhode Island because a drinking fountain is called a 'bubbler,' pronounced 'bubbla.'"

Immediately we see that we don't come to the course with the same assumptive grounds or contexts. The students have varied degrees, they come from all over North America—Oregon, Arizona, Utah, Alberta, and South Dakota for the westerners, and Massachusetts, Chicago, Tennessee, Indiana, and Maine for those from farther afield. One student responds this way: "I'd come to Montana with a 'way of being,' a '*minima aesthetica*' that *was* surprised that someone could be Republican, or that the majority of leaves in autumn would turn yellow instead of red; a way of being that didn't understand the term 'smoky,' and thought that deer ought to stay where they belong, in the woods, and not the lawn."[8]

Some have trouble identifying a hometown. Some of the prompts under-cut or complicate the early questions. We learn that the answer to "where are you from?" depends on where you are—one answer if one is in Tierra del Fuego and another if one is in Belfry, Montana. Nearly everyone has moved, some many times. The clarifying questions themselves are useful. Moved rooms? Dwellings? Locations? States? When one student, from New England, remarked how moisture-deprived she felt in Missoula—chapped lips, dry skin, thirsty—another, from Arizona, replied that Missoula felt humid to her. As we introduce ourselves, we begin to engage the everyday. The work of the course, then, is to make us connect our embodied experiences and those represented textually with the forces that bring them into being. Ben Highmore describes this process: "Our feelings, emotions and passions that seem so 'private' and 'internal' are, in actuality, social-material forces that circulate externally. These forces are constitutive of experience and of experiences that are felt to be 'internal.' It is the world that has got under our skin and has stirred us to the core."[9]

Theories in the Classroom

Reading works by Ben Highmore and Kathleen Stewart shifts our attention away from a course primarily about location—country, town, camp, or city—to one about feeling and the everyday. Moreover, this shift decenters the course—no longer a traditional survey of a topic but a workshop on process, on reading strategies, compositional and representational practices that address lives in place, embodied, social, and political. While place remains historically contingent, with this approach it is accessed through representations of everyday life. We also develop a more nuanced sense of time and duration. Rita Felski analyzes three kinds of time: "everyday-time," "life-time," and "large-scale time." For Felski, everyday-time includes punctuality, daily bodily rituals, and habits, while life-time includes all the minutiae "shaped into intimate narrative forms." Large-scale time consists of "larger time frames [that] allow us to talk about shared pasts and collective futures and to fashion larger narratives around group identities."[10] Literature commonly moves between these types of temporal conception, yet our analyses commonly don't. Why literary texts? Much of the interesting work on the everyday, as well as strong work on place-making, comes from other disciplines, and we read some of that work. But in literature, everyday life as embodied in character, in representation, comes together formally, through composed scene, narrative, description, and character, reaching out across a range of temporalities.

Many students come to the class with at least fundamental training in critical methods and the history of literary criticism, so for students who are working at the master's level, and now predominantly on a creative writing track, I tend to assign high theory and philosophical texts sparingly. Instead, I always include foundational and theoretical texts on the supplementary reading list and encourage students to be drawn back to those texts based on an interest ignited by something in the assigned readings. I find it crucial to supply an extensive bibliography and encourage students to use me as a resource as they follow a thread through the critical readings. Students who have preregistered for the course receive the reading lists well before the class begins. At preregistration I encourage them to do a little research on the list of secondary readings. Once the term begins, I bring those books to class, and they have time to look them over. Then I ask them to give me a short list of the books that most interest them. Based on their preferences, I create groups of students with matched or similar interests in secondary texts.

For those who are uncomfortable with "theory," the group offers a place to work through the texts in the company of colleagues with different skills. They learn from each other. Group tasks are adapted from "reading circles," with formal tasks for each group member.[11]

As a group they will do a little more research and prepare a presentation for the class. I offer up standard reading group tasks but do not require that they run their group with rigid roles for each member. For the presentation to the class I ask them to provide a 250-word summary of the book and distribute a copy of the summary to each class member. By the end of term all of the students have an annotated bibliography of several secondary works, as well as "experts" they might consult to see how a text might be useful in their own work. In a presentation of no more than 30 minutes, groups summarize the book and then characterize the critical reception of the book, noting where the book is reviewed and ascertaining if there are disciplinary turf wars and alliances. I ask them to see if they can discover the author's intellectual "friends" and "enemies." Books participate in conversations, and this is one way of figuring out the conversation, as is a careful perusal of front and back matter. Who appears in the acknowledgments? In the bibliography? Their presentations, along with the summary, force them to make choices. What is the book or article's thesis? Where do these ideas come from? What conversation do they join? Where does it fit with our course objectives? They articulate ways the book might be useful to our work and, finally, suggest how something from the book might inform the literary text under discussion. Each reading group works through an academic conversation, and each models how we might move from reading criticism alone to reading it in conversation with literary texts. In this process I break out several individual tasks for evaluation and credit. Students often go on to use the preparation for their presentation as grounding for the final project.

The presentations work to bring everyday life out of philosophical discourses (Certeau, Lefebvre, Heidegger, Deleuze and Guattari, Foucault) and access those discourses through application, more as method than theory.

Each group suggests links between their text and the literary texts, as we work together to emphasize constellations, matrices, and sticky bits, not genealogies and histories. As often discussed in American literary history, regionalism is a developmental phase rather than a useful term of classification. Dead letters.[12] The course, then, rejects strictly historical construction, either in foundational theories or in the sequencing of literary texts. For balance, I let the two foundational books for the course—Ben Highmore's *Ordinary Lives: Studies in the Everyday* (2011) and Kathleen Stewart's *Ordinary Affects* (2007) draw students into genealogies and histories of the ideas they engage. Now, with the addition of Neil Campbell's *Affective Critical Regionality* (2016), the course builds from a tripod of methodological books, with the advantage that Campbell's fine chapter on Stewart will clarify how her unusual style performs her thesis. Highmore and Campbell lay out their foundations in a clear and straightforward manner, while Stewart's approach is more oblique. Of Stewart's book, Highmore notes that "there is nothing explicit here that can simply be extracted and applied to something else, no easily borrowed system of thought or analysis, no quotable paragraph that would underwrite a methodology."[13]

The three texts together offer the grounding we need to practice new modes of reading and writing, for each insists that we attend to "worlding," or "becoming," rather than to fixing places, identities, or bodies to make them static, preserved specimens. Thus, for Stewart and then Campbell, our engagement with the North American West is not as region, with its concern for boundaries, insiders, and outsiders, but in terms of "regionality," which for Stewart is "something taking place . . . an event that jumps between landscape and bodies of all kinds. It is ambient and therefore atmospheric."[14] Together the three foundational texts use key elements from affect theory, philosophies of everyday life, cultural theory, cultural geography, and gender theories as they cite thinkers such as Adorno, Appadurai, Bakhtin, Barthes, Benjamin, Bennett, Butler, Crouch, Certeau, Deleuze and Guattari, Foucault, Haraway, Heidegger, Hume, Latour, Lefebvre, Massumi, Moran, Muecke, Rancière, Soja, Whitehead, and Williams among others. Students have many opportunities to pursue theoretical genealogies and byways.

Why the everyday? Focusing on the everyday accomplishes much. First, it opens up possibilities in all kinds of texts, not just novels. Second, it creates a space for us to attend to the representations of the lives of those who don't align with grand plots. We can see how lives are embodied in place outside grand narratives of conquest, migration, and conflict. And such a strategy works to undercut assumptions about what kinds of texts are western. By focusing on the particulars—how our everydays *in place* differ—we can begin to unpack how identity is placed. Also, the everyday has often been devalued as a site of repetition and habit, uneventful. And why not use a set of practices that values the overlooked and denigrated to read a group of texts by those "regional" writers frequently disparaged as regional?

Although used widely, "the everyday" is a slippery term, so we begin with a history of its use and some working definitions. Theorists have located within everyday life a set of topics or areas upon which to focus, locating them as "sites in which people do (perform, reproduce, and occasionally challenge) social life, day to day."[15] We read Rita Felski's "The Invention of Everyday Life," which offers some history of the term's use, its deployment in twentieth-century philosophy, and its appropriation by sociologists and cultural studies scholars, before going on to locate possibilities through her focus on three key aspects of the everyday: repetition, home, and habit.

Felski's essay gives us a way in as we begin to consider first Highmore and his elaborations of the everyday, and then Stewart, as she brings affect to bear on the ordinary, working toward both a poetics and a politics of the ordinary. Another advantage to employing the everyday is that what is commonplace, naturalized, and therefore invisible to one kind of community can be extraordinary or exotic to another. Again, one student, in a response to Stewart's essay "Regionality," writes:

> But when we view a region or a culture through the lens of this ordinary, even a region we're familiar with, there's nothing "not surprising" about it. Investigating the idea of "affect" means, inevitably and *necessarily*, being surprised by its characteristics and effects. Thus, while the words "dog-gentle, half-Holstein milk penner" (Blunt, 121) conjure no image for me whatsoever as a description or representation, there is a sense of understanding—albeit an intangible one, without the image to hold— that these words *do* conjure an image for those who would own a region in which they carry a very obvious connotation. The everyday is not universal, but understanding what is *considered* everyday is.

Western lives have often been represented as exotic or out of time, and the everyday can help bring these lives, represented, into different kinds of focus. Attention to the everyday adds contours and complexities to place, revealing the in-between places, waiting places, even what Marc Augé calls "non-places." For example, how might a reading of *Winter in the Blood* shift when we focus on the narrator's waiting, his hitchhiking, his hangovers, as they evoke liminal space? Another student uses Ben Highmore's thoughts about distraction, first in a short response to the Welch novel and later as the organizing idea for an extraordinary final paper. The following is from her response:

> When we adjust perception to accommodate what Highmore describes as dispersed and vacant forms of distraction, *Winter's* narrator emerges not as the emotionally and ethically blunted victim of alienation as sometimes perceived, but as hyper-attentive, ethically conflicted, and capable of sharing to a startling degree an alternative way of experiencing lived moments, and making choices. The dream becomes lucid, perception becomes reality, or, as *Winter's* narrator says, "the memory was more real than the experience." In *Winter*, something special happens in a confusion of ordinary moments, throw-away details, and lingering sensations of the reading experience that remain after the book is closed.

Reading/Writing against What?

Not all students will have a working knowledge of the myths this approach seeks to break down, so for the second class I ask students to prepare working definitions of the mythic West and the classic western. We engage these varied definitions and use them as a means for me to introduce the book list, including a brief description of some ways each book or handout disrupts or complicates classic ideas about the West. I have a short lecture prepared to supplement the definitions if I need to do so. I'll then turn to a handout with short sections from some classic westerns, *The Virginian*, for example, and we talk about principles of inclusion and exclusion in the passages. What is worth mentioning? What is excluded? This introductory work helps set up possibilities for counter- or alternative readings of the better-known books on our list. For my students, the best-known books on the reading list are Judy Blunt's *Breaking Clean*, Jeanne Wakatsuki Houston and James D. Houston's *Farewell to Manzanar*, and James Welch's *Winter in the Blood*.

Early in the course the readings lay out various reading and representational strategies available to us. We can move from Stewart's often elliptical strategies in *Ordinary Affects* to her thick description of a working-class town near Boston in the essay "Regionality," to Campbell's nuanced and more formally academic readings of literary work by western writers such as Rebecca Solnit, Willy Vlautin, and Karen Tei Yamashita, to Ben Highmore's analyses of everyday life. Each of these strategies opens up the literary texts to nuanced readings of how gender, sexuality, race, ethnicity, class, and other identity markers express themselves socially and in place. Attentive to the particularities both of place and of the everyday, to the pathologies of everyday life, to the way characters feel in place, we readers can connect these texts to other texts, to other places, to other bodies.

The Course Structure

The course I outline here is ambitious and demanding of students, but I think it can be easily adapted to particularities of place and other models of workload. There are many other ways of organizing a similar course. The class I present here can skew toward one geographical region (I think this would work as a "California" course, for example) or have an emphasis on urban literature, on genre, on period. Students could profit from a less extensive and more intensive reading list. One might cluster texts that consider a particular place or subregion, organize by geographical contrasts—wet versus dry, the country and the city, green versus brown—or by topographies. One might organize the texts based on flipped assumptions, with texts that figure whites as newcomers, outsiders, or exiles, for example.

This course places theories and methodologies (from critical regionalism, cultural geography, everyday studies, place studies, and affect theory) in conversation with a body of literary texts in which place—the North American West—matters. We look at "the West" as an imagined construct as well as a set of geographical locations, with particular attention on the ways in which location is embodied, as gendered, temporal, cultural, classed, raced, physical, psychological. How do the particularities of place engage with regional, national, and planetary histories, politics, environments, cultures, socialities, ideologies? How do writers represent place? Or bodies in place? How do a writer's historical, cultural, and embodied positions contribute to the representations of places? How much of a writer's project involves revision, reclamation, or redefinition of a place? How do writers represent their relationships with or to the land? And does that have anything to do with how a writer represents relations between humans or between humans and other beings or objects? How does a text work to make distinctions between places, to set a place apart, define it? What aspects of the everyday does a writer use to express humans in place? Where in these texts is there a move from the individual to the social? Is there a quotidian West, and, if so, how is it located textually? Are there strategies common to what we might call western writing, or is western writing too diverse for any generalization? In the contemporary period is there such a thing as a regional quotidian? A regional body? Regional aesthetic? Is western writing a genre or a set of practices, obsessions, habits, tendencies?

Through the term "western," we keep one hypothesis at the forefront of our considerations: western writing registers as "western" because of both its treatment of geography and its treatment of everyday life. Because all of us are thinking through these questions within a particular constellation of texts and from a range of backgrounds, each of us works in territory both familiar and strange. This leads us to question how a discipline's underlying assumptions and values are compromised or adapted when we borrow them for use in a different discipline. We discover which theoretical approaches work best for the reading of literature as region and place specific. For the group, specific chapters of books and particular essays emerge as most cited, most useful. What is opaque at the beginning of the term becomes clear and helpful by term's end. Thinking through our own habits, ordinary and quotidian, helps us see identity as an accumulation of place-based habits, behaviors, and assumptions that belong to the everyday.

What we read as the grounding for our interest in the everyday and in ordinary affect: Ben Highmore's *Ordinary Lives* and Kathleen Stewart's *Ordinary Affects*. We supplement these books with a selection from Joe Moran's *Reading the Everyday* and Kathleen Stewart's "Regionality." Now that Neil Campbell's *Affective Critical Regionality* has been published, it would be the third text to serve as a base for our explorations:

Our shared readings, those everyone in class reads, are as follows:

Ordinary Life: Studies in the Everyday, by Ben Highmore
Farewell to Manzanar, by Jeanne Wakatsuki Houston and James D.
   Houston
"Virgin Everything," by Deirdre McNamer
Introduction to *Reading the Everyday,* by Joe Moran
Affective Critical Regionality, by Neil Campbell
"The Dump Ground," from *Wolf Willow,* by Wallace Stegner
Ordinary Affects, by Kathleen Stewart
"Bears and Lions," by Mary Clearman Blew
"The Invention of Everyday Life," by Rita Felski
Winter in the Blood, by James Welch
Breaking Clean, by Judy Blunt
The Meadow, by James Galvin
"Regionality," by Kathleen Stewart
The Legend of Colton H. Bryant, by Alexandra Fuller
Medicine River, by Thomas King
Mountain City, by Gregory Martin
The Magic of Blood, by Dagoberto Gilb
The Faith Healer of Olive Avenue, by Manuel Muñoz
Holy Land, by D. J. Waldie

I place the critical foundational works early in the term but weave them among literary texts so we can practice thinking about the methods while engaging with a literary text. I break up the reading of *Affective Critical Regionality* with the chapter on Stewart appearing before *Ordinary Affects.* We move from the best-known books to ones I feel were likely to be unknown to my class, and I place the most formally experimental book last on the schedule. I begin with *Farewell to Manzanar* because so many students know it from middle school or high school. The prose isn't difficult, it is familiar, and it is a good showcase for the methods we will use throughout the semester. Through the lens of the everyday and ordinary affect, they see how complex a text it is and the way it plays with event, history, and domesticity. Several students wrote responses on this book, many emphasizing a collision of very different concepts of the ordinary. One student wrote,

Many "ordinary" aspects of Jeanne Wakatsuki Houston's experiences in the Manzanar internment camp were not ordinary for the inhabitants, but were portrayed in the memoir as uncomfortable readjustments and intrusions into an ordinary that had previously existed for the Japanese Americans imprisoned in this camp. The scene with the women's latrines sticks out particularly, in which "one old woman had already solved the problem (of privacy) for herself by dragging in a large cardboard carton. She set it up around one of the bowls, like a three-sided screen." (Houston 20). The old woman's solution of a partition for bathroom privacy seems like a small victory, but it's necessary to portray this "ordinary" seeking moment in order to explain the conditions and adaptations that came with them.

The environment, and geographic space, becomes a vessel to recreate an ordinary and everyday that is comfortable enough to not only survive in, but to make a real life in. When Houston describes the Sierra Nevadas as reminding her father of a mountain in Japan, the environment itself is creating a sense of normalcy and recreates familiarity in an adaptive way.

Another key element is regular, low-evaluative-stakes reflection, modeling the application of critical work to the literary texts. In a fourteen-week term, students must submit at least seven responses of five hundred to one thousand words. The responses are due the night before the class meeting so that I have time to read them and think about how to incorporate them into the class. All students must write on one or two of the most challenging texts. This way, we will have one or two texts for which all class members have composed their thoughts on the page before the class begins. These responses offer a chance to explore ideas and to think about the theories through texts. One student uses Joe Moran's essay on waiting to think about why Dagoberto Gilb's story "Al, in Phoenix," from *The Magic of Blood*, can be so unsettling when nothing much happens. The narrator, a working-class Latino, is in Phoenix when his car breaks down, and Gilb's story takes up the wait for the car repair and the affect of the mechanic, Al. Waiting, the narrator has the time to worry—about the cost, about whether the price will be fair, whether Al is racist. In other classes students have been more confident about judging the characters—"Al *is* racist," for example—but an attention to the ordinary helps students slow down, read with care, and attend to the significance of the choices the author has made.

Students produce a substantial work for the final project, either a critical analysis or a creative piece. As the culmination of a literature course, this project is where I want to see how students use what we have pursued over the term, so any creative work must include an analytical foreword or afterword that both analyzes students' own creative pieces in terms of the critical material for the class and discusses the ways their thinking and writing incorporate material from the class. The results vary. Some students, seeking to use the final project as part of their thesis work, don't fully integrate the theoretical work into the project. Two literature students write essays that they go on to present at Western Literature Association annual meetings. For the student who writes on *Winter in the Blood*, Ben Highmore's articulation of the uses of distraction leads her to find a place amid a substantial body of criticism. Her contrarian reading moves away from common readings that diagnose the narrator as alienated and finds a different perspective that, rather that rejecting the themes of alienation, adds to our understanding of him, adds another layer of complexity. She finds that

> the narrator seems to be wielding attention as "poison and cure," noticing ordinary, apparently meaningless things at moments life threatens to burst in. He sometimes seems bombarded by people, nature, and objects, peppering his rich perceptive field with details. Encountering the calf that might remind him of his brother's death, he concentrated on a tadpole in a tub. Challenged by his mother about fetching his wife, "'Are you going to go after her?'" he focuses on flies on the kitchen windowsill. Diverted from that chase once again, encountering Malvina, another woman he might pursue, he notices the blue bath beads on her bedside table. There are also the intermittent squeaks from grandmother's rocker, often heard from another room, dropped into scenes in which the narrator is struggling with choices, or avoiding memory. It is this that the narrator seems skilled at using as a means of dealing with the emotional realities of his life as he struggles to endure the bombardment of present experience and memory in everyday life.

Outcomes

By the end of the course most students adeptly read methodological, theoretical, or critical texts, including those outside their home discipline, and use those texts to become strong and subtle readers and producers of literary texts. They drill down to the constituent components of a place-based sensibility, embodiment, and microculture; have specific tools to connect the personal to larger frameworks—social, regional, national, and planetary; have a flexible, nuanced understanding of the ways in which place matters; understand and articulate the ways in which all human activities have a politics; understand the ways in which attention to the everyday can create a space for stories of seemingly unextraordinary people and places; can relinquish the strong desire for grand narratives and characters; can locate intersections of identities and places and articulate the ways identity is always in place, and always situational; read beyond the plot and find ways writers have created texts that have place deeply and complexly embedded in them; can disrupt literary habits and canons; understand that the literatures of the underrepresented come from the places where the underrepresented live and work; know that there are many wests, varied by geography, class, time, gender, sexuality, race, ethnicity, occupation; and know that these wests have rich literary traditions and deep archives, with only a few titles reaching national popular or scholarly notice. There are lots of good books out there by writers we have never heard of.

In class discussion I work to model a conversation between critical and literary text, often working through a passage, attending closely to it in terms of a claim or observation in the critical reading. I bring up comments and readings from students' responses, which they must turn in before class time. For example, we might discuss how waiting in everyday life expresses powerlessness, status or lack thereof, and the politics of waiting, as discussed by Joe Moran or Ben Highmore. One student writes,

> When Ben Highmore paints the picture of people waiting at a bus stop, he is giving an element of the everyday. Most of us have experienced it before: the delays, the body odor, the lack of heat in winter months, etc. It appears perfectly normal because it's been so ingrained as a way of life. But when broken down—the private intersecting with the public, the physical closeness to people you've never met and may never see again— the quotidian becomes complex, creating a "zone for analysis."

We might then create a close reading of a passage in Judy Blunt's book where she waits for the men to return from fighting a grass fire. After beginning the chapter with an anecdote concerning a young Judy, her grandfather, and the necessity of culling the "girl kittens," Blunt continues to list the ways in which the gender divide, both on the ranch and in public culture (the newly arrived TV), celebrated "the manly man for doing the work of two men and the little woman for whipping up man-sized meals." She catalogs the childhood games with siblings—all masculine roles, exciting, and in active voice, "reached," "rescued," and finally, closer to home, "We played Fire."[16] She then contrasts the excitement, danger, and agency she feels when the girls play fire to the actual fire started when her brother played the game and the flames got out of control. And of the repercussions she writes, "I think Dad could have forgiven Gail or me had one of us taken the blame for that fire, girls with too much time on their hands, girls whose stupidity and carelessness were explainable, but there were no words or excuse for any son of a cattleman who would willfully, deliberately, betray his land."[17] A series of observations about women's double duties, with the domestic home-work paramount, and Judy's efforts to stall her passage through puberty, when her ranch work will come second to housework—all these stories work to set up an account of a prairie fire when Judy races toward thirteen and the inevitability of womanhood.

The community comes together to fight the fire, and Judy is left behind, with the women. She wanders, she waits, fidgets, tries again to go with the men to fight the fire but is turned away. She retreats from the women to watch the fire and the men fighting it. She watches alone, first on a windbreak, then a haystack, where she sees and hears everything but remains apart from the action. She becomes the still point around which activity occurs. As she waits, for another hour, Judy imagines an active role for herself, as a fire scout, a job she sees as heroic. In her daydream, when the fire raced, inevitably, toward her ranch where the women had gathered, Judy would save them all. Long after the fire has been controlled, the men have returned, the neighbors have gone home, the dinner bell rung, she remains hidden in the haystack, waiting. She waits in part to delay her fate, to stay removed from the stories that reinforce gendered roles. Throughout this chapter Blunt has structured her topic, pacing, and sentences on a pendulum swinging between active and passive, the fire line and the home fires, and an in-between, a place of defiance, of fantasy, and of reflection.

At the end of the chapter she moves forward in time, to a different place, one with a playground, and with the role of mother.

It is the time, recounted in the chapter, between events and intentions—first with Judy waiting in contrast to the ranch women waiting for telephone calls, for news, for the men to return and then a kitten, Tiger, waiting for young Judy to return—that the deep work of the chapter takes place. Not everything waits, as Judy discovers. She finds the kitten dead, choked by the twine leash she had so carefully constructed. And so, as the blackened post-fire land echoes young Judy's arm, bruised by her own pinching as a means to keep from crying, the unintended consequences play out—her brother's runaway "play" fire, her inevitable maturation into a restrictive role in her ranch community, her fatal attempt to control the kitten's movements, all considered, ordered, and reflected upon in the waiting, the gap between each role. While waiting can neither speed nor delay action, it offers a pause and a place for reflection.

One student cataloged a series of similar moments in *Breaking Clean*:

> By and large, something in Judy herself creates a circuit break in the ordinary, but occasionally it comes from somebody else. . . . In another episode of childhood where Judy hits a break point, she interacts with a native family outside the diner where her family is eating. Judy's sense of the ordinary does not yet fall in line with the ordinary of the adult world where native people are seen as a potentially dangerous other with low morals and hygiene, and the extreme reaction of her parents to her innocent interactions fills her belly with "anger and shame" (87). Added to this visceral internalized reaction to the unseen affects surrounding ethnic tensions, she had come from the dentist that day, and the episode became even more "sticky" from that additional layer of physical discomfort. The collision of her own sense of ordinary and that of her parents was meant to bring her into alignment, such that her perception of native people would become tainted with a different affect and bring her emotions and connotations into agreement with theirs.

While this student foregrounds the scene in terms of other aspects of the ordinary, we could discuss it as another event that is occasioned by waiting: young Judy, mouth numb from Novocain and unable to eat at the café, a rare treat for her family, "slide[s] to the floor under the table and begin[s] to cry." Her father sends her to the car to wait and "straighten up." Waiting, her "attention wanders" to "where an Indian woman sits holding a baby." She watches, transfixed, as the woman feeds the baby food she has chewed for her.[18] In recounting a life where the work ethic dominated and people are valued for the work that they do, these moments of waiting are uncommon, and in Blunt's memoir they are significant.

Or we recall passages in *Farewell to Manzanar* that describe the long waits of internees for access to basic facilities, such as toilets. Classroom conversations such as these ground big-issue conversations, such as the ethics of internment or the inequities of gendered roles, in the specific ways in which injustices are administered, where and how they are felt and embodied. By looking through the lenses of the everyday and ordinary affect, we get at the "how" of things, the way policies, degradations, ideologies are registered bodily, socially, and emplaced.

For students from outside a particular set of regional discourses, these strategies offer a way in—readers might not know anything about raising beef cattle, but these strategies allow them a way to analyze structures and themes in books such as Blunt's *Breaking Clean*. Such approaches serve not to estrange or exoticize but to connect the remote life fifty miles from the nearest small town to larger networks and patterns, of gender inequality, for example. Several students wrote convincingly of patterns in Blunt's book that emerged from repetition of domestic scenes or her deployment of descriptions of the day-to-day at times of high stress.

Students often find new and surprising ways into texts that have long critical bibliographies. For example, several students developed new and innovative readings of *Winter in the Blood*, focusing on waiting, distraction, objects, and eating. One student tracked Jeanne's losses in *Farewell to Manzanar* through encounters with the ordinary. Another described the ways in which the everyday is pathologized in that text. With a new set of reading strategies, they also find their way into useful explication of critically ignored texts and readings attentive to how race, class, and gender are expressed through the particularities of place. They became attentive to different aspects of repetition in several of the books, whether conversation patterns, music, habits, chores, or labor. Several students produced work that could evolve into publishable essays.

Two literature students from this class went on to use these reading strategies for their theses, and some of the creative writing students found ways to use the everyday as a means to strengthen character development and embed characters in place rather than setting. This methodological approach breaks down insider/outsider barriers, for these strategies allow students to find and connect, through both similarities and differences, to the ways their own quotidian existence tells fundamental truths about their identities and their lives.

The final projects were as varied as the students. For the most part the fiction students figured out how to accrete details of ordinary life to develop character and scene, with some stunning results. One nonfiction essay riffed on Stewart's "Regionality" essay to build a richly layered portrait of her working-class town. Two poets turned to prose to better work through the theoretical ideas and then later sent me poems thickly immersed in observations of the ordinary. The critics wrote essays on *Winter in the Blood, The Legend of Colton H. Bryant,* and a western film. One fiction student wrote a story heavily influenced by supplemental reading of Marc Augé's theory of non-places—airports, stations, hotels. He writes of the transformation of his Thanksgiving break trip, with its weather delays, into fiction:

> It seemed I was in a constant state of transience, even as I had access to a comfortable, clean room in a good hotel, I took shuttles and trains, and the being in the hotel itself, alone, was fraught with the conflicting emotions Stewart tackles in *Ordinary Affects*. Though, having read Stewart, Moran, Jackson, and some of Augé, I noticed they had shaped the way I think about quotidian Non-space. I could not help but ruminate on the alternating sensations of glee and loneliness I felt in the hotel room. . . . It was an internal experience, and nothing remarkable had really happened. But this is my chance at grappling [with] the question of whether or not something remarkable really *did* happen. The experience was entirely provoked by place, Non-place. Had I made my flight, things could have gone very differently, and it's quite possible I wouldn't have thought of Stewart, Moran, or Jackson. It's possible I wouldn't have thought a thing about any of it at all.
>
> But it is the very sensitivity of that which shaped my desire to write about it. I did not want to forget about this unremarkable thirty-six hours in my life.

My first iteration of this class was too broad and too ambitious, the product of several writing projects I was working on simultaneously. When I teach this course again, I will focus on the everyday and ordinary affect with very close attention to the particularities of place, where a politics emerges. Several subthemes and correspondences between texts got lost in the complexities of our tasks. For example, I think the notion of the relation between country and city will be better served in a different class. With each year I am able to curtail, book by book, my love of the fat syllabus, and I think this course will be stronger with a less extensive and more intensive reading list.

As I continue to read more contemporary studies of the everyday, I am convinced that it is a useful way to approach certain kinds of western American literature and to refocus the way we look at some familiar texts. In the primary reading for the class, I select books where very little happens in terms of plot. Long sections of each of these books attend to the everyday, which by accumulation reaches some sort of claim about lives lived in the western United States. Even in the books or stories where something happens, usually a death, the writer refuses suspense, either by telegraphing those events (*The Legend of Colton H. Bryant*) or by situating them before the narrative begins (*Winter in the Blood*). By eschewing plot-driven texts for this class, I move us away from books that valorize closure and we embrace texts for the vibrant way they connect to worlds outside the text. Where narrow configurations of region might set texts off and isolate them, an attention to the everyday opens these texts to connections by means of their evocations of ordinary affects; in Kathleen Stewart's terms, "affects are not so much forms of signification, or units of knowledge, as they are expressions of ideas or problems performed as a kind of involuntary and powerful learning and participation."[19] With this approach to western literary texts, readers make momentary, confounding, affective connections to a text. From reading a book such as Gregory Martin's *Mountain City*, readers won't have the satisfied feeling of knowing the West; instead, they will experience a contingent, debatable version of a family in constellations of place and time through a series of intensities registered in the smallest moments of human lives. It is a West, but not *the* West.

My gratitude to the students in my 2013 version of this class: Catherine Bailey, Kimberly Bell, Robert Bosworth, Nathaniel Cox, Michelle Gullickson, Michael Hicks, JP Kemmick, Rachel Mindell, Jules Ohman, Brenden Oliva, Brett Puryear, Philip Schaefer, Lindsay Stephens, and Michèle Van Haecke. Thanks to readers of my drafts, including Tom Berninghausen and the anonymous readers for the press.

1. My course title has changed for this essay. I had to submit a title nearly six months before teaching the course in fall 2013 and before I had had a chance to think about it in detail. The original course title was Rethinking the West as Region: The Urban, the Rural, and the Quotidian Wests in a Glocal World. I prefer this new title: Quotidian Wests: Exploring Regionality through the Everyday.

2. I borrow "getting under our skin," from critic Ben Highmore. The quotation appears later in this essay. Highmore, *Ordinary Lives*, 33.

3. Kowalewski, "Writing in Place," 174.

4. My own scholarly work considers problems with configuring region too broadly. See Cook, "Imagining the Rocky Mountain Region"; and Cook, "Making California's Small Cities and Towns Visible in the Twenty-First Century."

5. Stewart, *Ordinary Affects*, 127.

6. Kowalewski, *Reading the West*, 8.

7. Stewart, quoted in Campbell, *Affective Critical Regionality*, 13.

8. The student quotes the term *minima aesthetica* from a passage in Stewart, "Regionality," 282.

9. Highmore, *Ordinary Lives*, 33.

10. Felski, quoted in Highmore, *Ordinary Lives*, 92.

11. While literature or reading circles are common in K–12 education, they aren't currently common in the university classroom. For university teaching, see Gee, "Reading Circles Get Students to Do the Reading," 6.

12. Neil Campbell tracks the use of the terms "region," "regional," and "regionalism," finding that Kathleen Stewart's term "regionality" better conveys the sense of "*region-as-process*." Campbell, *Affective Critical Regionality*, 8. For Campbell, "to rethink region and regionalism with this in mind understands the local and specific to be interventionist in wider, more distanced or global projects and 'languages' and yet, at the same time, refuses to allow the local to become static, nostalgic, or reductive" (3).

13. Highmore, *Ordinary Lives*, 8.

14. Stewart, quoted in Campbell, *Affective Critical Regionality*, 118.

15. Scott, *Making Sense*, 1.

16. Blunt, *Breaking Clean*, 89–91.

17. Blunt, *Breaking Clean*, 94–95.

18. Blunt, *Breaking Clean*, 85–86.

19. Stewart, *Ordinary Affects*, 40.

Those entries marked with * indicate works on the course reading list.

*Adams, Paul C., Steven D. Hoelscher, and Karen E. Till. *Textures of Place: Exploring Humanist Geographies*. Minneapolis: University of Minnesota Press, 2004.

Allmendinger, Blake. *A History of California Literature*. New York: Cambridge University Press, 2015.

*Augé, Marc. *Non-places: Introduction to an Anthropology of Supermodernity*. London: Verso, 1995.

*Bachelard, Gaston. *The Poetics of Space*. 1961. Boston: Beacon Press, 1994.

*Basso, Keith H. *Wisdom Sits in Places: Landscape and Language among the Western Apache*. Albuquerque: University of New Mexico Press, 1996.

*Berlant, Lauren. *Cruel Optimism*. Durham NC: Duke University Press, 2011.

*Berry, Kate A., and Martha L. Henderson, eds. *Geographical Identities of Ethnic America: Race, Space, and Place*. Reno: University of Nevada Press, 2002.

*Bird, Jon. *Mapping the Futures: Local Cultures, Global Change*. New York: Routledge, 1996.

*Blew, Mary Clearman. "Bears and Lions." In *The Best of Montana's Short Fiction*, edited by William Kittredge and Allen Morris Jones. Guilford CT: Lyons Press, 2004.

*Blunt, Alison, and Gillian Rose, eds. *Writing Women and Space: Colonial and Postcolonial Geographies*. New York: Guilford Press, 1994.

*Blunt, Judy. *Breaking Clean*. New York: Vintage Books, 2003.

*Brosnan, Kathleen A., and Amy L. Scott, eds. *City Dreams, Country Schemes: Community and Identity in the American West*. Reno: University of Nevada Press, 2011.

*Campbell, Neil. *Affective Critical Regionality*. London: Rowman & Littlefield, 2016.

*Certeau, Michel de. *The Practice of Everyday Life*. Berkeley: University of California Press, 1988.

*Ching, Barbara, and Gerald Creed. *Knowing Your Place: Rural Identity and Cultural Hierarchy*. New York: Routledge, 1997.

Cook, Nancy S. "Imagining the Rocky Mountain Region." In *A History of Western American Literature*, edited by Susan Kollin, 162–76. New York: Cambridge University Press, 2015.

———. "Making California's Towns and Small Cities Visible in the Twenty-First Century." In *A History of California Literature*, edited by Blake Allmendinger, 358–70. New York: Cambridge University Press, 2015.

*Crang, Mike, and Nigel Thrift, eds. *Thinking Space*. New York: Routledge, 2000.

*Creswell, Tim. *In Place/Out of Place: Geography, Ideology, and Transgression*. Minneapolis: University of Minnesota Press, 1996.

*Domosh, Mona, and Joni Seager. *Putting Women in Place: Feminist Geographers Make Sense of the World*. New York: Guilford Press, 2001.

*Feld, Steven, and Keith H. Basso, eds. *Senses of Place*. Santa Fe NM: School for Advanced Research Press, 2000.

*Felski, Rita. *Doing Time: Feminist Theory and Postmodern Culture*. New York: New York University Press, 2000.

*———. "The Invention of Everyday Life." In *Everyday Life*, edited by Ben Highmore, 1:287–306. London: Routledge, 2012.

*Francaviglia, Richard V. *Main Street Revisited: Time, Space, and Image Building in Small-Town America*. Iowa City: University of Iowa Press, 1996.

*Fuller, Alexandra. *The Legend of Colton H. Bryant*. New York: Penguin Books, 2008.

*Galvin, James. *The Meadow*. New York: Henry Holt, 1992.

Gee, Jane. "Reading Circles Get Students to Do the Reading." *Teaching Professor* 27, no. 1 (2013): 6.

*Gilb, Dagoberto. *The Magic of Blood*. Albuquerque: University of New Mexico Press, 1993.

*Groth, Paul, and Todd W. Bressi, eds. *Understanding Ordinary Landscapes*. New Haven CT: Yale University Press, 1997.

*Gupta, Akhil, and James Ferguson, eds. *Culture, Power, Place: Explorations in Critical Anthropology*. Durham NC: Duke University Press, 1999.

*Harbison, Robert. *Eccentric Spaces*. Cambridge MA: MIT Press, 2000.

*Hayden, Dolores. *The Power of Place: Urban Landscapes as Public History*. Cambridge MA: MIT Press, 1995.

*Highmore, Ben, ed. *Everyday Life*. 4 vols. London: Routledge, 2012.

*———. *Ordinary Lives: Studies in the Everyday*. New York: Routledge, 2011.

*Houston, Jeanne Wakatsuki, and James D. Houston. *Farewell to Manzanar*. New York: Bantam Books, 1973.

*Jackson, John Brinckerhoff. *Discovering the Vernacular Landscape*. New Haven CT: Yale University Press, 1984.

*———. *Landscape in Sight: Looking at America*. New Haven CT: Yale University Press, 1997.

*———. *Landscape: Selected Writings of J. B. Jackson*. Amherst: University of Massachusetts Press, 1970.

*———. *A Sense of Place, a Sense of Time*. New Haven CT: Yale University Press, 1994.

*King, Thomas. *Medicine River*. New York: Viking, 1990.

*Kittredge, William, and Allen Morris Jones, eds. *The Best of Montana's Short Fiction*. Guilford CT: Lyons Press, 2004.

Kollin, Susan, ed. *A History of Western American Literature*. New York: Cambridge University Press, 2015.

Kowalewski, Michael. *Reading the West: New Essays on the Literature of the American West*. Cambridge: Cambridge University Press, 1996.

*———. "Writing in Place: The New American Regionalism." *American Literary History* 6, no. 1 (1994): 171–83.

*Lefebvre, Henri. *The Production of Space*. 1974. Malden MA: Blackwell, 2016.

*Lippard, Lucy. *The Lure of the Local: Senses of Place in a Multicentered Society*. New York: New Press, 1997.

*Low, Setha M. *The Anthropology of Space and Place: Locating Culture*. Malden MA: Blackwell, 2007.

*Martin, Gregory. *Mountain City*. New York: North Point Press, 2000.

*Massey, Doreen. *Space, Place and Gender*. Minneapolis: University of Minnesota Press, 1994.

*McNamer, Deirdre. "Virgin Everything." In *The New Montana Story: An Anthology*, edited by Rick Newby. Helena MT: Riverbend, 2003.

*Meinig, D. W. *The Interpretation of Ordinary Landscapes: Geographical Essays*. New York: Oxford University Press, 1979.

*Miller, Daniel. *The Comfort of Things*. Cambridge: Polity, 2013.

*Moran, Joe. *Reading the Everyday*. New York: Routledge, 2005.

*Muñoz, Manuel. *The Faith Healer of Olive Avenue*. Chapel Hill NC: Algonquin Books of Chapel Hill, 2007.

*Nazarea, Virginia. *Cultural Memory and Biodiversity*. Tucson: University of Arizona Press, 2005.

*Newby, Rick. *The New Montana Story: An Anthology*. Helena MT: Riverbend, 2003.

*Pink, Sarah. *Situating Everyday Life: Practices and Places*. Los Angeles: SAGE, 2012.

*Powell, Douglas. *Critical Regionalism: Connecting Politics and Culture in the American Landscape*. Chapel Hill: University of North Carolina Press, 2007.

*Preston, Christopher J. *Grounding Knowledge: Environmental Philosophy, Epistemology, and Place*. Athens: University of Georgia Press, 2003.

*Riegel, Christian, and Herb Wylie, eds. *A Sense of Place: Re-evaluating Regionalism in Canadian and American Writing*. Edmonton: University of Alberta Press, 1998.

*Sack, Robert David. *A Geographical Guide to the Real and the Good*. New York: Routledge, 2003.

*Scott, Susie. *Making Sense of Everyday Life*. Cambridge: Polity, 2013.

*Soja, Edward. *Postmetropolis: Critical Studies of Cities and Regions*. Malden MA: Blackwell, 2000.

*———. *Postmodern Geographies: The Reassertion of Space in Critical Social Theory*. London: Verso, 1989.

*———. *Thirdspace: Journey to Los Angeles and Other Real-and-Imagined Places*. Oxford: Blackwell, 1996.

*Stegner, Wallace. "The Dump Ground." In *Wolf Willow: A History, a Story, and a Memory of the Last Plains Frontier*. 1961. New York: Penguin Books, 2000.

*Stewart, Kathleen. *Ordinary Affects*. Durham NC: Duke University Press, 2007.

*———. "Regionality." *Geographical Review* 103, no. 2 (2013): 275–84.

*———. *A Space on the Side of the Road: Cultural Poetics in an "Other" America*. Princeton NJ: Princeton University Press, 1996.

*Stilgoe, John. *Outside Lies Magic: Regaining History and Awareness in Everyday Places*. New York: Walker and Company, 1998.

*Waldie, D. J. *Holy Land: A Suburban Memoir*. New York: Norton, 1996.

*Welch, James. *Winter in the Blood*. New York: Harper & Row, 1974.

*Wilson, Chris, and Paul Groth, eds. *Everyday America: Cultural Landscape Studies after J. B. Jackson*. Berkeley: University of California Press, 2003.

Wister, Owen. *The Virginian*. 1902. New York: Oxford University Press, 2009.

9

Western Writers in the Field

O. ALAN WELTZIEN

Literary Pilgrimages and Experiential Learning

I value the local. I learn the literary landscape nearby and often teach writers who were or are part of it, because such activity *grounds* students and teachers alike in many ways. The familiar organic metaphor is deliberate. For one thing, students learn that important writers don't all live in New York City or Seattle or Paris. And they learn that local literary or even biocentric knowledge affords us the best grasp of the planetary.[1] Leading a class off campus to sites associated with western writers represents a "value-added" pedagogy, one that echoes, for example, more than one "high-impact practice" (HIP) or "high-impact activity," as identified in Association of American Colleges and Universities (AAC&U) literature. HIP-inflected pedagogy has become the gold standard in early twenty-first-century educational theory, and because of my campus's innovative "X1" structure (which I define below), taking students on the road enhances their already enhanced course experience of particular western writers.

A literary pilgrimage can magnify a writer's spirit and particular sensibility, like a zoom lens that invites intimate connections between the texts, the life lived, and our own lives as readers and writers, scholars and students. Direct bodily contact with sites associated with writers constitutes one form of cultural tourism, which in my experience increases demand for a writer's work, enhancing its popularity. Literary sites inherently draw readers and create a personal bond different than that experienced through the novel or essay. Integrating a writer's real ground with before and after experiences, in the student's room and in the classroom, ties reading and writing, discussion and reflection with the visceral, sensory experience of writers on their home ground.

George D. Kuh, one of the primary figures in HIP pedagogy, uses as an epigraph for one of his path-breaking articles a passage from William Cronon's "Only Connect: The Goals of a Liberal Education": "Being an educated person means being able to see connections that allow one to make sense of the world and act within it in creative ways. Every one of the qualities I have described here . . . is finally about connecting."[2] To Kuh's and Cronon's lists of fundamental HIP teaching activities that enhance undergraduate education, I propose adding another: traveling off campus and visiting a writer's own ground (then returning to the campus "home"). Students who read a literary text and then take in through their senses the actual landscapes it animates will return to campus having made fundamental affective connections that deepen their intellectual encounters with the text and writer. This is value-added learning.

Such an activity constitutes an optimal version of place-based education. When students walk the actual settings or home turf of a text, they understand in new ways the writer's biography, the flavors of the text (including particular scenes within a plot), and ways in which these substantiate their own reading and understanding. By standing on the ground, they know more than they knew from the book or the classroom. Closing that imaginative distance makes all the difference.

Taking students on the road and down the path reinforces two of the ten HIPs Kuh and colleagues highlight: first-year seminars and experiences, as well as writing-intensive courses. With regard to the former, Kuh recommends "a human-scale first-year seminar" that features an enrollment cap of twenty-five and a pair of instructors.[3] Although the University of Montana–Western (UMW) for the most part lacks paired instructors for a single course, our average class size is twenty-five because of our "x1" or "block" schedule. Thus, our first-level English class (Writ 101) echoes two HIPs, and when we go on field trips, that activity echoes a third HIP, the one devoted to service learning or community-based learning, which I'd rewrite as follows: "A key element in this [field study] is the opportunity students have to both *apply* what they are learning [from the field trip] and *reflect* in a classroom setting on their [field trip] experiences."

In giving his reasons for supporting HIPs, Kuh argues that "participation in these high-impact activities provides opportunities for students to see how what they are learning works in different settings, on and off campus." He confirms what some have also known a long time: "it can be life changing" to participate in one or more HIPs as an undergraduate.[4] My students do not forget their course-based travels: for many, they are the course highlight.

UMW enables HIP pedagogy because back in 2006 the university adopted a block, or "one-course-at-a-time," curricular structure. Adapted from Colorado College's seasoned block program, UMW (Montana's old "normal school") remains the only public college or university in the United States using the block schedule.[5] In the X1 structure students take only one course at a time, with a class typically meeting every weekday for three hours (either in the morning, say, 8:15–11:15, or the afternoon, 12:15–3:15), for three and a half weeks. Flexibility is built into the system to accommodate such things as off-campus travel (sometimes students are gone all day or even longer). Students and instructor alike focus only on that one class (excepting semester-long "stringer" classes). Multiple preps or homework sets don't exist. Teaching and learning "in the block" proves heady, intensive, tiring. X1 was designed to highlight teaching and learning according to "authentic practice in the discipline."[6] In 2009 Rob C. Thomas and Sheila Roberts laid out the rationale: "A wealth of published educational research and assessment has documented that experiential learning, inquiry-based learning, and immersion learning all improve the depth of concept understanding, so we were confident that this was the right thing to do."[7]

The X1 plan incorporates the "flipped classroom" approach. It features small groups (e.g., three to five students) that carry out assigned tasks almost every day. Instructors design a range of discussion activities or even tasks to be completed outside the classroom, often interspersing small-group work with occasional lecturing. In X1 instructors recast their roles and off-load responsibilities to the small groups. X1 thus diffuses teaching responsibilities. In every class, optimal discussion unfolds to the extent the small groups undertake sustained conversation with each other, given their respective roles at any given hour. Of course it's not always optimal, but most students get the drift and at times take the lead. Attendance and participation figure as a larger percentage of one's course grade than in the traditional system. The locus and energy shift from *within* to *between* the small groups: student eyes don't remain fixed on the instructor.[8]

The larger blocks of time enable a range of activities more difficult or impossible in traditional class periods. This includes field trips. In xi English courses it's easy to schedule off-campus activities. I've led writing classes on walks to two prominent local landmarks or around our rural town. Writer-focused field trips are a natural extension of this approach. These field trips constitute a capstone experience for students, whose understanding of both writers and their work intensifies exponentially.

Thomas Savage and Norman Maclean Country Tours

Montana, a state known above all for big mountains, valleys, and prairies, proves excellent ground on which to explore an almost chthonic connection between writers and their native or chosen landscapes. In recent years I have taken students on day trips that explore the native soil of both a lesser-known and a well-known writer. Doing so enhances students' understanding of those authors' connection to place, as well as their own connections to those authors and places.

I lead first-year students on half- and full-day tours through what I have for years called Thomas Savage Country.

Students taking coursework in western American literatures must learn to distinguish the diversity and quality of voices critiquing and undermining popular cultural production about the American West from the ceaseless production of pop culture, with its hoary Old West lies. The novelist Thomas Savage always takes a hard look at his native country, and sometimes students are struck by his acerbic perspective that offers something other than naïve celebration and self-congratulation. The fact that Savage was homosexual and grew up on both cattle and sheep ranches in country that remains remote to this day renders his perspective, as both insider and outsider, all the more novel and valuable—and challenging.[9] I am stunned by the testimony of students, not all from farms or ranches, about the ways in which Savage's historical novels describe their lives in the 2010s, which points to literature's abiding relevance.

We first stop at the fishing access along old State Highway 91, on the south side of Clark Canyon Reservoir. The construction of Clark Canyon Dam in 1964 led to the inundation of the small town of Armstead (called Beech in Savage's novels); scenes from the three novels students read take place in Armstead/Beech, which I discuss as the class tracks the highway's yellow stripe under water and imagines the townsite.[10] Horse Prairie, a small dispersed village of ranchers (located at an elevation above 6,000 feet), is a forty-five-minute drive from Dillon, the county seat, even now; the valley remains distant from any population, as does Idaho's Lemhi River valley, just west over the Continental Divide, which we reach at midday.

We stop atop Bannock Pass (7,681 feet) on the divide, with its sweeping views north over Horse Prairie and beyond, and the Canyon Creek drainage to the south-southwest, through which the road descends to Leadore, Idaho. Students marvel at the classic Montana panorama, big and open, with very few structures or signs of human habitation anywhere in sight. Students intuitively grasp this comment made by the elderly Savage during an interview: "I think the difference in Westerners has to do with the fact that they feel it's impossible to look at the Rocky Mountains—or to look at the horizon, which is equally vast, and consider that there is such a thing as Europe or neighbors or anything else."[11] One response to this visual grandeur pitches into loneliness and isolation, and *The Power of the Dog* (the second novel they read) tingles with aching loneliness.

Later in the Lemhi valley we stop at the Shiner Ranch, formerly the Yearian Ranch, founded and built up by the writer's maternal grandparents and the main setting for his first novel, *The Pass* (1944).[12]

Before we reach Savage's home place (i.e., the former Brenner Ranch) in Horse Prairie, Montana, students have digested *The Power of the Dog*, Savage's greatest novel. They gather against a split-rail fence as I discuss the exact site of the "big house."[13] Later they wander through the 1892 barn and note the bunkhouse. The bunkhouse to which the main character, Phil, retreats, is unchanged despite the passage of time, and just beyond it, browse thickens along Horse Prairie Creek.[14]

Authenticity is one slippery critical concept in the history of the literary American West.[15] However, I have no doubt that students' experience of the text ratchets up a notch or two because of their physical encounter with the text's actual (and, in some ways, unchanged) setting. Many draw connections between particular scenes and characters and their own footsteps, and those connections linger well beyond the end of the course. In this place they adjust what they *imagine* with what they *discover*, then *integrate* their reflections back in the classroom. That's the kind of experiential intensification I'm after. According to a range of subsequent student testimony, students crave this brush with writers' specific, actual landscapes, which "make it real" and illustrate one high-impact activity.[16]

Norman Maclean and *A River Runs Through It* need no review, as the critical consensus about that work's place in contemporary American literature emerged quickly in the late 1970s. *Young Men and Fire*, which Maclean worked on years longer than he had *A River Runs Through It*, won the National Book Critics Circle Award for best nonfiction the year it was published (1992).

I want students to learn Maclean's Big Blackfoot River—the river that runs through it—firsthand, the way I've come to know Mann Gulch, scene of the devastating blaze chronicled in *Young Men and Fire*, after repeated hikes.

Years ago, in a senior seminar that included Maclean's works, we took a full-day field trip to Montana's Bitterroot Valley, specifically Blodgett Canyon just west of Hamilton, Montana. Blodgett serves, along with Hamilton, as the primary setting in Maclean's "other" novella, usfs 1919: *The Ranger, the Cook, and a Hole in the Sky*.[17] We hiked at least the first few miles of this long, east-west canyon lined with steep rock faces (a haven for big wall climbers), picnicked along the creek, talked about the place. With their bodies they knew the rock and the water. Some of the students incorporated their experience into their longer critical essays.

But taking a first-year English class on the road, twice, in their opening weeks as college students also serves as a retention strategy, for they've been viscerally treated to one version of UMW's experiential learning model. They know that encountering literary studies in the field places particular writers and texts very close to them. They discover that field trips aren't just for botany or biology or geology students, and they even learn that field trips represent but one mode of active learning.[18]

We take two day-long field trips. After studying *River* and screening Robert Redford's film adaptation, we spend several hours with Jerry O'Connell, riverkeeper of the Big Blackfoot River.[19] Together we visit three locations from *River*.[20] O'Connell describes the river in detail and reads from the novella as the students cluster along the bank. He reminds us that while individuals like himself or me cannot know with complete certainty that Maclean wrote those particular scenes with just these sites in mind, it is more than likely, based on a range of testimony, that these are representative or even accurate locations.

In each place the class spreads out along the river in the soft sunlight. In what ways is their understanding of *River* enhanced by standing, several times, alongside Maclean's River, as it's come to be known in Montana? These students know that they *authenticate* their interpretation of *River* in a privileged way available to few of its readers. They smell the river and listen to its riffles, skip rocks across clear flows and pools. They contrast these scenes with Robert Redford's versions in his film adaptation (filmed on the Yellowstone River) and what they imagined in the first place. This series of physical reference points renders their experience of this undisputed literary classic optimal. They are grounded in *River*. This is HIP.

I'm surprised to discover that most students, even the Montanans, have not passed through Montana's "Gates of the Mountains" (north of Helena, Montana).[21] At the mouth of Mann Gulch, near the north end of the Gates, they carefully jump off the port bow onto the simple rock trail. The first time I led a Writ 101 class into Mann Gulch, a UMW videographer accompanied us as we hiked along the bottom of the dry box canyon, then steeply upslope to the rim, threading through the grave markers of the thirteen dead smokejumpers from the infamous 1949 fire. I remember the quiet of Montana's Gates and the intense, yellowing light of a perfect Indian summer day and guess some students also remember that day's bright textures as a capstone of early college life. I still regard that instructional day as one of my best, thanks to high-pressure sunshine, an extraordinary book, and the haunted place itself.

Place-based teaching usually delivers high-impact power because of the range of critical and affective connections.

Another year, another class boards a tour boat in mid-September. I pause frequently, read brief passages from *Young Men and Fire*, and point out locations in light of Maclean's detailed map (i.e., the photo gallery in the book). Most of the students plunge upward past Joe Sylvia's "rock" and cross, breathe hard, reach the ridgetop in a gap between the rimrock, spread out. Students study Rescue Gulch, as it came to be known, the Missouri River's oxbow bend, the severe vegetation scheme of Mann Gulch, the ridges and canyons beyond that make up Montana's Gates of the Mountains Wilderness Area. After lunch some scramble with me down to James Hellman's cross; all traverse the path, just below the rim and upgulch, that links the crosses of Maclean's "Four Horsemen" (i.e., those four smokejumpers who ran the farthest). We stop at all the crosses.

Those readers who also hike Mann Gulch—in the process following in slow motion Ranger Robert Jansson's struggle to reach the crew, then slowly approaching the desperately fleeing firefighters (roughly the students' ages) in their final minutes—and pause at the crosses unquestionably engage with Maclean at deeper levels. This is one instance of HIP pedagogy. Mann Gulch remains an austere, haunted wild place.[22] I believe students' pilgrimage to Mann Gulch helps them understand, early on, one version of UMW's experiential learning and gives them a feeling of confidence in their college choice.

Beyond the Day Trip: Camping through Literary Regions

In taking upper-class English majors on the road, I have twice ventured outside of Montana on multiday trips. I matched an upper-level class with a sustained field experience, one with more demands for myself and students alike, including, for some, occasional personal discomfort or irritation. In these trips I collaborated with a longtime colleague and friend who is a (now-retired) geochemist, along with her husband, who is an amateur astronomer and professional storyteller. We represented an instructional team of two (and sometimes three), a number that is characteristic of some HIP teaching.

I use a junior-level course, Literary Regions, as the base for forays in the Intermountain West. In the first case I featured southern Idaho (an unlikely literary region). About fifteen students and I studied several writers whose fiction or nonfiction is set in southern Idaho: Vardis Fisher (*Mountain Man*, 1965), Ruth Ozeki (*All Over Creation*, 2003), Ron Nelson (*Five Skies*, 2007), Mitch Wieland (*God's Dogs*, 2009), and Evelyn Funda (*Weeds: A Farm Daughter's Lament*, 2013). Our four-day trip occurred during late spring (i.e., UMW Block VIII), so students had read the majority of the texts before traveling.

Our motto was English Majors *Can* Camp, and although a few English majors resisted some of geology's language and lessons, many subsequently declared this experience among their best at UMW. We camped at places like Craters of the Moon National Monument, and students were challenged (in ways different than I was) to bridge the disciplinary spaces between, say, the successive lava flows characterizing southern Idaho and a variety of narratives set in this region—the old story of rocks with the new stories of white settlers or inhabitants. They learned, though not at all well enough, a story of absence as well.[23] This was because I spent grossly insufficient time sketching the *long durée* of tribal peoples (e.g., the Bannock Shoshone), who of course were living here long before white settler-colonialism took hold.

Student-instructor interaction becomes far more frequent and informal, and personal bonds grow quickly in ways not possible on campus. When you repeatedly spend time with students around a campfire far from the college town, the quality of interaction tilts. For example, student pairs were assigned the task of leading a campfire discussion as a structured reflection about the day's learning experiences. Campfires of course remove barriers and inspire intimacy and candor—and storytelling.

Of the many slides in my memory from this trip, one of my favorites comes from a scene at the ruins of Vardis Fisher's home, near Hagerman, Idaho. We walk to the site, poke around the foundations, check out his lakeside view amid the arid southern Idaho landscape. In my group portrait students lie on the grass in front of the ruins, in casual posture, listening to Beethoven of all things on one student's portable electronic device. They've already studied Fisher's most famous novel, suffused with Old West clichés and virulent racism, but found some repose, if not sympathy, at Fisher's homeplace. We were a long way from a classroom, or rather, we had discovered a series of outdoor classrooms, this one a wet pocket in the middle of a sere landscape.

I heard informal testimony for the next year or two from majors or minors not enrolled in this course who voiced envy and regret that they'd missed out. That buzz, however indistinct, once again suggests the power of off-campus time with students, of bringing them into specific landscapes with literary associations.

These camping trips become capstone experiences for upper-level students because they provide a broader integration of learning styles than what is available in a classroom. For example, a final course project, a photojournalism essay, requires these majors to synthesize in some way their "before, during, and after" experiences, at home and onsite far away, between assigned books, their journals, and particular landscapes. The block class that culminates in the camping trip climax defines a (temporary) learning community, and the research about them, according to Jayne E. Brownell and Lynn E. Swaner, claims they "positive[ly] impact . . . behavioral outcomes (such as peer and faculty interaction and student engagement), and attitudinal outcomes (such as sense of belonging and perception of a positive campus climate)." From Brownell and Swaner's list of "liberal learning goals," I'd claim these camping trips directly promote "integrative thinking, and reading and writing skills; openness to new perspectives and ideas . . . [and] development of ethics and values."[24]

For the second camping trip I teach Literature of the Southwest (a survey of desert readings), and we study texts such as Mary Hunter Austin's *Land of Little Rain* (1903), the anthology *Getting Over the Color Green* (2001), and that model of contemporary environmental journalism, Mark Reisner's *Cadillac Desert* (1986; revised 1993). The students, mostly English majors, also buy Robert P. Sharp and Allen Glazner's *Geology Underfoot in Death Valley and Owens Valley* (1997), though most fail to read much of this text.

We fly, rent two vans, and drive to Death Valley National Park (DVNP), where we hike and camp over five days and four nights. I, with my two colleagues, again model interdisciplinarity in our explorations and rambles in DVNP. English majors are treated to many "geology moments"—brief site stops and talks—each day. Students stand in Badwater Basin (at 282 feet below sea level, the low point of North America), walk the sand dunes at Stovepipe Wells, explore debris fans and slot canyons and the shoulders of the Panamint Mountains. Students encounter through their senses, up close and personal, facets of desert topography that bring the texts alive as nothing else can.

It turns out none of these students has traveled in DVNP before, and based on feedback during the trip as well as detailed course evaluations, most (though not all) found it transformative. A couple disliked more than liked the desert, and at least one felt homesick, but most declared this one of the highlights of their college career. To walk up slot canyons or plunge down sand dunes, to stand on the crest of the Funeral Mountains or, conversely, the cracked white salt flats of Badwater Basin a mile west of the valley highway provided them experience, through their bodies, that married their reading and reflection more intensely than anything else I can imagine.

In my limited experience there's no question about the comparatively greater power of teaching students in the field, because their learning curves spike. When you hike with students or, in evenings, sit around a campfire a long way from town or city lights, you influence them in ways dramatically different from what is possible in a classroom. When I take students to sites associated with writers or their books, they gain a kind of quick biographical knowledge they'd otherwise lack, or they reread and grasp the text with new eyes because of their feet on the ground. Out of these kinds of experiences I form friendships that last beyond the students' class or sometimes even their undergraduate years.

Yet I am the only English Department member who takes students on off-campus literary trips. Such experiences naturally pose a range of logistical challenges and require extensive design and planning far beyond your usual class prep. And other challenges loom for this or other manifestations of HIP teaching. Researchers George D. Kuh, Ken O'Donnell, and

Carol Geary Schneider have cited three HIP teaching challenges, the first of which is money (no surprise). Travel and related logistics cost more for the institution or the students or both, as I'm painfully aware every time I reserve and use college vans or implement a special course fee. Second, they point out that planning and implementing such activities are "not a focus of institutional reward systems"—only a current expression of the disconnect between teaching as the primary criterion of professorial evaluation and academe's research-driven agenda. They also point out that HIP pedagogy remains "invisible on most transcripts," that is, there's no "institutional data system recognition."[25]

Despite these three challenges, or all the extra planning work, or the reality that time with students can approach 24/7 during travel, or the risk of many unforeseen problems (illness, injury, etc.), I have never hesitated. I feel charged anew every time I take students off campus or out of town. I have not the slightest question about the HIP impact of teaching while moving. This mode poses a contemporary adaptation of Aristotle's peripatetic style, wherein walking fuses diverse learning modes. There's something fundamental about riding away from campus, near or far, walking and talking, then returning to the classroom, distilling the travel, and integrating it with our reading and writing. It represents a species of literary biocentrism, and *any* opportunity to teach or practice biocentrism of any sort must be seized, given the level of ignorance of most of us (including students).

NOTES

1. In that spirit the anthology edited by Lynch et al., *Thinking Continental*, which includes personal and academic essays, as well as poems, represents a broad series of linkages between the local and the planetary.

2. Quoted in Kuh, "High Impact-Educational Practices," in *High-Impact Educational Practices*, 13.

3. Kuh, "High-Impact Educational Practices," in *College Learning*.

4. In his conclusions, Kuh recommends that campuses (1) "make it possible for every student to participate in *at least two high-impact activities*" during undergraduate years, that is, in both first-year and upper-level coursework, and (2) create curricular and course structures that make "one high-impact activity . . . available to every student every year." Kuh, "High Impact-Educational Practices," in *High-Impact Educational Practices*, 17. Further, in Kuh's appendix C, one of nineteen reported National Survey of

Student Engagement (NSSE) outcomes that promote involvement in opportunities for active and collaborative learning reads, "Discussed ideas from your readings or classes with faculty members outside of class." Taking students into the literary field directly supports this NSSE outcome. Due to UMW's small size and innovative block schedule, it routinely accomplishes these goals in the majority of its classes.

5. During 2001–5, the lifespan of a three-year FIPSE (Fund for the Improvement of Post-Secondary Education) grant, Montana Western converted to the one-course-at-a-time, "block schedule" model. By 2006 UMW had completely converted to this "X1" model. Rob C. Thomas and Sheila Roberts summarize the UMW transition: "After . . . 3 yr[s] operating the program with freshmen only, rigorous assessment of the results, vigorous campus discussion, contentious and exhaustive approval processes at meetings of the Board of Regents, and a unanimous vote in favor of adopting the system by the UMW Faculty Senate, the transition was approved. In 2005, the University of Montana–Western became the first public, four-year campus in the United States to adopt one-class-at-a-time immersion scheduling for the majority of classes." Thomas and Roberts, "Experience One," 66.

6. Thomas and Roberts, "Experience One," 66.

7. Thomas and Roberts, "Experience One," 66. In their work Thomas and Roberts cite six publications supporting this view, including Dewey, *Logic*, and Beard and Wilson, *Experiential Learning*.

8. In the X1 approach, Blocks I–IV occur in the autumn term and V–VIII in the spring term. Attendance problems diminish, as students have responsibilities with/for each other every day. Besides, missing a class day resembles missing a week in the traditional semester. A species of peer pressure contributes to steady attendance, as small group members don't want to let one another down, given their common tasks.

9. I have taught Savage's *The Pass*, *The Power of the Dog*, and *The Sheep Queen* several times, in both first-year composition classes (Writ 101, required of all students) and at least one upper-level course. *The Power of the Dog* takes place in 1924 in Dillon, which is where UMW is located (though in the novel it is thinly disguised as a town called Herndon), and in Horse Prairie, so in class discussion I probe ways in which the students' college town has changed—or not changed—in the intervening nine decades.

10. As drought conditions took hold early in the twenty-first century (the summers of 2003 and 2004), the reservoir was reduced to 10–15 percent "pool," which re-exposed Armstead, and I and many others explored the old school and depot sites, among others.

11. Savage, interview by Jean W. Ross, in *Contemporary Authors Online*.

12. This ranch was founded by Thomas and Emma Russell Yearian. Emma, known as Big Mama within the extended family, was also known as the Sheep Queen of Idaho, and in 1930 she became the first woman to serve in the Idaho legislature. Savage's photographic memory is suggested by the detail of recall about nooks and crannies in his grandparents' house in letters written decades later.

13. The house has been removed, intact, and trucked to a site in the Bloody Dick Creek canyon owned by Sandy James, the writer's nephew, and his son.

14. In the novel the prissy Phil—a repressed gay, homophobic misogynist—bathes in the creek and is spied by the young Peter Gordon, an autobiographical surrogate who in this novel becomes the avenger of his father (Dr. Johnny Gordon having been driven to drink and suicide after enduring persistent humiliation from Phil). Peter, ostensibly befriending the aloof Phil, in fact goes after him just as Hamlet goes after Claudius. Peter also seeks revenge for his poor mother, the attractive young widow Rose Gordon, whom George Burbank, Phil's stolid younger brother, has married. In his vitriolic contempt, Phil makes Rose's life a living hell and drives her to drink. I like to think students sense those tensions—and the novel's horrific climax—anew as they step exactly where Savage/Peter stepped.

15. In this regard see Handley and Lewis, *True West*.

16. The Writ 101 students' final papers reflect their geographical and topographical immersion. Sometimes their reflections from the trip precipitate into their final, "mini-research" essays, as I call them. (These essays typically run five to seven pages.)

17. When I teach *USFS 1919*, I always screen for students John Kent Harrison's sensitive 2006 adaptation, filmed in British Columbia.

18. The UMW University Relations team used myself, Maclean, and this first-year writing class in the inaugural video of a series of faculty profiles highlighting what some of us try and accomplish in the field. See "Alan and Maclean," University of Montana–Western, http://vimeo.com/195479168.

19. By the twenty-first century more than three hundred designated riverkeepers were promoting the goals of the Riverkeepers, a conservationist nonprofit established in 1966 to protect American rivers. For more information, see www.riverkeepers.org.

20. The three locations are (1) the broad sandbar where the frustrated brothers find Neal with Old Rawhide, who is drunk, naked, asleep, and seriously sunburned; (2) a "rock garden" section near the junction with the Clearwater River where O'Connell narrates that the young brothers escaped to spend their afternoons fishing; and (3) the spot featured in the climatic scene where the Reverend and Norman watch Paul, the great fisherman, plunge into the current, rod tip raised, to follow and land his ultimate trout.

21. Originally named by Meriwether Lewis in 1805, it is easily the deepest canyon along the Missouri River in Montana, with walls looming hundreds of feet high and a series of specialized plants growing within it. Mann Gulch, an undistinguished canyon only three miles long, gained notoriety after an August 5, 1949, wildfire that killed thirteen smokejumpers.

22. Mann Gulch became an "official" hike listed in the fifth edition of Schneider, *Hiking Montana*.

23. The Minidoka (Japanese-American) internment camp site, incorporated into the National Park System in 2001, is a racist symbol of presence and absence. The trip included a morning spent walking the grounds of the site.

24. Brownell and Swaner, "Outcomes of High-Impact Educational Practices," 2.

25. Kuh, O'Donnell, and Schneider, "HIPs at Ten," 14.

Beard, Colin, and John P. Wilson. *Experiential Learning: A Handbook for Education, Training and Coaching*. 2nd ed. London: Kogan Page, 2006.

Brownell, Jayne E., and Lynn E Swaner. "Outcomes of High-Impact Educational Practices: A Literature Review." *Diversity and Democracy* (AAC&U) 12, no. 2 (2009). https://www.aacu.org/publications-research/periodicals/outcomes-high-impact-educational-practices-literature-review.

Contemporary Authors Online. Detroit: Gale Research, 1999. https://www.gale.com/c/contemporary-authors-online.

Cronon, William. "Only Connect: The Goals of a Liberal Education." *Liberal Education* 85, no. 1 (1999): 6–13.

Dewey, John. *Logic: The Theory of Inquiry*. In *John Dewey: The Later Works, 1925–1953*, volume 12, edited by Jo Ann Boydston. Carbondale: Southern Illinois University Press, 1991.

Handley, William R., and Nathaniel Lewis, eds. *True West: Authenticity and the American West*. Lincoln: University of Nebraska Press, 2004.

Johnson, David W., Roger T. Johnson, and Karl A. Smith. *Active Learning: Cooperation in the College Classroom*. Edina MN: Interaction Book Company, 1998.

Kolb, Alice Y., and David A. Kolb. "Learning Styles and Learning Spaces: Enhancing Experiential Learning in Higher Education." *Academy of Management Learning & Education* 4, no. 2 (2005): 193–212.

Kolb, David A. *Experiential Learning: Experience as the Source of Learning and Development*. Englewood Cliffs NJ: Prentice Hall, 1984.

Kuh, George D. "High-Impact Educational Practices." In *College Learning for a New Global Century*. Washington DC: American Association of Colleges and Universities, 2007.

———. "High-Impact Educational Practices: Who Has Access to Them and Why They Matter for All Students." In *High-Impact Educational Practices: What They Are, Who Has Access to Them, and Why They Matter*. Washington DC: American Association of Colleges and Universities, 2008.

Kuh, George D., Ken O'Donnell, and Carol Geary Schneider. "HIPs at Ten." *Change* 49, no. 5 (2017). https://doi.org/10.1080/00091383.2017.1366805.

Lynch, Tom, Susan Naramore Maher, Drucilla Wall, and O. Alan Weltzien, eds. *Thinking Continental: Writing the Planet One Place at a Time*. Lincoln: University of Nebraska Press, 2017.

Maclean, Norman, *A River Runs Through It and Other Stories*. Chicago: University of Chicago Press, 1976.

———. *Young Men and Fire*. Chicago: University of Chicago Press, 1992.

Rogers, Carl R., and H. Jerome Freiberg. *Freedom to Learn*. 3rd ed. Upper Saddle River NJ: Prentice Hall, 1994.

Savage, Thomas. *The Pass*. 1944. Helena MT: Drumlummon Institute in conjunction with Riverbend, 2009.

———. *The Power of the Dog*. 1967. Boston: Little, Brown, 2001.

———. *The Sheep Queen* (*I Heard My Sister Speak My Name*). 1977. Boston: Little, Brown, 2001.

Schneider, Bill. *Hiking Montana.* 5th ed. Helena MT: Falcon Press, 1995.

Thomas, Rob C., and Sheila Roberts, "Experience One: Teaching the Geoscience Curriculum in the Field Using Experiential Immersion Learning." In *Field Geology Education: Historical Perspectives and Modern Approaches*, edited by Steven J. Whitmeyer, David W. Mogk, and Eric J. Pyle. GSA Special Papers, volume 461. Boulder CO: Geological Society of America, 2009.

10

Placing the Pacific Northwest on the Literary Map
Teaching Ella Rhoads Higginson's *Mariella, of Out-West*

LAURA LAFFRADO

This chapter offers strategies for teaching the early twentieth-century novel *Mariella, of Out-West* (1902), written by a neglected Pacific Northwest author, Ella Rhoads Higginson.[1] My discussion emerges from the vital intersection of literary recovery and pedagogy. A crucial stage of the recovery of a forgotten text is the informed teaching of that text. The act of teaching a work adds it to syllabi and to students' knowledge, both important to generating a more visible presence for a text, both in and out of the classroom. Additionally, when teaching an overlooked region-specific work, the literary and cultural studies of that region—here the Pacific Northwest—become further incorporated into broader disciplines of literary and cultural studies—in this case, those of the American West. Among pedagogical approaches included here are ways for students to become active agents in the work of literary recovery, joining their instructor in accessing new information that adds to a more thorough understanding and analysis of an underexamined text. This chapter provides new contributions to the confluence of recovery and pedagogy by promoting a dynamic mix of textual context and teaching strategies that make plain that recovered texts are readily teachable and will expand and diversify the range of canonical texts selected for course reading.

Within literary and cultural studies, the Pacific Northwest remains, as Susan Kollin writes, "largely undertheorized."[2] The theoretical implications

of recovering Higginson and her work reside in the expansion of the parameters and possibilities of both the West and of western writing. That is, to
plainly include the Pacific Northwest in the West and to include Higginson
and her writing in the body of work by western women authors is to invite
a refiguring of both the West and of western writing, one that incorporates
the sweeping region of mountains and trees bordering the Pacific Ocean,
as well as women's writing from that region.

In the absence of such a reimagining, scholars such as Cathryn Halverson
have understandably but mistakenly concluded that "the early twentieth-
century Pacific Northwest" had "a paucity of prominent Northwest writers
and narratives."[3] Correspondingly, John Cleman has argued that "a major
(or canonical) distinctly regionalist work of Pacific Northwest fiction—
comparable to *Country of the Pointed Firs*, *Adventures of Huckleberry Finn*,
My Ántonia, or *The Sound and the Fury*—has yet to appear."[4] This chapter extends such scholarship on western literature, pushing against these
narratives of scarcity and arguing for *Mariella* as a major work of fiction.

Two recent books on the literature of the American West also argue
against such scarcity. In *Re-imagining the Modern American West*, Richard
Etulain "discuss[es] key novelists," including earlier regional women writers
such as Mary Hunter Austin, Willa Cather, and Ruth Suckow, "who lived
during the century that stretched from the 1890s to the 1990s and whose
works help us understand the shifting interpretations of the modern West."[5]
Likewise, Nicolas Witschi's *A Companion to the Literature and Culture of
the American West* features a range of valuable essays on late nineteenth-
century U.S. western fiction, including texts by western women writers.
However, both of these far-ranging collections overlook Higginson and
her foundational work.

Important critical work performed specifically on women's literature of
the American West includes L. L. Lee and Merrill Lewis's pioneering study
Women, Women Writers, and the West, as well as work by scholars such as
Paula Gunn Allen, Melody Graulich, Annette Kolodny, Vera Norwood,
Tey Diana Rebolledo, Lois Rudnick, and others. In her foundational essay
"Western Biodiversity: Rereading Nineteenth-Century American Women's
Writing," Graulich perceptively argues that "the West is a vast, diverse,
rapidly changing region. Even the most commonly accepted geopolitical

definition today, that the West is defined by aridity, cannot encompass the whole region; what of the Pacific Northwest and hence the seaside stories and poems by Higginson and [Pauline] Johnson?"[6] My choice to teach Higginson as a western author and *Mariella* as a western novel is informed by these pioneering scholars, as well as by Nina Baym's *Women Writers of the American West, 1833–1927*. Baym's interests in the women writers she discusses "are governed by," among other issues, "how the authors showed women making lives for themselves in the West—what they gave to the West, and what it gave to them," as well as "how they represented the West."[7] Such concerns are central to the work Higginson performs in *Mariella*, a book in which the female protagonist is identified in the title as representing the West and, within the novel's text, as shaped and defined by the West.

Baym also addresses western regions, writing that "these authors tried to give detailed depictions of the western places where their accounts were set. There might be an overarching and abstract concept of the West, but on the ground there were many different Wests," that is, various parts of the West were "each distinct in history, landform, and climate."[8] Higginson's focus in *Mariella* on distinguishing Pacific Northwest characteristics provides readers with a specific western region, differing from other parts of the West, yet also one of "many different Wests."

In general Baym argues that "the West was seen to allow women to become capable, physically active, independent, honest, and forthright. Ideas of bigness and spaciousness, of freedom from convention, of physical development, contribute to a sense of the western heroine as a new kind of person." Further, "the West, with its supposed lack of class distinction, its acceptance of every person on his or her own merits, presumably allowed women without pedigrees to make something of themselves."[9] Baym's assessment of how the West was perceived to empower women closely corresponds with Higginson's portrayal of the lives of white western women in *Mariella*. Indeed, Baym's remarks may almost be read as a summary of Higginson's depiction of white women in *Mariella*.

My choice to teach Higginson as a western author and *Mariella* as a western novel is also influenced by Victoria Lamont's important *Westerns: A Women's History* (2016). Lamont's subject, the popular western, is not the genre in which *Mariella* is written. However, Lamont's argument "that the popular western, widely considered a male-authored tradition, was founded as much by women writers as by men and played a significant role in American women's literary history at the turn of the twentieth century" amplifies the ways that western women writers such as Higginson have been neglected across genres. That is, to teach Higginson as a western author and *Mariella* as a western novel is to reinscribe both back into their "significant role in American women's literary history at the turn of the twentieth century."[10] Further, reading *Mariella* as a western novel expands that category by explicitly incorporating the Pacific Northwest into the larger West and so augmenting that category with the possibilities of women's writing and fictive scripts of women's lives in the Pacific regions of the West.

This chapter provides approaches to teaching *Mariella* in six sections: first, author's background; second, *Mariella*'s status as the foundational novel of the Pacific Northwest; third, detailed summary of the text; fourth, proposed topics helpful for teaching *Mariella*; fifth, pedagogical uses of digital resources such as online databases and digital archives; and sixth, discussion of supplementary critical material regarding women's literary regionalism.

Background and Context

I begin by providing background and context for instructors, which is particularly necessary given the overlooked status of Higginson and her work. Although Higginson is little known today, more than a century ago she was the most influential Pacific Northwest literary writer in the United States. People across the nation and around the world were first introduced to the Pacific Northwest when they read Higginson's award-winning poetry, fiction, and nonfiction.[11] Higginson's descriptions of the majestic mountains, vast forests, and scenic waters of the Puget Sound presented the then-remote, unfamiliar Pacific Northwest to eager readers. Her distinctive characterizations of the white women and men who inhabited the region revealed to readers what it was like to live in this particular part of the United States as opposed to other, better-known regions such as New England or the American South.[12] Higginson's celebrated writings were the very first to prominently place the Pacific Northwest on the literary map of the United States.

Higginson's talent was widely recognized in her lifetime. Her publisher was New York's prestigious Macmillan Company. She was awarded best-short-story prizes from well-known magazines such as *Collier's* and *McClure's*. Her poetry was set to music and performed internationally by celebrated dramatic singers, including Enrico Caruso. And in 1931 Higginson was elected first poet laureate of Washington State. In her day Higginson and her writing attracted international literary attention to the Pacific Northwest. However, in the last decades of her life most of her books went out of print and her prominence dramatically diminished.

A mix of reasons informs this movement from celebrated to forgotten author. In broad terms, during the first half of the twentieth century many if not most once-popular U.S. women writers experienced a similar eclipse of their earlier literary success. They and their works became gendered casualties of the early U.S. twentieth century's standardization of the literary canon. Academic gatekeepers up to the late twentieth century ignored many previously well received works by women and by people of color, while also discounting numerous literary texts that they considered narrow due to a regionalist focus. My aim here is not to reiterate the useful arguments on this subject but rather to provide brief context for instructors to share with students regarding what became the decades-long scholarly neglect of *Mariella*.[13] As a consequence of such activity in the academy, the admiration early twentieth-century readers and reviewers accorded *Mariella* was displaced and muted. Destabilized by academic debates of canonicity, *Mariella* remained outside the margins of scholarly consideration. It lingered there even after prevailing academic assumptions were again reconsidered and recast.

With the 1970s feminist movement and subsequent efforts of feminist literary critics, new scholarly attention focused on forgotten women's writing. During this key moment the texts and literary reputations of women writers such as New England's Mary E. Wilkins Freeman and Sarah Orne Jewett, the American Southwest's and California's Mary Hunter Austin, and Appalachia's Mary Noailles Murfree were restored to prominence. Yet Higginson and her work remained overlooked. A factor in this continued neglect was Higginson's regional location in the West, far from the literary establishments of the Northeast and the literary locations of other writers. However, with the turn into the twenty-first century, scholars directed their attention to disregarded writings from areas of the United States that were less represented in well-known American literature. This welcome undertaking resulted in new attention to Higginson's writing and reputation, which has activated a recuperation of both Higginson and her work.

Foundational Novel of the Pacific Northwest

No matter the course in which I assign *Mariella*, I begin by positioning it as the foundational novel of the Pacific Northwest. In doing so, I put pressure on students' understandings of canonicity and I also present notions of literary regionalism. This introduction differs in degree depending on the course topic and level. I have successfully taught *Mariella* in a 200-level general-education survey of American literature for undergraduate non–English majors; a 300-level period course of texts from the U.S. Civil War to World War I for undergraduate English majors; a 400-level seminar on U.S. literary regionalism for advanced undergraduate English majors; a 400-level major authors course on Higginson for undergraduate English majors and nonmajors; and a graduate seminar on U.S. regionalist writing. I supply this list to provide readers with guidance regarding courses in which one might teach *Mariella* or indeed courses in which one might incorporate any other neglected text into the assigned reading.

While *Mariella* was once celebrated as the foundational novel of the Pacific Northwest, that status is long forgotten. Currently there is no critically accepted foundational novel of the region. Such a notable absence is largely due, I argue, to critical neglect of the Northwest as a literary region before the 1960s. In the many decades since *Mariella* appeared, novels by authors such as Ken Kesey, Sherman Alexie, and Ruth Ozeki have skillfully employed regionalist representations of the Pacific Northwest. However, it is imperative to integrate into our teaching the early twentieth-century beginnings of Pacific Northwest literature.

One of the earliest published novels written by a white woman born west of the Mississippi, *Mariella* was compared by critics to novels by Jane Austen, Leo Tolstoy, and Émile Zola, among others. Reviews across the United States highly praised *Mariella*. For example, a reviewer for the *San Francisco Examiner* wrote, "Jack London of Oakland and Ella Higginson of Seattle are putting forth more and better works of fiction than any other writers on the Coast."[14] A review in the *San Francisco Bulletin* read, "Her characters are as strong, as individual, as any created by Dickens or Thackeray."[15] The *Buffalo Express* reviewer wrote, "The author's style and breadth and power are American, and . . . 'Mariella' is a fine American novel."[16] Reviewers and readers alike judged Higginson's writing—its skill, artistry, and sympathetic character development—to be a valuable, appealing part of regionalist U.S. literature. As a result, *Mariella* rapidly went through multiple editions. In December 1902 the *Seattle Daily Times* informed readers that the book's publisher, Macmillan, was unable to ship more copies of *Mariella*: "Owing to the great demand in the East for the book they cannot bind them fast enough to anywhere nearly keep pace with orders."[17] *Mariella*'s international popularity was such that more than two years later the *Tacoma Daily News* reported that the Australian market was requesting a large order of the book.[18]

Having established *Mariella*'s critical reception and popularity for students, I then turn to excerpts from regional works with a largely uncontested foundational status, such as Willa Cather's *My Ántonia* and Mark Twain's *The Adventures of Huckleberry Finn*, in order to place *Mariella* in conversation with these texts. For example, I read aloud the openings of both *My Ántonia* and *Huckleberry Finn* followed by a reading of the opening of *Mariella*. I then ask students to identify and consider shared aspects among these novelistic beginnings. Students quickly discover the bildungsroman structure of all three texts, noting that the three main characters are young and inexperienced. They also identify the regional descriptions that color the opening sections. I ask students to reflect on the uses of first-person or third-person narration as well as the narrative voice employed in each novel. By comparing passages from these books with sections of *Mariella*, students recognize similarities among the texts in literary uses of region, dialect, and plot. *Mariella* thus is (re)positioned as an American bildungsroman among other novels with which it was classed in the early twentieth century.

Comparisons with (other) foundational U.S. novels lead to animated class discussions regarding the significant roles played by unexamined cultural biases and assumptions in canonization. Students begin to recognize the frequent disconnect between a text's popularity when initially published and its later literary status. Consideration of *Mariella* as the foundational novel of the Pacific Northwest unsettles students' received notions about literature, preparing them to read *Mariella* more critically.

Summary of the Text

A compelling drama of family struggle, romance, and cultural change, *Mariella* focuses on a strong white female protagonist in the early Pacific Northwest. It is important for students to recognize that in its attention to the social and economic struggles of the white Palmer family, the overall story line of *Mariella* maintains ethnocentrism and reinforces settler colonialism. As discussed in more detail below, though the Palmers occupy Straits Salish land, Indigenous groups appear in only a small portion of the text. Additionally, the novel examines significant marital constraints that limit both white women and female agency. These restrictions are echoed in portrayals of the Pacific Northwest region as equally confining because of its wild nature and sparse economic prospects. As discussed below, Higginson's figuring of region demonstrates that region is more than merely a setting for the story but is instead part of a larger discourse that offers disparate depictions of U.S. culture.

The narrative of the novel that drew the attention and admiration of critics and readers features as its main character fourteen-year-old Mariella Palmer, who grows to early adulthood in the book. Mariella lives with her parents on "an isolated ranch in Puget Sound."[19] This is "the land of forest and plain and desert; of deep-flowing, majestic rivers and vast spaces swimming from snow-mountain to snow-mountain."[20] Mrs. Palmer's stultifying marriage, secret adultery, and inability to respond to her sensitive, imaginative daughter run parallel in the text with Mariella's knowledge of her mother's deceit and Mariella's long engagement to a man whose poverty would force her into a life of drudgery were she finally to marry him.

Her parents' unhappiness and impoverished lives despite and because of the beautiful Pacific Northwest region in which they live confirm for Mariella how wretched her future life may be. As her mother's "high-pitched voice arose in hot and bitter dispute with her husband . . . Mariella leaned her elbows upon the table, and pressed her palms over her ears, so she could not hear. Her gaze went out the window; out to the blue stretch of sea. . . . Far to the west, across those miles of water, the majestic Olympian range of snow-peaks stood out in splendid fire. She was shaken with the longing to get away from the sordid, coarse tumult of her daily life."[21] Before escape can occur, two central conflicts established early in *Mariella* must be resolved.

First, early in the novel Mariella starts to discover the secret of her mother's adultery. This begins when an angry playmate "burst[s] out . . . 'anyhow—*Mr. Mallory don't come to see my ma!*'" Mariella "understood perfectly" that the outburst was "an insult . . . intended . . . for her mother; but she was in the dark as to its nature."[22] At another point, when her father is away, Mariella, watching from her bedroom window at night, sees a man "stepping stealthily across the porch."[23] As the novel proceeds, Mariella gradually comprehends the illicit nature of her mother's relationship with Mr. Mallory and struggles to come to terms with her mother's deceit.

Mariella is likewise deeply vexed by her pledge to marry her handsome longtime sweetheart, Mahlon, who had been her classmate before poverty forced him to end his formal schooling. Despite her love for Mahlon and her promise to marry him, as she reaches adulthood "Mariella's soul was yearning for something different."[24] Nonetheless, she valiantly tries "to imagine the future as his wife. She saw herself rising in the gray dawns, year after year, to cook his breakfasts; toiling all day at housework, cooking his dinner."[25]

Correspondingly, Mrs. Palmer is determined that her daughter use marriage as a means to escape the harsh western life she herself has endured. She insists Mariella "mak[e] the best match 'n town." Without such a marriage for her daughter, she fears for Mariella's future in the rugged Pacific Northwest, especially after she and Mr. Palmer are gone. She asks Mariella, "What are you goin' to do when you're left all alone in the world? . . . You're a delicate little thing—you ain't worth shucks."[26] Mariella's long, fraught engagement, Mrs. Palmer's adultery, and Mariella's knowledge of that adultery constitute the foremost pressures of the novel's plot.

Proposed Teaching Topics

Central features of *Mariella* provide rich opportunities for effective teaching that lead students to productive analysis, discussion, and understanding of the novel and its uses of region. Below I offer suggested teaching topics.[27]

Exclusions/Erasures

Although *Mariella* is set in the Indigenous Straits Salish region, all major characters are presented as being of Anglo European descent. This obvious exclusion/erasure of Indigenous peoples and cultures leads students to consider issues of race, gender, and genre. It also makes plain the raced effects of the novel's default whiteness. However, Higginson's accurate references to Straits Salish Native groups, precise descriptions of Lummi and Nooksack practices, and use of Chinook Jargon suggest her familiarity with details of these cultures. That is, the exclusion of Straits Salish material from *Mariella* is not due to Higginson's lack of knowledge. This deliberate omission leads to vital class discussions regarding raced exclusion and erasure.

To ground this discussion, I employ chapter 31 of *Mariella*, which is devoted entirely to a gambling event held by various Native groups passing through town. Mariella, reflecting Higginson's awareness of regional Native groups and practices, explains, "The Lummis and the Nooksacks are camped down on the beach; they are going to have a big sing-gamble game." She anticipates "canoe races" and the arrival of the Alaskas, whose "canoes are beautifully carven."[28] Higginson's knowledge of regional Native practices also appears in descriptions of types of sticks, chanting, and game rules. Such details mix with racialized language such as "squaws," "barbaric," "weird music with its fierce perfect rhythm," and "beating, chanting, and wild gesticulations."[29]

Higginson also describes "scarlet-blanketed" Native women "stolidly watching the game, their faces revealing neither triumph nor disappointment."[30] The women are marked by immobility (making plain that they are not Native men: the Native men are in motion playing the games) and their race- and gender-specific clothing (no white woman or Native man is described as wearing such blankets). The portrayal of unreadable faces and clothing of Native women contrasts sharply with the more conventional portrayal of white Mariella, who, "dressed for a walk," is "flushed and glowing with excitement."[31]

After drawing attention to these and other passages, I ask students to discuss implications of these descriptions. I also ask why this chapter is in *Mariella* and how, for example, the novel would change were the chapter to be omitted. Additionally, I explain that in some of her nonfiction Higginson foregrounds Native representation, and I ask how differences between Higginson's writing of fiction/nonfiction might lead to under/representation of Natives.

Opportunities for White Women

In *Mariella*, Higginson explores the narrow range of gendered scripts available to white women in the Pacific Northwest at the time. Her consideration of such restrictions implicitly invokes divergent notions of the fin-de-siècle idea of the New Woman, particularly women's right to sexual self-expression. It is thus unsurprising that a central tension of the novel occurs regarding marriage. Mrs. Palmer believes that marriage, while often unreliable as a means of economic security, nonetheless has the greatest potential to provide Mariella with a stable future. Mariella, having witnessed her parents' unhappy marriage as well as the cheerless marriages of neighbors, resists matrimony. After a man of stable income courts Mariella, she and her mother argue. Her mother exclaims, "The only man of any style that's ever looked at you! You keep your chin up in the air, an' you'll drive your pigs to a pretty market, or die an old maid"; Mariella replies, "I'd rather be an old maid fifty times over, than to have all this talk about marrying."[32] Mrs. Palmer's insistence that marriage is Mariella's sole chance for a better life emerges from her own bleak, premarital past as a harshly treated indentured servant. Mariella's defiance signals that regional culture has changed for white women during Mrs. Palmer's lifetime. Similarly, the older Mrs. Palmer's rough commodifying of Mariella's chastity as pigs driven to market reflects her pragmatic view of marriage as an exchange, just as the younger Mariella's avowal that remaining unmarried is a viable possibility indicates her more novice view of marriage as a woman's option.

A later scene portrays Mrs. Palmer's own constrained choices and the ways in which gendered restrictions may provoke a woman to transgress:

> In many ways she was a powerful woman; but she had the weakness that may be found in many women—the desire for love, the kind of love that bears ceaseless homage with it. . . . Mrs. Palmer, with her head high in the air and her mouth scornful, declined the milder and more comfortable attachment which is known as affection. She would have devotion from her husband, or she would have nothing. So for many years she had nothing. Then another man offered her devotion, and she accepted it.[33]

The language in this passage, perhaps unexpectedly for students, abstains from criticizing Mrs. Palmer's adultery and adultery itself.[34] Instead, Mrs. Palmer's affair with Mr. Mallory is characterized as "devotion" that is "offered" and "accepted." After "many years" on a lonely ranch, with no formal education, no one to advise her, and an affectionate but not ardent husband, Mrs. Palmer chooses the only path available to her that provides the love she craves.

Once we have reviewed these passages and others like them, I ask students to consider how the novel would differ if the early Pacific Northwest had offered more possibilities for poor white women. That is, what if Mariella had been able to leave home and attend college in New England? What if Mrs. Palmer had a life less arduous than one spent working the land around Puget Sound? What if both or either of the women had been exposed to the cultural possibilities of New Womanhood or ways that women's sexual self-expression was emerging in other regions of the nation? What kinds of women might have emerged from such changed regional circumstances?

Speech

Dialect or accent and regionalism figure significantly in *Mariella*. Language used by characters regularly serves as a site of tension, disruptively signaling a character's class status, lack of formal education, or provincial attitude, among other identity markers. This is displayed, for instance, when Mariella and her sweetheart, Mahlon, speak after a long absence during which her education has continued and his has not: "Mahlon pronounced the last two words 'a-tall.' Mariella noticed it, and loathed herself at once for noticing it. 'How could he be expected to pronounce words correctly?' she thought with fierce self-reproach. 'His parents talk that way, and he had to leave school and work.'"[35] In this complex scene that points both to speech and to speaking, Mariella detects provincialism in Mahlon's speech, berates herself for that detection, and understands that without formal education one's speech will likely resemble the (uneducated) speech of one's parents. Students sympathetically recognize this intersection of speech and formal education. In discussion of this passage and others like it, students describe their often painful awareness of (mis)pronunciation in their own or another's speech.

Higginson also uses speech to dramatize changes in class status that have emerged from the economic boom occurring in this region. Mrs. De Haro, a poor, uneducated local woman, has become wealthy after selling her suddenly valuable real estate. Higginson describes her as she attempts to impress new arrivals from Boston with her wealth: "I've always been crazy to hear Florence Nightingale sing. I've often thought, well, dear me! Why not charter a special car an' bring a troupe of big op'ry singers out here to Kulshan, an' let 'em just sing us up full for once?"[36] Mrs. De Haro's speech mixes dialect, boastfulness, and comic ignorance. Gains in economic status plainly have been unaccompanied by advances in her speech. Discussion of passages like this one leads students to examine the disconnect that often exists when monetary wealth, language use, and class status come into play.

To further explore the role of speech, I ask students to select any paragraph of dialogue from *Mariella* and rewrite that paragraph by conventionalizing its language. Afterward, in-class comparison of Higginson's paragraphs with students' rewritten paragraphs heightens understandings of strategic ways Higginson uses speech to classify her characters for readers.

Environment

In *Mariella* depictions of the Pacific Northwest region as markedly unlike other U.S. regions align the environment with broader themes of the novel and its larger historical moment. Higginson's precise descriptions of the Pacific Northwest environment significantly inform her portrayals of place. This usage extends well beyond providing scenery. For example, in the following passage Mariella travels with others to a nearby cove:

> They had sailed ten miles across the bay, rounded the Cape of the Wind-bent Trees, and were just entering the small but beautiful Smuggler's Cove. The entrance was narrow; on either side masses of long olive kelp coiled and twisted, and floated over dangerous rocks. Inside, the bay widened to the curve of a horseshoe; the heavily timbered shores sloped up steeply to a height of a thousand feet; there was a small beach of sand, pebbles, and agates. The shores were rocky, but the shallow-rooted firs had managed to get a footing to the water's edge, to grow straight and tall, and blend into the dark green background of forest.[37]

Higginson's rich descriptions deftly include measurements (ten miles, a thousand feet) size (small, narrow, masses), color (olive, dark green), shape (rounded, sloped, straight), and diverse natural objects such as kelp, rocks, timber, sand, pebbles, and agates. A distant history is implied, one in which kelp massed and coiled, shores became heavily timbered, and firs thrived despite rocks. The description of Smuggler's Cove so exactly portrays this particular region that the cove specifically and the region generally join the novel's roster of Pacific Northwest characters.

To help students appreciate the role of environment in *Mariella*, I ask them to name any descriptions of region that they recollect from the novel. The resulting list is typically quite extensive. After compiling these descriptions, we discuss why such details are so readily recalled from their reading and, correspondingly, why Higginson's depictions of the environment are sometimes more memorable for readers than other details in the book. I then extend our analysis of environment and place in the novel by inviting students to consider how *Mariella* would read were all environmental references eliminated or were the novel to be set in a different U.S. region.

Religious Education

Sin, confession, and prayer substantially inform *Mariella*'s plot. In particular, the novel makes plain that the opportunity to receive religious schooling, as with other forms of formal education in the text, depends on region and class status. The book promotes sympathy for those unable to access that schooling. For example, after a minister scolds young Mariella for what he perceives as spiritual ignorance, he is rebuked by her teacher: "Why not teach children to love and worship God through the sunshine and the flowers, the birds and the woods; through love and truth and kind hearts toward their neighbors; and leave the Bible with all its sublime beauty and divine mystery for them to read when they are old enough to interpret it for themselves?"[38] The teacher does not defend Mariella—who is poor and lives in an isolated region—as one for whom such religious schooling has been unobtainable, though that is the case. Rather, he broadly criticizes formal religious schooling itself, arguing instead for religious education grounded in more generally available realms of nature and community.

In another scene, as Mr. Palmer, Mariella's elderly father, is dying, he recalls the brief religious schooling of his childhood: "There was another prayer we used to say together. I hadn't thought of it for years an' years; but it seems as if I could say it clear through." He muses, "Seems as if God 'u'd hear a prayer an old dying man had learned, when he was such a little fellow, at his Sund'y-school teacher's knee."[39] Although Mr. Palmer barely recalls his prayers, he is not condemned for lack of religious knowledge. Instead, seeking prayer for solace as he dies is portrayed with pity and understanding. In *Mariella*, religious education, with its power to console and to encourage love of nature and people, is wrongly constrained by region and class status. Using scenes such as these, I ask students to consider how topics of organized religion, religious schooling, and region intersect in the novel and how such issues shape the text.

Pedagogical Use of Digital Archives and Online Databases

Working with an understudied text, as well as its corresponding lack of critical and pedagogical guidance, may be daunting for instructors and readers at all levels. However, with access to various online databases and archives that have become available in digital form, instructors are increasingly able to design assignments that lead students to fascinating material that is relevant to an understudied text. Such material may include, for instance, data reflecting demographics and regional laws. In this section I provide examples of digital sources that have proved fruitful in teaching *Mariella*.

Online U.S. Census Records

As I begin the use of census records, I foreground class discussion by making plain that earlier U.S. Census records undercounted Coast Salish peoples and left uncounted African Americans. I also make clear that because of government surveillance fueled by xenophobia, some Chinese immigrants sought to avoid being counted.[40] I then ask students how this knowledge will affect their reading and use of census records.

Within these racist parameters, U.S. Census records plainly reveal that the demographics of the region in which Higginson set *Mariella* differed significantly from those of other U.S. regions. Most fundamentally, the Pacific Northwest was markedly underpopulated compared to, for example, the U.S. Northeast. A straightforward examination of U.S. Census records from 1900 and 1930 is highly instructive for students. U.S. Census records list the population of the New England states as 5,592,017 in 1900 and 8,166,341 in 1930.[41] Conversely, U.S. Census records show the combined populations of Washington and Oregon totaling 931,639 in 1900 and 2,517,182 in 1930. Further, census lists for Washington and Oregon in these decades include a warning of high margins of error, underscoring the difficulty of an accurate tally given the then-remote nature of these regions.

Students' examination of such data leads to discussion regarding Pacific

Northwest demographics. I ask students to consider the effects of later white colonization of the Pacific Northwest compared to earlier white colonization of New England. I also pose questions regarding the nineteenth-century perception and reality of the Pacific Northwest as difficult to reach. Additionally, given that census data make it plain that Higginson's regional literary setting was far less populated than settings employed by most regionalist writers of the time, I invite students to consider the consequences of a less populated region for Higginson's writing of *Mariella*. Such consequences may include notions of a very limited literary community, the absence of publishing centers, and the later beginnings of a regional literature.

Continuing our use of census records, I direct students to the ratio between female and male populations. For example, students see that the 1860 U.S. Census, the first to attempt to formally calculate the population of Washington Territory, recorded a population that was nearly 75 percent male, almost all of those males being white. This sharp disparity resulted from events such as the Fraser River gold rush (1858), which drew thousands of white men unaccompanied by women, as well as from economic panics and natural disasters that rendered the region undesirable for further white colonialization. I then ask how this knowledge affects their reading and use of census records regarding female and male populations.

Additionally, sending students to other sections of census records will reveal, for example, that in 1900 the New England states had 98 men for every 100 women, while the Pacific Northwest had 128 men for every 100 women. Using these ratios, we see that Higginson located *Mariella* in a region occupied by significantly more white men than women, data that, given the number of available men, leads students to reexamine Mariella's and Mrs. Palmer's views of marriage. Such data generate productive discussion regarding the ways that Higginson in *Mariella* charts the social and material conditions of white women in the Pacific Northwest.

Women's Suffrage Records

While women's suffrage was finally achieved in 1920 with the Nineteenth Amendment to the U.S. Constitution, some individual states granted female suffrage significantly earlier than 1920. Using databases available through the women's studies online discussion network H-Women, students may examine such dates and recognize that western states and territories achieved more extensive female suffrage much earlier than eastern states did. For example, female suffrage was approved in Idaho in 1896, Washington in 1910, and Oregon in 1912. It is important to remind students that despite these achievements, various oppressive restrictions existed that were designed to deny many nonwhite women the right to vote.

After examining such data, we discuss the reasons for and the role of earlier female suffrage in the West. For example, Sherilyn Cox Bennion summarizes conjectures regarding the success of women's suffrage in the West, ranging from the less settled aspect of the West compared to the East, the role of "frontier spirit promot[ing] a sense of equality as women and men worked together," and the hope that suffrage would bring publicity and thus more settlers to the West.[42] Higginson's use of actual Pacific Northwest regional conditions of remoteness, a majority male population, and a predisposition toward white women's enfranchisement enabled her to depict in *Mariella* a less established region inhabited by fictive white women who were, like their region, often less settled and more self-determined.

Other databases that may be used are, for example, the free, open-source Chronicling America, which includes texts published through 1922 and can be searched for reviews of Higginson's works and interviews with Higginson. Searches of the free Google news archive yield a range of articles, advertisements, and notices of Higginson's periodical publications. Databases available by institutional subscription, such as the American Periodical Series and ProQuest Historical Newspapers, may be similarly mined for details concerning Higginson's literary career and publications. When pointed in these directions, students avidly engage the work of recovery and search databases with the zeal of treasure hunters. They embrace the role of partnering with their instructor in seeking new information, much of which is genuinely surprising and which contributes to a fuller awareness of the text.

Women's Literary Regionalism

Providing students with supplementary material on women's literary regionalism critically informs students' reading of *Mariella*. I use excerpts from, for example, Judith Fetterley and Marjorie Pryse's *Writing Out of Place:*

Regionalism, Women, and American Literary Culture to teach women's literary regionalism not "as a fixed literary category" but "as the site of a dialogical critical conversation." That is, as Fetterley and Pryse cogently put it, "just because a story adopts a regional setting, it does not necessarily take up the question of what 'region' means or how it is deployed."[43] I also assign excerpts from an essay by Frank Davey to introduce students to his identification of regionalism as less "a geographical manifestation" than a discourse "represent[ing] a general social or political strategy for resisting meanings generated by others in a nation-state, particularly those generated in geographical areas which can be constructed by the regionalism as central or powerful."[44]

Reading critically about literary regionalism enables students to discern Higginson's own use of literary regionalism. For example, in *Mariella*, Higginson demonstrates the region performing nationally as a distinct location that claimed recognition from readers and membership among more known, established U.S. regions. Further, Higginson's depictions of the Pacific Northwest as singular in its character disputed readings, "constructed by the nation-state to serve its own interests," of the region as inaccessible, unlike other U.S. regions, and thus less significant. Instead, Higginson's critical regionalism "offer[ed] alternative understandings" of U.S. culture, drawing readers into her regional discourse.[45]

I invite students to consider that Higginson's use of region "to foreground a critique of the location of women" enables her to construct Pacific Northwest white women as passionate, vexed products of their environment.[46] Throughout *Mariella*, Higginson portrays the Pacific Northwest region as emergent and unstable, a place that functions culturally by producing white women shaped by regional characteristics—less established and more emergent themselves. Higginson's use of the Pacific Northwest in *Mariella*—her incorporation of its qualities into her characters and narrative—introduced readers to ways that regional discourses about the unfamiliar, intriguing Pacific Northwest might function. In this manner and others *Mariella* enrolled in critical conversation with other regionalist discourses.

Finally, teaching *Mariella* draws vital attention to the overlooked position of the Pacific Northwest region in both U.S. literature in general and western American literature from the late nineteenth and early twentieth centuries. Working at the intersection of recovery and pedagogy results in the important addition of neglected texts such as *Mariella* that extend the literary canon. Thus, recovering Higginson and her work expands the parameters and the possibilities of both the West and of writing of the American West. That is, to incorporate the Pacific Northwest into the West and to locate Higginson and her writing alongside work by western women authors advances a reimagining of both the West and western American writing, a reimagining that includes this wide region that abuts the Pacific Ocean as well as the women's writing that emerges from that region.

When students read *Mariella*, the Pacific Northwest of more than a century ago springs to life in precise detail rarely found in other published writings of the time about the region. Higginson's pivotal uses of region in *Mariella* repositioned the Pacific Northwest from the far cultural margins, placing it instead on the literary map as a distinct and distinctive region of the West and of the larger United States. As *Mariella* declared its place with other literary regionalist texts, it compellingly spoke of and for the region to the larger nation. Teaching *Mariella* helps to reestablish Higginson's once celebrated literary reputation and contributes to the process of restoring both her name and her novel to their justly merited places in U.S. literary history.

NOTES

1. Various arguments exist for what states, territories, and/or provinces make up the Pacific Northwest; some definitions include Idaho, British Columbia, and Alaska. For my chapter's purposes, the Pacific Northwest is defined as the states of Oregon and Washington.
2. Kollin, "North and Northwest," 414.
3. Halverson, *Maverick Autobiographies*, 118–19.
4. Cleman, "Belated Frontier," 448.
5. Etulain, *Re-imagining the Modern American West*, xiv, xiii.
6. Graulich, "Western Biodiversity," 51.
7. Baym, *Women Writers of the American West*, 2.
8. Baym, *Women Writers of the American West*, 3.
9. Baym, *Women Writers of the American West*, 9.
10. Lamont, *Westerns*, 1.
11. Higginson's major works are *From the Land of the Snow Pearls and Other Stories* (1897; originally published as *The Flower That Grew in the Sand and Other Stories* [1896]); *A Forest Orchid and Other Stories* (1897); *When the Birds Go North Again* (poems,

1898); *Four-Leaf Clover* (poems, 1901); *Mariella, of Out-West* (novel, 1902); *The Voice of April-Land and Other Poems* (1906); *Alaska, the Great Country* (travel, 1908); and *The Vanishing Race and Other Poems* (1911). Higginson authored nearly six hundred short stories and poems, which appeared in leading periodicals such as *Collier's, Harper's Bazaar, Lippincott's,* and *McClure's.* Her work was reprinted widely and published alongside writings by prominent U.S. and British authors such as A. Conan Doyle, Thomas Hardy, Sarah Orne Jewett, Harriet Prescott Spofford, Robert Louis Stevenson, Mark Twain, and Walt Whitman. Higginson also published more than three hundred nonfiction essays and served as editor on periodicals including Portland, Oregon's literary magazine *West Shore*; Seattle's *Sunday Times* newspaper; the Seattle magazines *The Pacific* and *The Westerner*; and Portland, Oregon's *Pacific Monthly.*

12. Whiteness serves as the default race of characters in *Mariella.* In contrast, the non-fiction book *Alaska* features explicit explanation of the disastrous effects of settler colonialism on Native groups, as well as detailed discussion regarding the history and customs of Kwakiutl, Thlinkits, and Tinneh groups, among others. This noteworthy foregrounding of Native groups in *Alaska* may have emerged as Higginson turned to book-length nonfiction, a new literary task for her that required comprehensive research and detailed observation in order to accurately describe a region unfamiliar to her and her readers.

13. For detailed discussion of this subject, see, for example, Brodhead, *Cultures of Letters*; and Renker, *Origins of American Literature Studies.*

14. *San Francisco Examiner*, December 14, 1902.

15. Review of *Mariella* in *San Francisco Bulletin*, n.d.

16. Review of *Mariella* in *Buffalo Express*, November 22, 1902.

17. *Seattle Daily Times*, December 26, 1902, 4.

18. *Tacoma Daily News*, April 14, 1905, 6.

19. Higginson, *Mariella*, vii. This and subsequent quotations are from the 1902 first edition of *Mariella.*

20. Higginson, *Mariella*, viii.

21. Higginson, *Mariella*, 13–14.

22. Higginson, *Mariella*, 64.

23. Higginson, *Mariella*, 98.

24. Higginson, *Mariella*, 170.

25. Higginson, *Mariella*, 359–60.

26. Higginson, *Mariella*, 217.

27. In addition to secondary sources discussed in this chapter, other secondary sources I assign depend on the course in which I am teaching *Mariella.* For example, in a 200-level general-education introduction to American literature, I assign excerpts from U.S. novels such as Herman Melville's *Redburn* so that students may see how *Mariella* fits with more familiar texts on the syllabus. In a 400-level seminar on U.S. literary regionalism for advanced undergraduate English majors, I assign critical essays on U.S.

literary regionalism, as well as essays about works by other regionalist authors, such as Sarah Orne Jewett and Mary E. Wilkins Freeman.

My assignments regarding *Mariella* also depend on the course level. In upper-division courses I typically assign a fairly lengthy (ten- to twelve-page) research essay. In lower division courses, I typically assign shorter (five- to seven-page) essays of literary analysis. Because *Mariella* is a rich, fairly lengthy novel, it provides a wealth of material from which students may draw.

All of these assignments yield excellent results in the form of strong, well-written essays. Students are eager to analyze *Mariella*, to consider its similarities to other works, and to research sections of and topics from the text. Indeed, one of the perhaps unanticipated advantages of teaching a neglected text is the way that students become inspired to join in the act of literary recovery by exploring and writing about the text.

28. Higginson, *Mariella*, 299.
29. Higginson, *Mariella*, 302, 304.
30. Higginson, *Mariella*, 302.
31. Higginson, *Mariella*, 299, 302.
32. Higginson, *Mariella*, 216.
33. Higginson, *Mariella*, 228.
34. For discussion of the strikingly different treatment of adultery in Hawthorne's *The Scarlet Letter*, see Laffrado, "Pacific Northwest (Re)Writes New England."
35. Higginson, *Mariella*, 189.
36. Higginson, *Mariella*, 288–89.
37. Higginson, *Mariella*, 333.
38. Higginson, *Mariella*, 45.
39. Higginson, *Mariella*, 345.
40. McGlinn, "Early Chinese Immigrants," 113.
41. Data in this section are drawn from online U.S. Census records for relevant years.
42. Bennion, *Equal to the Occasion*, 56.
43. Fetterley and Pryse, *Writing Out of Place*, 16.
44. Davey, "Toward the Ends of Regionalism," 4.
45. Fetterley and Pryse, *Writing Out of Place*, 31.
46. Fetterley and Pryse, *Writing Out of Place*, 38.

BIBLIOGRAPHY

Baym, Nina. *Women Writers of the American West, 1833–1927*. Urbana: University of Illinois Press, 2011.

Bennion, Sherilyn Cox. *Equal to the Occasion: Women Editors of the Nineteenth-Century West*. Reno: University of Nevada Press, 1990.

Brodhead, Richard. *Cultures of Letters: Scenes of Reading and Writing in Nineteenth-Century America*. Chicago: University of Chicago Press, 1995.

Cleman, John. "The Belated Frontier: H. L. Davis and the Problem of Pacific Northwest Regionalism." *Western American Literature* 37, no. 4 (2003): 431–51.

Davey, Frank. "Toward the Ends of Regionalism." In *A Sense of Place: Re-Evaluating Regionalism in Canadian and American Writing*, edited by Christian Riegel and Herb Wyile, 1–18. Edmonton: University of Alberta Press, 1997.

Etulain, Richard W. *Re-imagining the Modern American West: A Century of Fiction, History and Art.* Tucson: University of Arizona Press, 1996.

Fetterley, Judith, and Marjorie Pryse. *Writing Out of Place: Regionalism, Women, and American Literary Culture.* Urbana: University of Illinois Press, 2003.

Graulich, Melody. "Western Biodiversity: Rereading Nineteenth-Century American Women's Writing." In *Nineteenth-Century American Women Writers: A Critical Reader*, edited by Karen Kilcup, 47–61. Hoboken NJ: Blackwell, 1998.

Halverson, Cathryn. *Maverick Autobiographies: Women Writers and the American West, 1900–1936.* Madison: University of Wisconsin Press, 2004.

Higginson, Ella. *Mariella, of Out-West.* New York: Macmillan, 1902.

H-Women. https://networks.h-net.org/h-women.

Kollin, Susan. "North and Northwest: Theorizing the Regional Literatures of Alaska and the Pacific Northwest." In *A Companion to the Regional Literatures of America*, edited by Charles Crow, 412–31. Hoboken NJ: Blackwell, 2003.

Laffrado, Laura. "The Pacific Northwest (Re)Writes New England: Civic Myth and Women's Literary Regionalism in Ella Higginson's Revision of *The Scarlet Letter.*" *Nathaniel Hawthorne Review* 40, no. 1 (2014): 18–40.

Lamont, Victoria. *Westerns: A Women's History.* Lincoln: University of Nebraska Press, 2016.

Lee, L. L., and Merrill Lewis, eds. *Women, Women Writers, and the West.* Albany NY: Whitston, 1980.

McGlinn, Lawrence A. "Early Chinese Immigrants and the United States Census." *Middle States Geographer* 24 (1991): 113–20.

Renker, Elizabeth. *The Origins of American Literature Studies: An Institutional History.* Cambridge: Cambridge University Press, 2007.

U.S. Federal Census of 1860. Ancestry.com, 2006.

U.S. Federal Census of 1900. Ancestry.com, 2006.

U.S. Federal Census of 1930. Ancestry.com, 2006.

Witschi, Nicolas S., ed. *A Companion to the Literature and Culture of the American West.* Hoboken NJ: Wiley-Blackwell, 2011.

PART 4

Hemispheric/Global Wests

11

National, Transnational, and Human Rights Frames for Teaching María Amparo Ruiz de Burton's *The Squatter and the Don*

TEREZA M. SZEGHI

My experiences teaching María Amparo Ruiz de Burton's 1885 novel *The Squatter and the Don* are in American literature survey courses with the daunting mandate of covering the most significant authors, genres, and periods of American literature in sixteen weeks. Of course significance is continuously debated and, given the long history of privileging Euro-American male writers, rightfully contested. Rather than try to cover a list of the ostensibly most significant texts, my approach to American literature survey courses has been to create conversations between authors from varied cultural, regional, and racial backgrounds who are actively negotiating questions pertaining to U.S. national formation.

Questions I organize these courses around include these: How should lands in the newly formed United States be distributed? What are, or should be, the rights of all residents of the nation? How can literature help realize the promise of our national ideals? How can literature be used to testify to and preserve cultures and lifeways threatened by assimilationist policies and practices of U.S. federal and state governments, as well as its dominant Euro-American population? Such questions lead me to assign a diverse range of writers who were in intentional or implicit conversation about these issues. These questions also allow me to create a narrative arc to follow over the course of the semester to provide a sense of continuity while moving through a daunting range of materials.

I have learned that it is crucial to be transparent with students about the rationale behind a course's construction and the criteria used to select texts, particularly in a course with a broad title like Survey of American Literature. I learned this lesson the hard way when, after first teaching the course, I received several evaluations from students lamenting the absence of writers like Ernest Hemingway and Edgar Allan Poe from the syllabus, with an indignation suggesting the view that any *real* American literature survey must include these writers. Although initially dispirited that some students did not see the value in being acquainted with texts they had not encountered before, rather than rereading those likely to have been assigned in high school, I ultimately decided to offer a clearer narrative for the course on day one. I also began to incorporate selected criticism from a range of disciplines, such as western American literary studies, Chicanx/Latinx studies, and American Indian studies, to help clarify the rationale for text selection and preview issues we would examine through our study of the literature.

Secondary scholarship I assign to supplement and frame our literary analyses helps students think critically about the U.S. literary canon and assumptions about U.S. nation formation that have been implied and perpetuated by the canon. For instance, in her landmark 1992 essay "Letting Go Our Grand Obsessions: Notes toward a New Literary History of the American Frontiers," Annette Kolodny calls upon scholars of U.S. literatures to "let go our grand obsessions with narrowly geographic or strictly chronological frameworks and instead recognize 'frontier' as a locus of first cultural contact, circumscribed by a particular physical terrain in the process of change *because of* the forms that contact takes."[1] Kolodny underscores the fact that first cultural contacts have been numerous throughout U.S. history, originating prior to Columbus and continuing well after Frederick Jackson's Turner's 1893 declaration of the end of the frontier. Moreover, she calls attention to the varied geographical locations in which these contacts occurred and the varied linguistic collisions that informed them.

Citing Kolodny's article, José Aranda argues that in a similar vein scholars of Chicanx literature "must move beyond the boundaries of a separatist literary history and locate Chicano/a literature within the broader discursive history that has often produced competing literary nationalisms and the cultural values that privileged publicly some narratives (even if politically dissenting) as symbolically meaningful to the nation-state, while relegating other narratives to the margins of denationalized history."[2] Aranda identifies Ruiz de Burton as an author whose recovery into U.S. letters by Beatrice Pita and Rosaura Sánchez has helped undermine the U.S. black-white racial binary, illustrating the fragility of any coherent notion of U.S. identity well into the late nineteenth century.[3] Thus, teaching Ruiz de Burton's work—notably the first published fiction in English written by a Mexican American woman—can be presented as part of a larger narrative of U.S. literature that highlights the varied and ongoing nature of first cultural contexts. It thus can be used to help us all "let go our grand obsessions" with a one-directional, teleological progression of U.S. origins beginning with New England Puritans and moving steadily westward until the alleged achievement of Manifest Destiny with the 1848 Treaty of Guadalupe Hidalgo (which concluded the U.S.-Mexican War and led to the U.S. acquisition of nearly half of Mexico's territory).

The Squatter and the Don, which Ruiz de Burton published in 1885, destabilizes dominant conceptions of the U.S. frontier while repeatedly castigating U.S. policies that perpetuate inequality and belie the U.S. ideal of equal opportunity. Drawing from her own similar experiences, *Squatter* details how one Californio family, the Alamars, are financially, physically, and emotionally decimated by protracted legal battles to defend their lands against Euro-American squatters.[4] William Darrell, the titular squatter, is a conflicted character who feels entitled to seize contested lands but who also sees himself as an honest, hardworking man simply trying to achieve a nineteenth-century version of the American dream. The novel shifts between Alamar and Darrell perspectives, including those of the titular characters' wives and children. All of the Darrells but William quickly come to recognize the Alamar family's virtues and lament how they have been wronged by squatters and U.S. laws and policies justifying heinous acts. Eventually, but only after Don Alamar suffers a series of illnesses arising from his defense of his fortune against the squatters, even William realizes his actions are unjustified and laments the treatment of Californios—as Ruiz de Burton, through her narrator and various characters, invites her readers to do.

In hopes of gaining a broad readership and awakening them to the plight of her people, Ruiz de Burton wrapped her scathing political critique in the trappings of an interracial sentimental romance novel that testifies to the equality, and often superiority, of the Californios to the best of Euro-American society, thereby advancing an argument about Californios' rightful inclusion among the U.S. elite. One of her strategies for advancing this argument is to naturalize the inequality of other marginalized groups, namely American Indians and African Americans.[5] As Aranda argues, Ruiz de Burton's comparative privilege and the elitism that imbues her fiction belie categorization of her as subaltern, as Sánchez and Pita have done, and instead invite a more varied presentation of Chicanx authors than overly simplified separatist and Chicanx nationalist narratives allow.[6] Presenting students with the complexities of Ruiz de Burton's life and work effectively positions them to engage in close readings of the novel to tease out what Alemán terms its "colonial contradictions" in its objection not to the colonial project but to being among the colonized, as Aranda observes.[7]

Below I detail three interlocking frames for teaching *Squatter*, which, as I discuss in closing, are useful for teaching many Chicanx texts situated in the western U.S. literary context.[8] These are the national frame, the transnational frame, and the human rights frame. For each, I overview how I situate the novel for students, offer examples of how I guide students to analyze the novel closely to address its relationship to the frame, and provide recommended in-class activities and assignments.

The National Frame

In light of Ruiz de Burton's interest in influencing emergent conceptions of the United States, its laws, and its social order, I find it works best to begin discussion of *Squatter* within a national, U.S. frame. Like many others who teach *Squatter*, I find it useful to contextualize the novel with a close reading of the 1848 Treaty of Guadalupe Hidalgo—particularly Articles 8 and 9—alongside other legal documents that affected the ability of new Mexican Americans to thrive in the United States.[9] Such legislation includes the California Land Act of 1851 and the federal Homestead Act of 1862. Moreover, due to the lack of attention given to Mexican American/Chicanx history and cultures in most elementary and high school curricula, previewing the book with a short lecture on the U.S.-Mexican War, what motivated the war, and the status of Californios before and after the war is essential to students' ability to engage meaningfully with Ruiz de Burton's project. Given *Squatter*'s consistent excoriation of laws that bred inequality for Californios, it also is important to acquaint students with the state's Vagrancy Law of 1855 (commonly termed the "Greaser Act"), which required unemployed Mexicans to pay fines in cash or indentured labor.[10] Moreover, Californianas faced a different, gender-based set of legal challenges in securing their land claims. As Amelia María de la Luz Montes rightly suggests, "Antonia I. Castañeda's writings especially assist students in learning how, under Mexican law, upper class Californianas could inherit land and litigate in court. U.S. law did not recognize women within the context of law and litigation. This was all the more frustrating for Ruiz de Burton[,] who drew up her own legal papers, yet because she was a woman, she was not recognized under U.S. law."[11] Castañeda's "The Political Economy of Nineteenth-Century Stereotypes of Californianas" is accessible for undergraduates and offers a useful context for *Squatter*. Although Ruiz de Burton does not forefront the particular experiences of Californianas asserting land claims in court, the added gender-based legal challenges she faced are nonetheless significant for appreciating some of the urgency with which she wrote her book, and they can lead to generative discussion with students about why she chose not to forefront gender in *Squatter*'s political critiques. Moreover, Ruiz de Burton's emphasis on the refinement, beauty, and virtue of the Alamar women can be better understood when presented against the backdrop of prevailing stereotypes about Mexicanas/Californianas that Castañeda overviews, inclusive of the notion that they were sexually and financially promiscuous.[12]

I find it effective to divide students into groups to discuss the Treaty of Guadalupe Hidalgo, which, in my experience teaching at a majority white midwestern U.S. university, few students have previously encountered.

Each group is asked to address the following questions by providing a clear claim in response and offering the support of textual evidence and detailed analysis of that evidence. This claim-evidence-analysis structure also invites students to begin practicing some of the foundational maneuvers they will need to execute in a range of assigned papers, which I discuss in more detail below.

1. In a nutshell, what does the treaty communicate? What is its core mandate?
2. How does the treaty communicate its core idea/s? Identify specific language that seems important to the values, assumptions, and/or ideologies that underlie the document's mandate.
3. What expectations does the treaty set up for Mexicans now in U.S. territories?

To offer some illustration of how students might perform this work, let us look at portions of Article 8 of the treaty:

> Mexicans now established in territories previously belonging to Mexico, and which remain for the future within the limits of the United States, as defined by the present treaty, **shall be free** to continue where they now reside, or to remove at any time to the Mexican Republic, *retaining the property which they possess in the said territories, or disposing thereof, and removing the proceeds* **wherever they please**, *without their being subjected, on this account, to any contribution, tax, or charge whatever.*
>
> . . . In the said territories, property of every kind, now belonging to Mexicans not established there, *shall be inviolably respected.* The present owners, the heirs of these, and all Mexicans who may hereafter acquire said property by contract, **shall enjoy** with respect to it guarantees **equally ample as if the same belonged to citizens of the United States.**[13]

Students might infer that this article's core idea is that Mexicans living in what has become U.S. territory will retain their rights as property owners, full stop. The boldface portions of the above article emphasize the idea of freedom being associated with landownership within the United States. Indeed, Mexicans' ability to "enjoy" landownership or sales of that land, and the varied benefits associated with either, is presented in language that resonates with U.S. national ideals and mythologies, particularly those associated with the U.S. West or the frontier.

The boldface portions of the second paragraph of Article 8 communicate that Mexicans in the United States will enjoy property rights in the same way as U.S. citizens—whether or not they accept citizenship (which the omitted portion of the article makes optional for one year, after which all Mexicans in the newly acquired territories will be given U.S. citizenship). Unlike American Indians in these and other U.S. territories, Californios and their rights ostensibly will not be effaced in the interest of offering allegedly unpopulated lands to Euro-American settlers. The italicized sections of Article 8, in turn, emphasize that Mexican land rights are absolute. The promise here seems straightforward and can be understood as leading newly formed Mexican Americans to expect neither legal challenge to those land rights from any quarter nor any fees to pay should they sell their lands.

This work on the Treaty of Guadalupe Hidalgo positions students to think about California land rights from the perspective of Mexicans who, as bumper stickers say, were crossed by the border. It gives students a sense of what expectations Californios may have had as the United States assumed authority over the region, while also building awareness of California not as an open frontier but as a space in which individuals already owned land. With this perspective in mind, students often are surprised to learn that so soon after the signing of the treaty in 1848, the new state of California passed the Land Law of 1851, which established a commission to review the validity of prior Spanish and Mexican land grants and which was quick to invalidate these grants.

The benefits of this activity are multiple, as it encourages a detailed engagement with the law and its implications for different categories of U.S. citizens. It also demonstrates how basic literary analysis techniques can be applied productively to nonliterary texts. Indeed, our comparative analysis of the law and the novel demonstrates the permeability of such genre distinctions. Given Ruiz de Burton's repeated and detailed castigations of U.S. legal hypocrisy, as well as Euro-Americans' use of the law to create and perpetuate inequality, it also is important to discuss with students how she joined a growing group of nineteenth-century women—including, most famously, Harriet Beecher Stowe, author of *Uncle Tom's Cabin* (1852)—who seized the sentimental novel as a socially acceptable vehicle for advancing political arguments and seeking to effect social change. This helps to crystallize for students the ways in which the law, politics, and literature informed one another during this period.

With some orientation to the expectations Californios had after the Treaty of Guadalupe Hidalgo went into effect, students are well positioned to work closely with sections of the novel that address this treaty and the subsequent legislation that undermined its promises. For example, with the following speech Don Mariano Alamar calls out the failure of the United States to live up to its promises and the mean-spiritedness that has motivated the ruination of his people:

> They [legislators] are teaching the people to lose all respect for the rights of others—to lose all respect for their national honor. Because we, *the natives* of California, the Spano-Americans, were, at the close of the war with Mexico, left in the lap of the American nation, or, rather, huddled at her feet like motherless, helpless children, Congress *thought* we might as well be kicked and cuffed as treated kindly. [. . .] It ought to have been sufficient that by the treaty of Guadalupe Hidalgo the national faith, the nation's honor was pledged to respect our property. They never thought of that. With very unbecoming haste, Congress hurried to pass laws to legalize their despoliation of the conquered Californians, forgetting the nation's pledge to protect us.[14]

Don Mariano's pathos-ridden speech provides opportunities for students to examine the disparities between the language of the Treaty of Guadalupe Hidalgo and the lived experiences of Californios, as Ruiz de Burton represents them. One rhetorical strategy they may observe is Don Mariano's repeated placement of responsibility for "the despoliation of the conquered Californians" on Congress—a body he presents as acting in direct violation of its treaty-bound promises to his people. I ask students why Ruiz de Burton might opt to have Don Mariano hold Congress, rather than squatters who claim his lands, responsible in light of her target readership. The conclusion we generally work toward is that Euro-American readers might be more willing to see the government as corrupt than they would the average American. At the same time, Don Mariano's references to the United States breaking its treaty with Mexico, through policies that disadvantage Mexicans who, by the treaty's terms, suddenly are residents of the United States, is an enactment of the novel's repeatedly articulated thesis that most Americans do not know what is happening to Californios and would be outraged if they did. Here Don Mariano educates readers, presumably to spark their outrage and prompt action.

I find it effective when teaching *Squatter* to follow the dialogic structure Ruiz de Burton constructs, as indicated with the novel's repeated shifts back and forth between Alamar and Darrell perspectives. She encourages readers to think about how the novel's landed Californios and the squatters who lay claim to their property are positioned by U.S. law and policy to see one another as enemies. Notably, although Ruiz de Burton's sympathies clearly favor the Californios and it is their cause she advances, she also is careful to allow that the best of the squatters are not malicious thieves but rather are misled by their government. In fact *Squatter* opens with a sympathetic focus on William Darrell and his lament to his wife, Mary, about his failure to provide her with the lifestyle for which he aimed:

> In a few days it will be twenty-four years since we crossed the plains. [. . .] I firmly believed then, that with my fine stock and my good bank account, and broad government lands, free to all Americans, I should have given you a nice home before I was five years older; that I would have saved money and would be getting more to make us rich before I was old. But see, at the end of twenty-four years, where do I find myself? I am still poor, all I have earned is the name of "*Squatter*."[15]

In a novel primarily focused on the plight of the Californios and constructed to motivate action on their behalf, Ruiz de Burton is savvy in first presenting the injustice of encouraging Euro-Americans to settle on lands already claimed by prior occupants as *an injustice against Euro-Americans*. In this way, as I noted above and argue elsewhere, Ruiz de Burton astutely targets a broad U.S. audience by positioning average Euro-Americans as virtuous people being set up to engage—often unwittingly—in unethical actions that too often fail to bring them the promised financial reward.[16]

Thus, Manifest Destiny and the American dream have failed Euro-Americans while harming Californios.

This preface to the novel's more extensive detailing of the gradual impoverishment and physical decline of the Alamar family targets a broad audience in presenting a rationale for ending policies such as the Homestead Act of 1862, which was used to promote settlement in the western U.S. through the promise of 160 acres of ostensibly public land. After residing on the land for five years and making improvements on it, settlers were to receive full ownership of the land. However, Mary and William Darrell's conversation in the opening chapter of the novel indicates that time and again they settled on land still claimed by another owner and ultimately lost their legal battle.[17] As a result, they were little better off than when they first headed west as settlers twenty-four years prior.

To further engage students in thinking about the varied ideologies, expectations, and legal issues that came to bear in first encounters and conflicts between Euro-American settlers and Californios, Montes recommends an effective in-class activity in which students are divided into two groups: Californios and Euro-American settlers.[18] The latter group is further divided into squatters who appropriate land without payment and settlers who pay for the lands they occupy when they are already owned. The squatter group members must place their desks close to those of the Californios, and the Californios must determine how to explain that the land is taken already. As Montes notes, through this activity students can better understand that language barriers and lack of documentation for their land claims created significant challenges for Californios. I find this activity makes more vivid for students the real-world context in which Ruiz de Burton sought to intervene.

In a survey of American or western American literature, it is useful to reference texts students may have read earlier in the course, such as J. Hector St. John de Crèvecoeur's *Letters from an American Farmer* or Thomas Jefferson's *Notes on the State of Virginia*, to look at how the mythos of the heroic American pioneer was constructed and how someone like William Darrell might have been seduced by the promise this national ideal seemingly provided.[19] Such references to the larger U.S. literary tradition that Ruiz de Burton engaged and challenged helps students think critically about deep debates regarding such issues as national identity and multicultural inclusiveness versus white supremacy, as they have been litigated throughout U.S. history and literature. Moreover, *Squatter*, along with Ruiz de Burton's life experience, can be used to help students reexamine entrenched national mythologies. For instance, national loyalties during the U.S.-Mexican War were more complex than students generally expect. Ruiz de Burton and her family, along with other Baja Californios, allied themselves with the United States with the expectation that Baja California would be incorporated into the country at the war's conclusion. When Baja California remained in Mexican hands after 1848, Ruiz de Burton's future husband, Capt. Henry S. Burton, and his fellow officers appealed to their superiors to shield them from reprisals from the Mexican government and evacuate them to Monterey, California.[20] The cross-cultural, transnational affinity that developed during the U.S. occupation of Baja California "destabilizes easy notions of nineteenth-century political, cultural, and military hegemony in North America."[21] Aranda continues,

> Thus, a more differentiated model of historical agency would address why certain peoples of Mexican descent opted to align themselves with Anglo Americans, while others did not. Equally important, under this revised model, is to understand anew those moments during which Anglo Americans recorded either their ambivalence about Manifest Destiny or their admiration for the different colonial project they encountered in both Alta and Baja California. In both regions, Anglo Americans evidenced a willingness to realign their own nationalist loyalties during a political period otherwise dedicated to the consolidation of a continental United States.[22]

Here Aranda offers a valuable way of framing for students the historical moment Ruiz de Burton operated in and sought to influence through her fiction. Although she published her novels toward the end of the nineteenth century, decades after the war, she nonetheless protests the failures of the U.S. government to live up to its promises to peoples of Mexican descent now within U.S. national boundaries. At the same time, it is crucial to highlight for students that she attempts to shape the U.S. social order and popular views of Mexicanas/os and Californianas/os during a moment when, as Aranda notes, ideas about U.S. national identity were unsettled.

Because of the novel's dialogic nature—moving between varied Euro-American and Californio perspectives—and its overt intervention in U.S. policies and contemporaneous arguments about the place of different ethnic groups within the U.S. socioeconomic hierarchy, *Squatter* is a good subject for a rhetorical analysis paper. Students can appreciate Ruiz de Burton's rhetorical situation and be directed to assess her strategies for reaching a broad and varied U.S. audience. Moreover, the novel contains a range of rhetorical strategies, such as the narrator's direct appeals to readers to act on behalf of Californios; various characters calling out the need for legislative reforms; the merits of Californios being evidenced largely through their proper dress, refined manners, physical beauty (which notably is presented as European, with an emphasis on Don Mariano's blue eyes and Mercedes's blond hair and fair skin); and, related to the prior point, the repeated identification of the Californios as Spaniards (read: Europeans).

The Transnational Frame

In the context of his discussion of Ruiz de Burton's other novel, *Who Would Have Thought It?*, first published in 1872, Aranda writes, "Like those of many of her Californio peers, Ruiz de Burton's observations and judgments about New England society and U.S. politics are informed by her prior status as a Mexican citizen."[23] Certainly this also is the case with *Squatter* and is just one way the novel communicates a transnational sensibility as important to a judicious worldview. This is how I construct the transnational frame for students in approaching *Squatter*: as a way of thinking about Ruiz de Burton's negotiations across cultural and national lines in the context of newly constructed borders and renegotiations of racialized socioeconomic hierarchies. However, it is paramount, in my view, first to firmly situate Ruiz de Burton within the *U.S.* literary tradition and demonstrate her participation in national debates as a *U.S. citizen* before shifting to the transnational dimensions of *Squatter*.

Because U.S. citizens and residents of Mexican descent frequently continue to be positioned within national discourse as immigrants, it is important not to present Ruiz de Burton as an outsider but as the active participant she was within national debates during a time when insider and outsider status was actively contested. Students are interested to know, for instance, that the Burtons attended President Abraham Lincoln's 1861 inauguration and that Ruiz de Burton was a close friend of Mary Todd Lincoln. In short, Ruiz de Burton circulated within upper-class social circles. The perception of Mexican Americans as immigrants can be destabilized further by teaching the novel with emphasis on its central focus on the Alamar family's long-standing ownership of their lands and the incursion of Euro-Americans onto those lands. The Alamars did not move; they found themselves in the United States when they were crossed by the redrawn border.

In several ways the novel asserts the value of the insights Californios bring to dominant U.S. conceptions of how western lands should be organized and used. While Euro-American squatters on the Alamar estate doggedly pursue the Jeffersonian ideal of a nation of agrarian farmers through their attempts to plant wheat, Don Mariano repeatedly argues that the land is not suited for this type of agriculture and is better for raising cattle and cultivating orchards. Rather than being responsive to the climate of Southern California, however, the squatters are further incentivized to persist as farmers and impoverish Don Mariano by shooting his cattle with impunity under protection of the No-Fence Law (which permitted the killing of unfenced cattle that wandered onto land usurped by squatters). Ultimately, the respectable Euro-Americans in the novel are differentiated from the rest because they pay Don Mariano for the land *and* because of their validation of Don Mariano's argument about the natural use of Southern Californian lands. As William Darrell's son Clarence states to Mathews, one of the more opportunistic and sadistic squatters on the Alamar estate, "Plant wheat, if you can do so without killing cattle. But do not destroy the larger industry with the smaller. If, as the Don very properly says, this is a grazing county, no legislation can change it."[24] Here Clarence extends the novel's broader castigation of U.S. law by observing its failure to respond to the laws of nature. He depicts the squatters' dogged pursuit of wheat growing in California as a foolish errand motivated at least partly by foolish policy. Short of asking the squatters to adapt to the land, Clarence makes the more modest request that they not damage Don Mariano's fortunes while pursuing their doomed agricultural enterprises.

Don Mariano's experiences with the organization of California lands under the Spanish and Mexican governments also are offered to denaturalize U.S. distribution of lands in 160-acre individual land allotments and—as he pointedly observes—the granting of vast tracts of land to avaricious railroad monopolies. He responds to the charge that Californio land allotments, granted by Spain and Mexico, are too vast by pointing to the hypocrisy of the charge when the U.S. government grants large tracts—to corporations rather than individuals—and by arguing that the size of the Spanish and Mexican land grants had a much worthier rationale, namely, to bring order to the region. He argues,

> The land-owners were useful in many ways, though to a limited extent they attracted population by employing white labor. They also employed Indians, who thus began to be less wild. Then in times of Indian outbreaks, the land-owners with their servants would turn out as in feudal times in Europe, to assist in the defense of the missions and the sparsely settled country threatened by the savages. Thus, you see, that it was not a foolish extravagance, but a judicious policy which induced the viceroys and Spanish governors to begin the system of giving large land grants.[25]

Don Mariano places the history of California and its settlement under Spanish and Mexican rule within the genealogy of European civilization, and it is part of the novel's larger argument that Californios and Euro-Americans share a common ancestry. Likewise, he identifies his people as participants in Europe's long history of conquering and civilizing allegedly savage lands and peoples. Rather than Californios being savages to be civilized, they are part of the civilizing mission, as it was the Spaniards who established missions and cities within the presumed California wilderness, which was inhabited by American Indians. I will say more about the novel's representation of American Indians in the section on human rights below. For students, the material point I focus on in terms of the novel's transnationalism is how Don Mariano undermines dominant U.S. thinking about proper land use as it is constructed in opposition to other national systems—particularly how this thinking is used to invalidate the land claims of conquered peoples.

To help students negotiate how Ruiz de Burton positions Californios as full members of the United States, deserving of rights equal to those enjoyed by the Euro-American elite, while offering their transnational perspectives as a means of critiquing the U.S. social order, I ask the class to engage in a silent chalk talk.[26] I write relatively broad questions on the board to prompt a range of responses and encourage students to work toward narrower ideas and arguments in written conversation with one another. Broad questions might include the following:

Is this a transnational novel? Why/why not?
How does Ruiz de Burton define what it means to be a Californio?
How do the Californios' relationships to the United States versus Mexico compare in the novel?
How is Mexico represented in the novel in comparison to the United States?
What do the novel's references to Spain and Mexico accomplish relative to Ruiz de Burton's objective in writing it?

Students are instructed to write on the board their brief responses, tied to specific textual references. They are to continue returning to the board in cycles and may opt to add to another student's post, such as underlining something they want to emphasize, putting a question mark next to something that is unclear or that they disagree with, citing counterevidence, and so on. One of the merits of this activity is that it changes the dynamic of the classroom; it slows the pace, encourages thinking and reflection, and allows for reflective pauses while students process what others have written and think of their responses. Everyone is expected to continue participating until the time is up. I do not predetermine how much time to allot for the activity but note that we will continue until the process runs its course. When the board is full and students stop returning to the board, I ask them to read over all the ideas once more and add another contribution. I then talk through key themes, questions, and debates they have raised and ask the class to weigh in, as a way of delving deeper into the novel. For continued reference, I post pictures of the board to the classroom support platform.

The ideas generated through the chalk talk can be used as the germ for a variety of assignments, including a straightforward literary analysis paper organized around a thesis-driven argument and careful analysis of the novel, as well as in-class poster presentations in which students continue to develop their ideas and present them in conversation with one another.

The Human Rights Frame

Given the primacy of human rights in national and international discourse, engaging the novel's relationship to human rights is an effective way of addressing its continued relevance, alongside its limitations. I ask students to consider to what degree Ruiz de Burton anticipates contemporary understandings of human rights and whether or not she situates her arguments for Californio rights in a human rights frame. I find that the combination of Ruiz de Burton's advocacy for Californio equality *and* her elitism make her work ideal for this interrogation of what human rights advocacy can look like in the context of literature. In short, human rights arguments and their spokespersons are rarely pure. Having to grapple with the complex mix of deafening calls to eradicate laws that perpetuate racial inequality, paired with offhand comments about American Indian alleged savagery and depictions of African Americans as happily engaging their servitude, can prompt students into a nuanced consideration of human rights advocacy.[27] Rather than thinking in dichotomous terms about saviors and victims or advocates and villains, *Squatter* can be used to help students grapple with the complexities and frequent messiness of human rights advocacy.

In order to evaluate *Squatter* vis-à-vis contemporary human rights discourse, I assign the United Nations' Universal Declaration on Human Rights (UDHR) of 1948 and ask students to identify articles they see as most relevant to the novel. Students often are quick to point to the UDHR's universal language, as it repeatedly asserts that "everyone," without exception, is entitled to the rights detailed therein. This emphasis on universality accords with the novel's frequent censuring of laws that favor one group over another. For instance, as Don Mariano explains,

There are some enactments so obviously intended to favor one class of citizens against another class, that to call them laws is an insult to law, but such as they are, we must submit to them. By those laws any man can come to my land, for instance, plant ten acres of grain, without any fence, and then catch my cattle which, seeing the green grass without a fence, will go to eat it. Then he puts them in a "*corral*" and makes me pay damages and so much per head for keeping them, and costs of legal proceedings and many other trumped up expenses, until for such little fields of grain I may be obliged to pay thousands of dollars.[28]

It is not simply, in Don Mariano's view, that inequality exists within the United States but that it is *legislated*—contrary to U.S. national ideals of equality, as articulated in the Declaration of Independence, for instance, and in violation of the Treaty of Guadalupe Hidalgo. Moreover, the passage above can be placed in productive dialogue with Article 7 and Article 17, section 2, of the UDHR, which stipulate that "all are equal before the law and are entitled without any discrimination to equal protection of the law" and that "no one shall be arbitrarily deprived of his property," respectively.[29]

At the same time, *Squatter*'s arguments on behalf of Californio equality, as indicated above, are based on the assertion of a naturalized racial hierarchy in which Californios rightfully belong at the top and American Indians and African Americans at the bottom—obvious deviations from the UDHR and subsequent human rights documents.[30] Once more Ruiz de Burton did not object to colonization generally but to being among the colonized. When, for instance, Don Mariano attempts to persuade the squatters to take up cattle raising, squatter Mathews objects, saying, "I ain't no '*vaquero*' to go '*busquering*' around and *lassooing* cattle," to which Don Mariano replies, "You can hire an Indian boy to do that part. They know how to handle *la reata* and *echar el lazo* to perfection."[31] Don Mariano's recommendation of the use of American Indians for menial labor is presented as an unproblematic and obvious answer to the squatters' concerns. Moreover, the Darrell family's engagement of a black servant, Tish, likewise is presented as unproblematic.

A human rights frame also is useful for addressing the novel's argument on behalf of the allegedly besieged upper classes in the post–Civil War

Southeast and post–U.S.-Mexican War Southwest. Another of Ruiz de Burton's strategies for appropriating the prevailing U.S. racial hierarchy while asserting the Californios' rightful place within it is by presenting southern whites and Californios as joint victims of Yankee greed, as evidenced by northern Congress members working to defund the proposed Texas Pacific Railroad (which would have run through the Southwest and terminated in San Diego). As Don Mariano tells Clarence, who had just been reflecting to himself that the "southern people" are entitled to the same privileges of a railroad that the North enjoys, "The prospect is perfectly good, and I would have entire confidence in it, if the fate of the railroad did not depend upon right and just legislation. The Congressmen from the north do not seem to feel all the interest they should in reviving the south. They are angry yet."[32] The novel's view of U.S. legislation is so dim, and of northern members of Congress as so petty and corrupt, that there is little hope a railroad that would economically benefit the downtrodden elite in the southern and southwestern parts of the United States will be supported. Of course this fatalistic view is validated when the Texas Pacific fails to attract the governmental support it needs and the Alamar estate is dealt a final blow (as Don Mariano had invested heavily in San Diego).

Alemán notes the irony of Ruiz de Burton's conception of Californio and southern "white slavery" at the hands of monopoly interests, as it "comes at a time when the nation is reconstructing itself following the end of black slavery. And this is the catch to the novel's geopolitical reconstructing of whiteness. In much the same way that the Don's neocolonial venture relies on Indian labor, the narrative's re-mapping of whiteness forgets about black freedom."[33] Here again, to whatever degree Ruiz de Burton's appeals on behalf of Californios echo ideas in the UDHR, she simultaneously and strategically makes the case that other groups of people—African Americans and American Indians, just not Californios—should perform the hard labor to support the leisured classes.

Even the novel's distinction between types of Euro-Americans—the "riff-raff" who flooded California during the gold rush and began appropriating Californio lands versus the more refined and sympathetic figures like Clarence—bolsters an argument for Californio inclusion among the elites by advancing a social hierarchy.[34] Ruiz de Burton's presentation of Californios as superior to most of the Euro-American squatters who lay claim/siege to the Alamar estate renders absurd the notion that Californios should be at a legal, political, social, or economic disadvantage to them. Don Mariano's eloquent, logical, and generous proposal to squatters to advance them cattle to support a shift from wheat growing to cattle raising, for example, contrasts sharply with the rough and ungrammatical language of most of the squatters with whom he speaks. Ultimately, the novel as a whole does not predicate its argument on the human rights ideal that, by virtue of being human, all people are entitled to equal rights. Rather, it expresses outrage at structural inequalities that disenfranchise Californios.

As we work through the human rights frame in class, I assign either papers or group presentations in which students must generate an argument about *Squatter* by viewing it through a human rights lens. I ask them to select one article from the UDHR or another relevant human rights document (such as the United Nations' Declaration on the Rights of Indigenous Peoples) and assess the novel's advancement and/or undermining of the principles of the article. I ask them to utilize their comparative close reading to dig deeper in their analysis by addressing the implied basis on which the rights asserted in the novel and the article are made. Ultimately students must answer the question of whether or not we can rightfully regard Ruiz de Burton as operating within the human rights tradition or as opportunistically using some of the language we now find ubiquitous in human rights discourse to achieve selective and discriminatory ends. Either way, they must grapple with opposing views and negotiate the novel's complex web of democratic appeals combined with racialized and elitist arguments.

Conclusion

The three frames I have offered for teaching *The Squatter and the Don* can be used individually, as best fits the context of a given course, or in conjunction with one another. If all three are utilized, I recommend the sequence I have suggested here (national, transnational, and then human rights), as each builds upon the previous frame and can be interconnected through the theme of literary activism. Moreover, because many texts within the Chicanx and Latinx literary traditions also have an activist intent and negotiate issues of national inclusion, cultural identity, and transnational perspectives and critiques, I have found that these frames are effective for teaching a range of texts within these traditions. It also can be valuable, in a survey of American or western American literature, for example, to extend the dialogic structure of *Squatter* by placing it in conversation with literature written by members of other cultural groups within the United States during this same period of history while using one or more of my suggested frames.

One way or another, it is critical not to let pass or fall under the radar the implications of Ruiz de Burton's negations of American Indian land claims or her casual suggestion that American Indians are best suited to menial labor and thus are properly situated at the bottom of the U.S. socio-economic hierarchy. I recommend reading her work alongside Alexander Posey's *Fus Fixico Letters* (just one or two letters can be selected if time is short), given their discussion of how members of the Muscogee (Creek) Nation negotiated the forced allotment of the lands by the U.S. government through the Curtis Act of 1898. Posey's emphasis on Creek agency and the imperative for the continuance of his people as a distinct people *and* participants within the United States effectively problematizes Ruiz de Burton's selective erasure of American Indians and stereotyping of them as savages best utilized as servants.

Another effective pairing, which several scholars have engaged, is *The Squatter and the Don* with Helen Hunt Jackson's *Ramona*.[35] Like *Squatter*, *Ramona* protests late nineteenth-century California's emerging social order, only with an eye toward upholding the land claims and rights of American Indians. A more canonical author like Mark Twain can be put in conversation with Ruiz de Burton as well, given his negotiations of race, Euro-American identity, and agency as forged against the backdrop of racial inequality, as well as romanticization of the U.S. frontier as a site of individual and U.S. identity formation. This is not an exclusive list of potential pairings of texts with *Squatter*, but it suggests how Ruiz de Burton can be put in effective dialogue with other U.S. authors in a way that disrupts teleological notions of U.S. identity formation as a steady march from Puritan New England to an unpopulated western frontier. *The Squatter and the Don*, both in spite and because of its flaws and complexities, highlights the highly contested, geographically dispersed, and ongoing nature of U.S. identity formation and the considerable role literature has always played in this process.

NOTES

1. Kolodny, "Letting Go Our Grand Obsessions," 3.
2. Aranda, *When We Arrive*, xix.
3. Aranda, *When We Arrive*, 90, 99. Working with the Recovering the U.S. Hispanic Literary Heritage Project through Arte Público Press, Sánchez and Pita edited and provided detailed introductions for republications of Ruiz de Burton's *Who Would Have Thought It?* (1995) and *The Squatter and the Don* (1992, with a second edition in 1997).
4. The term "Californio" refers to a person of Spanish or Mexican descent born in California.
5. Several critics, including myself (Szeghi, "Vanishing Mexicana/o"), have commented on Ruiz de Burton's strategic and problematic use of race to advance her arguments. See also Alemán, "'Thank God Lolita Is Away'"; Aranda, "Contradictory Impulses"; Luis-Brown, "'White Slaves' and the 'Arrogant *Mestiza*'"; and Pita, "Engendering Critique."
6. Sánchez and Pita, introduction to *Squatter and the Don*; Aranda, *When We Arrive*, 87.
7. Alemán, "Citizenship and Colonial Whites," 27; Aranda, "Contradictory Impulses," 11.
8. By "frame" I mean a way of contextualizing the novel by constructing particular questions and concerns that will guide our interpretations of it.
9. See, for instance, Montes and Tuttle's recommendations in the subsection "Strategies for the Classroom," in Montes and Goldman, *María Amparo Ruiz de Burton*, section 5, "Teaching Ruiz de Burton."
10. Alemán, "Citizenship and Colonial Whites," 7.
11. Montes, "Teaching María Amparo Ruiz de Burton," 297.
12. See Castañeda, "Political Economy of Nineteenth-Century Stereotypes of Californianas."
13. "Treaty of Guadalupe Hidalgo: February 2, 1848" (emphases added, both italics and boldface).
14. Ruiz de Burton, *Squatter and the Don*, 142.
15. Ruiz de Burton, *Squatter and the Don*, 4–5.
16. See Szeghi, "Vanishing Mexicana/o."
17. Ruiz de Burton, *Squatter and the Don*, 5–6.
18. Montes, "Teaching María Amparo Ruiz de Burton," 296–97.
19. Although neither Crèvecoeur nor Jefferson was located in the western United States, their conceptions of American identity, forged through archetypal frontier experiences, have influenced much western American literature. I thus find it valuable to include even just brief excerpts from their writing in surveys of western American literature.
20. Aranda, *When We Arrive*, 91.
21. Aranda, *When We Arrive*, 99.

22. Aranda, *When We Arrive*, 99.
23. Aranda, *When We Arrive*, 88.
24. Ruiz de Burton, *Squatter and the Don*, 51.
25. Ruiz de Burton, *Squatter and the Don*, 144.
26. I borrowed the concept of the silent chalk talk from Dr. Eric Gary Anderson, associate professor in the English Department at George Mason University.
27. Similarly, Karen Kilcup, in her evaluation of *Squatter* as an environmental justice novel due to its advocacy of sustainable land use and Californios' agency in their ownership and occupation of California lands, sees the novel's simultaneous elitism, racism, and celebration of "sophisticated indoor activities" as important for grappling with the internal contradictions and fractures within social movements. Kilcup, "Writing against Wilderness," 373–74. For all of *Squatter*'s contradictions, Kilcup argues, Ruiz de Burton "anticipates the contemporary principle of environmental justice that 'considers governmental acts of environmental injustice a violation of international law, the Universal Declaration on Human Rights, and the United Nations Convention on Genocide'" (366).
28. Ruiz de Burton, *Squatter and the Don*, 15.
29. United Nations, Universal Declaration of Human Rights, 1948.
30. See Szeghi, "Vanishing Mexicana/o," for a detailed examination of Ruiz de Burton's racial hierarchies.
31. Ruiz de Burton, *Squatter and the Don*, 48.
32. Ruiz de Burton, *Squatter and the Don*, 147–48.
33. Alemán, "Citizenship and Colonial Whites," 22.
34. Regarding the "riff-raff," see Ruiz de Burton, *Squatter and the Don*, 17.
35. See Luis-Brown, "'White Slaves' and the 'Arrogant *Mestiza*'"; and Alemán, "Historical Amnesia and the Vanishing Mestiza."

BIBLIOGRAPHY

Alemán, Jesse. "Citizenship and Colonial Whites: The Cultural Work of María Amparo Ruiz de Burton's Novels." In *Complicating Constructions: Race, Ethnicity, and Hybridity in American Texts*, edited by David S. Goldstein and Audrey B. Thacker, 3–10. Seattle: University of Washington Press, 2007.

———. "Historical Amnesia and the Vanishing Mestiza: The Problem of Race in *The Squatter and the Don* and *Ramona*." *Aztlán: A Journal of Chicano Studies* 27, no. 1 (2002): 59–93.

———. "'Thank God, Lolita Is Away from Those Horrid Savages': The Politics of Whiteness in *Who Would Have Thought It?*" In *María Amparo Ruiz de Burton: Critical and Pedagogical Perspectives*, edited by Amelia María de la Luz Montes and Anne Elizabeth Goldman, 95–111. Lincoln: University of Nebraska Press, 2004.

Aranda, José F., Jr. "Contradictory Impulses: María Amparo Ruiz de Burton, Resistance Theory, and the Politics of Chicano/a Studies." *American Literature* 70, no. 3 (1998): 551–79.

———. *When We Arrive: A New Literary History of Mexican America*. Tucson: University of Arizona Press, 2003.

Castañeda, Antonia I. "The Political Economy of Nineteenth-Century Stereotypes of Californianas." In *Three Decades of Engendering History*, edited by Linda Heidenreich with Antonia I. Castañeda, 37–64. Denton: University of North Texas Press, 2014.

Crèvecoeur, J. Hector St. John de. *Letters from an American Farmer and Sketches of Eighteenth Century America*. 1782. New York: Penguin, 1981.

González, John M. "Romancing Hegemony: Constructing Racialized Citizenship in María Amparo Ruiz de Burton's *The Squatter and the Don*." In *Recovering the U.S.-Hispanic Literary Heritage*, volume 2, edited by Erlinda Gonzales-Berry and Chuck Tatum, 23–39. Houston: Arte Público Press, 1996.

Haas, Lisbeth. *Conquests and Historical Identities in California, 1769–1936*. Berkeley: University of California Press, 1995.

Jefferson, Thomas. *Notes on the State of Virginia*. 1785. New York: Penguin, 1998.

Kilcup, Karen. "Writing Against Wilderness: María Amparo Ruiz de Burton's Elite Environmental Justice." *Western American Literature* 47, no. 4 (2013): 360–85.

Kolodny, Annette. "Letting Go Our Grand Obsessions: Notes toward a New Literary History of the American Frontiers." *American Literature* 62, no. 1 (1992): 1–18.

Limerick, Patricia Nelson. *The Legacy of Conquest: The Unbroken Past of the American West*. New York: Norton, 1987.

Luis-Brown, David. "'White Slaves' and the 'Arrogant *Mestiza*': Reconfiguring Whiteness in *The Squatter and the Don* and *Ramona*." *American Literature* 69, no. 4 (1997): 813–40.

Montes, Amelia María de la Luz. "Teaching María Amparo Ruiz de Burton." In *Latino/a Literature in the Classroom: Twenty-First-Century Approaches*, edited by Frederick Luis Aldama, 295–98. New York: Routledge, 2015.

Montes, Amelia María de la Luz, and Anne Elizabeth Goldman, eds. *María Amparo Ruiz de Burton: Critical and Pedagogical Perspectives*. Lincoln: University of Nebraska Press, 2004.

Pita, Beatrice. "Engendering Critique: Race, Class, and Gender in Ruiz de Burton and Martí." In *José Martí's "Our America": From National to Hemispheric Cultural Studies*, edited by Jeffrey Belnap and Raúl Fernandez, 129–44. Durham: Duke University Press, 1998.

Pitt, Leonard. *The Decline of the Californios: A Social History of the Spanish-Speaking Californians, 1846–1890*. Berkeley: University of California Press, 1966.

Posey, Alexander. *The Fus Fixico Letters*. Edited by Daniel F. Littlefield Jr. and Carol A. Petty Hunter. 1902–8. Norman: University of Oklahoma Press, 1993.

"Principles of Environmental Justice." Environmental Justice/Environmental Racism. http://www.ejnet.org/ej/principles.html.

Ruiz de Burton, María Amparo. *Conflicts of Interest: The Letters of María Amparo Ruiz de Burton*. Edited by Rosaura Sánchez and Beatrice Pita. Houston: Arte Público Press, 2001.

———. *The Squatter and the Don*. 1885. New York: Random House, 2004.

Sánchez, Rosaura, and Beatrice Pita. Introduction to *The Squatter and the Don*, 5–51. Houston: Arte Público Press, 1992.

Stowe, Harriet Beecher. *Uncle Tom's Cabin*. Edited by Elizabeth Ammons. 1852. New York: Norton, 2018.

Szeghi, Tereza M. "The Vanishing Mexicana/o: (Dis)Locating the Native in Ruiz de Burton's *Who Would Have Thought It?* and *The Squatter and the Don*." *Aztlán* 36, no. 2 (2011): 89–120.

"Treaty of Guadalupe Hidalgo: February 2, 1848." Avalon Project: Documents in Law, History, and Diplomacy, Yale Law School. Accessed April 25, 2019. https://avalon.law .yale.edu/19th_century/guadhida.asp.

Turner, Frederick Jackson. *The Significance of the Frontier in American History.* 1894. Eastford CT: Martino Fine Books, 2014.

Tuttle, Jennifer. Commentary in *María Amparo Ruiz de Burton: Critical & Pedagogical Perspectives*, edited by Amelia María de la Luz Montes and Anne Elizabeth Goldman, 232. Lincoln: University of Nebraska Press, 2004.

United Nations. Declaration on the Rights of Indigenous Peoples. September 13, 2007. https://www.un.org/development/desa/indigenouspeoples/wp-content/uploads/sites /19/2018/11/UNDRIP_E_web.pdf.

———. Universal Declaration of Human Rights. December 10, 1948. http://www.un.org /en/universal-declaration-human-rights/.

12

Able-Bodies, Difference, and Citizenship in the West

Teaching James Welch's *The Heartsong of Charging Elk* in a Global Context

ANDREA M. DOMINGUEZ

What makes a man? What makes a man whole? Where do definitions of masculinity and wholeness emerge from? How are these definitions normalized? Perhaps more importantly, what is the result when one deviates from these expected normalizations? Within the realm of literary and regional studies of the West, these questions continue to shape our study and perceptions of space and identity formations. Today these questions are more complex—and pressing—than ever as educators continue to struggle with these abstractions in such a regionally and politically divisive time. As an educator, I find that confronting issues of gendered forms of normativity and structures of power in the classroom often means engaging current social constructions. Today we must lead discussions and scaffold understandings that more directly address toxic masculinity, rape culture, and "pussy grabbers." Thus, it is no surprise that students are even more daunted by—and even more in need of—thoughtful instruction that helps them read and understand the nuances of difference and the politics of normalcy in an increasingly intersectional world. While these are not new questions or constructions, they continue to be difficult to understand, engage with, and deconstruct in ways that make students better participants in our classrooms and our communities.

The Heartsong of Charging Elk, by James Welch, provides a rich case study with which to deconstruct constructions of normalcy in the West and connect the literary tradition of regionalism to contemporary conversations about difference and power. In the novel Welch tells the story of Indigenous identity through a chronicle of one man's performance of able-bodied masculinity. Set in 1889, the novel traces the story of Charging Elk, a Lakota man who is part of the second European tour of Buffalo Bill's Wild West Show. After suffering a disabling accident during the show and then falling victim to an influenza epidemic in France, Charging Elk is left for dead by his cohort, stranded in a foreign land, and forced to negotiate his rehabilitation as a man without cultural or national connections. The novel tells the tale of his rehabilitation, from the beginning of his illness to his ultimate assimilation into French society. This process of rehabilitation and assimilation is ultimately achieved through the exercise of western, heteronormative masculinity that is directly linked to the cultural institution of the family. It is only through this rehabilitation that Charging Elk can gain access to French citizenship and full human status in order to end his quest for a modified and negotiated sense of wholeness based on perceptions of normalcy in the West.[1] Through these shifts in culture, language, and identity politics, Welch weaves a tale of body-based discourse that radically complicates the notions of identity, wellness, and citizenship by positioning Indigenous bodies at the center of historical debates about marked otherness.[2]

Within the canons of western literature and Native American and Indigenous literatures, *The Heartsong of Charging Elk* provides a unique opportunity to guide students through a lesson in global colonialism that still has dramatic repercussions for how we understand race, cultural citizenship, and cultural capital in the Global West. Welch's body of work itself situates the Indigenous body in relation to constructed national fantasies of race and space. In *Winter in the Blood*, *Fools Crow*, and *The Indian Lawyer*, Welch uses the Indigenous body—and the masculine form—to build a narrative of colonial legacy that is dependent on bodily formations. As part of this narrative canon, *The Heartsong of Charging Elk* takes a closer look at the body politics of Indigenous Americans in a newly defined western landscape that transcends the borders of space and nation to focus on a cultural citizenry at the heart of discourses of colonialism and assimilation. By situating this text in a global context for students, the goal is to facilitate a broader understanding of the complex tropes of western literature to question the geographical and cultural boundaries of how we define the West in the literary imaginary. This globalized view of the novel helps us frame lines of inquiry that include questions such as the following:

What is the role of place in identity politics?

How is geography framed in relationship to citizenship and culture?

How are regions defined culturally and geographically? What does this suggest about political and cultural discourses of power?

How can we place this narrative in conversation with global colonial narratives?

This chapter considers these complex questions to help frame a pedagogical lens that advocates investigating the multifaceted relationship between able-bodiedness and discourses of citizenship. By situating Welch, Indigenous literatures, and regional studies of the West within the frameworks of postcolonial theory, cultural studies, and disability studies, this chapter identifies theoretical scaffolds for instruction. Each section of this chapter provides a context for discussing key themes in Welch's novel that revolve around questions of able-bodiedness and normalcy, as well as sample course activities or assignments along with suggested guidelines that can help shape extended dialogues. Furthermore, by engaging the novel through a global lens, this framework creates a forum in which discussions of Indigenous literatures are placed in contact with global conceptions of difference, systemic structures of power, diaspora, and resistance. In this context disability becomes a metaphor for physical and cultural diaspora, and students can use it to deconstruct and understand systemic forms of racialization and othering. Moreover, this chapter argues that such lines of inquiry within the humanities are central to discussions about how educational institutions and diverse course offerings contribute to and promote global cultural competence. Through applications of critical thinking skills to produce thoughtful analysis, overcome cultural divides, and make connections to contemporary perceptions of place, students are forced to contend with not only the legacies of colonial processes but with contemporary manifestations of the haunted racial past of the West, both in the United States and abroad. By facilitating these connections for students, the instructional methods suggested in this chapter aim to promote a globalized view of the West through critical analysis, historical contextualization, and comparative study.

Building a Framework for Student Engagement:
Disability and *The Heartsong of Charging Elk*

In approaching *The Heartsong of Charging Elk* through the lens of disability studies, it is important to consider the context of colonial and postcolonial studies and the relationship of that discipline to heteronormative constructions of masculinity in the West. This context is centered on the abnormalization of Charging Elk's body. From the beginning of the novel Charging Elk is disoriented and disconnected from his own body because of his unclear national and cultural positionality. More importantly, he is characterized as helpless due to his lack of national connection. In the opening passage of the novel Charging Elk wakes up in a French "sickhouse," where "he could smell the damp, ashy odor of the bodies mixed with the sharp smell of wasicn medicine."[3] Unable to care for himself or communicate, he is at the mercy of those staffing the sickhouse. Charging Elk considers his situation: "He was not of these people. He was a different color and he couldn't speak their tongue. He was from somewhere a long way off. And he was here, alone, in this house of sickness. He tried to fight off the panic by remembering something about himself."[4] His disorientation marks him as a foreign body by signaling his illness, heritage, and cultural difference as fundamentally different from normative constructions. This sense of foreignness renders him as the "other" in the text and drives him to become a "well" and rehabilitated citizen.

This sense of disorientation, and the resulting desire for rehabilitation, is a central narrative thread through which to engage disability studies theory and constructions. In their book *Narrative Prosthesis*, David Mitchell and Sharon Snyder explain, "While stories rely upon the potency of disability as a symbolic figure, they rarely take up disability as an experience of social or political dimensions."[5] In the context of the nineteenth century, in which the novel takes place, disability is informed by rigid discourses of normalcy and difference that shape social categories and conventions. In the nineteenth century "the social process of disabling arrived with industrialization and with the set of practices and discourses that are linked to late eighteenth and nineteenth century notions of nationality, race, gender, criminality, sexual orientation, and so on."[6] As a result, disability gets understood as a "sickness" that renders those marked by disability as "invalids," or those incapable of representing or controlling their own bodies.[7] In considering disability as a way to map gender and racial formations during this period, educators may create scaffolds for exploring the following ideas as part of supplemental readings and lecture materials. One potential model is represented in table 1.

Table 1. Tracing key themes in *The Heartsong of Charging Elk*

CONCEPT	KEYWORDS	THEMES IN NOVEL
Foucault's *History of Sexuality*	Sex and power Masculinity	Charging Elk's rehabilitation Citizenship
Cult of domesticity	Gender Performativity Public vs. private spheres	French masculinity Definitions of wellness Performativity
Social Darwinism	Natural selection Survival of the fittest	Representations of race Reproduction
Scientific racism	Racial classifications Racial hierarchies	Representations of race Charging Elk's rehabilitation

Tracing the concepts and themes outlined in table 1 allows instructors to build a foundation on which students can begin to think through concepts central to disability studies; they will begin to see the problems inherent in narratives of normalcy and learn to question default methods of categorizing marked and unmarked identity signifiers. These themes also scaffold a key premise of disability studies, which is that "disability signals that the body cannot be universalized."[8] As Lennard Davis suggests in his landmark study "Constructing Normalcy," "the emphasis on nation and national fitness obviously plays into the metaphor of the body."[9] In this context the body becomes an allegorical narrative for the nation, where citizenship is literally inscribed on the body through perceptions of wellness and health. As Davis notes, "if individual citizens are not fit, if they do not fit into the nation, then the national body will not be fit."[10] It is not merely a bodily sense of wellness that dictates the relationship between the disabled and the state but an ideological one as well. Charging Elk's illness and injury mark him as "sick" or unwell, further complicating his status as a foreign other. A disabled body becomes a marked body that does not and, perhaps more importantly, cannot conform to the norms of society.

Sample Activity: Constructing Normalcy

Description: When introducing students to key—and sometimes new—concepts, it is critical to build a strong foundation for activities and assignments that both prompt understanding and allow students to stretch their analytical skills to deconstruct, interrogate, and reconstruct meaning. Such skills are the bedrock of close reading and critical thinking. An effective method of facilitating this is a basic "think-pair-share" discussion. This activity is not intended to supply a close reading of the text but to allow students to use their fields of knowledge and cultural constructs to begin initial discussions about key themes that the text engages. As a result, this is an ideal activity for starting discussions that preface close readings of the novel.

Facilitation: In this activity students can work in pairs, larger groups, or individually to focus on a specific keyword for a five- to ten-minute period of reflection and discussion that is then briefly summarized for the class. This is an activity that can take place at the beginning of class to help situate the conversation for the day or in the middle of class to help reinforce key aspects of the lecture material. To help prepare students for engagement, instructors may suggest students take notes and be prepared to share key points of their discussion or reflection with the class. For this initial think-pair-share activity, pose the following prompt: *Define "normal" using three keywords. What are the terms that you think describe what "normal" means?*

Students should consider this prompt and propose three key terms to each other and discuss. If working in pairs, they can select three key terms from their brainstorming, then discuss and present them to the class. If using the prompt for an individual reflection, instructors may ask students to spend three to four minutes building a list and then lead them to narrow their list of words to three key terms to focus on and present to the class. One way to provoke a wide variety of responses is to have students focus not on the novel but on ways to culturally define normalcy in general. This activity is an excellent way to introduce key themes of *The Heartsong of Charging Elk* and to prompt students to interrogate forms of normalcy both in the novel and in contemporary society. Thus, this activity supports not only close reading of specific narrative threads and themes but supports students' cultural competence development through dialogues in the humanities.

As students present their terms to define normalcy, instructors can extend this activity by recording key terms and using them to build a word map for students. This can be done by creating a simple list on the classroom whiteboard, or the list can be electronically produced using a platform such as WordCloud or Wordle. When using this activity in any context or course, I often create a word map and post it to the course website or create handouts that can be distributed to the class for future reference. This provides a powerful and useful reference that will help guide students through subsequent activities. In addition, it provides a glimpse into the complexity levels of key concepts—in this case, normalcy—that will help instructors revise lecture material, focus on key points to aid understanding, and plan supplemental support materials as necessary.

This initial think-pair-share activity can then form the foundation of more nuanced close reading activities that bridge constructions of normalcy and the politics of dependency. Such activities will facilitate more specific and in-depth discussions couched in disability studies criticism. As Eva Kittay suggests in her work on the relationship between gender and dependence, "inequality of power is endemic to dependency relations."[11] This issue of inequality is directly related to constructions of normalcy and is foundational to Charging Elk's rehabilitative narrative. Once students have completed a think-pair-share activity, they can focus on more detailed close reading methodology. Consider asking students to perform their own close reading of a passage that highlights one of the following themes: masculinity, citizenship, wellness, performance, reproduction (or any additional themes that highlight key tropes in disability studies). Students may search individually or in pairs for a passage that highlights their selected or assigned theme and discuss these questions:

How does Charging Elk imagine his body and identity?

How do others in the scene imagine Charging Elk's body and identity?

What is the relationship of this theme to constructions of normalcy?

Depending on the time available or the desired depth, students can spend anywhere from ten to thirty minutes developing their responses.

Guided Case Study: Place, Space, and Nation

While the introductory think-pair-share activity is an excellent way to generate discussion and allow students to explore key concepts, it doesn't offer the opportunity for students to connect historical context with the narrative. Using a guided case study is a way to further engage students with the foundational concepts illustrated in table 1. Doing so also provides a model of the connection between theory and practice that will guide students through complex literary analysis via a focused theoretical lens. With an initial case study, the goal is to contextualize the key themes of the novel through a close look at the historical context of the period in which *The Heartsong of Charging Elk* is set. Much of this anxiety over bodily normalcy is represented in Charging Elk's shifting forms of masculinity in the novel. While getting students to openly discuss sexuality can be challenging, the goal is to contextualize it within the historic structures of power in which the novel is set.

Close Reading: Highlighting Historical Context

The goal of this close reading activity is to highlight examples of Charging Elk's "rehabilitation" that facilitate his journey to French identity and citizenship. This narrative is present from early on in the novel. When Charging Elk leaves the hospital and becomes a ward of the court, a form of dependency is established and repeated when he is left in the charge of the Soulas family, who are appointed guardian of his care and rehabilitation. Madeleine and René Soulas "were equipped to deal with vagabonds and orphans, it was their calling to care for indigents."[12] As Christians and missionaries in the community, the Soulas family is capable of administering not only Charging Elk's physical rehabilitation but his cultural and moral rehabilitation as well. As a result of their care, he will no longer be a vagabond or an orphan or a man without country, home, or cultural support. Rather, he will be transformed into a member of French society, one who knows his place and has subjugated his body to the ruling structures of power.

More importantly, the relationship between Charging Elk and the Soulas family mirrors the ward/guardian relationship that influences Charging Elk's positionality in both the United States and France and is indicative of Western perceptions of "otherness" in the nineteenth century that continue to reverberate in today's global political climate. In the novel Welch specifies that "Charging Elk wasn't a citizen of the United States. Because of the treaties, the Indian tribes were their own nations within the United States. But the individuals were wards of the government and as such were entitled to diplomatic representation in foreign countries."[13] In this passage Welch makes it clear that Charging Elk's national identity is a complex matter that has been left unresolved by the U.S. government.

This ambiguity is rooted in the legal and political climate of the period. In *Cherokee Nation v. Georgia* (1831), the Supreme Court of the United States declared that individual Indian tribes were neither a state nor a foreign nation; rather, each was a "domestic dependent nation."[14] As the ruling details, "They occupy a territory to which we assert a title independent of their will, which must take effect in point of possession when their right of possession ceases; meanwhile, they are in a state of pupilage. Their relations to the United States resemble that of a ward to his guardian. They look to our Government for protection, rely upon its kindness and its power, appeal to it for relief to their wants, and address the President as their Great Father."[15] After this landmark case, uneasy questions about citizenship lingered until 1924, when U.S. citizenship was finally extended to Indigenous people who possessed tribal affiliations. These vague stipulations over citizenship and nationalism help frame both Charging Elk's quest for a sense of identity and his rehabilitative process. During the era in which *The Heartsong of Charging Elk* takes place, "as citizens of dependent domestic nations, there were no laws dealing with the status of individual Indians. Thus, Indians were nonentities and had no legal status."[16] As a "nonentity," Charging Elk becomes a body that can be molded to any country, any era, and any culture. His transformability makes him the perfect possibility for rehabilitation. Thus, disability and unwellness in the novel act as a meta-metaphor for assimilative fantasies.

Case Study: Narratives of Rehabilitation

In the context of disability studies we can define rehabilitation as "society's wish to make identical without making equal."[17] Rehabilitation creates the appearance of equality as a way to regulate bodies and preserve hegemonic norms and the accompanying structures of power. Rehabilitation becomes a "'normalizing' strategy in which bio-medical authorities took the view that the impaired body could never benefit from rationalization or reform. The goal of rehabilitation is to fix or improve the 'performance' of broken bodies and make them 'fit.'"[18] Charging Elk is subject to this kind of rehabilitation methodology on multiple levels: as a man afflicted by illness, as an Indigenous person in France, as a linguistic minority, and as a vagabond in a society of citizens. His illness is continually extended in the novel as one form of rehabilitation leads to another. For Charging Elk, rehabilitation becomes a way for him to perform a sense of identity in order to function in French society. The goal of his rehabilitation is not only to recover from the affliction that plagues him at the beginning of the novel but also to not "feel much like a 'wild' Indian anymore."[19]

In deconstructing rehabilitation for the case of Indigenous identity in the U.S. West, it is crucial to contextualize this notion of the "wild Indian" within the sociopolitical framework of colonial processes and ideologies in the United States. Perhaps the most central of these ideologies—and certainly one with the deepest reach—is that of the noble savage. As Ter Ellingson explains in *The Myth of the Noble Savage*, "the idea that 'wild' or 'savage' native peoples were brought to a state of 'domestication' was widespread in the rhetoric of both racist anthropology and colonial administration."[20] Welch makes it clear in his narrative that Charging Elk is not "cruel or inhuman," as the "savage" designation might suggest, but rather "was gentle, even pliable."[21] This sense of being "pliable" is foundational to Charging Elk's process of rehabilitation.

Sample Activity: Context and Culture

Description: The "context and culture" assignment allows students to engage with a specific historical context and apply complex histories to close readings of key areas of the novel. This activity is designed to provide students

Table 2. Suggested topics for context and culture assignment

THEME	HISTORICAL CONTEXT	KEY QUESTIONS
Law	Marshall Trilogy	What are some of the key mandates and definitions formulated in the Marshall Trilogy? How did these cases help shape Indigenous-U.S. relations and Indigenous identity? How do these cases define "dependency"? What are some potential consequences? How is Charging Elk "dependent" in the novel?
Health	Nineteenth-century disease in Europe	What were some major public health concerns in Europe during the nineteenth century? What was the standard of care? In the novel, how is physical health related to mental and emotional wellness?
Culture	Buffalo Bill's Wild West Show	What was the purpose of the Wild West shows? What was the role of Indigenous performers? For a performer like Charging Elk, what are the potentials and limits of agency?
Space	Paris, 1889	How would you characterize Paris in 1889? What are some of the key differences between urban centers and rural areas? What are some experiences that Charging Elk may have had there?

with an opportunity to explore historical connections to the novel, build research and digital literacy skills, share information, and practice visual communication and oral presentation skills. Depending on class size and the length of the course, this assignment can be constructed for individual

Table 3. Suggested requirements for context and culture assignment

RESEARCH	PRESENTATION
Two secondary scholarly sources	5–7 slides, 10–15-minute presentation
One primary source	Specific examples: analysis that illustrates the connections between the text and key themes
Specific examples from *The Heartsong of Charging Elk*	Minimum of one visual or multimedia element

Students must provide a works cited page listing all sources used, including visual sources.

students or as a group project. As a method, this activity can be adapted to any text in your course. For this specific context and culture assignment, students select a key historical feature or event and conduct research to present to the class to help contextualize the novel.

Facilitation: To help frame the context of the novel, students should be provided with specific contextual and historical lenses to guide their research and analysis. Table 2 details potential prompts for the context and culture assignment.

In investigating these potential topics, students can conduct academic research focused on peer-reviewed and primary sources and design a presentation that helps situate these various contextual forms of the novel. Table 3 illustrates suggested requirements for this assignment.

In asking students to provide a short presentation on their selected context, instructors are able to create an environment in which students are able to share resources, express research in a multimedia form, and practice key analytical and communication skills. Consider giving students at least one week to complete the assignment and reserving a class meeting for student presentations. If your classroom has a technology station, students can present using PowerPoint, Prezi, or Google Slides. Alternatively, handouts can be used to help provide a visual guide for the presentation. Thoughtful and constructive feedback on content, close readings, and presentation style will help students become more aware of key analytical and communication skills and will also provide an avenue for improvement.

Contemporary Connections: Indigenous Spaces, Refugees, Immigration

More advanced students, or those who have already been led through the processes of close reading and contextualization, may be prompted to develop a more detailed critical analysis of the text by applying key themes and construction to contemporary conversations about normalcy, wellness, and race. Doing so will help students trace historical continuums and bridge the gap between cultural theory and pragmatic application. A key theme to anchor this analysis is that of passing. Charging Elk's narrative of rehabilitation is predicated on the concept of "passing." Because of his travels with the Wild West show, Charging Elk is "a seasoned performer."[22] His presence in France is established as performative in nature from the beginning, when he is passing as a performer—passing for what western Europe thinks an "Indian" is. Yet it is also through passing that rehabilitation becomes possible and tangible in the narrative. The novel offers rich examples of performance and even passing narratives, which can help shape students' understanding of these key constructs of critical race theory and disability studies. While the first two activities described in this chapter focus on understanding themes and concepts, an assignment centering on performativity allows students to apply the concepts they have learned to larger social and global concerns related to disability studies and constructions of hetero-able-bodied normativity.

Case Study: Passing

In the novel, passing is delineated through a close exploration of Charging Elk's sexuality and masculinity. Charging Elk's sexuality is constantly in question, marking him as a nonbinary figure with a fluid form of sexuality. In the novel there are multiple examples of homoeroticism from his past, and a turning point in his rehabilitation comes when he is on trial as a result of a violent sexual encounter with another man. These incidents in the narrative continually queer Charging Elk's body and identity, further marking him as "other" in a foreign land. His sexuality thus becomes a way to prove not only his masculinity but his normativity, as he becomes a rehabilitated body. Charging Elk must have a sense of "compulsory heterosexuality" that creates an image of "compulsory able-bodiedness." In his book *Crip Theory*, Robert McRuer explains that, "like compulsory heterosexuality, then, compulsory able-bodiedness functions by covering over, with the appearance of choice, a system in which there actually is no choice."[23] In reality Charging Elk has no choice but to pass, to be "compulsive" in the way he imagines and presents his body as a rehabilitated man. His gender becomes what critics such as Judith Butler have described as "performative." Engaging in a heteronormative sexual relationship is part of being able to imagine a life in France. As Butler suggests, "sex is always produced as a reiteration of hegemonic norms."[24]

The rules of masculinity that Charging Elk follows are thus directly linked to conceptions of nationhood and citizenship in the novel. In *The History of Sexuality*, Foucault explains that when sex is a police matter, it has the power to determine both nationhood and citizenship. The systems of canonical law, marriage, and the laws of desire govern and determine what is licit and illicit. These three systems, and the laws that enforce them, produce the idea of the citizen, or one who can surrender personal desires to the desires of a nation. As an Indigenous man, Charging Elk is not considered a citizen of the newly formed United States, but he is also not a French citizen. He is a man without country, without home, without a place to belong. The only way that Charging Elk can remedy his situation is through asserting his sexuality through marriage. While staying with the Grazier family during his rehabilitation, he falls in love with Nathalie, the young Grazier daughter. Nathalie "made him feel young again and more alive than he had ever been since he left the stronghold fifteen years before."[25] Their affair allows Charging Elk to be free from both affliction and restriction. This development in the novel signals Charging Elk's wellness as an assimilated member of French society. When Charging Elk speaks of his marriage, he explains, "I speak the language of these people. My wife is one of them and my heart is her heart. She is my life now and soon we will have another life and the same heart will sing in all of us."[26] His marriage to Nathalie and the coming birth of their child represent a submission to the hegemonic norms of France. Charging Elk's body has conformed to the rules of French society. It is only through marriage and reproduction that the process of assimilation and citizenship becomes possible. The union between Charging Elk and Nathalie symbolizes his final conquest in his desire for

Western masculinity because it signals his identification—and passing—as a French man. The canonical laws of the state, marriage, and the role of desire all serve to help craft Charging Elk into a model European citizen.

Sample Activity: Current Events

Description: This activity allows students to translate the themes of the novel into readings of contemporary current events. The goal is for students to identify and source contemporary issues and social debates that illustrate key themes in the novel that persist with regard to the notion of passing. This assignment also helps create a continuum with the long legacy of criminalizing difference in the West: views of disabled bodies as morally deficient and deviant, the criminalization of homosexuality, racial segregation, police brutality, and the criminalization of homelessness. Some sample themes students may wish to investigate are summarized in table 4.

Table 4. Sample current events for study

THEME	CURRENT EVENT TOPIC
Sickness/wellness	Disability rights
	Women's health
	Universal health care
Masculinity	Toxic masculinity
	Sexual harassment
	LGBTQ+ rights
Immigration and citizenship	Global migration
	Refugee rights
	Immigration debates/reform (U.S.)

Facilitation: The goal of this assignment is to guide students in facilitating connections between the major themes they are examining in *The Heartsong of Charging Elk* and the world around them. Students may select one news or social commentary article from a recent publication, such as the *Atlantic*, the *Economist*, or the *New Yorker*, which all cover a wide selection of current events that may be viewed through a social commentary lens.

Consider having students provide a two- to three-paragraph summary that highlights the main argument of the text, key supporting claims that help develop the argument, and specific case studies or examples that ground the argument. This will help students deconstruct their selected text and engage in thoughtful academic summary techniques. This summary can then form the foundation for a more detailed two- to three-page analysis of how the themes in their selected current event intersect with major themes from the novel. Instructors may prompt students to consider the following questions:

> In what ways are identities performative? In what complex histories are these performances rooted?
> What are the current ways that people can "pass"? How does passing influence legal and cultural citizenship?
> How are contemporary conflicts illustrative of modern discourses of power?
> Are there potential solutions to these conflicts? What theories can help people increase awareness and establish agency?

To provide extra support as students begin this process, instructors may consider presenting a short current event case study to the class and walk through some of the analysis questions together to help establish the scope of the assignment and provide a sample analysis. Alternatively, for smaller seminars, students may be given time in class to brainstorm current event ideas with their classmates as a point of departure for the assignment.

Conclusions: Moving Forward

In *The Heartsong of Charging Elk*, Welch traces a narrative of sickness and wellness, citizenship and vagabondage, disability and normalcy. The assignments described in this chapter are designed to help students translate and transfer these complex definitions and constructions of power to reveal historical trends and question contemporary realities. In deconstructing the text to question the politics and implications of definitions of normalcy and able-bodiedness, students are uncovering not only histories of the body but histories of a body politic that continue to delineate the way we imagine the relationship between space and race in the globalized West. In guiding students through *The Heartsong of Charging Elk* to navigate the global landscape of rehabilitation and passing, educators can guide them into expanding the scope of regionalism beyond physical geography to consider the epistemological constructions that are foundational to ideologies that shape perceptions of the West. *The Heartsong of Charging Elk* offers a revision of the boundaries of the West, alongside its revisions of the boundaries of the Indigenous body. By following this trajectory, students not only become more aware of the inherent contradictions of the positionality of the West but also gain analytical skills they can use to challenge those contradictions and apply critical analysis across space and time. Thus, a close reading of the novel through the lens of disability studies is not just about reading the text but about reading the world that the text emerges from, as well as the world that continues to shape the way we think collectively and critically about the relationship between race and space.

Further Resources

As you design and refine assignments, consider these resources (listed in order of relevance) for your course and students:

Disability Studies in the Humanities, https://listserv.umd.edu/archives/ds -hum.html.
   This Listserv includes information on themes and trends in the academic field of disability, both nationally and internationally.

Society for Disability Studies, https://disstudies.org/.
   An international, interdisciplinary organization dedicated to promoting scholarly investigation into disability. sds organizes academic conferences and publishes *Disability Studies Quarterly*.

Museum of Disability History, http://museumofdisability.org/.
   This resource provides detailed historical and timeline information to help contextualize perceptions of normalcy and able-bodiedness.

"Disability Studies: A New Normal," http://www.nytimes.com/2013/11 /03/education/edlife/disability-studies-a-new-normal.html?pagewanted= all&_r=0.

Accessible *New York Times* article that places disability studies in context with educational goals of equality and social justice.

Krupat, Arnold, ed. *Companion to James Welch's "The Heartsong of Charging Elk."* Lincoln: University of Nebraska Press, 2015. http://www.nebraskapress .unl.edu/university-of-nebraska-press/9780803254329/.
This collection includes recent academic works on *The Heartsong of Charging Elk.*

The Heartsong of Changing Elk Reader's Guide, https://www.penguinrandomhouse .com/books/188448/the-heartsong-of-charging-elk-by-james-welch /9780385496759/readers-guide/.
Publisher's reading guide with questions that can be adapted for the classroom.

Cherokee Nation v. Georgia, 30 U.S. 1 (1831), https://supreme.justia.com /cases/federal/us/30/1/case.html.
Complete ruling of *Cherokee Nation v. Georgia,* which established Indigenous tribes as "domestic dependent nations."

Native Times, https://www.nativetimes.com/.
Indigenous news outlet and excellent source for Indigenous current events.

NOTES

1. Ferguson, "Europe and the Quest for Home," 37.
2. I have elected to use the word "Indigenous" when referring to the Native peoples of the United States as a collective group. My purpose in utilizing this collective term is not to gloss over the extreme cultural, geographical, and linguistic diversity of Indigenous people within North America but to make clear distinctions between the various population groups—and national identities—discussed in this chapter. When appropriate, I use the name Lakota to discuss Charging Elk's particular identification, favoring the Indigenous nation affiliation. You are encouraged to discuss terminology with your students and to prompt them to select their preferred terms and supply ample reasoning for their choices.
3. Welch, *Heartsong of Charging Elk,* 8. *Wasicn* is a Lakota word meaning "white man."
4. Welch, *Heartsong of Charging Elk,* 9.

5. Mitchell and Snyder, *Narrative Prosthesis*, 205.

6. Davis, "Constructing Normalcy," 3.

7. Hughes, "Disability and the Body," 58.

8. Thomson, *Extraordinary Bodies*, 24.

9. Davis, "Constructing Normalcy," 9.

10. Davis, "Constructing Normalcy," 9.

11. Kittay, *Love's Labor*, 34.

12. Welch, *Heartsong of Charging Elk*, 111.

13. Welch, *Heartsong of Charging Elk*, 80.

14. This section is not designed to provide an exhaustive examination of *Cherokee Nation v. Georgia* or the foundational Marshall Trilogy of Supreme Court decisions that form the basis of federal policy shaping U.S.-Indigenous relations to this day. The goal is to supply students with a general understanding of the case that will inform their close reading of the novel.

15. Cherokee Nation v. Georgia, 30 U.S. 1, 17 (1831).

16. Martin, "Neither Fish, Flesh, Fowl, nor Good Herring," 52.

17. McRuer, *Crip Theory*, 113.

18. Hughes, "Disability and the Body," 63.

19. Welch, *Heartsong of Charging Elk*, 130.

20. Ellingson, *Myth of the Nobel Savage*, 229.

21. Welch, *Heartsong of Charging Elk*, 388.

22. Welch, *Heartsong of Charging Elk*, 51.

23. McRuer, *Crip Theory*, 8.

24. Butler, *Bodies That Matter*, 107.

25. Welch, *Heartsong of Charging Elk*, 387.

26. Welch, *Heartsong of Charging Elk*, 437.

BIBLIOGRAPHY

Butler, Judith. *Bodies That Matter: On the Discursive Limits of "Sex."* New York: Routledge, 1993.

Cherokee Nation v. Georgia, 30 U.S. 1 (1831). *Oxford Reference*. Accessed January 29, 2019. https://www.oxfordreference.com/view/10.1093/oi/authority.20110810104604575.

Davis, Lennard J. "Constructing Normalcy: The Bell Curve, the Novel, and the Invention of Disability in the Nineteenth Century." In *The Disability Studies Reader*, edited by Lennard J. Davis, 3–16. 2nd ed. New York: Routledge, 2006.

Donahue, J. J. "'A World Away from His People': James Welch's *The Heartsong of Charging Elk* and the Indian Historical Novel." *Studies in American Indian Literatures* 18, no. 2 (2006): 54–82.

Ellingson, Ter. *The Myth of the Noble Savage*. Berkeley: University of California Press, 2001.

Ferguson, Suzanne. "Europe and the Quest for Home in James Welch's *The Heartsong of Charging Elk* and Leslie Marmon Silko's *Gardens in the Dunes*." *Studies in American Indian Literatures* 18, no. 2 (2006): 34–53.

Foucault, Michel. *The History of Sexuality*. Volume 1. New York: Vintage Books, 1978.

Hughes, Bill. "Disability and the Body." In *Disability Studies Today*, edited by Colin Barnes, Mike Oliver, and Len Barton, 58–76. Cambridge: Polity Press, 2002.

Kittay, Eva Feder. *Love's Labor: Essays on Women, Equality, and Dependency*. London: Routledge, 1998.

Martin, Jill E. "Neither Fish, Flesh, Fowl, nor Good Herring: The Citizenship Status of American Indians, 1830–1942." In *American Indians and U.S. Politics: A Companion Reader*, edited by John M. Meyer, 51–72. London: Praeger, 2002.

McRuer, Robert. *Crip Theory: Disability, Globalization, and Resistance*. New York: New York University Press, 2006.

Mitchell, David T., and Sharon L. Snyder. *Narrative Prosthesis: Disability and the Dependencies of Discourse*. Ann Arbor: University of Michigan Press, 2000.

Thomson, Rosemarie Garland. *Extraordinary Bodies: Figuring Physical Disability in American Culture and Literature*. New York: Columbia University Press, 1997.

Welch, James. *The Heartsong of Charging Elk*. New York: Anchor Books, 2000.

13

Teaching Western Canadian Literature in the Croatian Context

A Case Study

VANJA POLIĆ

In the 2013–14 academic year I developed an undergraduate course for students of English at the University of Zagreb. I called it Contemporary Canadian Literature in English: Wild West the Canadian Way. It is the only course in Canadian literature offered in the English curriculum, and it is an alternative to the well-established anglophone canons of American and British literatures. As the title reveals, the course had two equally important aims: to acquaint students with contemporary Canadian literature in English in terms of its distinctive socio-historical context and to provide an insight into a (renovated) genre of western that has gained currency in Canada in recent years. The Canadian context together with the postmodern western would offer students new reading strategies and paradigms enabling them not only to recognize that narratives are constantly shifting sites of production and reception, be they literary, political, economic, or ideological, but also to approach them as constructs of meaning with a particular agenda. Since participation and feedback during the course and evaluations at the end of the semester revealed that students really enjoyed and benefited from the topics, I decided to continue with the course. In view of those positive outcomes, this chapter first briefly discusses the course's structure and the challenges of teaching such a course in the Croatian setting. It then elaborates on the theoretical framework and the teaching methods used for each of the texts on the syllabus. I also discuss the results achieved in class. Overall my experiences teaching this course have led me to conclude that students benefit from gaining insight into a multicultural society that espouses cultural, religious, ethnic, and racial diversity, as it makes them better aware of the discourses of power and otherness and the constructs of nation in a society and culture. They come out of the course better able to perceive Croatia as a society that comprises similar diversities but is often perceived as homogenous. They are also able to consider the complexity of the European Union as a supranational structure that is currently managing a large influx of immigrants while at the same time renegotiating its own borders and makeup.

Mapping the Main Issues of the Course

The course is designed as a version of a rhizome, defined by Gilles Deleuze and Félix Guattari as a means of connecting "any point to any other point" where the rhizome's traits are "not necessarily linked to traits of the same nature," thus bringing "into play very different regimes of signs, and even nonsign states."[1] The analogy with the rhizome is invoked here because the course simultaneously explores several mutually intertwined and interfunctional areas, which will be examined separately here to show the multiple fields of interest and objectives of the course.[2] The first area of study concerns literary theory and criticism; students analyze the ways in which the genre of the traditional western has been transformed into a postmodernist text, in this case most prominently into historiographic metafiction and fictocriticism. The western's postmodern metamorphosis from a popular genre into a genre of "serious" literature shows the typically postmodern strategy of invalidating the distinction between the high and the low. Other strategies of textual destabilization are also observed: multiple, unreliable, and ex-centric narrators, fragmentation of narrative and the Chinese box structure, pastiche, anachrony, foregrounding of narrative gaps, parody, irony, heteroglossia, and dialogism, to name but a few.[3]

Students observe the western's transmutation from a popular genre into an experimental prose form that is today variously called new western, postwestern, or antiwestern, its prefixes indicating the subversion of the genre and the dominant myth with which it is associated. This leads to another important questioning about the received history of the North American West around the forty-ninth parallel. For this purpose the western Canadian texts chosen for this course probe the boundaries of the genre, recalling Tzvetan Todorov's claim that the best examples of a genre bend its boundaries but never break them.[4] The texts are all examples of post-modern disruptions of the traditional narrative structure and tropes of the western, and they function as counterhistories to the grand narrative of the Canadian settlement of the West. The novels selected for in-class discussion are Guy Vanderhaeghe's *The Englishman's Boy* (1996), George Bowering's *Shoot!* (1995) and *Caprice* (1987), followed by Aritha van Herk's short story "Leading the Parade" (2006) and a performance piece/fictocritical text, "Shooting a Saskatoon (Whatever Happened to the Marlboro Man?)" (2004), all of which undermine the conventions of the western and bring socio-historical contestation points to the fore. The novels' chronotope, or "the intrinsic connectedness of temporal and spatial relationships that are artistically expressed in literature," spans the last decades of nineteenth-century Western Canada, juxtaposing the myth of the (Wild) West with the "situation on the ground" in the British North American region soon to be the Canadian Northwest Territories, across the very soft border with the United States.[5] The works that cover the contemporary moment are van Herk's texts, which focus on the performance and lived experience of the West in present-day Calgary.

Thus, the selected works are meant to make students aware of and to stimulate them to explore counterhistories to the grand narrative (that is, to the official history) of the ordered settlement of the Canadian West.[6] The selected antiwesterns offer rewritten histories that challenge the dominant discourses while at the same time they lay bare the inherently narrative pro-cesses of the production of historiographic texts, that is, of metahistory.[7] Here the relation between history and its representation is foregrounded, as is the concept of authenticity, which is "associated with authority and originality" rather than with truth.[8] Conceived in this way, the notion of metahistory is almost inseparable from the third topic, which investigates mythopoeia, or the strategies of myth-making, and the closely related discourse of the emergence of national identity. This topic includes the comparison of the myths of the "Mild West" and the Wild West, or the insistence on a western

Canadian identity as separate from the western American one.[9] The notion of performativity and the carnivalization of the myth is dealt with here as well, explicating the myth's simultaneous perpetuation and subversion from within, which, while celebrating the myth, also reveals its own artifice.[10]

The fourth topic stems from the analysis of the western leitmotifs and chronotope that the antiwestern uses to question and critique the received monolithic grand narrative of history and propose instead a heteroglossia and dialogism of different histories.[11] For this topic Laura Moss's *Is Canada Postcolonial?* and Cynthia Sugars's *Unhomely States* and *Home-Work* prove most useful. The students have to read the selected chapters in advance and prepare for in-class discussion. This topic serves as a site for investigating the idea of Canada's postcolonialism and related issues of internal and external colonialism, as well as those of neocolonialism, probing not only the power relations inside of Canada but also those between Canada and its southern neighbor. The selected historical novels in particular exhibit the power of political transformation inherent in postcolonial criticism, which "juxtapose[s] the imperial production of texts with the decolonizing process of critically re-reading them" instead of just being the latest model of "litcrit," to use the Canadian theorist Richard Cavell's term.[12]

A course designed in such a way also, in a manner of speaking, presents students with a game of detection: while appearing prima facie as a course on a popular genre, this course in fact uses that genre as a gateway for probing, confronting, and destabilizing the received truths about western Canadian history and then replacing them with alternative histories. The student-detectives have to follow the gradual deconstruction of the traditional western and understand how it functions in postmodern times before engaging the complex and unresolved issues of the dominant version of Canadian history. They tackle the postmodern paradox that the Canadian literary theorist Linda Hutcheon, with regard to historiographic metafiction, so famously referred to as "the paradox of the *reality* of the past but its *textualized accessibility* to us today."[13] In other words, she discusses the impossibility of finding out what "actually happened" in the past, since the only remnant left is a text (a representation or interpretation of the past). Hutcheon's concept of historiographic metafiction, as a dominant mode of writing in postmodernism, foregrounds the constructed nature of any text because such texts possess a "theoretical self-awareness of history and fiction as human constructs (historio*graphic meta*fiction) [which] is made the grounds for its rethinking and reworking of the forms and contents of the past."[14] Consequently, any narrative is observed as a site of production of knowledge, history, and culture.

In the end the various problem fields the syllabus explores are gradually shown as overlapping, over- and underlying each other. The rhizome metaphor is evoked here because the course functions very much like "a map that must be produced, constructed, a map that is always detachable, connectable, reversible, modifiable, and has multiple entrance ways and exits and its own lines of flight."[15] As stated earlier, one of the main goals of the course is to apprise the students of the constructed nature not only of history but also of contemporary locations of culture, society, politics, and economics as discourses that are first of all intersections and complications of points of views, race, class, gender, and colonialism. Once alerted, they are encouraged to question and critically think about rather than simply accept received truths about national identity and identity politics, multiculturalism and myth-making. The students uncover and navigate the course map gradually, through the reading and analysis of texts, participation in discussions, and collaborative learning (group work) for which I act as a facilitator of their learning processes. Finally, students have to complete a small research project and three-thousand-word research paper on a topic they select. I offer a choice of topics for critical analysis, and they may either choose one or formulate one of their own and apply it to one text of their choosing. If their proposal contains sound arguments, they are allowed to pursue it. Some of the topics I offer are as follows: the deconstruction of western myth and history, challenging the dominant discourse of gender or identity, the notion of silences and narrative gaps in official history, the colonial subject, and others. The aim of the paper is to have the students focus on a thorough analysis of a specific aspect of a work and to write a critical essay supporting their hypotheses with not only reference to scholarly criticism but also quotes from the chosen literary text. In this way they exhibit their close reading techniques and the ability to use critical texts to meaningfully substantiate their arguments. For this purpose they have to conduct individual research in online databases to find academic articles (a maximum of two or three) relevant to the chosen text, and they have to combine the information from them with the results of group work and in-class discussions. I am available for consultation at every stage of their research and writing process and often read through their drafts and half-finished papers. The research papers stimulate their individual research and hone their articulation skills, thus providing an exercise in synthesis, critical thinking, and application of key concepts from literary theory to a given text.

Fulfilling all of these course assignments accounts for two-thirds of their final grade (the other third is acquired through a midterm and a final exam), in accordance with the principle of continuous assessment. In this manner the course develops students' skills beyond merely the required elements of the course primarily by fostering critical thinking, independent and group research, and listening to and respecting the opinions of others.

Introducing "Canada" into the Croatian Context:
Challenges and Benefits to Croatian Students

The challenges of teaching a course about a country as complex as Canada to Croatian students are several. One of them is the uniqueness of such a Canada-related course on both the undergraduate and graduate levels of the English curriculum in Zagreb. Despite the fact that Wild West the Canadian Way is not a survey course, it has to include a framework of general information about Canada as well as the more specific context of the late nineteenth-century Canadian West, knowledge of which will enable students to have a better understanding of the course material. The complexity of the rhizome-like course framework presents yet another challenge because the issues discussed in the course require the undergraduate students to make a great leap in knowledge and awareness. A further challenge concerns preexisting knowledge and assumptions about Canada that students may possess. About twenty-eight Croatian students (a slightly higher than average number for a literary course) generally enroll, and they tend to have a vague but favorable perception of contemporary Canada, thanks to media outlets that usually present images of Canada as a peaceful, ordered, and multicultural country. Some students have relatives in Canada, a circumstance that naturally affects their views, mostly in a positive manner. Overall, however, Canada presents an unknown.

With this in mind, the course plan must address the role that location plays as "a significant aspect of pedagogical practice."[16] The concept of location here includes both the country of the students' origin as well as the country targeted by the course. In other words, in order to avoid projecting their assumptions about Croatian society onto Canada, the students have to be made aware that "space/place/location are *produced* and, therefore, inflected by their historical moment and social context."[17] The challenge here is to alert the students to their tendency to equate two very different societies: one that is, for better or for worse, "visibly" monocultural, even though the constitution states otherwise, and another that is as diverse as a society can get. The goal is to teach them not only about the otherness of Canada but also to become cognizant of their own space as *produced*. They must learn to apply the strategies acquired for the study of "an-other" country to the critical study of their own. This issue is most obvious in the students' ready use of the pronoun "we" when discussing various cultures and societies. In order to alter their ingrained modes of thinking, I ask questions about their geographic location as citizens of a southern European country, about their backgrounds and their age, race, ethnicity, religion, and gender versus those of the country studied. There are, however, other reasons for this ready identification of Western culture as "us," one being that they perceive Croatia as mostly homogenous in terms of race, national identity, and religion, despite the fact that Croatia defines itself as a multicultural state with twenty-two ethnic minorities recognized by the constitution.

Another reason for this perceived uniformity of cultures is the familiarity the students feel toward the culture they perceive as North American. Accordingly, Canada seems familiar to them as well, and they readily gloss over the differences in favor of perceived similarities between Croatian and Canadian (and American) cultures. It needs to be emphasized here, however, that the students do not consciously and rationally believe that these societies are identical—after all, they take the course to learn about another culture—but rather that their inexperience and assumptions occasionally get the best of them. In this sense the course proves to be very important for denaturalizing the acquired concepts of the term "American" as a happy-go-lucky cultural identifier of the North American continent and "western culture" as a unifier of the multifarious cultures and peoples in the Western Hemisphere.[18]

The Course: Introducing Canadian Geography, History, and Culture

The course itself begins with a brainstorming exercise: the students are asked to say what they know about Canada. There is no restriction concerning the type of information they can share; they can call on their prior knowledge, ranging from popular artists to stereotypes of Canada. Predictably, they mention hockey, maple syrup, snow, beaver, Margaret Atwood, certain singers and groups, various actors, but not much else. This session is followed by a ten-minute multiple-choice quiz about Canada, with questions on cultural topics such as famous artists, sports, and stereotypes of Canada and others about Canada's official languages, the capital, provinces and territories, founding nations and First Nations, natural resources, and so on. After answering the questions individually, the students discuss their responses in class. Even though their knowledge of Canadian culture is slightly better than their grasp of Canada's politics and society, they still end up listing Canadian stereotypes. They are then asked to disclose their expectations about the course; these differ depending on the students' interests and backgrounds, as well as on their second major.

At the Faculty of Humanities and Social Sciences in Zagreb, undergraduate students choose two majors from any discipline in the humanities (about twenty-three languages and literatures) and from a fair range of social sciences (history, sociology, archaeology, art history, ethnology, psychology, anthropology, and information sciences, to name but a few). These majors inflect their interests and contribute creatively to the course, opening it up to ever more diverse points of view. It is perhaps interesting to note here that my course, conceived as a seminar, is of a familiar format to students, as in the English department the literary courses, beginning with sophomore year, are structured as one-third lecture and two-thirds seminar and graded through continuous assessment. The lecture part is obviously intended to provide the theoretical and sociocultural framework for the new material that is then expanded by students during seminar periods. However, since the number of students enrolled in the seminars is smaller than that of the lecture courses, which have 120 students (i.e., the whole cohort of, say, sophomores enrolled in the English curriculum), these seminar courses are more relaxed and tend to turn into discussions. Formal lecture courses in the English curriculum are reserved for the introductions to linguistics, literary theory, and history of literature and are mandatory courses for first-year students.[19]

The introductions over, the following two weeks of classes consist of more formal lectures intended to provide students with a general understanding of the main factors that have shaped contemporary Canada. First on the agenda is a brief geographical analysis of the Canadian landscape and the regions, provinces, and territories of the country. Second is a historical overview, starting with the three arrivals: Indigenous peoples across Beringia, the Vikings, and John Cabot. A useful tool here is the map showing the gradual migrations of the Indigenous peoples across North America some fifteen thousand years ago. Students are then shown a present-day map of the Indigenous linguistic families of North America, and I then place over it a current political map of North America. The emerging palimpsest—because the two maps are visible simultaneously—consists of the hypotext of the Indigenous organization of the North American continent according to languages, onto which is superimposed the hypertext of a geometric grid of boundaries across the majority of the North American continent.[20] The grid delimits the provinces in the Canadian West, mirrored by a similar pattern in the western United States across the international boundary of the forty-ninth parallel. The hypertext shows the consequence of an organized plan of conquest and settlement of the territory instead of a "natural" development of states according to the boundaries between nations or geographical regions. The purpose of inserting this palimpsest is to offer the students at the very beginning an alternative perspective of an apparently straightforward "fact" and to entice them to approach critically the materials they receive. Thus, with the aim of moving the course beyond a settler-colonial historical narrative, the students are given information about an Indigenous cosmology that opposes the colonial violence of mapping. The course provides an introduction to the First Nations, their linguistic and cultural diversity and multiplicity, political configurations and confederacies, followed by their colonization and submission, forced assimilation and residential schools, the issues of treaties and present-day land rights and struggles for equality, and the status of First Nations in Canada today.

The historical overview consists of certain touchstones of Canadian history. The task of an extreme reduction of history is of course an ungrateful one, and there are bound to be omissions, but they are for the most part patched up as the course progresses. Students are also encouraged to watch documentaries such as *Canada: A People's History* to obtain more detailed information. Indeed, the overview is meant to provide students with basic working facts on which to build their base of knowledge on Canada. Thus, the course continues with the causes for the accidental (third) "discovery" of a large landmass (North American continent); the priority of finding a northwest passage to India; the relatively late interest in the exploration of the lands that would become Canada (an interest spurred by the fur trade); the doctrine of imperialism from which emerged the Hudson's Bay Company, which for centuries owned almost half of present-day Canada; the differences in the French and British settlements and exploitations of the territories; the treatment of First Nations by the French and British and the power relations among First Nations; the gradual relinquishing of the French territories to the British; the 1867 constitution of the Dominion of Canada and its planned expansion from the Atlantic to the Pacific. Twentieth-century developments such as the Quiet Revolution, Pierre Elliott Trudeau, and the Multiculturalism Act are briefly explained, and twenty-first-century Canada is introduced.[21] At each juncture students are asked what they know about that particular period of history and are then invited to pose queries of their own. Students who have already taken the postcolonial course on Australian literature and film are more knowledgeable than others, as British colonial politics were similar in both territories.

The overview then moves on to Western Canada and how the sale of the Hudson's Bay Company lands to the Canadian government and the building of the Canadian Pacific Railway were part of the effort to create a transcontinental state. The coursework analyzes the Northwest Territories around the forty-ninth parallel—the setting of the novels studied in the course—together with the concept of the forty-ninth parallel itself. Better known as the Medicine Line, due to the absence of any natural landmark to indicate its existence and yet the symbol of a clear demarcation between the Northwest Territories and the United States, the forty-ninth parallel was a "soft" barrier, its existence recognized and yet the flow of goods and people across it undisturbed. The importance of the permeability of the border is explained in the context of U.S.-Canadian relations at the end of the nineteenth century and the Canadian fear of the United States spreading northward, just as it was spreading westward.[22]

Introducing the Canadian and American West(s) and the Western Genre and Myth

At the end of the first two weeks of the course this rather intense introduction into Canadian history and politics is over, so the class turns once more toward collaborative learning.[23] The students are invited to a brainstorming session to produce tropes of the Wild West myth and the western genre. John Cawelti's *The Six-Gun Mystique Sequel* proves invaluable for this part of the course, as it provides a detailed analysis of the western genre and its history. Tropes that the students supply—cowboys and Indians, horses, the prairie, a small town in the middle of nowhere, a sheriff, outlaws, a school mistress, hurdy-gurdy girls, a saloon, an injustice that a lone ranger can rectify, the rule of the gun, maleness, individualism, conflict between usually poor farmers versus ranchers who want more land, and so on—are all noted.[24] They will serve as points of reference for the systematic subversion and deconstruction of both the western genre and the Wild West myth during the course.

For this class the students have to read and extract the main points from the American historian Frederick Jackson Turner's "The Significance of the Frontier in American History," the text that in many ways fostered the American national identity, and from the Canadian historian J. M. S. Careless's "Frontierism, Metropolitanism, and Canadian History," which offers a different paradigm for the settlement of the Canadian West. Their main points are discussed in class, the purpose being to reveal the differences in the conceptualizations of the West by the American and Canadian governments. The students conclude that while the ultimate goal of the invasion and settlement of the West was the same for both countries, the strategies used were different: Canadians undertook an organized settlement of the West, basically colonizing it with the railway, legislature, and the North-West Mounted Police, emulating Britain (its imperial mother country) and othering itself in this way from the United States just south of the border. The Americans prided themselves on the free spirit, individualism, entrepreneurship, and Manifest Destiny of forging a new nation unbeholden to Europe.

Having established the basic differences between the American and Canadian ideologies behind the conquest of the Wests, the course then proceeds with students being asked to find the similarities: both Wests celebrated the notions of masculinity and whiteness, the conquest of nature, and the advent of frontier capitalism, while only cursorily mentioning Indigenous peoples as a thing of the past. Here I add that one of the strategies of conquest is the older myth of the "vanishing Indian," which went hand in hand with the planned destruction of the Indigenous peoples. I show them some photos by Edward S. Curtis and ask them to analyze their "atmosphere" and contrived air (in the photos the "Indians" are carefully arranged into romanticized images of a vanishing race). The students' findings are then compared to the tropes of the western genre; the goal is to reveal the western's role as a means of the authentication of the Wild West myth, globally recognizable as epitomizing the United States as a whole.

The ideologies conceptualized in Turner's and Careless's texts are then opened to discussion through Lorry Felske and Beverly Rasporich's introduction to their volume *Challenging Frontiers*, which reexamines the myth by making visible the elements erased by the frontier thesis: the relevance of the Indigenous peoples, women, and settlers of different ethnicities; the contributions of domesticity, femininity, and community in the creation and survival of the West; and the subsequent creation of the very myth that erased them from historical representations of the settlement of the West. In this way the students begin to differentiate between the Canadian and American Wests while at the same time starting to unveil the narrative gaps in the grand narratives of both history and constructs of national identities. Two volumes of *One West, Two Myths*, edited by C. L. Higham and Robert Thacker, are particularly useful here and are offered as supplemental literature.

Textual Analysis: Group Tasks and Key
Concepts for *The Englishman's Boy*

After the general introduction to the course, our focus shifts to analysis of
the novels and short pieces on the reading list. What follows is a detailed
analysis of the group work and key concepts for each of the texts from the
reading list. Guy Vanderhaeghe's *The Englishman's Boy* is the first novel
analyzed in class. After the prerequisite reading check and introductory
discussion, the class is divided into three groups, with each group receiv-
ing a different task. The first group has to connect the novel's epigraphs
about the relation of story and history to the main body of the novel. The
second group has to enumerate and define the narrative structure of the
novel (narrative frames, story lines, types of narrators) and explain their
importance for the overall meaning of the novel. The third group's task is
to consider the relationships between Canada and the United States in all
of the story lines. The reports from the three groups are then assembled
into a bricolage, and I proceed to explain the theoretical background of
their findings. That background consists of the concepts of story, history
and emplotment, Chinese box structure of narrative, monologism versus
dialogism and heteroglossia, mythopoeia, narrative fragmentation, narrative
gaps and sutures of the text, unreliable narrators, and, finally, historiographic
metafiction.[25]

The students see in the example of *The Englishman's Boy* how counterhistories allow for the suppressed historical material to emerge, and we proceed
to discuss the relevance of the multiple frames through which the narrative
is related and which render it unreliable and open-ended. Attention is paid
to the outermost frame of the novel, which includes a parallel history of
the two horse thieves and its significance for the main body of the novel.
We also address the center of the Chinese box structure, which contains
silence, that is, an absence instead of a possible resolution of the narrative,
a narrative of the Cypress Hills massacre that cancels itself through the
manipulated representation. Connected to this is the significance of the
foregrounding of self-reflexivity and fragmentation of the narrative, which
is then analyzed in light of the historical events depicted in the novel. This
analysis focuses on the construction of the myth of law and order associated

with the Canadian state (a myth that originates in the Cypress Hills massacre), the paradox of lawlessness engendering the law and order myth, Canadian complicity in the massacre even though the violence toward the Indigenous peoples is othered onto the United States. From this evident construction and manipulation of historical "facts" ensues the explanation of the Wild West myth as a simulacrum, "substituting signs of the real for the real itself."[26] This is followed by the topic of the discrepancy between the myth and lived experience at the end of the nineteenth century, which poses another locus of contestation and another forum for discussion.

The critical texts that the students are assigned for this novel are an article by Alison Calder on the nation and genre in *The Englishman's Boy* and Patricia Linton's article on the novel's narrative geography.[27] Additionally, the students are asked to read Basil Johnston's "Cowboys and Indians" and watch the documentary *Reel Injun* in order to open further the intersections of histories, race, and colonialism. These alternative accounts of Canada are meant to introduce to students the importance of the speaker's place of utterance: despite the fact that the novels read in class are counterhistories that destabilize the official history, they are still novels written by white men. Therefore the students are also assigned to read a critical essay, "Godzilla vs. Post-Colonial," by the Canadian Indigenous writer Thomas King, because it points to the dangers of indiscriminately applying literary theories and worldviews from Western civilization to the interpretation of Indigenous texts.

Textual Analysis: Group Tasks and Key Concepts for *Shoot!*

The second novel on the course reading list is George Bowering's *Shoot!*, which continues the history of settlement and invasion of the Canadian West but with a greater dose of irony. One group of students is tasked with enumerating all the story lines and narrators in the novel, identifying the "story-now," or the present narrative moment in the novel, commenting on the ways in which the story lines and narrators are assembled into a pastiche, and the purpose of this narrative strategy. The second group has to find references to the processes of mythopoeia (the exaggerated stories of the West traveling eastward, only to be returned westward in the form of newspapers and dime novels; white men's insistence on being turned into stories, thereby inscribing themselves into the landscape; the authority of orality versus recorded history). They also have to look for the role the media (photography and newspaper articles) played in the mythopoeia and comment on their part in the authentication of the emerging myth. The third group needs to find the tropes of the western genre in the novel and note the possible metamorphoses they undergo in *Shoot!* as the author criticizes the politics of colonization. Once again, as the reporters for each group bring forth their findings, I write down key concepts and ask the students to use the theoretical terms acquired in the previous session. Then I introduce the concept of white civility as an important part of the Canadian politics of colonization; the premise of Canadian white civility lies in the perception of Canada as the daughter country of Britain, emulating all of its civilizational institutions.[28] White civility in the novel is parodied in the justice system, which is turned into a farce, particularly in the power politics that hide behind "civility" but are used to appropriate the land and so on. Other concepts include the Métis and the absence of place in the colonial politics of the province of British Columbia; the notion of the ex-centric; irony as a double-coded discourse that operates within the existing (dominant) discourse and contests it from within (as detailed by Hutcheon in *Irony's Edge*); pastiche; metahistory and emplotment; dislocation, *terra nullius*, and indigenization; colonial frontier and contact zone; the idea of "half-breed" and its historical and colonialist underpinning; Indian; the western trope of the outlaws at the center of *Shoot!*, which Bowering constantly deconstructs and reconstructs to juxtapose the myths of the Canadian and American Wests and to break down the illusion that the treatment of Indigenous peoples was more "civilized" in Canada than south of the forty-ninth parallel; and the blurring of boundaries between narrative and history in historiographic metafiction by thematizing its own discursive processes.[29] The self-reflexivity of the novel is discussed, as is the postmodernist emphasis on the text as a process.[30] All of these elements are then compared to their counterparts in *The Englishman's Boy*, and a pattern of narrative strategies and thematic concerns starts to emerge.

The three critical texts the students have to read concerning *Shoot!* are Sherrill Grace's article on the strategies of autobiography and landscape and her afterword to the 2008 edition of *Shoot!*, as well as W. F. Garrett-Petts's article on Bowering's postmodern reading strategies. John Thompson has written a brief historical article that also serves as a good reference point. For those interested in learning more, I suggest Bowering's companion "diary" to his novel *Shoot!*[31]

Textual Analysis: Group Tasks and Key Concepts for *Caprice*

The last novel on the reading list is Bowering's *Caprice*, which the students have read by this point in the course. However, they are first shown the film *Shane*, and I ask them to identify as many western tropes as they can, to pay attention to the opening and closing scenes in the film, focalization and visuality, as well as the basic plotline. After the reading check the discussion immediately turns into a comparison of *Shane* and *Caprice*, during which they identify different intertextual moments in the hypertext of *Caprice*. The first group has to identify the different kinds of gazes in the novel because this is a novel about watching and seeing. The second group is in charge of identifying the stereotypes of the West and their parodies and, related to them, the differences between the Mild West and the Wild West, while the third group analyzes puns and wordplay and the two Indians who appear as commentators throughout the novel and as catalysts for the final scene in the novel. The discussion after the group reports includes the role of visuality in both *Shane* and *Caprice*; other hypotexts of *Caprice* and their role in the parodying of the genre; the character of Caprice as the central axis of the parody of the genre; the deployment of humor and irony, lighter in tone than in *Shoot!*; mythopoeia and the role of photography (the character of the photographer from *Shoot!* reappears here); an Austro-Hungarian writer who searches for adventures and not factual reports of life in the West; and the presence of the alternative gaze upon white settlers/invaders of the Canadian West. The critical texts assigned to students are van Herk's afterword to the 2010 edition of *Caprice* and my article on the transformations of the western genre in *Caprice* because critical texts about *Caprice* are sparse.[32] Of course having already read *Shoot!* and related critical articles, the students can draw analogies and venture into their arguments on the basis of the knowledge gathered in the course by that point.

Textual Analysis: Group Tasks and Key Concepts for
"Leading the Parade" and "Shooting a Saskatoon"

The last two texts in the syllabus are Aritha van Herk's short story "Leading the Parade" and her fictocritical text "Shooting a Saskatoon." Modifying the methodological approach I have used thus far, I make the introductory talk about the Calgary Stampede and the performativity and carnivalization of this rodeo and western-themed spectacle. I show them some promotional materials for the event and explain its doubleness of performance and lived experience for the participants. They are informed that van Herk deconstructs the western myth by emphasizing the performativity of the Calgary Stampede. As is to be expected, the students usually have few problems with the short story, since it is a straightforward text, but "Shooting a Saskatoon" baffles them. Here is a text that does not follow the rules of either strictly scholarly or fictional work. It contains too much "inside" information on a specific locale of the Canadian West, and they simply do not know where to begin. The first time I taught the course I included this work experimentally because I wanted to see how the students would cope with it after a full semester of western Canadian literature, and I later retained it because the students seemed to profit from that initial bafflement at the end of the course, when they thought they were already quite knowledgeable. This text produced yet another shift in their assumptions, reaffirming the need to constantly question and adapt their knowledge according to new information and perspectives.

Group tasks were laid out as follows. The first group looks for the figure of the cowboy in "Shooting" and identifies his role in the text, while the second group describes the narrator, her attitudes toward the myth of the West, and the "reality" of living in the West. The third group searches for the postmodern traits of the text that keep reappearing in the novels. The groups usually conclude as follows. The first group reveals the role of the cowboy as a formerly iconic but now obsolete and absent figure of the West. The second group identifies the narrator as a woman and teacher who replaces the cowboy on center stage. The analogy is then made to the role reversal in *Caprice* (Caprice's boyfriend being the teacher while she is a "cowperson") and further linked to the female protagonist of the short story. As the last group relays their findings, we start unpacking both texts with special regard to their marked traits of performance and performativity, the laying bare of the myth, and its continued albeit somewhat transformed presence in contemporary life. The myth's topicality in the Canadian West is speculated upon, and in general the texts are observed as yet another postmodern transformation of the western genre. The accompanying critical texts that the students are given include Katherine Roberts's article on van Herk's new West and her text on the Calgary Stampede.[33]

In this way the course symbolically ends in the present day, in which the myth of the Wild West is recognized as myth and performance, its discursive practices revealed and parodied and yet owned as a marker of regional identity. The concluding session serves to compare the texts from the reading list, as well as to detect shared narrative strategies and topical concerns. The list of western tropes from the beginning of the course is pulled out and the unraveling of each trope discussed. Overall, the postmodern strategies of destabilization of grand narratives, fragmentation, unreliable and multiple ex-centric narrators, narrative gaps and absences, metafiction, open-endedness of postmodern texts, and the contrapuntal readings of history as analyzed through the novels all comment on the politics of colonialization in the Canadian West. They also serve, in the words of Marta Dvořák, to subvert the "traditional understanding of history and biography, reexamining and contesting the totalizing master narratives" of the historical and political events "that have become New World myths."[34] Those strategies also concern questions of "territory, (de)possession, and appropriation, and interrogating the Eurocentric assumptions that have been offered and accepted as objective truth."[35] The course thus combines theories of postmodernism, postcolonialism, feminism, and new histories of the West with western Canadian literature, and the course's rhizomatic structure reveals itself as a complex network of interconnections that examine questions about the production of history, identity, and society.

The Final Aim of the Course

The objective of this course on the Wild West in Canada is therefore to inspire students to take their theoretical knowledge and analytical skills outside of the classroom and apply them to current affairs in Croatian politics, the economy, society, and culture, that is, to become critical of any account presented as a received truth. They have, I hope, become more aware of the illusion of Croatia as a homogenous mononational society, of social inequality, of the relations of power in society and culture disguised by grand narratives. Canada, the general model for a multicultural state, serves as a specific model for multiculturalism in the European Union and for an imminent reality in Croatia. The course thus teaches students to accept the fluidity of the notions of nation and national and individual identity, to realize that, with the increased immigration of refugees of various ethnic and religious denominations, society needs to become a multicultural space, one that incorporates these "others" into its whole. It is hoped that in a small way the course will contribute to the students' navigation and shaping of Croatian society, since it is on its way to becoming a multicultural space in this very generation.

NOTES

1. Deleuze and Guattari, *Thousand Plateaus*, 21.
2. Neil Campbell uses the rhizome as a paradigm of the western genre in his book *The Rhizomatic West*.
3. See Hutcheon, *Poetics of Postmodernism*; McHale, *Postmodernist Fiction*; and Bakhtin, *Dialogic Imagination*.
4. Todorov, "Typology of Detective Fiction," 121.
5. The chronotope definition is from Bakhtin, *Dialogic Imagination*, 84.
6. Grand narrative or metadiscourse is, according to Jean-François Lyotard, "a discourse of legitimation with respect to its own status," which the institutions of power produce in order to assign themselves legitimating power. Lyotard, *Postmodern Condition*, xxiii. Grand narratives "create" a version of knowledge that privileges certain kinds of information while suppressing others that they perceive as threatening or subversive.
7. See White, *Metahistory*. To put it simply, the historian Hayden White claims that the concept of metahistory indicates that historical texts are constructed by the same narrative strategies that are used for the creation of literary texts. Thus, metahistory undermines the illusion behind the alleged authority, objectivity, and truthfulness of historical texts.
8. Handley and Lewis, *True West*, 3.
9. The American Wild West is stereotypically characterized as "the rule of the gun" or "life, liberty, and the pursuit of happiness," while the Canadian "Mild West" was defined with the motto "peace, order, and good government." For a more detailed explanation, see Katerberg, "Northern Vision," 65–68. For the sake of brevity, the adjective "American" will be used in reference to the United States and "Canadian" in reference to Canada.

When both countries are collectively referenced, the syntagm "North American" will be used.

10. On carnivalization, see Bakhtin, *Rabelais and His World*.

11. Heteroglossia is "a multiplicity of social voices and a wide variety of their links and interrelationships (always more or less dialogized)." Bakhtin, *Dialogic Imagination*, 263. Dialogism denotes a discourse that "becomes relativized, de-privileged, aware of competing definitions for the same things" (427) and stands in opposition to monologism or a "single hermetic context" (274).

12. Cavell, "Transvestic Sites," 339.

13. Hutcheon, *Poetics of Postmodernism*, 114.

14. Hutcheon, *Poetics of Postmodernism*, 5. The concept of historiographic metafiction has undergone revision since the 1980s, but with due deference to these revisions, it is extremely useful for the analysis of the novels chosen for this course. For Hutcheon's revision of her prior theoretical paradigm, I use her essay "The Glories of Hindsight."

15. Deleuze and Guattari, *Thousand Plateaus*, 21.

16. Cavell, "Transvestic Sites," 338.

17. Cavell, "Transvestic Sites," 338.

18. Speaking of cultural diversity, it is interesting to note that Canada and Croatia were among the first countries to contribute to a legally binding instrument regarding the protection of cultural diversity and of cultural goods and services in the global economy. They did so together with a small number of countries that were members of the World Trade Organization but acted outside it, within the International Network on Cultural Policy. See Burri, "Cultural Diversity as a Concept of Global Law."

19. According to the English curriculum, beginning with the sophomore year literary courses fall into the so-called mandatory-elective category because the students are given certain parameters but are allowed to choose the courses they want. The parameters include, for example, having to take one early modern, one postmodern, one American, and one British or other non-American anglophone literature course.

20. See Genette, *Palimpsests*.

21. The Quiet Revolution (Révolution tranquille) denotes the 1960s secularization and modernization of politics, industry, culture, and society in Québec. Governance in the province prior to that time was unofficially controlled by the Catholic Church. The Multiculturalism Act, first passed in 1971 by Pierre Elliott Trudeau's government and amended in 1988, was created for the preservation and enhancement of the equality of all cultural and ethnic groups in Canada.

22. Books on the history of Canada are numerous. I primarily use Ferguson's *Canadian History for Dummies* and Riendeau's *A Brief History of Canada* for my notes, as well as the internet (e.g., the online Canadian Encyclopedia, the National Film Board of Canada, and other, more content-specific websites). To students I give introductory texts from *Insight Guides: Canada* (chapters titled "History," "People," "Features") as review materials because they provide a very concise historical survey with a list of important years.

23. It is worth mentioning that because students do not read their course materials in advance, these two weeks of introduction, for which their participation and preparation for the class are limited, give them time to read the first assigned novel.

24. I have used the term "cowboys and Indians" with full awareness of its racist onus, but I use it deliberately to deconstruct its discourse, which has affected much of North American history. I also use it to point out the many ways in which the binary and the imbalance of power it carries are still present in contemporary cultural, historical, political, and economic discourses.

25. Some of these terms have already been explained, but I offer here brief identifications of others. "Emplotment" is the American historian Hayden White's term, connected with metahistory, for the various narrative strategies used to transform historical data into stories of a particular kind. The "Chinese box structure" of narrative is when one or more narratives are placed within a narrative, or multiple frames of narrative, which has "the effect of interrupting and complicating the ontological 'horizon' of the fiction, multiplying its worlds, and laying bare the process of world-construction." McHale, *Postmodernist Fiction*, 112. "Mythopoeia" is the discursive and ideological processes of myth-making, whether the myth of national identity or the myth of the West. All of these are metafictional narrative strategies laying bare the processes of the text's construction and are thus useful for the deconstruction of any narrative or discourse: societal, historical, political, economic, cultural, or ideological.

26. Baudrillard, *Simulations*, 4.

27. These works are Calder, "Unsettling the West"; and Linton, "Narrative Geography in Guy Vanderhaeghe's *The Englishman's Boy*."

28. See Coleman, *White Civility*.

29. "Ex-centric" refers to off-center, marginalized groups that are identified with the center they desire but are denied it because the center uses the ex-centric to define itself. In the postmodern world they become the decentered center, or the pluralized world where there is only ex-centricity. Hutcheon, *Poetics of Postmodernism*, 60–61. The term "colonial frontier" may be defined as an imperial concept that "implies not only a hierarchy of colonizer (European and political center of power) over colonized (non-European and marginal) but, more importantly, a one-way process of influence in which the colonizer remains immune from any contact with the colonized." Grace, "Calling Out the McLean Boys," 14. A contact zone is "the space in which peoples geographically and historically separated come into contact with each other and establish on-going relations, usually involving conditions of coercion, radical inequality, and intractable conflict." Pratt, *Imperial Eyes*, 6.

30. Hutcheon, *Canadian Postmodern*, 61.

31. These works are Grace, "Calling Out the MacLean Boys"; Grace, "'Stories That Never End'"; Garrett-Petts, "Novelist as Radical Pedagogue"; Thompson, "Canadianizing the Myth of the West"; and Bowering, "Parashoot!"

32. These works are van Herk, "A Lot of Beautiful Things Are Dangerous"; and Polić, "Of Wests, Quests and Bullwhips."

33. These works are Roberts, "Sundance Style"; and van Herk, "Half a Mile of Heaven's Gate."
34. Dvořák, "Fiction," 165.
35. Dvořák, "Fiction," 165–66.

BIBLIOGRAPHY

Bakhtin, Mikhail M. *The Dialogic Imagination: Four Essays.* Translated by Caryl Emerson and Michael Holquist. Edited by Michael Holquist. Austin: University of Texas Press, 1981.
———. *Rabelais and His World.* Translated by Hélène Iswolsky. 1968. Bloomington: Indiana University Press, 1984.
Baudrillard, Jean. *Simulations.* Translated by Paul Foss, Paul Patton, and Philip Beitchman. Los Angeles: Semiotext(e), 1983.
Bowering, George. *Caprice.* Markham ON: Penguin Books, 1987.
———. "Parashoot! Diary of a Novel." In *Fresh Tracks: Writing the Western Landscape*, edited by Pamela Banting, 159–70. Victoria BC: Polestar, 1988.
———. *Shoot!* 1995. Vancouver BC: New Star Books, 2008.
Burri, Mira. "Cultural Diversity as a Concept of Global Law: Origins, Evolution and Prospects." *Diversity* 2, no. 8 (2010): 1059–84.
Calder, Alison. "Unsettling the West: Nation and Genre in Guy Vanderhaeghe's *The English-man's Boy*." *Studies in Canadian Literature* 25, no. 2 (2000): 96–107.
Campbell, Neil. *The Rhizomatic West: Representing the American West in a Transnational, Global, Media Age.* Lincoln: University of Nebraska Press, 2008.
Canada: A People's History. Created by Mark Starowicz. Aired on CBC, 2000–2001.
Careless, J. M. S. "Frontierism, Metropolitanism, and Canadian History." In *One West, Two Myths II: Essays on Comparison*, edited by Carol Higham and Robert Thacker, 193–214. Calgary AB: University of Calgary Press, 2006.
Cavell, Richard. "Transvestic Sites: Postcolonialism, Pedagogy, and Politics." In *Unhomely States: Theorizing English-Canadian Postmodernism*, edited by Cynthia Sugars, 335–48. Peterborough ON: Broadview Press, 2004.
Cawelti, John. *The Six-Gun Mystique Sequel.* Bowling Green OH: Bowling Green State University Popular Press, 1999.
Coleman, Daniel. *White Civility: The Literary Project of English Canada.* Toronto: University of Toronto Press, 2006.
Deleuze, Gilles, and Félix Guattari. *A Thousand Plateaus: Capitalism and Schizophrenia.* Translated by Brian Massumi. Minneapolis: University of Minnesota Press, 1987.
Dvořák, Marta. "Fiction." In *The Cambridge Companion to Canadian Literature*, edited by Eva-Marie Kröller, 155–76. Cambridge: Cambridge University Press, 2005.
Felske, Lorry, and Beverly Rasporich. "Introduction: Challenging Frontiers." In *Challenging Frontiers: The Canadian West*, edited by Lorry Felske and Beverly Rasporich, 1–11. Calgary AB: University of Calgary Press, 2004.
Ferguson, Will. *Canadian History for Dummies.* 2nd ed. Mississauga ON: John Wiley & Sons Canada, 2005.

Garrett-Petts, W. F. "Novelist as Radical Pedagogue: George Bowering and Postmodern Reading Strategies." *College English* 54, no. 5 (1992): 554–72.

Genette, Gérard. *Palimpsests: Literature in the Second Degree.* Translated by Channa Newman and Claude Doubinsky. Lincoln: University of Nebraska Press, 1982.

Grace, Sherrill. "Calling Out the MacLean Boys: George Bowering's *Shoot* and the Autobiography of British Columbia History." *Canadian Literature* 184 (Spring 2005): 11–25.

———. "'Stories That Never End': Listening to *Shoot!*" Afterword to *Shoot!,* by George Bowering, 254–60. Vancouver BC: New Star Books, 2008.

Handley, William R., and Nathaniel Lewis, eds. *True West: Authenticity and the American West.* Lincoln: University of Nebraska Press, 2004.

Higham, Carol, and Robert Thacker, eds. *One West, Two Myths: A Comparative Reader.* Calgary AB: University of Calgary Press, 2004.

———. *One West, Two Myths II: Essays on Comparison.* Calgary AB: University of Calgary Press, 2006.

Hutcheon, Linda. *The Canadian Postmodern: A Study of Contemporary English-Canadian Fiction.* Don Mills ON: Oxford University Press, 1988.

———. "Glories of Hindsight: What We Know Now." In *RE: Reading the Postmodern: Canadian Literature and Criticism after Modernism,* edited by Robert D. Stacey, 39–53. Ottawa: University of Ottawa Press, 2010.

———. *Irony's Edge: The Theory and Politics of Irony.* New York: Routledge, 1995.

———. *A Poetics of Postmodernism: History, Theory, Fiction.* New York: Routledge, 1988.

Insight Guides: Canada. 2nd ed. London: APA Publications, 2008.

Johnston, Basil. "Cowboys and Indians." In *Think Indian: Languages Are Beyond Price,* 316–21. Wiarton ON: Kegedonce Press, 2011.

Katerberg, William H. "A Northern Vision: Frontiers and the West in the Canadian and American Imagination." In *One West, Two Myths II: Essays on Comparison,* edited by Carol Higham and Robert Thacker, 63–83. Calgary AB: University of Calgary Press, 2006.

King, Thomas. "Godzilla vs. Post-Colonial." In *Unhomely States: Theorizing English-Canadian Postmodernism,* edited by Cynthia Sugars, 183–90. Peterborough ON: Broadview Press, 2004.

Linton, Patricia. "Narrative Geography in Guy Vanderhaeghe's *The Englishman's Boy.*" *American Review of Canadian Studies* 31, no. 4 (2001): 611–21.

Lyotard, Jean-François. *The Postmodern Condition: A Report on Knowledge.* Translated by Geoff Bennington and Brian Massumi. Minneapolis: University of Minnesota Press, 1984.

McHale, Brian. *Postmodernist Fiction.* New York: Routledge, 1987.

Moss, Laura, ed. *Is Canada Postcolonial? Unsettling Canadian Literature.* Waterloo ON: Wilfrid Laurier University Press, 2003.

Polić, Vanja. "Of Wests, Quests and Bullwhips: Caprice Rides through the Western Genre." *Umjetnost riječi* 58, no. 3–4 (2014): 369–89.

Pratt, Mary L. *Imperial Eyes: Travel Writing and Transculturation.* London: Routledge, 1992.

Reel Injun. Directed by Neil Diamond and Catherine Bainbridge. Performances by Adam Beach, Chris Eyre, and Russell Means. Montreal: National Film Board of Canada, 2009.

Riendeau, Roger. *A Brief History of Canada*. Markham ON: Fitzhenry & Whiteside, 2000.

Roberts, Katherine A. "Sundance Style: Dancing with Cowboys in Aritha van Herk's (New) West." *Journal of Canadian Studies* 44, no. 3 (2010): 26–52.

Sugars, Cynthia, ed. *Home-Work: Postcolonialism, Pedagogy and Canadian Literature*. Ottawa: University of Ottawa Press, 2004.

———. *Unhomely States: Theorizing English-Canadian Postmodernism*. Peterborough ON: Broadview Press, 2004.

Thompson, John H. "Canadianizing the Myth of the West." *Canadian Issues* (Winter 2005): 38–40.

Todorov, Tzvetan. "Typology of Detective Fiction." In *The Narrative Reader*, edited by Martin McQuillan, 120–28. New York: Routledge, 2000.

Turner, Frederick Jackson. *The Frontier in American History*. 1920. Tucson: University of Arizona Press, 1994.

Vanderhaeghe, Guy. *The Englishman's Boy*. Toronto: McClelland & Stewart, 1996.

van Herk, Aritha. "The Half a Mile of Heaven's Gate." In *Icon, Brand, Myth: The Calgary Stampede*, edited by Max Foran, 235–25. Edmonton AB: Athabasca University Press, 2008.

———. "Leading the Parade." In *One West, Two Myths II: Essays on Comparison*, edited by Carol Higham and Robert Thacker, 153–62. Calgary AB: University of Calgary Press, 2006.

———. "A Lot of Beautiful Things Are Dangerous: Caprice Dreams a Western." Afterword to *Caprice*, by George Bowering, i–xi. Vancouver BC: New Star Books, 2010.

———. "Shooting a Saskatoon (Whatever Happened to the Marlboro Man?)." In *Challenging Frontiers: The Canadian West*, edited by Lorry Felske and Beverly Rasporich, 15–25. Calgary AB: University of Calgary Press, 2004.

White, Hayden. *Metahistory: The Historical Imagination in Nineteenth-Century Europe*. Baltimore: Johns Hopkins University Press, 1975.

CONTRIBUTORS

Chadwick Allen (PhD, University of Arizona) is professor of English, adjunct professor of American Indian studies, and associate vice provost for faculty advancement at the University of Washington. Author of the books *Blood Narrative: Indigenous Identity in American Indian and Maori Literary and Activist Texts* and *Trans-Indigenous: Methodologies for Global Native Literary Studies*, he is a former editor of the journal *Studies in American Indian Literatures* and a past president of the Native American and Indigenous Studies Association (NAISA).

Nancy S. Cook (PhD, University at Buffalo) is professor of English at the University of Montana. Her publications include work on the language of U.S. water policy, on Montana writing, on ranching, and on authenticity. She is a past president of the Western Literature Association. Currently she is working on twentieth-century U.S. ranching cultures.

Andrea M. Dominguez (PhD, University of California, San Diego) is a professor and national faculty chair of curriculum development for the College of Liberal Arts and Sciences at DeVry University, San Diego. She teaches composition and humanities courses, oversees curriculum development and assessment, and has published multiple articles and delivered many talks on humanities, cultural studies, and pedagogical practices in the digital age.

Kalenda Eaton (PhD, Ohio State University) is an associate professor of African American studies at the University of Oklahoma. Her scholarship and research interests include African American literature, the black American West, womanist theory, and Afro-descendants in the Americas. She is the author of *Womanism, Literature, and the Transformation of the Black Community, 1965–1980*, as well as a forthcoming coedited volume titled *New Directions in Black Western Studies* (with Michael Johnson and Jeannette Eileen Jones). She was an associate professor of English and pan-African studies at Arcadia University in Glenside, Pennsylvania, from 2010 to 2019, hence her reference to teaching in the eastern United States in the text she has contributed to this volume.

Amanda R. Gradisek (PhD, University of Arizona) is professor of English at Walsh University. She has been published in *Mississippi Quarterly*, *Southwestern American Literature*, and other notable journals.

Melody Graulich (PhD, University of Virginia) is emeritus professor of English and American studies (Utah State University) and a former editor of *Western American Literature* (1997–2015). Among her published books is an edited collection, *Dirty Words in "Deadwood": Literature and the Postwestern* (2013). She has published several essays on Wallace Stegner.

Amy T. Hamilton (PhD, University of Arizona) is professor of English at Northern Michigan University, where she teaches classes on Indigenous American literature, ecocriticism and environmental justice, early American literature, and western American literature. She is the author of *Peregrinations: Walking in American Literature* (2018) and coeditor with Tom J. Hillard of *Before the West Was West: Critical Essays on Pre-1800 Literature of the American Frontiers* (2014).

Brady Harrison (PhD, University of Illinois at Urbana-Champaign) is professor of English at the University of Montana. He is the author of *Agent of Empire: William Walker and the Imperial Self in American Literature* (2004), editor of *All Our Stories Are Here: Critical Perspectives on Montana Literature* (2009), and coeditor of *These Living Songs: Reading Montana Poetry* (2014) and *Punk Rock Warlord: The Life and Work of Joe Strummer* (2014). He is also the author of *The Dying Athabaskan* (2018), a novella set in the West.

Michael K. Johnson (PhD, University of Kansas) is professor of American literature at the University of Maine–Farmington, and he is a past president of the Western Literature Association. He is the author of *Hoo-Doo Cowboys and Bronze Buckaroos: Conceptions of the African American West*, and he is coeditor (with Kalenda Eaton and Jeannette Eileen Jones) of a special issue of the *American Studies Journal*, "New Directions in Black Western Studies."

Laura Laffrado (PhD, University at Buffalo) is professor of English at Western Washington University. Her most recent book is *Selected Writings of Ella Higginson: Inventing Pacific Northwest Literature* (2015), which received the 2018 Society for the Study of American Women Writers Edition Award. Her essays have appeared in *Legacy: A Journal of American Women Writers*, *a/b: Auto/Biography Studies*, *ESQ*, and other journals and collections.

Vanja Polić (PhD, University of Zagreb) is an associate professor in the Department of English at the University of Zagreb in Croatia. She is a member of the editorial board of *Canadian Literature*. She coedited a volume on Canada and the North and two special issues of the journals *Text Matters* and *London Journal of Canadian Studies*. Her current research focuses on the postmodern revisions of the history and myth of the West in contemporary western Canadian literature.

Her essays have appeared in the journals *Cultural Studies–Critical Methodologies* and *British Journal of Canadian Studies*, as well as in other edited volumes.

Mark C. Rogers (PhD, University of Michigan) is professor of communication at Walsh University. He has written extensively about genre and political economy in relation to comics and television. His work has appeared in the *International Journal of Comic Art* and in collected volumes about *The Sopranos, The X-Files*, and other television programs.

Karen R. Roybal (PhD, University of New Mexico) is an assistant professor of Southwest studies at Colorado College. She is the author of *Archives of Dispossession: Recovering the Testimonios of Mexican American Herederas, 1848–1960* (2017) and has been published in *Chicana/Latina Studies, Southwestern American Literature*, and *Aztlán: A Journal of Chicano Studies*, among other notable journals.

Tereza M. Szeghi (PhD, University of Arizona) is associate professor of comparative literature and social justice at the University of Dayton in Ohio. Her research focuses on ways American Indian and Latinx writers use literature to achieve social and political change pertaining to their human rights. Her publications have appeared in such journals as *Aztlán, Studies in American Indian Literature, Comparative Literature*, MELUS, and *Western American Literature*.

Randi Lynn Tanglen (PhD, University of Arizona) is an associate professor of English and director of the Johnson Center for Faculty Development and Excellence in Teaching at Austin College in Sherman, Texas. Her articles have appeared in *Western American Literature, Southwestern American Literature*, and various edited volumes.

Lisa Tatonetti (PhD, Ohio State University) is professor of English at Kansas State University. She is coeditor of *Sovereign Erotics* (2011) and author of *The Queerness of Native American Literature* (2014). She is currently completing work on a book titled *Indigenous Knowledges Written by the Body: Female, Two-Spirit, and Trans Masculinities*.

O. Alan Weltzien (PhD, University of Virginia), a longtime professor of English at the University of Montana–Western in Dillon, has published two chapbooks and nine books. These include a memoir, *A Father and an Island* (2008), and three poetry collections, most recently *Rembrandt in the Stairwell* (2016). He has also completed work on a biography of the neglected Montana novelist Thomas Savage.

INDEX

AAC&U. *See* American Association of Universities and Colleges (AAC&U)

"The Abandoned Wife Gives Herself to the Lord" (Glancy), 117–18

Abbey, Edward: *Desert Solitaire*, 136–37, 139, 141n32

able-bodiedness, 252–53, 255–56, 263–64, 266

absences: of historical memory, 107; of minorities in westerns, 66, 71, 108, 111, 113, 136–37, 195, 200n23; of resolution in narrative, 283

activism: African American, 78; environmental, 7–8, 70, 152, 156; feminist, 148; literature and, 101; Native American, 70; organizations involved in, 7–8; people of color and, 148, 159, 245–46; students and, 17, 155; Wallace Stegner and, 51

activities, course: agricultural, 150; chalk talks as, 241–42; close reading as, 258; current events in, 265–66; discussions in, 158–59; environmental justice and, 147; high-impact, 192, 193–95, 197–98, 198n4; literary devices and, 156–58; maps in, 154–55; normalcy considered in, 256–57; presentations as, 260–63; race issues and, 78, 236–37; related reading as, 230–32, 242; research as, 260–63; theoretical approaches and, 156–58

adultery, 210–11, 213

The Adventures of Brisco County, Jr. (television series), 68

"The Adventures of Col. Daniel Boon," 25–28, 38

The Adventures of Huckleberry Finn (Twain), 14, 48–49, 209

affect: in classroom setting, 92, 96–102, 182; in coursework, 11; definition of, 91–92; environmental studies and, 93–95; feminist studies and, 92–93; Indigenous studies and, 95–96; in memoirs, 179–80; novels and, 96–99; ordinary, 163, 165, 181, 182; place-based teaching and, 188–89; poems and, 99–101; short stories and, 175; texts on, 173–74

Affective Critical Regionality (Campbell), 169, 173, 183n12

African Americans: in art, 77; census records on, 217; coursework about, 7, 10–11, 76, 81; in literature, 64–65, 67, 70–72, 73–76, 78, 79–80, 230, 242, 243; in music, 64, 71, 77, 79; as soldiers, 64; in visual media, 64, 66–67, 68, 69, 72–73, 77–79; in white narrative, 63

African Americans on the Great Plains (Glasrud and Braithwaite), 74

Afrocentrism, 70

Afrofuturism, 69

agency, personal, 148, 210, 246

Ahmed, Sara, 91

AIM. *See* American Indian Movement (AIM)

Akiwenzie-Damm, Kateri, 113–14

Ak'shaar, Neranda (fictional character), 119

Alamar, Don Mariano (fictional character), 229, 234–35, 239–41, 242–43, 244, 245

Alamar family (fictional characters), 229–30, 236, 239

Alaska (Higginson), 222n12

Aldama, Frederick Luis, 7, 155

Alemán, Jesse, 230, 244

Alexie, Sherman, 208

Alias Smith and Jones (television series), 68

Allen, Chadwick: aural media used by, 35–38; course development by, 35; course overview of, 10, 25; exam development by, 32–33; formal writing taught by, 29–32, 33–34; grading system of, 27, 33; informal writing taught by, 26–28; methods of, 25–26, 30, 32, 36; reading guidance by, 25–26, 30, 31–32; teaching experience of, 24–25; *Trans-Indigenous*, 7

alliances, 125, 168, 236–37

All Over Creation (Ozeki), 195

American Association of Universities and Colleges (AAC&U), 187

American Daughter (Thompson), 67, 74

American dream, 229, 236

American Indian Movement (AIM), 17

American Indians, 105, 230, 240, 242, 243, 244, 246. *See also* Indigenous peoples; Native Americans

analysis: affective response and, 93, 96; in claim-evidence-analysis structure, 232; as course basis, 24; critical, 37, 176, 263, 267; emotion and, 97–98; of films, 37; genre and, 128, 139; in group work, 154, 232; guidance for, 262–63, 274–75; importance of, 6, 267; of literature, 75, 223n27, 228, 233, 242, 245, 258, 281, 290n14; of photos, 282; quotidian as zone for, 177; rhetorical, 25, 238; by students, 73; textual, 139, 283–88

Anderson, Eric Gary, 248n26

Angle of Repose (Stegner): *The Adventures of Huckleberry Finn* compared to, 49; citizenship and, 51; controversy about, 43–44, 58n9; in coursework, 10; as fictional biography, 42–44; "quirky little things" concept and, 44–45, 50–51, 54–58; *The Rise of Silas Lapham* compared to, 48–49; as thick description, 41, 45, 46–47

Anishinaabe people, 100, 105

anomaly, 106, 120n1

anthropology, 148, 260

"Apache (Jump on It)" (song), 79

Aranda, José, 228–29, 230, 237–38

Arches National Park, 141n32

archives, 74–75, 120, 177, 206, 217–19

Arellano, Juan Estevan, 145–46

Aristotle, 198

Armstead MT, 191, 199n10

art, visual, 50, 55–56, 77

Arte Público Press, 247n3

Article 8 of Treaty of Guadalupe Hidalgo, 230, 232–33

Article 9 of Treaty of Guadalupe Hidalgo, 230

assimilation, 65, 227, 252, 259, 264

Association for the Study of Literature and Environment (ASLE), 7–8

As some things appear on the Plains . . . (Young), 74

Atlantic, 265

Augé, Marc, 171

Augusta (fictional character), 131–32

Austen, Jane, 208

Austin, Mary Hunter, 204, 207; *Land of Little Rain*, 196

authenticity, 140n7, 189, 192, 193, 273, 282, 285

Bad Indians (Miranda), 109, 116

Baja California, 237

The Ballad of Little Joe (film), 38

Bannock Pass, 191

Baritz, Loren, 127

Bashō, 89

Bautista, José, 90

Baym, Nina, 14; *Women Writers of the American West, 1833–1927*, 8, 205

Beatty, Paul: *The Sellout*, 79

Before the West Was West (Hamilton and Hillard), 18n9

Belafonte, Harry, 66

Bennett, Brit: *The Mothers*, 79

Beringia, 279

Beyond the Hundredth Meridian (Stegner), 43, 54

bibliographies, 33, 119, 167, 168, 180. *See also* reading lists

Big Blackfoot River, 192, 193

bildungsroman, 209

Bill Pickett Invitational Rodeo, 78

biocentrism, 198

bioregionalism, 12, 164–65

The Birth of a Nation (film), 67

Bitterroot Valley, 192

The Blacker the Berry (Thurman), 77

Blackfeet Indians, 32, 35

blackness, 75, 139

The Black Panthers (documentary), 78

Black Wall Street (H. Johnson), 77

Blazing Saddles (film), 38, 78

blinks and winks, 45–46

block schedules, 13, 188, 189, 196, 199n5, 199n8

Blodgett Canyon, 192

Blunt, Judy: *Breaking Clean*, 171–72, 177–80

boarding schools, 115, 116

bodies: colonialism's effect on, 98; disabled, 254–55, 256, 265; environmental issues and, 155, 157; experiential learning by, 192, 197; female brown, 155, 157; Indigenous, 112, 252, 254, 256, 259, 266–67; land compared to female, 140n8; landscape and, 169; as metaphor for nation, 255–56; place and, 165, 173; queering of, 263; rehabilitation of, 260, 263–64; subjugation of, 259

body politics, 153, 157, 159, 252

Bold, Christine: *The Frontier Club*, 8, 124–25, 140n5

Book, Shepherd (fictional character), 69

books, 41, 48–49, 126, 168

Boone, Daniel, 25–27, 28, 38

borders: crossings by, 233, 239; crossings of, 90, 102; in European Union, 272; national, 6, 76, 273, 281, 282; sense of place and, 158; significance of, 124; soft, 273, 281; transnational frame and, 238

Bordwell, David: *Film Art*, 36

botany, study of, 95–96

Boudinot, Elias, 118

Bourdieu, Pierre, 141n21

Bowering, George: *Caprice*, 273, 286; *Shoot!*, 273, 284–86

Bowler, Lord (fictional character), 68

brainstorming, 106, 107, 108, 112, 256, 266, 278, 281

Braithwaite, Charles: *African Americans on the Great Plains*, 74

Brant, Beth, 12, 109, 114, 115; *Writing as Witness*, 119–20

Breaking Clean (Blunt), 171–72, 177–80

"The Bride Comes to Yellow Sky" (Crane), 63

A Brief History of Canada (Riendeau), 290n22

Britain, 280, 282, 285

The Bronze Buckaroo (film), 77

Brower, David, 51–52

Brown, Bill: *Reading the West*, 28

Brownell, Jayne E., 196

Buck and the Preacher (film), 11, 66, 78

Buffalo Bill's Wild West Show, 252, 263

Buffalo Dance (Walker), 11, 65–66

Buffalo Express, 209

"Buffalo Soldier" (song), 79

buffalo soldiers, 64

Burbank, George (fictional character), 200n14

Burbank, Phil (fictional character), 200n14

Burnett, Charles, 70
Burns, Neal (fictional character), 200n20
Burton, Henry S., 237
Butler, Judith, 264
Butler, Octavia: *Parable of the Sower*, 79

Cabot, John, 279
Cadillac Desert (Reisner), 196
Calamity Jane, 29
Calder, Alison, 284
Calgary Stampede, 287
Califia, Queen (fictional character), 72
California, 72, 79, 116, 151, 233, 244, 246, 248n27
California Land Act (1851), 231, 233
Californios: coursework incorporating, 236, 238, 241–42; definition of, 247n4; in history, 234, 237, 240; legal issues and, 233, 236; in literature, 229–30, 231, 234–35, 238, 239–40, 243–45; race issues and, 243–45
Campbell, Neil, 6, 172; *Affective Critical Regionality*, 169, 173, 183n12; *The Rhizomatic West*, 289n2
camping trips, 194–98
Canada: British influence in, 280, 285; constitution of, 280; in Croatian context, 276–78, 288–89; cultural diversity and, 290n18, 290n21; deconstruction of traditional history of, 274–75; French influence in, 280; immigration policies of, 76, 77; in literature, 271, 286–87, 288; literature on, 290n22; overview of, 279–80; stereotypes about, 278, 284, 289n9; United States and, 6, 15, 273–74, 279, 280–82, 283, 284, 285
Canada: A People's History (documentary), 280
Canadian History for Dummies (Ferguson), 290n22
Canadian Pacific Railway, 280
CANVAS (learning management system), 73, 75

Caprice (Bowering), 273, 286
Careless, J. M. S., 281, 282
Caridad (fictional character), 151
Caruso, Enrico, 207
Castañeda, Antonia I., 231
Castillo, Ana, 152, 156, 160n12; *So Far from God*, 13, 146, 151–53, 154–59
Cather, Willa, 141n27, 204; *My Ántonia*, 14, 209; *The Professor's House*, 12, 130–33, 139
Catholicism, 116, 126, 160n12, 290n21
cattle, 133, 239, 243, 245
cattle rights, 140n5
Cawelti, John, 126, 128; *The Six-Gun Mystique Sequel*, 129, 281
census records, 217–18
Century Magazine, 47–48
Ceremony (Silko), 12, 137, 138
chalk talks, 241–42, 248n26
Challenging Frontiers (Felske and Rasporich), 282
Charging Elk (fictitious character), 252, 254, 256, 258–60, 263–65
Cherokee Nation, 96–99, 117–19, 120n1
Cherokee Nation v. Georgia, 259
children, 115, 129, 149
Chinese box structure, 272, 283, 291n25
Chinese people, 44, 217
Christianity, 115, 117, 129, 258–59. *See also* Catholicism
chronotopes, 273, 274
Cinema Journal, 77
cinematography, 136
citizenship: cultural, 100, 252; government policy on, 232–33, 238–39, 259, 264–65; personal change and, 252, 254, 255–56, 264; rehabilitation and, 258–59, 260; responsible actions as, 42, 51–54
civilization: Britain associated with, 285; East associated with, 63, 68; Europe associated with, 240; outsiders protecting, 133–34; reading associated with, 48; Wallace Stegner on, 54;

emplotment, 283, 285, 291n25
English courses, 278–79, 290n19
The Englishman's Boy (Vanderhaeghe), 15–16, 273, 283–84, 285
environment, 136–37, 141n32, 145, 146, 215–16
environmentalism, 7, 160n9
environmental justice: activism for, 155–56; in coursework, 13, 92, 146–47; emotions and, 94–95; as field of study, 7–8; injustice and, 146–49, 150, 151, 152, 155, 156–58, 159, 160n4; in interdisciplinary studies, 146, 160n4; minorities and, 93–94, 148–49, 151, 152, 154, 157–58; in novels, 151–53, 154–55, 156–57, 158, 248n27; overview of, 147; place-based learning and, 152–54, 160n4; in plays, 151
environmental racism, 160n4
equality, 260, 290n21
Esperanza (fictional character), 151, 154–55
essays: on environmental issues, 149; on the everyday, 170–71, 175–76, 180–81; on historical narratives, 26–28; on injustice, 159; mini-research, 200n16; on nonprint media, 36, 68; on novels, 31, 47; photojournalism, 196; presentations of, 31–32; on queer West, 111, 113; on regionalism, 220, 222n27; on West, 127; on western writing, 204–5; as writing assignments, 27–31, 33–35, 37–38, 74, 80–81, 223n27
ethics, 92, 94, 96, 102, 180
ethnic groups, 75, 238, 277, 282, 290n21
Etulain, Richard: *Re-imagining the Modern American West*, 204
Euro-Americans, 227, 229–30, 233, 234–36, 239–41, 244–45
Eurocentricism, 108–9, 288
European Union, 272, 289
Everett, Percival: *Watershed*, 70
the everyday: access to, 168; in coursework, 5, 13, 165, 172–73, 176–77, 181; definition of, 170; feeling and, 167; foundational

texts for, 173–74; importance of, 169–71, 172, 182; in literature, 174–75, 177–80; place and, 166–67
everyday-time, 167
ex-centricity, 272, 285, 291n29
exclusions, 76, 124–25, 171, 211–12
Exodusters (Painter), 73
expansionism, 66, 108, 117, 128, 140n8
Eyes on the Prize (television series), 78

family as institution, 67, 108, 134, 252
Famuyiwa, Rick, 79
fantasy, 117, 118, 119
Farewell to Manzanar (Houston and Houston), 165, 171–72, 174–75, 180
farmers and farming, 133, 150, 239
Fe (fictional character), 151
Felske, Lorry: *Challenging Frontiers*, 282
Felski, Rita, 167, 170
females. *See* women
femininity, 92, 133, 136–37, 140n10
feminism, 8, 92–93, 124, 125–26, 129, 152, 156, 207
Ferguson, Will: *Canadian History for Dummies*, 290n22
Fetterley, Judith: *Writing Out of Place*, 219–20
fictocriticism, 272, 273, 287
Fiedler, Leslie, 126; *Love and Death in the American Novel*, 140n10
field experiences, 12, 194–98
Film Art (Bordwell, Thompson, and J. Smith), 36
films, 23–24, 37–38, 71, 76, 77–78, 79, 121n10, 128
Filson, John: "The Adventures of Col. Daniel Boon," 25–28, 38; *The Discovery, Settlement and Present State of Kentucke*, 25
finding aids, 33–34
FIPSE. *See* Fund for the Improvement of Post-Secondary Education Grant (FIPSE)
Firefly (television series), 69

Indigenous peoples: in historical narratives, 27; ignorance about, 105–6, 107–8; invisibility of, 106–9, 125, 210; migration of, 279; myths about, 282; in novels, 38, 96–99; overview of, 7, 12; in poems, 99–101, 117–18; queer literature and, 106, 109–12, 113–15, 116–17; rehabilitation of, 252, 260; stereotypes about, 211–12, 260; terms for, 268n2; undercounted, 217. *See also* American Indians; Native Americans

"In 1864" (Tapahonso), 11, 96, 99–101

In Motion: The African Migration Experience (interactive map), 73

inquiry, 4, 6, 11, 125, 148, 189, 253

In Search of the Racial Frontier (Taylor), 72–73, 76, 78

Insight Guides: Canada, 290n22

interactive maps, 73

interdisciplinary approach, 124, 126–27, 136, 139, 146–47, 150–51, 155, 159, 160n4, 197

International Network on Cultural Policy, 290n18

internet, 290n22

intersectional approach, 106, 115, 125, 138–39, 151, 158–59

Invisible Man (Ellison), 78

Ireland, Justina: *Dread Nation*, 68, 69

irony, 272, 284, 285

Is Canada Postcolonial? (Moss), 274

Jackson, Andrew, 118

Jackson, Helen Hunt: *Ramona*, 14, 246

Jacobs, Harriet, 64; *Incidents in the Life of a Slave Girl*, 64

Jacobs, Sue-Ellen: *Two-Spirit People*, 109–10, 113

Jaji, Tsitsi, 71

James, Sandy, 199n13

Jansson, Robert, 194

Japanese Americans, 200n23

Jefferson, Thomas, 247n19; *Notes on the State of Virginia*, 236

Jerome, Father (fictional character), 151–52

Jewett, Sarah Orne, 207, 223n27

Johnson, Hannibal: *Black Wall Street*, 77

Johnson, Michael K.: contemporary West in course of, 70; course overview of, 10–11, 63–64; cultural studies in course of, 68–69; expansion in course of, 64–66; goals of, 61; *Hoo-Doo Cowboys and Bronze Buckaroos*, 62, 68; migration in course of, 64–66; region in course of, 66–67; writings of, as teaching aids, 74

Johnson, Pauline, 205

Johnston, Basil, 284

Jones, Adam Garnet: *Fire Song*, 121n10

Jones, Allyson, 50–51

journaling, 150

Justice, Daniel Heath, 106, 119, 120n1; *Sovereign Erotics*, 109–11, 114; *The Way of Thorn and Thunder*, 117, 118

Kansas State University, 105–6

Karush, Deborah, 141n30

Katapodis, Christina, 101

Kenny, Maurice, 12, 109, 114

Kesey, Ken, 208

Kilcup, Karen, 248n27

Kimmerer, Robin Wall, 95–96

King, Thomas, 284

Kittay, Eve, 257

Knobowtee (fictional character), 97

knowledge, 102, 289n6

Kollin, Susan, 6, 14, 203

Kolodny, Annette: gender studies and, 125–26, 127–28, 140n8; *The Land Before Her*, 8, 128; writings of, as teaching aids, 17n3, 27–28, 127, 228

Kool Moe Dee, 71, 79

Kowalewski, Michael, 164

Kuh, George D., 188–89, 197–98; *High-Impact Educational Practices*, 198n4

Kwakiutl tribe, 222n12

Kyn (fictional tribe), 118, 119

Melville, Herman: *Redburn*, 222n27
memoirs, 67, 90, 116, 172, 179–80
men: black, 66; in census count, 218; as
    characters in film, 133–35; as characters
    in historical narratives, 25, 26, 140n10;
    as characters in memoirs, 90, 177–79;
    as characters in novels, 28, 132; as
    characters in songs, 79; as characters in
    westerns, 126; Indigenous, 108; objectiv-
    ity and, 93; power and, 118; as readers,
    128; stereotypes about, 92–93, 129; as
    students, 38–39, 45; West's influence
    on, 206; white, 25, 26, 124–25, 140n5;
    women and, 118, 129–30, 133, 140n10,
    177–79, 219; as writers, 128, 227, 284
metadiscourse, 289n6
metafiction, 272, 274–75, 283, 290n14,
    291n25
metahistory, 273, 285, 289n7, 291n25
methodologies: educational, 172;
    feminist, 130; Indigenous, 110–11;
    interdisciplinary, 42–43; intersectional,
    130; multiple-perspective, 127; regional,
    124–25, 140n3; student-developed, 45
Métis, 285
Mexican Americans, 229, 230–31, 233, 239.
    See also Californios
Mexico, 229, 235, 240–41
Micheaux, Oscar, 77–78; *The Homesteader*,
    66–67
microregions, 164–65
Midnight Ramble (film), 77–78
migration, 62, 64–66, 72–73, 76–77,
    117, 279. *See also* immigrants and
    immigration
Mild West, 273–74, 286, 289n9
Minidoka internment camp, 200n23
minima aesthetica (term), 166, 183n8
minority groups, 93–94, 157, 159, 260, 277.
    See also African Americans; American
    Indians; Charging Elk (fictitious
    character); disabilities; Indigenous
    peoples; Native Americans; women

Miranda, Deborah, 113–14; *Bad Indians*,
    109, 116; *Sovereign Erotics*, 109–11, 114
missions, Catholic, 116, 240, 258–59
Mississippian nations, 120n1
Missouri River, 194, 200n21
Mitchell, David: *Narrative Prosthesis*, 254
monogamy, 108, 109, 114, 115–16, 117, 118
monologism, 283, 290n11
Montana, 165, 190, 191
Montana Board of Regents, 199n5
Montes, Amelia María de la Luz, 231, 236
Monument Valley, 36
Moraga, Cherríe, 160n9; *Heroes and Saints*,
    151, 160n11
Moran, Joe: *Reading the Everyday*, 173
Morgensen, Scott Lauria: *Queer Indigenous
    Studies*, 109–11
Morrison, Toni: *Paradise*, 76
Moss, Laura: *Is Canada Postcolonial?*, 274
Mother Eve (fictional mummy), 132
The Mothers (Bennett), 79
Mountain City (Martin), 182
Mountain Man (Fisher), 195–96
Moya, Paula, 93, 101
multiculturalism, 276, 277, 289
Multiculturalism Act, 280, 290n21
Murfree, Mary Noailles, 207
music, 64, 71, 79
My Ántonia (Cather), 14, 209
The Myth of the Noble Savage (Ellingson),
    260
mythopoeia, 273, 283, 284–85, 286, 291n25
myths: African American, 70; Canadian,
    283–84, 288; in coursework, 275; Euro-
    pean influence on, 108–9; foundational,
    6, 107–8; frontier, 125–26, 141n30;
    inverting of, 66; national, 237; pioneer,
    236; savage war as, 120n3; violence and,
    64, 65; of the West, 5, 15, 62, 125, 171,
    273–74, 281–82, 284–85, 287–88

Nama, Adilifu, 69
narrative maps, 80

Ruiz de Burton, María Amparo: activism
in writings of, 229–31, 233–36, 238–39,
242; citizen issues of, 237; as elite,
241, 242; environmental issues and,
248n27; legal affairs of, 231; race issues
and, 243–45, 246, 247n5; as recovered
author, 229; *Who Would Have Thought
It?*, 238, 247n3. See also *The Squatter
and the Don* (Ruiz de Burton)

Sánchez, Rosaura, 229, 230, 247n3
Sandoval, Chela, 156
San Francisco Bulletin, 208–9
San Francisco Examiner, 208
Savage, Thomas, 13, 190–92, 199n12; *The
Pass*, 191, 199n9; *The Power of the Dog*,
191–92, 199n9; *The Sheep Queen*, 199n9
"savage war" concept, 108, 120n3
Sawyer, Tom (fictional character), 48–49
scaffold approach, 112, 150, 153, 251, 253, 254
Schneider, Carol Geary, 197–98
scholarship, 5, 124–25, 126, 140n7
science fiction, 69, 118, 119
The Searchers (film), 12, 136
Seattle Daily Times, 209
The Sellout (Beatty), 79
sense of place, 13, 145–46, 152–54, 157,
161n32
settler colonialism, 6–7, 106–8, 124, 141n33,
210, 222n12
Seven Samurai (film), 23
sexism, 92, 141n32
sexuality, 114, 258, 264
Shane (fictional character), 134–35
Shane (film), 12, 130, 133–35, 286
Sharp, Robert P.: *Geology Underfoot in
Death Valley and Owens Valley*, 196
The Sheep Queen (Savage), 199n9
Shepard, R. Bruce: *Deemed Unsuitable*,
76–77
Shoot! (Bowering), 273, 284–86
short stories, 115, 287–88
Shulman, Robert, 30

Sierra Club, 51
Silko, Leslie Marmon: *Ceremony*, 12, 137, 138
Silverado (film), 78–79
single hermetic context. *See* monologism
Singleton, John, 79
The Six-Gun Mystique Sequel (Cawelti),
129, 281
slaves and slavery, 65–66, 68, 69, 72, 74,
105–6, 138, 244
Slotkin, Richard, 108, 120n3, 125, 129, 133;
Gunfighter Nation, 64
Smith, Henry Nash: *Virgin Land*, 17n3
Smith, Jeff: *Film Art*, 36
Smith, John, 108
smokejumpers, 194, 220n21
Smuggler's Cove, 215
Smyth, John, 148
Snyder, Sharon: *Narrative Prosthesis*, 254
So Far from God (Castillo): in coursework,
13, 146; overview of, 151–52; in
place-based learning, 152–53; student
activities and, 154–59
Sorry to Bother You (film), 11, 69
Soulas, Madeleine (fictional character),
258–59
Soulas, René (fictional character), 258–59
The Souls of Black Folks (Du Bois), 64
Southwest, 146, 147, 161n32, 196–97
Southwest Organizing Project (swop),
156, 161n24
Sovereign Erotics (Tatonetti, Miranda, and
Justice), 109–11, 114
sovereignty, 106, 114
Spain and the Spanish, 72, 153, 233, 240–41
speeches, 64, 118
The Squatter and the Don (Ruiz de
Burton): contexts of, 245–46; in
coursework, 14, 227; environmental
issues in, 248n27; frontier concept in,
229; gender in, 231; human rights frame
for, 242–45; national frame for, 230–31,
234–38; republication of, 247n3; texts
compared with, 236, 246; transnational

frame for, 238–42; U.S. policy and, 229–30

Stagecoach (film), 36, 135–37

Stanfield, LaKeith, 69

Starrett, Joe (fictional character), 133–34

Starrett, Marian (fictional character), 134, 135

Stegner, Page, 42

Stegner, Wallace: appropriative actions of, 43–44, 58n9, 140n3; Bernard DeVoto and, 42, 43; *Beyond the Hundredth Meridian*, 43, 54; in coursework, 3–4, 10; as observer, 42–44, 47–48; reading and, 49; *This Is Dinosaur*, 52; *The Uneasy Chair*, 43; values of, 50, 51–54. See also *Angle of Repose* (Stegner)

Stephens, Ann: *Malaeska: The Indian Wife of the White Hunter*, 28, 38

Stevens, George, 133

Stewart, Kathleen: in coursework, 13; influence of, 163, 183n8, 183n12; *Ordinary Affects*, 169, 172, 173; writings of, as teaching aids, 165, 167, 170, 181, 182

Stowe, Harriet Beecher: *Uncle Tom's Cabin*, 233

St. Peter, Godfrey (fictional character), 130–33

St. Peter, Lillian (fictional character), 131

St. Peter, Rosamond (fictional character), 131

Straight Outta Compton (Cruz), 79

Stryker clan (fictional characters), 133

subjugation, 120n3

Suckow, Ruth, 204

suffrage records, 218–19

Sugar, Cynthia: *Home-Work*, 274; *Unhomely States*, 274

Sugarhill Gang, 79

Supreme Court, 259

Swaner, Lynn E., 196

swop. *See* Southwest Organizing Project (swop)

syllabi, 4, 10, 14, 24, 81, 124, 182, 203, 275

Sylvia, Joe, 194

The Symbol of the Unconquered (film), 67

Szeghi, Tereza M.: course overview of, 14, 227–28, 230; human rights frame used by, 242–45; laws in national frame used by, 230–34; literature in national frame used by, 234–38; on race issues, 247n5; teaching experience of, 227; transnational frame used by, 238–42

Tacoma Daily News, 209

Tapahonso, Luci: "In 1864," 11, 96, 99–101

Tara'deshae (fictional character), 118

Tarantino, Quentin, 69

Tatonetti, Lisa: course overview of, 12; methods of, 106, 108, 110–16; *The Queerness of Native American Literature*, 7; readings chosen by, 109–11; *Sovereign Erotics*, 109–11, 114; teaching experience of, 105

Tatum, Stephen: *Reading "The Virginian" in the New West*, 31, 33–34

Taylor, Quintard: *In Search of the Racial Frontier*, 72–73, 76, 78

Tayo (fictional character), 137, 138

teachers and teaching, 1–5, 17, 17n1, 42, 92, 123, 203

television, 36, 64, 68, 69, 78–79

Testimony (Williams and Trimble), 52

Texas Pacific Railroad, 244

Thacker, Robert: *One West, Two Myths*, 282

"thick description" concept, 10, 41, 45–47, 172

"thin description" concept, 46

thinking, critical: emotions and, 93; environmental issues and, 155; fostering, 32, 39, 123, 228, 256, 275, 276; gender and, 137, 139, 155; globalization and, 253; legal issues and, 236–37

Thinking Continental (Lynch), 198n1

think-pair-share discussion, 256–58

This Is Dinosaur (Stegner), 52

Thlinkit tribe, 222n12

Thomas, Rob C., 189, 199n5

Vagrancy Law (1855), 231

Vanderhaeghe, Guy: *The Englishman's Boy*, 15–16, 273, 283–84, 285

van Herk, Aritha, 16, 273, 286–87

Veracini, Lorenzo, 107

videos, 64, 115, 121n10, 200n18

Vikings, 279

violence, 64, 65, 125, 126, 129–30, 133, 140n8

The Virginian (Wister), 10, 25, 30–32, 35, 38, 49

Virgin Land (H. N. Smith), 17n3

virtual reality, 146, 160n3

visual maps, 154–55

A Voice of My Own (Hinojosa-Smith), 145–46

Walden (Thoreau), 146

Walker, Frank X: *Buffalo Dance*, 11, 65–66

Ward, Lyman (fictional character), 41, 43–44, 47

Ward, Molly (fictional character), 43–44

Ward, Oliver (fictional character), 43–44, 49

Ward, Susan (fictional character), 47, 49, 58n9

Washburne, Zoë (fictional character), 69

Washington (state), 207, 217, 219, 221n1

Washington (territory), 218

Washington, Booker T., 65; *Up from Slavery*, 64

Watershed (Everett), 70

Watkins, Mel: *On the Real Side*, 66

Wayne, John, 36

The Way of Thorn and Thunder (Justice), 117, 118

Weeds (Funda), 195

Welch, James: background of, 25, 32; characters of, 259, 260; in coursework, 253; *Fools Crow*, 10, 25, 32–35, 38–39, 252; *The Indian Lawyer*, 252; themes of, 266; *Winter in the Blood*, 165, 171–72, 176, 180, 252. See also *The Heartsong of Charging Elk* (Welch)

wellness and health, 255–56, 264

Wells, Ida B., 73–74

Welty, Eudora, 141n27

Weltzien, O. Alan: approach of, 187; block scheduling by, 13; goals of, 192; methods of, 13, 190–91, 194–95, 196–97; in public relations video, 200n18; self-evaluation of, 193–94, 196, 198; student interaction with, 197

West, American: African American, 63–65, 67, 70, 71–80, 81; associations with, 63; authenticity in, 192; Canadian West compared to, 273–74, 281–82, 285, 289; contemporary, 70, 78–79; in coursework, 5–6, 172–73; East compared to, 63, 67, 68, 219; environmental activism in, 152, 156; expanded perceptions of, 17n3, 18n9, 117, 124–25, 163–64, 204–5, 221; gender and, 128–30, 132–39, 140n5, 219, 264–65; globalized view of, 252–54, 266–67; importance of, 125; incomplete perceptions of, 106, 108–9, 163; Indigenous people in, 7, 106, 108, 112–20; normalcy in, 251–52; Pacific Northwest as part of, 203–4, 205–6, 221; queerness in, 106, 111–20; quotidian, 165, 166–67, 169–70, 173, 181; race issues in, 140n5; traditional perceptions of, 126–28, 171, 190, 232–33, 254, 260; Wallace Stegner and, 42–44, 47, 49, 51

West, Canadian, 15, 276, 280, 281–82, 284, 285, 286, 287–89, 289n9

West, North American, 1–2, 15, 109, 164, 169, 172, 273

Western Literature Association (WLA), 4, 7–8, 17, 17n1, 176

westerns, film, 23–24, 36–38, 66–67, 69, 71, 77–79, 128, 133–36, 137–38

westerns, music, 71, 79

westerns, print: autobiographies as, 65, 136–37, 139; blacks and, 62; historical narratives as, 25–27; memoirs as, 67, 172; novels as, 25, 28–29, 30–35, 66–67, 70–72, 130–33, 135–39, 171–72, 205–6; poems as, 65–66; postmodernism and, 272; revisionist, 141n33; short stories as, 63; weird, 68–69; women in, 114, 125, 129–30

Ybarra, Priscilla Solis, 7, 150–51, 152–53, 157; *Writing the Good Life*, 160n9

Yearian, Emma Russell "Big Mama," 199n12

Yearian Ranch, 191, 199n12

The Year of Decision (DeVoto), 43

York (enslaved person), 65–66

Young, Kenneth: *As some things appear on the Plains . . .*, 74

Young Men and Fire (Maclean), 192, 194

Zane Grey Theatre (television series), 64

Zola, Émile, 208

*Dirty Wars: Landscape, Power, and
Waste in Western American Literature*
John Beck

Post-Westerns: Cinema, Region, West
Neil Campbell

*The Rhizomatic West: Representing the
American West in a Transnational,
Global, Media Age*
Neil Campbell

Weird Westerns: Race, Gender, Genre
Edited by Kerry Fine, Michael
K. Johnson, Rebecca M. Lush,
and Sara L. Spurgeon

*Positive Pollutions and Cultural
Toxins: Waste and Contamination in
Contemporary U.S. Ethnic Literatures*
John Blair Gamber

Dirty Words in Deadwood:
Literature and the Postwestern
Edited by Melody Graulich
and Nicolas Witschi

*True West: Authenticity and
the American West*
Edited by William R. Handley
and Nathaniel Lewis

Teaching Western American Literature
Edited by Brady Harrison and
Randi Lynn Tanglen

*We Who Work the West: Class, Labor, and
Space in Western American Literature*
Kiara Kharpertian
Edited by Carlo Rotella and
Christopher P. Wilson

*Captivating Westerns: The Middle
East in the American West*
Susan Kollin

*Postwestern Cultures:
Literature, Theory, Space*
Edited by Susan Kollin

Westerns: A Women's History
Victoria Lamont

*Manifest and Other Destinies:
Territorial Fictions of the Nineteenth-
Century United States*
Stephanie LeMenager

*Unsettling the Literary West:
Authenticity and Authorship*
Nathaniel Lewis

Morta Las Vegas: CSI *and
the Problem of the West*
Nathaniel Lewis and Stephen Tatum

Late Westerns: The Persistence of a Genre
Lee Clark Mitchell

*María Amparo Ruiz de Burton:
Critical and Pedagogical Perspectives*
Edited by Amelia María de la Luz
Montes and Anne Elizabeth Goldman

*In the Mean Time: Temporal
Colonization and the Mexican
American Literary Tradition*
Erin Murrah-Mandril

To order or obtain more information on these or other University
of Nebraska Press titles, visit nebraskapress.unl.edu.

CPSIA information can be obtained
at www.ICGtesting.com
Printed in the USA
LVHW012349010520
654848LV00003B/425